Penguin Education

Penguin Critical Anthologies
General Editor: Christopher Ricks

William Carlos Williams

Edited by Charles Tomlinson

William Carlos Williams
A Critical Anthology

Edited by Charles Tomlinson
Penguin Books

Penguin Books Ltd, Harmondsworth,
Middlesex, England
Penguin Books Inc, 7110 Ambassador Road,
Baltimore, Md 21207, USA
Penguin Books Australia Ltd, Ringwood,
Victoria, Australia

First published 1972
This selection copyright © Charles Tomlinson, 1972
Introduction and notes copyright © Charles Tomlinson, 1972

All excerpts from William Carlos Williams's poetry
books are reprinted by permission of New Directions
Publishing Corporation and MacGibbon & Kee; all
excerpts from *Selected Essays*, *Selected Letters* and *The
Wedge* by permission of New Directions Publishing Corporation,
publishers and agents for Mrs William Carlos Williams

Made and printed in Great Britain by
Hazell Watson & Viney Ltd, Aylesbury, Bucks
Set in Monotype Bembo

To Gael Turnbull

Contents

Part Two The Debate on *Paterson*

9 Contents

How Some of the Poems Work

The Question of Measure

Later Poetry

The Novels and Other Prose

Further Views

Preface

For reasons of space I was compelled to omit the items by Burke, Duncan, Fiedler, Lechlitner, Taupin, Sereni, Weaver, as given in the bibliography. The same applies to Kenner's 'The Drama of Utterance' (see page 208) and his 'A Note on The Great American Novel', and to Tony Tanner's 'Transcendentalism and Imagism'.

I should like to record my gratitude to the following persons for their helpful kindness: Karl H. Darenberg, Ruth Grogan, who compiled the Table of Dates, Hugh Kenner, James Laughlin, Diana Surman and Christopher Ricks.

List of Plates

Table of Dates

Few events of Williams's life effected an immediate and
obvious change of direction in his art; his response has to
ripen, sometimes for years, before finding concrete
realization. The turning points of his literary development
are best conceived, in his own metaphorical usage, as
recurrent 'descents' into different aspects of reality. In the
following chronology dates are 'interpreted' by remarks
drawn for the most part from Williams's own
autobiographical works, to emphasize this and other
patterns of growth.

1883   *17 September* William Carlos Williams born in
          Rutherford, New Jersey, to William George Williams
          (English) and Raquel Hélène Hoheb Williams (Puerto
          Rican). Spanish and French heard habitually in the home.

1889–96   Attends elementary schools in Rutherford. 'Going to
          school, Ed [brother] and I grew up together to become
          as one person.'

1897–9   'Our first European sally': attends school near Geneva,
          and for a short time in Paris. 'We were mere infants,
          hundreds of years younger than most of the sixty-two
          other boys there.'

1899–1902 Attends Horace Mann High School in New York City.
          Interest in poetry begins, so Williams claims, with the
          discovery of a heart murmur: 'I was forced back on
          myself. . . . I began to read.'

1902–6   Studies medicine at University of Pennsylvania in
          Philadelphia. Meets Ezra Pound ('before meeting Ezra
          Pound is like B.C. and A.D.'), Hilda Doolittle and
          Charles Demuth (on whose death in 1935 he wrote one
          of his best poems, *The Crimson Cyclamen*). Develops
          interest in drama. Records Whitmanesque 'thoughts' and

writes monumental imitation of Keats's *Endymion* (both later burned). Sometime during these years he acquires an 'inner security' which will inform all his work: 'It is something which occurred once when I was about twenty, a sudden resignation to existence, a despair ... which made everything a unit and at the same time a part of myself.'

1906–9   Intern at old French Hospital and at Nursery and Child's Hospital in New York City.

1909   *Poems*: '... not one thing of the slightest value in the whole thin booklet – except the intent ..., full of inversions of phrase, the rhymes inaccurate, the forms stereotype'.

1909–10   Studies paediatrics in Leipzig. Visits Pound in London, and his brother in Rome. Begins general practice in Rutherford.

1912   *12 December*   Marries Florence Herman: '... the end of my passionate identification with my brother.... Something profound did happen, something moving and final.... On the other hand there is Flossie, my wife, who is the rock on which I have built.'

1913   *The Tempers*: '... influenced by my meeting with Pound, but even more by *Palgrave's Golden Treasury*.... The orderliness of verse appealed to me ... but even more I wanted a new order.' During the next few years Williams contributes poems to many 'little magazines', among them the *Glebe*, *Poetry*, *Others* (the last issue of which he edited), the *Little Review*, the *Egoist*, *Dial*, *Broom*. Meets Walter Arensberg, Alfred Kreymborg, Marianne Moore, Kenneth Burke, Marsden Hartley, Charles Sheeler and others. 'Painting took the lead. It came to a head for us in the famous "Armory Show" of

1913'; 'impressionism, dadaism, surrealism applied to both painting and the poem'.

1914   *The Wanderer*, precursor of *Paterson*, published in the *Egoist*.

1917   *Al Que Quiere! A Book of Poems*: 'the struggle to get a form without deforming the language'.

1919   Begins steady, life-long publication of critical and 'improvisatory' prose essays.

1920   *Kora in Hell: Improvisations*. Frontispiece by Stuart Davis. Represents a 'plunge' into nonsense, into the 'dark void' of his own imagination; 'it is to loosen the attention . . . that I write these improvisations'. Had discussed Persephone with Pound; 'I thought of myself as springtime and felt I was on my way to Hell (but I didn't go very far).'

1920–23   Edits *Contact* with Robert McAlmon: 'We, *Contact*, aim to emphasize the local phase of the game of writing.'

1921   *Sour Grapes*: 'All the poems are poems of disappointment, sorrow.' But 'sour grapes are just as beautiful as any other grapes'.

1922   T. S. Eliot publishes *The Waste Land*: for Williams 'the great catastrophe . . . which gave the poem back to the academics'.

1923   *The Great American Novel*: A travesty.
Spring and All: Poems interspersed with improvisatory prose, 'a mixture of philosophy and nonsense', attempting a definition of the imagination.

1924   Third trip to Europe; renews friendship with Hilda Doolittle and Pound, and meets Philippe Soupault, George Antheil, James Joyce, Sylvia Beach, Valéry Larbaud, Ernest Hemingway, Ford Madox Ford and others.

1925   *In the American Grain*: A 'descent' (the title of one
            chapter) into America's historical sources, written
            partly in Europe.

1926   *Dial* publishes his poem called *Paterson*, another
            precursor of later extended poem. Receives the *Dial*
            Award for poetry.

1927   Fourth trip to Europe.

1928   *A Voyage to Pagany*: A 'travel' novel following the
            itinerary of Williams's 1924 trip, and examining the
            relationship of an American writer to European life and
            tradition.

1928–34   Meets Louis Zukofsky, and is loosely associated with the
            'objectivist' poets, Charles Reznikoff, George
            Oppen and others. Objectivism, as Williams later
            defined it, 'recognizes the poem, apart from its meaning,
            to be an object. . . . [It] looks at the poem with a special
            eye to its structural aspect.'

1929   *Last Nights of Paris*, by Philippe Soupault. Translated
            from the French by William Carlos Williams.

1931   Wins Guarantors Prize from *Poetry* magazine. A short
            cruise from Montreal to Newfoundland 'deeply
            influenced my later writing'.

1932   Edits *Contact II* with Nathaniel West.
            A Novelette and Other Prose (1921–1931): shows 'the
            influence of Dadaism'; the improvisatory method again
            but 'more sophisticated'.
            The Knife of the Times and Other Stories. Short stories:
            'I was impressed by the picture of the times, depression
            years, the plight of the poor. . . . I felt as if I were a
            radical without being a radical.'

1934   *Collected Poems 1921–1931*. Preface by Wallace Stevens
            Williams was nettled by Stevens's use of the term

'anti-poetic': 'I have never been satisfied that the anti-poetic had any validity or even existed.'

1935 *An Early Martyr and Other Poems*. Dedicated to John Coffey, a young radical who wanted to help the poor.

1935–44 Series of articles, reviews, letters reflecting the political interests of the time.

1936 *Adam and Eve and the City*: 'tributes to my father and mother'.
The First President. Libretto for an Opera. Published in *The New Caravan* (edited by Alfred Kreymborg).
Writes to Pound that he is considering a form for 'that magnum opus I've always wanted to do: the poem PATERSON'.

1937 *White Mule*: a novel based on his wife's babyhood. 'Tired, for the moment of writing poetry, I turned for relief to prose....' Although begun ten years earlier as an improvisation, in the end it was 'write, rewrite, correct and write again'.

1938 *Life Along the Passaic River*. More short stories: 'still obsessed by the plight of the poor'.
The Complete Collected Poems 1906–1938: '... gave me a chance to sit back and appraise not only the poetry but what I had learned about life'. In a letter Williams admits that 'I haven't written anything to speak of for almost a year.... Maybe I am drying up.'

1939 Sees Pound again during his visit to the United States.

1940 *In the Money*. Part Two of *White Mule*.

1941 *The Broken Span*. Poems old and new, including a short stanza, 'For the Poem Paterson', to be used later in *Paterson*. In an essay Williams remarks: 'Make no mistake, war releases energy', but 'the idiotic belief that the arts must be put aside for arms – UNTIL a time or peace . . . must give way to a triple fury of activity, to steel the released energy for constructions.'

1942 *Trial Horse No. 1* (later entitled *Many Loves*). A play.

1943 'Paterson, I know, is crying to be written; the time demands it.'

1944 *The Wedge*: ' . . . probably the best yet'. Williams considered the Introduction, written 'in a period of great conviction and excitement', one of the two most important essays to be reprinted in his *Selected Essays*.

1946 *Paterson*, Book One. A metaphorical fusion of man and city. The Great Falls of the Passaic River, which flows through Paterson, NJ, represents the failure ('the catastrophe of the descent'), and possible recovery, of language.
Receives honorary degree from University of Buffalo; *Briarcliff Quarterly* issues a 'W.C.W. Number'; *Quarterly Review of Literature* prints largest group of poems he has ever published together.

1947 Lectures at University of Washington, one engagement among many in these later years to lecture and read his poetry.

1948 In February Williams suffers a heart attack, the first of several, and possibly his first strong apprehension of death. Begins autobiographical notes, published in *Poetry*. *Paterson*, Book Two: ' . . . a milestone for me'. The passage beginning 'The descent beckons | as the ascent beckoned' sometime later 'brought all my thinking about free verse to a head'.
The Clouds.
A Dream of Love. A play.

1949   *Selected Poems.* Introduction by Randall Jarrell.
        The Pink Church.
        Paterson, Book Three.

1950   *The Collected Later Poems.*
        Make Light of It: Collected Stories.
        Teaches short-story seminar at University of
        Washington.

1951   *Paterson*, Book Four.
        Autobiography.
        The Collected Earlier Poems. Suffers stroke; retires from
        medical practice. Reads *The Desert Music* before the Phi
        Beta Kappa Society of Harvard University: 'many of my
        culminating ideas as to form have entered into this poem'.

1952   *The Build-Up.* Third novel based on his wife's family; a
        continuation of his descent into memory, as one of the
        daughters (based on his wife) is courted by a young
        intern: 'I found much of what I was writing was too
        personal.'

1953   Receives the Bollingen Award for Poetry.

1954   *The Desert Music and Other Poems.* The volume opens
        with a reprint of 'The descent beckons | as the ascent
        beckoned'; these and subsequent poems are a further
        investigation of 'measure' and the 'variable foot', his
        major formal preoccupations of these years, as well as a
        final 'descent' into personal memory, apprehension of
        death and love.
        A Dog and the Fever. A perambulatory novella by Don
        Francisco de Quevedo. Translated by William Carlos
        Williams and Raquel Hélène Williams.
        Selected Essays.

1955   A reading tour of colleges across the country.
        Journey to Love.

1957   *The Selected Letters*. Edited by John C. Thirlwall.
       The Lost Poems of William Carlos Williams. Collected by
       John C. Thirlwall in *New Directions 16*.

1958   *I Wanted to Write a Poem*. Edited by Edith Heal. A
       descriptive bibliography, transcript of the poet talking
       about his own books.
       Paterson, Book Five. In the ten years since *Paterson*, Book
       Four 'I have come to understand not only that many
       changes have occurred in me and the world, but I have
       been forced to recognize that there can be no end to such
       a story I have envisioned . . .' (from note on dust jacket).

1959   *Yes, Mrs Williams: A Personal Record of My Mother*.

1961   *The Farmers' Daughters*. The Collected Stories.
       Introduction by Van Wyck Brooks.
       Many Loves and Other Plays.

1962   *Pictures from Brueghel and Other Poems*.

1963   *4 March* Williams dies in Rutherford, NJ. Receives
       posthumously the Pulitzer Prize for *Pictures from Brueghel*
       and the Gold Medal for Poetry of the National Institute
       of Arts and Letters.
       Paterson. Including Notes for Book Six.

1966   *The William Carlos Williams Reader*. Edited by M. L.
       Rosenthal.

1970   *Imaginations*. Edited by Webster Schott. Miscellaneous
       prose and verse including *Kora in Hell, Spring and All,
       The Great American Novel, The Descent of Winter, A
       Novelette and Other Prose*.

Note on Quotations

All quotations (except from *Kora in Hell*, reprinted in W. Schott (ed.), *Imaginations*, New Directions, 1970) are from the English editions of Williams's work.

The publication dates are as follows:

1963 *Pictures from Brueghel*
1964 *Paterson*, Books One to Five
1965 *Collected Later Poems, White Mule*
1966 *In the Money, The William Carlos Williams Reader*
1967 *Collected Earlier Poems, In the American Grain, I Wanted to Write a Poem*
1969 *Autobiography, The Build-Up*

With the exception of *I Wanted to Write a Poem* (Cape), all are published by MacGibbon & Kee. *White Mule, In the Money* and *In the American Grain* are also published by Penguin.

Part One The Beginnings to the 1940s

Introduction

'The permanent expatriate type is extinct. The act of Ezra Pound in 1908 need not be repeated. The young American can now function in his home *milieu*.' Thus Gorham Munson in 'Mechanics for a Literary "Secession"' of 1922 (see p. 65). Among the nucleus of writers Munson counted on to give substance to this conviction was William Carlos Williams, whose choice of the home *milieu*, the raw merging of American pastoral and urban squalor, was to temper the whole of his life's work. In an essay, 'The Renaissance', first published in 1914, Ezra Pound had hoped for an American reawakening which would 'overshadow the quattrocento': 'our opportunity is greater than Leonardo's ... we have more aliment.' But Pound's flight to Europe seemed, in the eyes of Williams, to belie the prediction and the hopes behind it, as did T. S. Eliot's.

'A poet of the quattrocento,' wrote Marianne Moore of Williams in 1927, wryly indicating that perhaps some of Pound's prediction had come true (see p. 92). Others thought so, too, among them Munson who published one of the first full-scale essays on Williams in *Destinations* (1928), reprinted here, and Paul Rosenfeld whose *Port of New York* had attempted to survey the American situation as it appeared in 1924. With all their differences (Munson disliked Rosenfeld's writing as can be seen from his attack on him in 'Mechanics'), the work of these two tells us much about the background of this phase. Williams occupied an important part in the argument of Rosenfeld's book (it is an argument that is to be refurbished by J. Hillis Miller in his *Poets of Reality* forty years on (see p. 373). According to it, art having emerged from a period of transcendentalism, Williams's poetry, along with the paintings of Marsden Hartley and John Marin, stands for a reconquest of the actual, a marriage with things. In Rosenfeld's version, it is the paintings of Ryder with their ethereal other-worldliness, that marked for the American artist the end of 'a long cycle of wandering', the end of 'the modern malady, the pathos of farness', and the beginning of an era when

Hartley, Marin, Williams are 'at home', 'in contact'. In the sort
of poetic prose that was to make Williams wince when he
reviewed Rosenfeld's *The Boy in the Sun*,[1] Rosenfeld sums it all up:
'Today, perhaps, still the oceanic waste, and the flight under the
inhuman sorcerer's moon. Tomorrow the inhabited solid earth,
and the faces of men.' Overwriting apart, *Port of New York* is one
of the fascinating forgotten books. A measure of its breadth of
intelligence is that Rosenfeld should have placed Williams in the
company of the painters, for Williams shared with them not only
a common subject matter but the vocabulary of muscular tension
that dominates their written statements. One of the most moving
passages in Rosenfeld on coming to terms with the American
present – it might almost be notes for a Williams poem – occurs in
his description of the 'slatey weed-garden of wharves, gas-tuns,
church-spires, chimneys, gash-like streets' seen from the Staten
Island ferry boat, a passage that concludes with the returning
American confronting 'a fume of strangling smoke' and deciding
to make something of it (see p. 86).

The resolve here points forward to Munson's proud title,
'William Carlos Williams, A United States Poet' (see p. 95). Yet
Munson, with his stress on literary quality, shows himself to be
clearly aware of the dangers in any mere Americanism for its own
sake. He speaks of the nationalistic impulse as revealing itself 'most
blatantly in Vachel Lindsay, most ravenously in Robert J. Coady
and his *Soil* magazine, most generalized in the allied phenomena
of the group that animated the *Seven Arts*, and most mystically in
Alfred Stieglitz'. In placing the 'Americanism' of Williams, one
must distinguish it from that of the group behind the *Seven Arts*
magazine – a group that included Rosenfeld, Van Wyck Brooks
and Waldo Frank, and which tended to look on Marianne Moore,
Pound and Williams as tainted by their Europeanism. Williams
belongs far more in the world of the *Little Review* with its strong

1 In *Dial*, vol. 85, November 1928, pp. 431–2.

French and European connection and its relations with Dada. When Williams's *In the American Grain* pleads the American cause it is in reported conversation with a strong-minded Frenchman, Valéry Larbaud. Pound and Eliot stayed on in Europe. Williams transferred what he wanted of Paris to the American scene: speaking of Whitman in *Spring and All*, he assimilates him to the company of Gris and Cézanne. Thus in his early phase he focused the cubist tradition on 'the home *milieu*', aligning cubist fragmentations with those of American photography (Stieglitz, Steichen), and making poetry out of the awareness that came to him, in part, from these sources.

In *Mechanics*, Munson values Dada for its endeavour 'to put Machinery into a positive equilibrium with man and nature', whereas 'the aggravating thing about our *milieu* is its negative attitude towards modern life'. This negativism was the trademark of the great figure who, for Rosenfeld and for Williams, seemed to deny the possibility of a renaissance that would come to terms with the present and on American soil – namely, T. S. Eliot. Rosenfeld says of Williams's poetry, 'There is no blame laid on time, custom, environment for his leanness, as there is blame in the writings of . . . T. S. Eliot.' He implicitly criticizes Eliot for casting an 'egoistical veil over the world' and for an imperiousness towards places and objects (compare Karl Shapiro's 'Our True Contemporary' in *In Defense of Ignorance*, 1952).

It was the stress on place ('Place is the only reality, the true core of the universal . . .') in terms of the native scene, that most deeply divided Williams from his life-long friend, Pound, 'with his artificial pearl' and from Eliot who 'has philosophically, I think, renounced America much more fully'. Both quotations are from the 'Tentative Statement' of 1929,[1] but Williams's feeling that Eliot's choice of Europe was 'a betrayal' goes back much further. It is there already in the 1918 *Prologue to Kora in Hell* (p. 40),

1 *Little Review*, vol. 12, May 1929, pp. 95-8.

Williams's anger having been kindled by Edgar Jepson's, 'Could anything be more US, more soul of that modern land than *The Love Song of J. Alfred Prufrock*?'[1] Williams experienced an added bitterness when he came to realize how complete was Pound's approval of Eliot's work; it grew with the publication of *The Waste Land* and, once the fact of 'the age of Eliot' had been ratified by critic after critic, Williams's vituperation became almost a reflex. (It seems to have been Robert Lowell, in a letter acknowledged by Williams, who finally mellowed the attitude of the latter.)[2] Our need is less to take sides than to understand Williams's sense that Eliot stood for a kind of poetry and a kind of criticism that left little room for his own kinds. Eliot's 'Place is only place' of *Ash Wednesday* could well be taken to be the antithesis of Williams's view of place – and both Sister Bernetta Quinn's *The Metamorphic Tradition in Modern Poetry* (1955) and Linda Wagner's *The Poems of William Carlos Williams* (1963) read the matter this way. Again, Williams's stress on place needs to be seen in its historical perspective, as coming at a given moment of cultural development. One cannot imagine any future American writer feeling the necessity of stressing place in precisely the way Williams did. His attitude to the local scene and language have, in the course of time, been absorbed by subsequent writers; they can afford to be less tense, but only because Williams was tense for them.

Eliot's criteria – and they were the influential criteria of an epoch – do not aid one much in the reading of Williams's work. Temperamentally antipathetical, Williams thought consistently in terms of new beginnings (hence *Spring and All*), Eliot in terms of endings. (Hence in his *Last Words*, in the final issue of the *Criterion*, he even decides that the artistic impetus of the twenties 'had been rather the last efforts of an old world, than the first

1 'The Wild West School', *Little Review*, vol. 5, September 1918, pp. 4–9.
2 *Selected Letters*, pp. 311–13.

struggles of a new'.) Parker Tyler imagines Williams replying to Eliot's 'objective correlative', that once fashionable catchword, with

My theory of poetry was that it arises from immediate environment, and in the case of *my* environment, America, the poetic formulas for familiar (or 'objective correlative') emotions did not exist. Why not? Because the emotions themselves, and the very imagery of their implicit situations, were elusive and unformed (see p. 157).

The sheer fact of Eliot overshadowed the existence of Williams as it did the productions of Hart Crane and Wallace Stevens. But how directly – that is, consciously – did Eliot impede Williams's critical recognition? There is no easy answer to this. Eliot's reaction to Williams consisted mostly of silence. Editing Pound's essays for publication in 1954, Eliot saw fit by this date to include 'Dr Williams's Position'. There exist at least two direct references to Williams by Eliot and both of them occur when the battle has long been decided in Eliot's favour. In his *The American Language and American Literature*, given as a lecture at the University of Washington in 1953, arguing that 'the pioneers of twentieth-century poetry were more conspicuously the Americans than the English', and stating 'the most dangerous tendency of American versifiers' as being one 'towards eccentricity and formlessness', Eliot concludes with his list of pioneers – Pound, Williams, Stevens and Marianne Moore. The second reference occurs in a letter to Richard A. Macksey, of 15 February 1959, where Eliot writes of Williams: 'Poetry springs from the most unexpected soil. . . . He continues to split rocks and find poems.'[1] What of the years of silence before these mild instances of recognition? Pound insisted that Eliot 'don't even like the best of the *Active Anth.* or

1 Quoted in *William Carlos Williams* ed. J. Hillis Miller, Prentice Hall, 1966, p. 77.

"admit" any of it, save him, me an' Marianne'.[1] Williams was interestingly represented in *The Active Anthology* (1933) and Pound's contention is also backed up by Eliot's curiously uninformed and derogatory pronouncements on contemporary American verse in both the *Dial* and the *Nouvelle Revue Française* in the early twenties. Again, why was it, during Eliot's editorship of the *Criterion*, Herbert Read's promise in those pages (February 1924 issue) that Moore's and Williams's work 'will be considered in future numbers', was never honoured as far as Williams was concerned? Perhaps there is no answer to this question that would stand up in a court of law, but Pound's continual championing of Williams remains strikingly in contrast to Eliot's apparent indifference.

It was not, however, Pound's championing which won in the early stages of the establishment of Williams's reputation in England, although things seemed to begin promisingly for him here, *The Tempers* (1913) being published in London, characteristically introduced by his friend (see p. 39). After this, little happened: an appearance in Pound's anthology, *Des Imagistes* (1914); *The Wanderer* in Conrad Aiken's *Modern American Poets* (1922); Robert Graves and Laura Riding is *A Survey of Modernist Poetry* (1927) mentioned Williams but failed to take his measure; 1926 saw D. H. Lawrence's brilliant review of *In the American Grain* ('And this, this sensitive touch upon the unseen America, is to be the really great adventure in the New World.'), but the review appeared in New York[2] and forty years were to elapse before *In the American Grain* received English publication. When Pound's *Active Anthology* came out from Faber in 1933, Williams was represented there by a number of his best poems. His appearance did little to establish him as a literary fact. F. R. Leavis wrote

Mr Pound's notion of good general intentions are both inadequate and out-of-date. There might, for instance, have been

1 *Letters of Ezra Pound, 1907–1941*, ed. D. D. Paige, Faber & Faber, 1951, p. 331.
2 Reprinted in *Phoenix*, 1936.

some show of point in presenting William Carlos Williams to the British public fifteen years ago. But it isn't the wordy debility of Georgianism that needs reacting against today.[1]

For *Scrutiny* the issue was closed, until Marius Bewley briefly re-opened it almost twenty years later in 'Aspects of Modern American Poetry'[2] only to thrust Williams aside as an example of 'rampant' Americanism, and turn to Robert Lowell. (And *Scrutiny* never saw fit to admit Williams's name to its rather bizarre index of authors.) Williams did marginally better in the *Criterion*[3] in Hugh Gordon Porteus's tiny review of *An Early Martyr*, kindly meant yet a little glib:

His verse has considerable vitality, almost no body, no dexterity, and a sentimentality so slight and so transparent that it can be accepted at once. He wears no disguises, deliberate or otherwise. You get a bit of sentiment and a bit of poetry, both quite genuine and direct, as in *An Elegy for D. H. Lawrence.* . . .

Ignored by Michael Roberts's *Faber Book of Modern Verse* in 1937, Williams had a sizeable appearance in *The Oxford Anthology of American Literature* (1939), but curiously this anthology was never distributed in England by Oxford. Williams contributed a note on his intentions that pointed out the differences between British and American English ('Pace is one of the most important of its manifestations. This is particularly significant in versification since it is the direct forerunner of poetic form'). Hugh Kenner[4] has argued that the very differences of language were to be against Williams for a long time in England: 'It is difficult for a reader who comes to these writers [Moore and Williams] with Shakespearian expectations not to find them bare and astringent to

1 *Scrutiny*, vol. 2, 1933–4, p. 300.
2 *Scrutiny*, vol. 17, 1950–51, pp. 334–52.
3 *Criterion*, vol. 15, January 1936, p. 355.
4 'Words in the Dark', *Essays by Divers Hands*, vol 29, 1958.

the point of incompetence.' Kenner maintains that the English of
Moore and Williams – very unlike the multiple levels implicit in
Shakespeare's 'strong toil of grace' or in an Empsonian teasing out
of ambiguities – is written 'out of the logic of their real world, in
which the Elizabethans in fact really did not exist.' Of course,
Kenner exaggerates, but not fantastically. And elsewhere he brings
home the point in relation to Williams when he says: 'that words
set in Jersey speech rhythms mean less but mean it with greater
finality, is Williams's chief technical perception.' Essentially, then,
Williams made no impact in England, and by the forties his works
had disappeared from notice here. It was not until the fifties that
the situation began to change and not until 1963 that a British
publisher finally brought out his work.

If Williams's recognition was largely an American affair, in the
USA this recognition was for many years confined to an
intellectually outstanding but small circle. Besides Munson,
Rosenfeld, Burke, Williams received the attention of some of the
finest practitioners of his time – Marianne Moore, Wallace Stevens,
Louis Zukofsky, Ezra Pound – yet their opinions were slow to
penetrate the general literary consciousness and the universities.
Besides this indigenous group, a French critic, René Taupin, turned
his attention to Williams in L'Influence du Symbolisme Français sur
la Poésie Américaine.[1] Although Taupin overestimates the influence
of French literature, particularly Rimbaud, on Williams, and
underestimates that of French visual art, his essay is both historically
and intrinsically important. He was early to see the nature of
Williams's dissatisfaction with 'pure imagism' and to recognize the
importance of Kora in Hell in the poet's development. This work,
according to Taupin, although not one of Williams's most
successful, provided the means whereby he came into closer contact
with his gifts. Taupin's perspective makes clear for us the way
Williams's own 'dérèglement', his deliberately oblique approach in

1 Champion, Paris, 1929.

Kora in Hell, prepared for the jagged asymmetries of *Spring and All*
where the writer is in full possession of those gifts. Here Williams
is his own best critic and the *Prologue to Kora in Hell* and the prose
sections of *Spring and All* contain some of his finest *aperçus*. In the
Prologue we get:

> ... a poem is tough by no quality it borrows from a logical
> recital of events nor from the events themselves but solely from
> that attenuated power which draws perhaps many broken things
> into a dance giving them thus a full being.

The methods of both the prose and poetry of *Spring and All* are
foreseen in this Prologue. One perceives there how Williams's
sense of a form that would resemble – he borrows Marcel
Duchamp's image – a stained glass window 'that had fallen out
and lay more or less together on the ground', and of a movement
that travels resolutely athwart, place him close to the cubist spirit,
which prevails in the 'brokenness' of composition of *Spring and All*:

> The stream of things having composed itself into wiry strands
> that move in one fixed direction, the poet in desperation turns
> at right angles and cuts across current ...
> (*Kora in Hell*, note on XV)

The perceptiveness of a Pound or Taupin carried Williams's
reputation little further than a writer's world. The publication of
his novel, *White Mule*, in 1937, promised to do for Williams what
criticism had failed to do: it drew enthusiastic notices from the
New York press (some of them of real intelligence – see, for
example, Kazin and Rahv p. 134 and p. 136) and Williams said:

> I thought I was *made*. All the lady reviewers were flocking to
> me. But this is what happened. Mr Laughlin [Williams's
> publisher] was also a skier, and right before *White Mule* was
> published he went to New Zealand as manager of a ski team.

He had published only a small quantity of the books which were sold out immediately and there were no more copies available. I got in the car and drove up to Norfolk to see Mr Laughlin senior. All he said was, 'Well, what are *you* going to do about it?' What *could* I do. There were no books and the whole thing blew up.

(*I Wanted to Write a Poem*, p. 73)

Often the tone of criticism about Williams was one of grudging approval. Thus he was chosen to play Primitivism opposite Hart Crane's Decadence in Yvor Winters's *Primitivism and Decadence: A Study of American Experimental Poetry* (1937) where one finds some interesting if idiosyncratic remarks on his poems, including a system of scansion for reading them which seems at once arbitrary and unnecessary. Winters points to the Tenochtitlan passage of *In the American Grain* as an example of great prose ('superior in all likelihood to nearly any other prose in our time and to most of the verse'), but this passage is entirely divorced by Winters from its structural context and the rest of the book is ignored. Winters reviewed the *Collected Poems* of 1938[1] concluding that '[Williams's] own excellent ear has made of free verse a complex accentual metre, very difficult to control and creating very binding conventions of feeling', and venturing the prediction, 'Williams will prove as nearly indestructible as Herrick'. When the review was reprinted in J. Hillis Miller's *William Carlos Williams* in 1966, Winters added a postscript narrowing his choice of successful poems and emphasizing his limiting judgements: 'To say that Williams was anti-intellectual would be almost an exaggeration: he did not know what intellect was.' R. P. Blackmur, in an essay of 1939, 'John Wheelwright and Dr Williams', (see p. 138) qualifies some of Winters's views – he is not sure of the justice of the Herrick comparison, but agrees that Williams has written some fine poems. Blackmur's own later 'postscript'[1] returns to Winters's charge of primitivism: 'He is contact without tact; he is objectivism without objective; l'anima semplicetta run wild . . .' But this kind of statement is possible only if you ignore Williams's best work. It was usual, as in Frederick Morgan's 'William Carlos Williams: Imagery, Rhythm, Form'[2] to look on Williams as a survivor from imagism (Blackmur even granted, 'He is . . . the imagism of 1912 self-transcended'). Morgan, like Blackmur and Winters – his tone owes something to the latter – finds felicitous poems but insists: 'Poetic statement in the free-verse form never achieves the power that metrical verse may give even in the work of a poet not of the first rank.' Never? What was needed, and what is still needed in Williams's criticism, was a clearer recognition of what a Williams poem *does*, how its recovery of weight in the syllabic components (a term like 'free verse' does little to account for this) brings a new care into both music and syntax. It is only in the fifties and sixties (see Robert Lowell, and Hugh Kenner's 'Syntax in Rutherford' pp. 366 and 306) that attention has moved in this direction and that such poetry begins to be seen, as in Robert Duncan's 'Notes on Poetics'[3] in its fuller implications for other poets – and not only American ones.

1 'Lord Tennyson's Scissors', reprinted in *Language as Gesture*, 1954.
2 *Sewanee Review*, vol. 55, October–December 1947, pp. 675–90.
3 *Black Mountain Review*, vol. 3, Spring 1956, pp. 201–11.

Ezra Pound

Introduction to *The Tempers* 1913 (reprinted in E. Heal (ed.), *I Wanted to Write a Poem*, 1958, 1967)

God forbid that I should introduce Mr Williams as a cosmic force.

To give sound criticism of a man's work after it is published is so difficult a task that we find it rarely done well, but to criticize a man's work before it is written is a task so very difficult that even I hesitate before the undertaking.

Having said recently that no man now living in America writes anything that is of interest to the serious artist, my position is none the more easy.

Mr Williams may write some very good poetry. It is not every one of whom one can say that.

Mr Williams has eschewed many of the current American vices; I therefore respect him. He has not sold his soul to editors. He has not complied with their niminy-piminy restrictions.

He apparently means what he says. He is not overcrowded with false ornament. He seems to have found his art very difficult and to be possessed of some sort of determination which has carried him through certain impasses, one can only hope that his grit is not yet exhausted.

His cadence is, to my sense, genuine, and his verse is sound as a bell – at least in places (e.g. *Homage*, second strophe[1]).

But above all these he has one virtue pre-eminent: he has not the magazine touch.

And for this I welcome him. And when I received the sheaf of his verse six months ago, I was glad. I was more glad than I can rationally explain to a critical English audience. I had found at least one compatriot to whom I could talk without a lexicon; some one who has been through somewhat the same mill that I have been through; some one who has apparently a common aim with me. And I would rather confess to a feeling of companionship than to proceed with analysing verses which the gentle reader may very well judge for himself. Yet I would mention one beautiful simile from another poem, not here printed, where he speaks of a thousand freshets

1 *Collected Earlies Poems*, p. 18.

```
                    ... crowded
Like peasants to a fair
Clear skinned, wild from seclusion.
(23-4)
```

William Carlos Williams

from *Prologue to Kora in Hell*, 1918 (reprinted in
Selected Essays, 1954)

When Margaret Anderson published my first improvisations Ezra
Pound wrote me one of his hurried letters in which he urged me to
give some hint by which the reader of good will might come at
my intention.

Before Ezra's permanent residence in London, on one of his trips
to America – brought on I think by an attack of jaundice – he was
glancing through some book of my father's. 'It is not necessary,' he
said, 'to read everything in a book in order to speak intelligently of it.
Don't tell everybody I said so,' he added.

During this same visit my father and he had been reading and
discussing poetry together. Pound has always liked my father. 'I of
course like your old man and I have drunk his Goldwasser.' They
were hot for an argument that day. My parent had been holding
forth in downright sentences upon my own 'idle nonsense' when
he turned and became equally vehement concerning something Ezra
had written: what in heaven's name Ezra meant by 'jewels' in a
verse that had come between them. These jewels, – rubies, sapphires,
amethysts and whatnot, Pound went on to explain with great determination and care, were the backs of books as they stood on a man's
shelf. 'But why in heaven's name don't you say so then?' was my
father's triumphant and crushing rejoinder.

The letter:

... God knows I have to work hard enough to escape, not
propagande, but getting entered in *propagande*. And America?
What the h—l do you a blooming foreigner know about the
place. Your *père* only penetrated the edge, and you've never
been west of Upper Darby, or the Maunchunk switchback.

Would H., with the swirl of the prairie wind in her underwear, or the Virile Sandburg recognize you, an effete easterner as a REAL American? INCONCEIVABLE!!!!!

My dear boy you have never felt the woop of the PEEraries. You have never seen the projecting and protuberant Mts. of the SIerra Nevada. WOT can you know of the country?

You have the naive credulity of a Co. Claire emigrant. But I (*der grosse Ich*) have the virus, the bacillus of the land in my blood, for nearly three bleating centuries.

(Bloody snob. 'eave a brick at 'im!!!) ...

I was very glad to see your wholly incoherent unamerican poems in the L.R.

Of course Sandburg will tell you that you miss the 'big drifts', and Bodenheim will object to your not being sufficiently decadent.

You thank your blookin gawd you've got enough Spanish blood to muddy up your mind, and prevent the current American ideation from going through it like a blighted colander.

The thing that saves your work is opacity, and don't forget it. Opacity is NOT an American quality. Fizz, swish, gabble and verbiage, these are *echt americanisch*.

And alas, alas, poor old Masters. Look at Oct. Poetry.

Let me indulge the American habit of quotation:

'Si le cosmopolitisme littéraire gagnait encore et qu'il réussit à éteindre ce que les différences de race ont allumé de haine de sang parmi les hommes, j'y verrais un gain pour la civilisation et pour l'humanité tout entière. ...

'L'amour excessif d'une patrie a pour immédiat corollaire l'horreur des patries étrangères. Non seulement on craint de quitter la jupe de sa maman, d'aller voir comment vivent les autres hommes, de se mêler à leurs luttes, de partager leurs travaux, non seulement on reste chez soi, mais on finit par fermer sa porte.

'Cette folie gagne certains littérateurs et le même professeur, en sortant d'expliquer le Cid ou Don Juan, rédige de gracieuses injures contre Ibsen et l'influence, hélas, trop illusoire, de son oeuvre, pourtant toute de lumière et de beauté.'[1] et cetera. Lie down and compose yourself.

I like to think of the Greeks as setting out for the colonies in Sicily and the Italian peninsula. The Greek temperament lent itself to a certain symmetrical sculptural phase and to a fat poetical balance of line that produced important work but I like better the Greeks setting their backs to Athens. The ferment was always richer in Rome, the dispersive explosion was always nearer, the influence carried further and remained hot longer. Hellenism, especially the modern sort, is too staid, too chilly, too little fecundative to impregnate my world.

Hilda Doolittle before she began to write poetry or at least before she began to show it to anyone would say: 'You're not satisfied with me, are you Billy? There's something lacking, isn't there?' When I was with her my feet always seemed to be sticking to the ground while she would be walking on the tips of the grass stems.

Ten years later as assistant editor of the *Egoist* she refers to my long poem *March*,[2] which thanks to her own and her husband's friendly attentions finally appeared there in a purified form:

14 August 1916

Dear Bill,

I trust you will not hate me for wanting to delete from your poem all the flippancies. The reason I want to do this is that the beautiful lines are so very beautiful – so in the tone and spirit of your *Postlude* – (which to me stands, a Nike, supreme among your poems). I think there is *real* beauty – and real beauty is a rare and sacred thing in this generation – in all the pyramid, Ashur-ban-i-pal bits and in the Fiesole and in the wind at the very last.

I don't know what you think but I consider this business of writing a very sacred thing! – I think you have the 'spark' – am sure of it, and when you speak *direct* are a poet. I feel in the hey-ding-ding touch running through your poem a derivative tendency which, to me, is not *you* – not your very

1 Remy de Gourmont, *Epilogues, Réflexions Sur la Vie*, Paris, 1903.
2 *Collected Earlier Poems*, p. 43.

self. It is as if you were *ashamed* of your Spirit, ashamed of your inspiration! – as if you mocked at your own song. It's very well to *mock* at yourself – it is a spiritual sin to mock at your inspiration –

Hilda

Oh well, all this might be very disquieting were it not that 'sacred' has lately been discovered to apply to a point of arrest where stabilization has gone on past the time. There is nothing sacred about literature, it is damned from one end to the other. There is nothing in literature but change and change is mockery. I'll write whatever I damn please, whenever I damn please and as I damn please and it'll be good if the authentic spirit of change is on it.

But in any case H. D. misses the entire intent of what I am doing no matter how just her remarks concerning that particular poem happen to have been. The hey-ding-ding touch *was* derivative, but it filled a gap that I did not know how better to fill at the time. It might be said that that touch is the prototype of the improvisations.

It is to the inventive imagination we look for deliverance from every other misfortune as from the desolation of a flat Hellenic perfection of style. What good then to turn to art from the atavistic religionists, from a science doing slavery service upon gas engines, from a philosophy tangled in a miserable sort of dialect that means nothing if the full power of initiative be denied at the beginning by a lot of baying and snapping scholiasts? If the inventive imagination must look, as I think, to the field of art for its richest discoveries today it will best make its way by compass and follow no path.

But before any material progress can be accomplished there must be someone to draw a discriminating line between true and false values.

The true value is that peculiarity which gives an object a character by itself. The associational or sentimental value is the false. Its imposition is due to lack of imagination, to an easy lateral sliding. The attention has been held too rigid on the one plane instead of following a more flexible, jagged resort. It is to loosen the attention, my attention since I occupy part of the field, that I write these improvisations. Here I clash with Wallace Stevens.

The imagination goes from one thing to another. Given many things of nearly totally divergent natures but possessing one-thousandth part of a quality in common, provided that be new, distinguished, these things belong in an imaginative category and not in a gross natural array. To me this is the gist of the whole matter. It is easy to fall under the spell of a certain mode, especially if it be remote of origin, leaving thus certain of its members essential to a reconstruction of its significance permanently lost in an impenetrable mist of time. But the thing that stands eternally in the way of really good writing is always one: the virtual impossibility of lifting to the imagination those things which lie under the direct scrutiny of the senses, close to the nose. It is this difficulty that sets a value upon all works of art and makes them a necessity. The senses witnessing what is immediately before them in detail see a finality which they cling to in despair, not knowing which way to turn. Thus the so-called natural or scientific array becomes fixed, the walking devil of modern life. He who even nicks the solidity of this apparition does a piece of work superior to that of Hercules when he cleaned the Augean stables.

Stevens's letter applies really to my book of poems, *Al Que Quiere* (which means, by the way, 'To Him Who Wants It') but the criticism he makes of that holds good for each of the improvisations if not for the *oeuvre* as a whole.

It begins with a postscript in the upper left-hand corner: 'I think, after all, I should rather send this than not, although it is quarrel-somely full of my own ideas of discipline.'

9 April

My dear Williams,

[. . .]
What strikes me most about the poems themselves is their casual character. . . . Personally I have a distaste for miscellany. It is one of the reasons I do not bother about a book myself.

[Wallace Stevens is a fine gentleman whom Cannell likened to a Pennsylvania Dutchman who has suddenly become aware of his habits and taken to 'society' in self-defense. He is always immaculately dressed. I don't know why I should always associate

him in my mind with an imaginary image I have of Ford Madox Hueffer.]

... My idea is that in order to carry a thing to the extreme necessity to convey it one has to stick to it; ... Given a fixed point of view, realistic, imagistic or what you will, everything adjusts itself to that point of view; the process of adjustment is a world in flux, as it should be for a poet. But to fidget with points of view leads always to new beginnings and incessant new beginnings lead to sterility.

(This sounds like Sir Roger de Coverley)

                                   A single manner
or mood thoroughly matured and exploited is that fresh thing ... etc.

One has to keep looking for poetry as Renoir looked for colors in old walls, woodwork and so on.

Your place is

                 – among children
        Leaping around a dead dog.
A book of that would feed the hungry ...

Well a book of poems is a damned serious affair. I am only objecting that a book that contains your particular quality should contain anything else and suggesting that if the quality were carried to a communicable extreme, in intensity and volume, etc. ... I see it all over the book, in your landscapes and portraits, but dissipated and obscured. Bouquets for brides and Spencerian compliments for poets .... There are a very few men who have anything native in them or for whose work I'd give a Bolshevik ruble. ... But I think your tantrums not half mad enough.

[*I am not quite clear about the last sentence but I presume he means that I do not push my advantage through to an overwhelming decision. What would you have me do with my Circe, Stevens, now that I have double-crossed her game, marry her? It is not what Odysseus did.*]

I return Pound's letter ... observe how in everything he does he proceeds with the greatest positiveness, etc.

Wallace Stevens

I wish that I might here set down my 'Vortex' after the fashion of London, 1913, stating how little it means to me whether I live here, there or elsewhere or succeed in this, that or the other so long as I can keep my mind free from the trammels of literature, beating down every attack of its *retiarii* with my *mirmillones*. But the time is past.

I thought at first to adjoin to each improvisation a more or less opaque commentary. But the mechanical interference that would result makes this inadvisable. Instead I have placed some of them in the preface where without losing their original intention (see reference numerals at the beginning of each) they relieve the later text and also add their weight to my present fragmentary argument.

V. No. 2. By the brokenness of his composition the poet makes himself master of a certain weapon which he could possess himself of in no other way. The speed of the emotions is sometimes such that thrashing about in a thin exaltation or despair many matters are touched but not held, more often broken by the contact.

II. No. 3. The instability of these improvisations would seem such that they must inevitably crumble under the attention and become particles of a wind that falters. It would appear to the unready that the fiber of the thing is a thin jelly. It would be these same fools who would deny tough cords to the wind because they cannot split a storm endwise and wrap it upon spools. The virtue of strength lies not in the grossness of the fiber but in the fiber itself. Thus a poem is tough by no quality it borrows from a logical recital of events nor from the events themselves but solely from that attenuated power which draws perhaps many broken things into a dance giving them thus a full being.

It is seldom that anything but the most elementary communications can be exchanged one with another. There are in reality only two or three reasons generally accepted as the causes of action. No matter what the motive it will seldom happen that true knowledge of it will be anything more than vaguely divined by some one person, some half a person whose intimacy has perhaps been cultivated over the whole of a lifetime. We live in bags. This is due to the gross fiber of all action. By action itself almost nothing can be imparted. The world of action is a world of stones.

XV. No. 1. Bla! Bla! Bla! Heavy talk is talk that waits upon a deed. Talk is servile that is set to inform. Words with the bloom on them run before the imagination like the saeter girls before Peer Gynt. It is talk with the patina of whim upon it makes action a bootlicker. So nowadays poets spit upon rhyme and rhetoric.

The stream of things having composed itself into wiry strands that move in one fixed direction, the poet in desperation turns at right angles and cuts across current with startling results to his hangdog mood.

XI. No. 2. In France, the country of Rabelais, they know that the world is not made up entirely of virgins. They do not deny virtue to the rest because of that. Each age has its perfections but the praise differs. It is only stupid when the praise of the gross and the transformed would be minted in unfit terms such as suit nothing but youth's sweetness and frailty. It is necessary to know that laughter is the reverse of aspiration. So they laugh well in France, at Coquelin and the *Petoman*. Their girls, also, thrive upon the love-making they get, so much so that the world runs to Paris for that reason.

XII. No. 2B. It is chuckleheaded to desire a way through every difficulty. Surely one might even communicate with the dead – and lose his taste for truffles. Because snails are slimy when alive and because slime is associated (erroneously) with filth, the fool is convinced that snails are detestable when, as it is proven every day, fried in butter with chopped parsley upon them, they are delicious. This is both sides of the question: the slave and the despoiled of his senses are one. But to weigh a difficulty and to turn it aside without being wrecked upon a destructive solution bespeaks an imagination of force sufficient to transcend action. The difficulty has thus been solved by ascent to a higher plane. It is energy of the imagination alone that cannot be laid aside.

Rich as are the gifts of the imagination bitterness of world's loss is not replaced thereby. On the contrary it is intensified, resembling thus possession itself. But he who has no power of the imagination cannot even know the full of his injury.

VIII. No. 3. Those who permit their senses to be despoiled of the things under their noses by stories of all manner of things removed and unattainable are of frail imagination. Idiots, it is true nothing is possessed save by dint of that vigorous conception of its perfections which is the imagination's special province but neither is anything possessed which is not extant. A frail imagination, unequal to the tasks before it, is easily led astray.

IV. No. 2. Although it is a quality of the imagination that it seeks to place together those things which have a common relationship, yet the coining of similes is a pastime of very low order, depending as it does upon a nearly vegetable coincidence. Much more keen is that power which discovers in things those inimitable particles of dissimilarity to all other things which are the peculiar perfections of the thing in question.

But this loose linking of one thing with another has effects of a destructive power little to be guessed at: all manner of things are thrown out of key so that it approaches the impossible to arrive at an understanding of anything. All is confusion, yet it comes from a hidden desire for the dance, a lust of the imagination, a will to accord two instruments in a duet.

But one does not attempt by the ingenuity of the joiner to blend the tones of the oboe with the violin. On the contrary the perfections of the two instruments are emphasized by the joiner; no means is neglected to give to each the full color of its perfections. It is only the music of the instruments which is joined and that not by the wood-worker but by the composer, by virtue of the imagination.

On this level of the imagination all things and ages meet in fellow-ship. Thus only can they, peculiar and perfect, find their release. This is the beneficent power of the imagination.

Age and youth are great flatterers. Brooding on each other's obvious psychology neither dares tell the other outright what mani-festly is the truth: your world is poison. Each is secure in his own perfections. Monsieur Eichorn used to have a most atrocious body odor while the odor of some girls is a pleasure to the nostril. Each quality in each person or age, rightly valued, would mean the freeing of that age to its own delights of action or repose. Now an evil odor can be pursued with praiseworthy ardor leading to great natural activity whereas a flowery skinned virgin may and no doubt often does allow herself to fall into destructive habits of neglect.

XIII. No. 3. A poet witnessing the chicory flower and realizing its virtues of form and color so constructs his praise of it as to borrow no particle from right or left. He gives his poem over to the flower and its plant themselves, that they may benefit by those cooling winds of the imagination which thus returned upon them will refresh them at their task of saving the world. But what does it mean, remarked his friends?

VII. *Coda.* It would be better than depriving birds of their song to call them all nightingales. So it would be better than to have a world stript of poetry to provide men with some sort of eyeglasses by which they should be unable to read any verse but sonnets. But fortunately although there are many sorts of fools, just as there are many birds which sing and many sorts of poems, there is no need to please them.

All schoolmasters are fools. Thinking to build in the young the foundations of knowledge they let slip their minds that the blocks are of gray mist bedded upon the wind. Those who will taste of the wind himself have a mark in their eyes by virtue of which they bring their masters to nothing.

All things brought under the hand of the possessor crumble to nothingness. Not only that: He who possesses a child if he cling to it inordinately becomes childlike, whereas, with a twist of the imagination, himself may rise into comradeship with the grave and beautiful presences of antiquity. But some have the power to free, say a young matron pursuing her infant, from her own possessions, making her kin to Yang Kuei-fei because of a haunting loveliness that clings about her knees, impeding her progress as she takes up her matronly pursuit.

As to the sun what is he, save for his light, more than the earth is: the same mass of metals, a mere shadow? But the winged dawn is the very essence of the sun's self, a thing cold, vitreous, a virtue that precedes the body which it drags after it.

The features of a landscape take their position in the imagination and are related more to their own kind there than to the country and season which has held them hitherto as a basket holds vegetables mixed with fruit.

VI. No. 1. A fish swimming in a pond, were his back white and his belly green, would be easily perceived from above by hawks against the dark depths of water and from below by larger fish against the penetrant light of the sky. But since his belly is white and his back green he swims about in safety. Observing this barren truth and discerning at once its slavish application to the exercises of the mind, a young man, who has been sitting for some time in contemplation at the edge of a lake, rejects with scorn the parochial deductions of history and as scornfully asserts his defiance.

XIV. No. 3. The barriers which keep the feet from the dance are the same which in a dream paralyse the effort to escape and hold us powerless in the track of some murderous pursuer. Pant and struggle but you cannot move. The birth of the imagination is like waking from a nightmare. Never does the night seem so beneficent.

The raw beauty of ignorance that lies like an opal mist over the west coast of the Atlantic, beginning at the Grand Banks and extending into the recesses of our brains – the children, the married, the unmarried – clings especially about the eyes and the throats of our girls and boys. Of a Sunday afternoon a girl sits before a mechanical piano and, working it with her hands and feet, opens her mouth and sings to the music – a popular tune, ragtime. It is a serenade. I have seen a young Frenchman lean above the piano and looking down speak gently and wonderingly to one of our girls singing such a serenade. She did not seem aware of what she was singing and he smiled an occult but thoroughly bewildered smile – as of a man waiting for a fog to lift, meanwhile lost in admiration of its enveloping beauty – fragments of architecture, a street opening and closing, a mysterious glow of sunshine.

VIII. No. 1. A man of note upon examining the poems of his friend and finding there nothing related to his immediate understanding laughingly remarked: After all, literature is communication while you, my friend, I am afraid, in attempting to do something striking, are in danger of achieving mere preciosity. – But inasmuch as the fields of the mind are vast and little explored, the poet was inclined only to smile and to take note of that hardening infirmity of the imagination which seems to endow its victim with great solidity and rapidity of judgement. But he thought to himself: And yet of what other thing is greatness composed than a power to annihilate half-truths for a thousandth part of accurate understanding.

I have discovered that the thrill of first love passes! It even becomes the backbone of a sordid sort of religion if not assisted in passing. I knew a man who kept a candle burning before a girl's portrait day and night for a year – then jilted her, pawned her off on a friend. I have been reasonably frank about my erotics with my wife. I have never or seldom said, my dear I love you, when I would rather say:

My dear, I wish you were in Tierra del Fuego. I have discovered by scrupulous attention to this detail and by certain allied experiments that we can continue from time to time to elaborate relationships quite equal in quality, if not greatly superior, to that surrounding our wedding. In fact, the best we have enjoyed of love together has come after the most thorough destruction or harvesting of that which has gone before. Periods of barrenness have intervened, periods comparable to the prison music in *Fidelio* or to any of Beethoven's pianissimo transition passages. It is at these times our formal relations have teetered on the edge of a debacle to be followed, as our imaginations have permitted, by a new growth of passionate attachment dissimilar in every member to that which has gone before.

It is in the continual and violent refreshing of the idea that love and good writing have their security. . . .

A somewhat petulant English college friend of my brother's once remarked that Britons make the best policemen the world has ever witnessed. I agree with him. It is silly to go into a puckersnatch because some brass-button-minded nincompoop in Kensington flies off the handle and speaks openly about our United States prize poems. This Mr Jepson – 'Anyone who has heard Mr J. read Homer and discourse on Catullus would recognize his fitness as a judge and respecter of poetry' – this is Ezra! – this champion of the right is not half a fool. His epithets and phrases – slipshod, rank bad workmanship of a man who has shirked his job, lumbering fakement, cumbrous artificiality, maundering dribble, rancid as *Ben Hur* – are in the main well-merited. And besides, he comes out with one fairly lipped cornet blast: the only distinctive US contributions to the arts have been ragtime and buck-dancing.

Nothing is good save the new. If a thing have novelty it stands intrinsically beside every other work of artistic excellence. If it have not that, no loveliness or heroic proportion or grand manner will save it. It will not be saved above all by an attenuated intellectuality.

But all US verse is not bad according to Mr J., there is T. S. Eliot and his *Love Song of J. Alfred Prufrock.*

But our prize poems are especially to be damned not because of superficial bad workmanship, but because they are rehash, repetition – just as Eliot's more exquisite work is rehash, repetition in another way of Verlaine, Baudelaire, Maeterlinck – conscious or unconscious –

just as there were Pound's early paraphrases from Yeats and his constant later cribbing from the Renaissance, Provence and the modern French: Men content with the connotations of their masters.

It is convenient to have fixed standards of comparison: all antiquity! And there is always some everlasting Polonius of Kensington forever to rate highly his eternal Eliot. It is because Eliot is a subtle conformist. It tickles the palate of this archbishop of procurers to a lecherous antiquity to hold up Prufrock as a New World type. Prufrock, the nibbler at sophistication, endemic in every capital, the not quite (because he refuses to turn his back), is 'the soul of that modern land', the United States!

Blue undershirts,
Upon a line,
It is not necessary to say to you
Anything about it—

I cannot question Eliot's observation. Prufrock is a masterly portrait of the man just below the summit, but the type is universal; the model in his case might be Mr J.

No. The New World is Montezuma or, since he was stoned to death in a parley, Guatemozin who had the city of Mexico leveled over him before he was taken.

For the rest, there is no man even though he dare who can make beauty his own and 'so at last live', at least there is no man better situated for that achievement than another. As Prufrock longed for his silly lady, so Kensington longs for its Hardanger dairymaid. By a mere twist of the imagination, if Prufrock only knew it, the whole world can be inverted (why else are there wars?) and the mermaids be set warbling to whoever will listen to them. Seesaw and blindman's buff converted into a sort of football.

But the summit of United States achievement, according to Mr J. – who can discourse on Catullus – is that very beautiful poem of Eliot's, *La Figlia Che Piange*: just the right amount of everything drained through, etc., etc., etc., etc., the rhythm delicately studied and – IT CONFORMS! *ergo*, here we have 'the very fine flower of the finest spirit of the United States'.

Examined closely this poem reveals a highly refined distillation.

Added to the already 'faithless' formula of yesterday we have a conscious simplicity:

Simple and faithless as a smile and shake of the hand.

The perfection of that line is beyond cavil. Yet, in the last stanza, this paradigm, this very fine flower of US art is warped out of alignment, obscured in meaning even to the point of an absolute unintelligibility by the inevitable straining after a rhyme, the very cleverness with which this straining is covered being a sinister token in itself.

And I wonder how they should have been together!

So we have no choice but to accept the work of this fumbling conjurer.

Upon the Jepson filet Eliot balances his mushroom. It is the latest touch from the literary cuisine, it adds to the pleasant outlook from the club window. If to do this, if to be a Whistler at best, in the art of poetry, is to reach the height of poetic expression then Ezra and Eliot have approached it and *tant pis* for the rest of us.

The Adobe Indian hag sings her lullaby:

The beetle is blind
The beetle is blind
The beetle is blind
The beetle is blind, etc., etc.

and Kandinsky in his, *Ueber das Geistige in der Kunst*, sets down the following axioms for the artist:

Every artist has to express himself.
Every artist has to express his epoch.
Every artist has to express the pure and eternal
    qualities of the art of all men.

So we have the fish and the bait, but the last rule holds three hooks at once – not for the fish, however.

I do not overlook De Gourmont's plea for a meeting of the nations, but I do believe that when they meet Paris will be more than slightly abashed to find parodies of the Middle Ages, Dante and *langue d'oc* foisted upon it as the best in United States poetry. Even Eliot, who is too fine an artist to allow himself to be exploited by a blockheaded grammaticaster, turns recently toward 'one definite false note' in his quatrains, which more nearly approach America than ever *La Figlia Che Piange* did. Ezra Pound is a Boscan who has met his Navagiero.

One day Ezra and I were walking down a back lane in Wyncote. I contended for bread, he for caviar. I became hot. He, with fine discretion, exclaimed: 'Let us drop it. We will never agree, or come to an agreement.' He spoke then like a Frenchman, which is one who discerns.

Imagine an international congress of poets at Paris or Versailles, Remy de Gourmont (now dead) presiding, poets all speaking five languages fluently. Ezra stands up to represent US verse and De Gourmont sits down smiling. Ezra begins by reading *La Figlia Che Piange*. It would be a pretty pastime to gather into a mental basket the fruits of that reading from the minds of the ten Frenchmen present; their impressions of the sort of United States that very fine flower was picked from. After this Kreymborg might push his way to the front and read *Jack's House*.

E. P. is the best enemy United States verse has. He is interested, passionately interested – even if he doesn't know what he is talking about. But of course he does know what he is talking about. He does not, however, know everything, not by more than half. The accordances of which Americans have the parts and the colors but not the completions before them pass beyond the attempts of his thought. It is a middle-aging blight of the imagination.

I praise those who have the wit and courage, and the conventionality, to go direct toward their vision of perfection in an objective world where the signposts are clearly marked, viz. to London. But confine them in hell for their paretic assumption that there is no alternative but their own groove.

Dear fat Stevens, thawing out so beautifully at forty! I was one day irately damning those who run to London when Stevens caught me up with his mild: 'But where in the world will you have them run to?'

Nothing that I should write touching poetry would be complete without Maxwell Bodenheim in it, even had he not said that the *Improvisations* were 'perfect', the best things I had ever done; for that I place him, Janus, first and last.

Bodenheim pretends to hate most people, including Pound and Kreymborg, but that he really goes to this trouble I cannot imagine. He seems rather to me to have the virtue of self-absorption so fully developed that hate is made impossible. Due to this, also, he is an unbelievable physical stoic. I know of no one who lives so completely in his pretenses as Bogie does. Having formulated his world neither toothache nor the misery to which his indolence reduces him can make head against the force of his imagination. Because of this he remains for me a heroic figure, which, after all, is quite apart from the stuff he writes and which only concerns him. He is an Isaiah of the butterflies.

Bogie was the young and fairly well acclaimed genius when he came to New York four years ago. He pretended to have fallen in Chicago and to have sprained his shoulder. The joint was done up in a proper Sayre's dressing and there really looked to be a bona fide injury. Of course he couldn't find any work to do with one hand so we all chipped in. It lasted a month! During that time Bogie spent a week at my house at no small inconvenience to Florence, who had two babies on her hands just then. When he left I expressed my pleasure at having had his company. 'Yes,' he replied, 'I think you have profited by my visit.' The statement impressed me by its simple accuracy as well as by the evidence it bore of that fullness of the imagination which had held the man in its tide while we had been together.

(7–25)

Marianne Moore

'*Kora in Hell*', *Contact*, no. 4   1921

'The unready would deny tough cords to the wind because they cannot split a storm endwise and wrap it upon spools.'

This statement exemplifies a part of what gives to the work of William Carlos Williams, 'a character by itself'. It is a concise, energetic disgust, a kind of intellectual hauteur which one usually associates with the French.

The acknowledgement of our debt to the imagination, constitutes, perhaps, his positive value. Compression, colour, speed, accuracy and that restraint of instinctive craftsmanship which precludes anything dowdy or laboured – it is essentially these qualities that we have in his work. Burke speaks of the imagination as the most intensive province of pleasure and pain and defines it as a creative power of the mind, representing at pleasure the images of things in the order and manner in which they were received by the senses or in combining them in a new manner and according to a different order. Dr Williams in his power over the actual, corroborates this statement. Observe how, by means of his rehabilitating power of the mind, he is able to fix the atmosphere of a moment:

It is still warm enough to slip from the weeds into the lake's edge . . . and snakes' eggs lie curling in the sun on the lonely summit.

Calvary Church with its snail's horns up sniffing the dawn – o' the wrong side!

Always one leaf at the peak twig swirling, swirling and apples rotting in the ditch.

By the brokenness of his composition (he writes) the poet makes himself master of a certain weapon which he could possess himself of in no other way.

We do not so much feel the force of this statement as we feel that there is in life, as there is in Sir Francis Bacon – in the ability to see resemblances in things which are dissimilar; in the ability to see such differences, a special kind of imagination is required, which Dr Williams has. Despite his passion for being himself and his determination not to be at the mercy of 'schoolmasters', it is only one who is academically sophisticated who could write:

Fatigued as you are, watch how the mirror sieves out the extraneous, (and)

Of what other thing is greatness composed than a power to annihilate half truths for a thousandth part of accurate understanding.

Often (he says) a poem will have merit because of some one
line or even one meritorious word. So it hangs heavily on
its stem but still secure, the tree unwilling to release it.

Such an observation certainly is not the result of pure intuition or of
any informally, semi-consciously exercised mental energy. It is not,
after all, the naïve but the authentic upon which he places value. To
the bona fide artist, affectation is degradation and in his effort to
'annihilate half truths', Dr Williams is hard, discerning, implacable
and deft. If he rates audacity too high as an aesthetic asset, there can
be no doubt that he has courage of the kind which is a necessity and
not merely an admired accessory. Discerning the world's hardness,
his reply is the reply of Carl Sandburg's boll weevil to threats of
sand, hot ashes and the river: 'That'll be ma HOME! That'll be ma
HOME!'

Where does this downhill turn up again? (he says).

Driven to the wall you'd put claws to your toes and make a
ladder of smooth bricks.

Though restive under advice, he is resigned under the impersonal,
inevitable attrition of life.

One need not be hopelessly cast down (he says) because he
cannot cut onyx into a ring to fit a lady's finger. . . . There is
neither onyx nor porphyry on these roads – only brown dirt.
For all that, one may see his face in a flower along it – even in
this light. . . . Walk in the curled mudcrusts to one side, hands
hanging. Ah well.

To discuss one's friends in print may or may not be necessitated by
fealty to art but whether there is beauty or not in Dr Williams's
discussion of persons as there is in his discussion of life – in citing the
idiosyncrasies of friends, note his calmness:

B. pretends to hate most people, . . . but that he really goes
to this trouble I cannot imagine.

Additional marks of health are to be found in his use of idiom.
He says:

If a woman laughs a little loudly one always thinks that way
of her.

Throw two shoes on the floor and see how they'll lie if you
think it's all one way.

The sharpened faculties which require exactness, instant satisfaction
and an underpinning of truth are too abrupt in their activities sometimes to follow; but the niceness and effect of vigour for which they
are responsible are never absent from Dr Williams's work and its
crisp exterior is one of its great distinctions. He again reminds one of
the French. John Burroughs says of French drivers of drays and
carts,

They are not content with a plain matter-of-fact whip as an
English or American labourer would be, but it must be a
finely modeled stalk, with a long tapering lash, tipped with
the best silk snapper.

It is silly to go into a 'puckersnatch' (Dr Williams says)
because some brass-button-minded nincompoop in Kensington
flies off the handle and speaks openly about our United
States prize poems.

In the following passage, the words 'black and peculiar' would
seem to be the snapper:

A mother will love her children most grotesquely. . . . She
will be most willing toward that daughter who thwarts her
most and not toward the little kitchen helper. So where one
is mother to any great number of people she will love best
perhaps some child whose black and peculiar hair is an exact
replica of that of the figure in Velásquez's Infanta Maria
Theresa or some Italian matron whose largeness of manner
takes in the whole street.

Despite Dr Williams's championing of the school of ignorance, or
rather of no school but experience, there is in his work the authori-
tativeness, the wise silence which knows schools and fashions well
enough to know that completeness is further down than professional
intellectuality and modishness can go.

Lamps carry far, believe me (he says) in lieu of sunshine.

What can it mean to you that a child wears pretty clothes
and speaks three languages or that its mother goes to the best
shops? . . . Men . . . buy finery and indulge in extravagant
moods in order to piece out their lack with other matter.

Kindly stupid hands, kindly coarse voices, . . . infinitely
detached, infinitely beside the question . . . and night is done
and the green edge of yesterday has said all it could.

In middle life the mind passes to a variegated October. This
is the time youth in its faulty aspirations has set for the
achievement of great summits. But having attained the
mountain top one is not snatched into a cloud but the descent
proffers its blandishments quite as a matter of course. At this
the fellow is cast into a great confusion and rather plaintively
looks about to see if any has fared better than he.

Dr Williams's wisdom, however, is not absolute and he is sometimes petulant.

'Nowadays poets spit upon rhyme and rhetoric,' he says. His work
provides examples of every rhetorical principle insisted on by
rhetoricians and one wonders upon what ground he has been able to
persuade himself that poets spit upon rhyme? Possibly by rhetoric, he
means balderdash; in this case then, we are merely the poorer by one,
of proofs for his accuracy.

It is folly (he says), to accept remorse as a criticism of
conduct.

One's manners, good or bad, are conventionalized instincts and
conduct as a combination of manners and volition, predicates whatever is the result of it, so that remorse is automatically a criticism of
conduct; but Dr Williams is essentially a poet. It is true, as he says,
that 'by direct onslaught or by some back road of the intention the
gifted will win the recognition of the world.' His book is alive with
meaning; in it, 'thoughts are trees' and 'leaves load the branches'. But
one who sets out to appraise him has temerity, since he speaks
derisively of the wish of certain of his best friends to improve his

work and, after all, the conflict between the tendency to aesthetic anarchy and the necessity for self-imposed discipline must take care of itself.

As for leaving nothing unsaid – or to be accurate, something unsaid – there is no topic which a thoughtful person would refuse to discuss if gain were to result; but so far as one can see, the peculiar force of Dr Williams's work does not gain by an allusion to topics of which the average person never thinks unless inescapably for humanitarian reasons. Dr Williams is too sincere to wish to be fashionable and that one so rich in imagination should have to be thrifty in the use of poetic material is preposterous. One's perspicacity here meets a stone wall.

So disdainful, so complex a poet as Dr Williams, receives at best half treatment from the average critic or from the ambitious critic, such untruthful, half specific approbation as, 'Ah, quite deep; I see to the bottom.' This is to be expected. There is in Dr Williams an appetite for the essential and in how many people may one find it? How many poets, old or new, have written anything like *January Morning*[1] in *Al Que Quiere!*, like the second paragraph of Improvisation XVII in the present volume, and pre-eminently, the *Portrait of the Author*[2] in a recent number of *Contact*? Withholding comment upon the title, this poem is a super-achievement. It preserves the atmosphere of a moment, into which the impertinence of life cannot intrude. In the sense conveyed, of remoteness from what is detestable, in the effect of balanced strength, in the flavour of newness in presentation, it is unique.

(5–8)

1 *Collected Earlier Poems*, p. 162.
2 p. 228.

Kenneth Burke

'Heaven's First Law', a review of *Sour Grapes*, *Dial*, vol. 72   1922

It had once been my privilege to see a page written by William Carlos Williams on which he undertook to reproduce nine times the lovely sunshine thought, 'Order is Heaven's first law'. Now, by the fifth time, the poet became noticeably impatient, and from the seventh on the copy was completely unreadable. The ninth version was a mere wavy line, broken in four places. At first I took this to be quite damning; but on second thought, what use could Williams make of order? He thinks in an entirely different set of terms. To add organization to his poetry would have no more meaning than to insist that his lines begin in alphabetical rotation.

What Williams sees, he sees in a flash. And if there is any correlation whatsoever, it is a certain determined joyousness in a poet who would find it awkward to weep. For as his arch-enemy has noted, Williams is a bad Freudian case whose poetry is certainly not allowed to come out the way it came in. But beyond this very reasonable pudency, which he shares with no less an artist than Flaubert, consistency falls away.

No, Williams is the master of the glimpse. A line of his, suddenly leaping up out of the text, will throw the reader into an unexpected intimacy with his subject, like pushing open a door and advancing one's nose into some foreign face. Given a subject, he will attack it with verve, striking where he can break through its defence, and expecting applause whenever a solid, unmistakable jolt has been landed. It would be mere idleness to give his *ars poetica* in more presumptuous terms. The process is simply this: There is the eye, and there is the thing upon which that eye alights; while the relationship existing between the two is a poem.

The difficulty here lies in conveying the virtues of such a method. For the method itself is as common as mud. The minute fixating of a mood, an horizon, a contrast; if one finds there any unusual commendation for Williams it is not in the excellence of his poetics, but in the excellence of his results. His first virtue, therefore, lies in the superiority of *his* minute fixations over those of his ten million competitors. He is a distinguished member of a miserable crew.

Honest people who really think highly enough of words to feel unhappy when they are vague will rejoice that Williams's new volume, Sour Grapes, is more sober in this respect than the Improvisations. For the Improvisations were not finally satisfactory. Clear notes were there in abundance, but they were usually preceded and followed by the usual modern data for mental tests. (How beautiful the association of ideas would have been in art if used in one work, by one man, for one page, and for some end other than that of a beautiful association of ideas.) True, by the mere dissatisfaction of their context, such momentary beatitudes of expression received their full share of enthusiasm, but having twenty sentences of chaos to heighten one sentence of cosmos is too much like thanking God for headaches since they enable us to be happy without them.

Sour Grapes, however, skips a generation and takes after the volume, Al Que Quiere. And in these two works, it seems to me, Williams is at his best, since here he is not handicapping his remarkable powers of definition, of lucidity. You may wonder, perhaps, just why the poet is going off in some particular direction; but you are always aware just what this direction is. Here also his inveterate lustiness is up to par; for Williams knows Walt Whitman's smile down to the last wrinkle. If there are logs in the grate, he puts a match to them; if it is a warm Easter morning, he throws off his coat. And if, behind it all, there is evidence of a strong tendency towards transgression, towards, let us say, the mountains of Tibet or a Negro harem in Madagascar, such things are there as an irritant rather than as a subject. The face value of the poems will always remain the definition of the poet's own gatepost. His peculiar gifts of expression, if nothing else, dictate this simplification. Williams evidently realizes that his emotions are one thing and his art another, and that those who wish to go beyond his minute fixations can find a great deal more implicated in them; but in the meantime, let the minute fixations suffice.

I should say, therefore, that Williams was engaged in discovering the shortest route between object and subject. And whether it is a flamingo befouling its own tail, or the tired ogling at little girls, or trees stark naked in a wind, one must always recognize the unusual propriety of his poetry, the sureness and directness with which he goes at such things. A fact with him finds its justification in the trimness of the wording.

If a man is walking, it is the first principle of philosophy to say that he is *not* walking, the first principle of science to say that he is placing one foot before the other and bringing the hinder one in turn to the fore, the first principle of art to say that the man is *more than* walking, he is *yearning*: then there are times when scientist, philosopher and poet all discover of a sudden that by heavens! the man is walking and none other. Now, a good deal of this discovery is in Williams's poetry, and, if I understand the word correctly, is contained in his manifesto praising Contact in art. For I take Contact to mean: man without the syllogism, without the parode, without Spinoza's Ethics, man with nothing but the thing and the feeling of that thing. Sitting down in the warmth to write, for instance, Kant might finally figure it out that man simply must have standards of virtue in spite of the bleakness of the phenomenon–noumenon distinction, and that this virtue could be constructed on the foundations of a categorical imperative. But Williams, sitting down in the warmth to write, would never get over his delight that the wind outside was raging ineffectually; and, in his pronounced sense of comfort, he would write:

January

Again I reply to the triple winds
running chromatic fifths of derision
outside my window:
                  Play louder.
You will not succeed. I am
bound more to my sentences
the more you batter at me
to follow you.
             And the wind,
as before, fingers perfectly
its derisive music.[1]

Seen from this angle, Contact might be said to resolve into the counterpart of Culture, and Williams becomes thereby one of our most distinguished Neanderthal men. His poetry deals with the coercions of nature – and by nature I mean iron rails as well as iron

1 *Collected Earlier Poems*, p. 197.

ore – rather than with the laborious structure of ideas man has erected above nature. His hatred of the idea in art is consequently pronounced, and very rightly brings in its train a complete disinterest in form. (Note: Form in literature must always have its beginnings in idea. In fact, our word for idea comes from a Greek word whose first meaning is 'form'.) The Contact writer deals with his desires; the Culture writer must erect his desires into principles and deal with those principles rather than with the desires; the *Urphenomen*, in other words, becomes with the man of Culture of less importance than the delicate and subtle instruments with which he studies it.

Williams, however, must go back to the source. And the process undeniably has its beauties. What, for instance, could be more lost, more uncorrelated, a closer Contact, a greater triumph of anti-Culture, than this poem:

The Great Figure

Among the rain
and lights
I saw the figure 5
in gold
on a red
firetruck
moving
with weight and urgency
tense
unheeded
to gong clangs
siren howls
and wheels rumbling
through the dark city.[1]
(197–200)

1 p. 230.

Gorham B. Munson

'The Mechanics for a Literary "Secession"', *S4N*, Year 4
November 1922

In the spring of 1922 I founded in Vienna, after many talks in Paris
with Matthew Josephson, a small literary review named *Secession*. If
this were an isolated personal venture, I should hesitate to claim
importance for it. But as it was, I believe, predicated by American
literary activity at large, and as it may link up with possible important
developments in American letters, and as it aims to focus the energies
of six or eight interesting young writers into an organ all their own,
I am perhaps justified in mentioning it here.

I begin with a general call to writers to secede.

And literary secession, in the sense it conveys to me, is a calm
intelligent resolute swerving aside, an emotional sloughing-off of
irrelevant drains upon our energies and a prompt deviation into
purely aesthetic concerns. It is that rather than the direct violent
opposition we mean by revolt.

The first requisite for a secession has been established. We have
something from which to secede. The last decade has seen a literary
milieu created in America. A corps of novelists, poets and critics has
thrust up, whose members one can take as seriously as, say, Arnold
Bennett or Octave Mirbeau or John Drinkwater or Sudermann or
A. B. Walkley. That is a great advance over previous American
decades. A public, numbering by the wildest estimate 20,000, has
come into being for these writers. And a number, too few by far,
of magazines and publishers have closed the gap between writers and
audience. The bondage to a stultifying amalgam brightly named
genteelness – (its constituents were a pioneer-puritan-industrialist
moralism and a servility to English Victorianism) – has now been
shattered, for a minority anyway. Russian and French influences have
sifted in. Finally, a considerable total of activity in writing, reading,
publishing, collecting, gossip has been generated.

The net result may be indicated by saying that the permanent
expatriate type is extinct. The act of Ezra Pound in 1908 need not be
repeated. The young American can now function in his home *milieu*.

If he doesn't like it, he has another and less distorting alternative than revolt into exile; he can secede.

The second requisite is, of course, the presence of bitter necessities demanding secession. And these today's scene, for all the nourishment it provides, protrudes amply. One of them is the aesthetic sterility of the present directions of American letters. The counter-attack on puritanism which absorbs a number of critics is useful to an artist, as the acquisition of the means of living is useful to him. And naturalism and realism up to, but not including, Dostoevsky have received their maximum aesthetic exploitation in Europe. Dostoevsky murdered them. Possibly Waldo Frank will perform their *coup de grâce* for us. Consequently, Sinclair Lewis, Floyd Dell, Zona Gale, Sherwood Anderson, Theodore Dreiser, *et al.* are merely giving us more or less duplicate effects: they are laboring within exhausted forms. The most interesting values of their work are social rather than aesthetic: they are a means for a candid unflinching examination by us of American life. Incidentally, Europe has been through all this: we are merely catching up. Whitman, like Shakespeare, was a full stop to a period. Both periods have passed, and a full stop bars progression and makes departure imperative. The psychological school, too, is for the most part on a barren tack, since it makes a means, psychology, into an ultimate. Social dynamics, psychological dynamics, how much of our letters they include!

The bitterest thing is the 'good taste' that has been erected on these conditions. Genius, remember, is at first always in 'bad taste'. For 'good taste' takes only the dominant literary tendencies of the day, generalizes from them, and condemns the unfamiliar. Canons based on Sinclair Lewis, James Branch Cabell and Robert Frost and pasted up solemnly each week in the *New Republic* or the *Nation* recognize creation only within these canons. They concentrate (although that is not wholly the fault of Messrs Cabell and Frost) the attention upon materials rather than presentation and upon the non-aesthetic rather than the aesthetic. Let us say with that tiresome ass, Picabia, 'All people of good taste are rotten'. We shall be, at least, in a better position to recognize a new genius.

Another bitter necessity is the general flabbiness of American criticism. It is united and vigorous towards a stupid reactionaryism. Within its own general faction, it is too enervatingly harmonious.

There is no effective pacemaking for it: there are no mortal duels fought. It has a disgusting uniformity. Its amiability, one often suspects, covers a nervous ignorance. In their lack of questioning each other, American critics reveal an absence of a refined intensity of interest in their problems. To cap it, their audience is of unparalleled docility. It does not disturb slowness and softness. Let a critic like Paul Rosenfeld once gain its ear regularly through the columns of the *Dial* and *Vanity Fair* and no rude voice will arise to interrupt his dreams of competence. His huge mud-bed of undisciplined emotionalism, his inflated windbag of premature ejaculations no one, apparently, thinks of dredging or pricking. Blithely complacent, he goes undisturbed. This docility does not even protest against smartish, gossipy, men-about-town journalistic critics (e.g. Burton Rascoe) posing as 'advanced' critics: it does not flip off the froth which conceals their sub-surface sub-academicism. Truly, here is a situation which calls for the tonic injection of a little ferocity!

Finally, the aggravating thing about our *milieu* is its negative attitude towards modern life. Machinery is recognized only as a necessary evil against which one is to erect counter-forms or anti-bodies, generally to the accompaniment of eloquent whines and lamentations. There is a dualism here – Machinery and the values of life – which may be as pernicious as the man-and-nature dualism of the puritan. The glory of the French dadaists to my mind rests principally upon their endeavor to put Machinery into a positive equilibrium with man and nature.

The last requisite is a nucleus of writers who are ripe for a secession. And this nucleus, I believe, our youngest generation, the chaps from twenty to twenty-six or so, provide. They have been able to mature much more rapidly than their predecessors: they owe these a debt of gratitude for making it easy to throw off preliminary entanglements and strike out freely into immediate aesthetic interests. So that it was possible for one of them, Malcolm Cowley, to say:

Form, simplification, strangeness, respect for literature as an art with traditions, abstractness . . . these are the catchwords that are repeated most often among the younger writers.

Form, first. That brings in the intellect and rejects purely intuitional emotional work as insufficient. The desire for it makes it an aim to produce work that not only has an emotional appeal, but that can exhaust a surveying intelligence. It leads to research in the inherent properties of words, it sets up an expression as its desideratum that shall be purely literary and non-transferable into any other art. It says No to Mallarmé's 'musicality of literature' theory. One of the distinguishing marks of 'secessionist' writing is its cerebral quality, manifested particularly by Kenneth Burke and Malcolm Cowley.

Simplification. That means the replacement of hazy vague states of mind by stark hard definition, by the accurate rendering of immediate sensations. Concretely, this is exemplified by the work of an older poet with a strong following among the young men, William Carlos Williams. Somewhat differently, E. E. Cummings also simplifies.

Strangeness. The movement away from naturalism and realism, the deliberate imposition upon a basically realistic attitude of romantic materials for the intellect to exploit and arrange. It includes the subjection of new materials such as exclusively modern sensations produced by machinery. The true meaning of romanticism is the crusade for new materials. The example is Matthew Josephson, who deliberately negates logic with his intellect and becomes an intellectual freebooter.

Respect for literature as an art with traditions. That is to say, the youngest writers go back of Shaw and Ibsen. Their favorite source-books are Elizabethan. And their principal foreign influence is French in two opposed tendencies – one from de Gourmont, the other from Apollinaire and the dadaists.

Finally, abstractness, the concomitant of form. Literature, while remaining representative, must also have an abstract significance. Its parts – introductions, transitions, progressions, conclusions – must all function as such, must relate to each other with thrusts, suspensions, recoils, intersections and masses.

Here, then, is a program in the rough. It would probably be endorsed by all the writers I have named as I thought of them exemplifying one catchword or another in a special degree. There are other ingredients. I mention two employed by individuals rather than by a group. One is a new reorganization of consciousness (that is, a new primitiveness) represented by such diverse precultural writers as William Carlos Williams, Waldo Frank and E. E. Cummings. Williams I have spoken of. Frank, more instinctive and emotional though still very intelligent, locates on the fringes of the *Secession* group. He has definitely left behind the older slope of consciousness, so gigantically summed up in Joyce's *Ulysses*, and out of chaos is formulating a new slope. Cummings is a naif boy whose 'intelligence functions at intuitional velocity', to quote his words on Lachaise. Cummings too, is the only one so far to declare himself favorably on the American language, the literary use of which is the second ingredient I had in mind.

It is for this group and kindred writers like Slater Brown, Hart Crane and Foster Damon that I founded *Secession*. In a limited way it prints them and combats 'good taste' and wages a ferocious tangential warfare.

I invite the readers of *S4N* to partake as they see fit in a necessary movement.

(Unpaginated)

William Carlos Williams

from *Spring and All*   1923 (reprinted in W. Schott (ed.), *Imaginations*, 1970)

It is spring. That is to say, it is approaching THE BEGINNING.

In that huge and microscopic career of time, as it were a wild horse racing in an illimitable pampa under the stars, describing immense and microscopic circles with his hoofs on the solid turf, running without a stop for the millionth part of a second until he is aged and worn to a heap of skin, bones and ragged hoofs – In that majestic progress of life, that gives the exact impression of Phidias's frieze, the men and beasts of which, though they seem of the rigidity of marble are not so but move, with blinding rapidity, though we do not have the time to notice it, their legs advancing a millionth part of an inch every fifty thousand years – In that progress of life which seems stillness itself in the mass of its movements – at last SPRING is approaching.

(94)

The fight is on: These men who have had the governing of the mob through all the repetitious years resent the new order. Who can answer them? One perhaps here and there but it is an impossible situation. If life were anything but a bird, if it were a man, a Greek or an Egyptian, but it is only a bird that has eyes and wings, a beak, talons and a cry that reaches to every rock's center, but without intelligence? –

The voice of the Delphic Oracle itself, what was it? A poisonous gas from a rock's cleft.

Those who led yesterday wish to hold their sway a while longer. It is not difficult to understand their mood. They have their great weapons to hand: 'science', 'philosophy' and most dangerous of all 'art'.

(98)

The man of imagination who turns to art for release and fulfilment of his baby promises contends with the sky through layers of demoded words and shapes. Demoded, not because the essential vitality which begot them is laid waste – this cannot be so, a young man feels, since he feels it in himself – but because meanings have been lost through laziness or changes in the form of existence which have let words empty.

Bare handed the man contends with the sky, without experience of existence seeking to invent and design.

Crude symbolism is to associate emotions with natural phenomena such as anger with lightning, flowers with love, it goes further and associates certain textures with

Such work is empty. It is very typical of almost all that is done by the writers who fill the pages every month of such a paper as. Everything that I have done in the past – except those parts which may be called excellent – by chance, have that quality about them.

It is typified by use of the word 'like' or that 'evocation' of the 'image' which served us for a time. Its abuse is apparent. The insignificant 'image' may be 'evoked' never so ably and still mean nothing.

(100–101)

The better work men do is always done under stress and at great personal cost.

It is no different from the aristocratic compositions of the earlier times, The Homeric inventions

but

these occurred in different times, to this extent, that life had not yet sieved through its own multiformity. That aside, the work the two-thousand-year-old poet did and that we do are one piece. That is the vitality of the classics.

So then – Nothing is put down in the present book – except through weakness of the imagination – which is not intended as of a piece with the 'nature' which Shakespeare mentions and which Hartley speaks of so completely in his *Adventures:*[1] it is the common thing which is anonymously about us.

Composition is in no essential an escape from life. In fact if it is so it is negligible to the point of insignificance. Whatever 'life' the artist may be forced to lead has no relation to the vitality of his compositions. Such names as Homer, the blind; Scheherazade, who lived under threat – Their compositions have as their excellence an identity with life since they are as actual, as sappy as the leaf of the tree which never moves from one spot.

What I put down of value will have this value: an escape from crude symbolism, the annihilation of strained associations, complicated ritualistic forms designed to separate the work from 'reality' – such as rhyme, meter as meter and not as the essential of the work, one of its words.

But this smacks too much of the nature of – This is all negative and appears to be boastful. It is not intended to be so. Rather the opposite.

The work will be in the realm of the imagination as plain as the sky is to a fisherman – A very clouded sentence. The word must be put down for itself, not as a symbol of nature but a part, cognizant of the whole – aware – civilized.

(101–102)

There is only 'illusion' in art where ignorance of the bystander confuses imagination and its works with cruder processes. Truly men feel an enlargement before great or good work, an expansion but this is not, as so many believe today a 'lie', a stupefaction, a kind of mesmerism, a thing to block out 'life', bitter to the individual, by a 'vision of beauty'. It is a work of the imagination. It gives the feeling of completion by revealing the oneness of experience; it rouses rather than stupefies the intelligence by demonstrating the importance of personality, by showing the individual, depressed before it, that his

1 Marsden Hartley, *Adventures in the Arts*, Boni & Liveright, 1921.

life is valuable – when completed by the imagination. And then only. Such work elucidates –

Such a realization shows us the falseness of attempting to 'copy' nature. The thing is equally silly when we try to 'make' pictures –

But such a picture as that of Juan Gris, though I have not seen it in color, is important as marking more clearly than any I have seen what the modern trend is: the attempt is being made to separate things of the imagination from life, and obviously, by using the forms common to experience so as not to frighten the onlooker away but to invite him,

(107)

Things with which he is familiar, simple things – at the same time to detach them from ordinary experience to the imagination. Thus they are still 'real' they are the same things they would be if photographed or painted by Monet, they are recognizable as the things touched by the hands during the day, but in this painting they are seen to be in some peculiar way – detached

Here is a shutter, a bunch of grapes, a sheet of music, a picture of sea and mountains (particularly fine) which the onlooker is not for a moment permitted to witness as an 'illusion'. One thing laps over on the other, the cloud laps over on the shutter, the bunch of grapes is part of the handle of the guitar, the mountain and sea are obviously not 'the mountain and sea', but a picture of the mountain and the sea. All drawn with admirable simplicity and excellent design – all a unity –

This was not necessary where the subject of art was not 'reality' but related to the 'gods' – by force or otherwise. There was no need of the 'illusion' in such case since there was none possible where a picture or a work represented simply the imaginative reality which existed in the mind of the onlooker. No special effort was necessary to cleave where the cleavage already existed.

I don't know what the Spanish see in their Velázquez and Goya but

Today where everything is being brought into sight the realism of art has bewildered us, confused us and forced us to re-invent in order to retain that which the older generations had without that effort.

Cézanne –

The only realism in art is of the imagination. It is only thus that the work escapes plagiarism after nature and becomes a creation

Invention of new forms to embody this reality of art, the one thing which art is, must occupy all serious minds concerned.

From the time of Poe in the US – the first American poet had to be a man of great separation – with close identity with life. Poe could not have written a word without the violence of expulsive emotion combined with the in-driving force of a crudely repressive environment. Between the two his imagination was forced into being to keep him to that reality, completeness, sense of escape which is felt in his work – his topics. Typically American – accurately, even inevitably set in his time.
(110–111)

Whitman's proposals are of the same piece with the modern trend toward imaginative understanding of life. The largeness which he interprets as his identity with the least and the greatest about him, his 'democracy' represents the vigor of his imaginative life.
(112–13)

Understood in a practical way, without calling upon mystic agencies, of this or that order, it is that life becomes actual only when it is identified with ourselves. When we name it, life exists. To repeat physical experiences has no –

The only means he has to give value to life is to recognize it with the imagination and name it; this is so. To repeat and repeat the thing without naming it is only to dull the sense and results in frustration.

this makes the artist the prey of life. He is easy of attack.

I think often of my earlier work and what it has cost me not to have been clear. I acknowledge I have moved chaotically about refusing or rejecting most things, seldom accepting values or acknowledging anything.

because I early recognized the futility of acquisitive understanding and at the same time rejected religious dogmatism. My whole life has been spent (so far) in seeking to place a value upon experience and the objects of experience that would satisfy my sense of inclusiveness without redundancy – completeness, lack of frustration with the liberty of choice; the things which the pursuit of 'art' offers –

But though I have felt 'free' only in the presence of works of the imagination, knowing the quickening of the sense which came of it, and though this experience has held me firm at such times, yet being of a slow but accurate understanding, I have not always been able to complete the intellectual steps which would make me firm in the position.

So most of my life has been lived in hell – a hell of repression lit by flashes of inspiration, when a poem such as this or that would appear

What would have happened in a world similarly lit by the imagination

Oh yes, you are a writer! a phrase that has often damned me, to myself. I rejected it with heat but the stigma remained. Not a man, not an understanding but a WRITER. I was unable to recognize.

I do not forget with what heat too I condemned some poems of some contemporary praised because of their loveliness –

I find that I was somewhat mistaken – ungenerous

Life's processes are very simple. One or two moves are made and that is the end. The rest is repetitious.

The *Improvisations* – coming at a time when I was trying to remain firm at great cost – I had recourse to the expedient of letting life go completely in order to live in the world of my choice.

I let the imagination have its own way to see if it could save itself. Something very definite came of it. I found myself alleviated but most important I began there and then to revalue experience, to understand what I was at –

The virtue of the improvisations is their placement in a world of new values –

their fault is their dislocation of sense, often complete. But it is the best I could do under the circumstances. It was the best I could do and retain any value to experience at all.

Now I have come to a different condition. I find that the values there discovered can be extended. I find myself extending the understanding to the work of others and other things –

I find that there is work to be done in the creation of new forms, new names for experience

and that 'beauty' is related not to 'loveliness' but to a state in which reality plays a part

Such painting as that of Juan Gris, coming after the impressionists, the expressionists, Cézanne – and dealing severe strokes as well to the expressionists as to the impressionists group – points forward to what will prove the greatest painting yet produced.

– the illusion once dispensed with, painting has this problem before it: to replace not the forms but the reality of experience with its own – (115–17)

I suppose Shakespeare's familiar aphorism about holding the mirror up to nature has done more harm in stabilizing the copyist tendency of the arts among us than –

the mistake in it (though we forget that it is not S. speaking but an imaginative character of his) is to have believed that the reflection of nature is nature. It is not. It is only a sham nature, a 'lie'.

Of course S. is the most conspicuous example desirable of the falseness of this very thing.

He holds no mirror up to nature but with his imagination rivals nature's composition with his own.

He himself become 'nature' – continuing 'its' marvels – if you will

I am often diverted with a recital which I have made for myself concerning Shakespeare: he was a comparatively uninformed man, quite according to the orthodox tradition, who lived from first to last a life of amusing regularity and simplicity, a house and wife in the suburbs, delightful children, a girl at court (whom he really never confused with his writing) and a café life which gave him with the freshness of discovery, the information upon which his imagination fed. London was full of the concentrates of science and adventure. He saw at 'The Mermaid' everything he knew. He was not conspicuous there except for his spirits.

His form was presented to him by Marlow [sic], his stories were the common talk of his associates or else some compiler set them before him. His types were particularly quickened with life about him.

Feeling the force of life, in his peculiar intelligence, the great dome of his head, he had no need of anything but writing material to relieve himself of his thoughts. His very lack of scientific training loosened his power. He was unencumbered.

For S. to pretend to knowledge would have been ridiculous – no escape there – but that he possessed knowledge, and extraordinary knowledge, of the affairs which concerned him, as they concerned the others about him, was self-apparent to him. It was not apparent to the others.

His actual power was PURELY of the imagination. Not permitted to speak as W.S., in fact peculiarly barred from speaking so because of his lack of information, learning, not being able to rival his fellows in scientific training or adventure and at the same time being keen enough, imaginative enough, to know that there is no escape except in perfection, in excellence, in technical excellence – his buoyancy of imagination raised him NOT TO COPY them, not to holding the mirror up to them but to equal, to surpass them as a creator of knowledge, as a vigorous, living force above their heads.
(121-2)

The imagination uses the phraseology of science. It attacks, stirs, animates, is radio-active in all that can be touched by action. Words occur in liberation by virtue of its processes.

In description words adhere to certain objects. and have the effect on the sense of oysters, or barnacles.

But the imagination is wrongly understood when it is supposed to be a removal from reality in the sense of John of Gaunt's speech in Richard the Second: to imagine possession of that which is lost. It is rightly understood when John of Gaunt's words are related not to their sense as objects adherent to his son's welfare or otherwise but as a dance over the body of his condition accurately accompanying it. By this means of the understanding, the play written to be understood as a play, the author and reader are liberated to pirouette with the words which have sprung from the old facts of history, reunited in present passion.

To understand the words as so liberated is to understand poetry. That they move independently when set free is the mark of their value

Imagination is not to avoid reality, nor is it description nor an evocation of objects or situations, it is to say that poetry does not tamper with the world but moves it – It affirms reality most powerfully and therefore, since reality needs no personal support but exists free from human action, as proven by science in the indestructibility of matter and of force, it creates a new object, a play, a dance which is not a mirror up to nature but –

As birds' wings beat the solid air without which none could fly so words freed by the imagination affirm reality by their flight

Writing is likened to music. The object would be it seems to make poetry a pure art, like music. Painting too. Writing, as with certain of the modern Russians whose work I have seen, would use unoriented sounds in place of conventional words. The poem then would be completely liberated when there is identity of sound with something – perhaps the emotion.

I do not believe that writing is music. I do not believe writing would gain in quality or force by seeking to attain to the conditions of music.

I think the conditions of music are objects for the action of the writer's imagination just as a table or –

According to my present theme the writer of imagination would attain closest to the conditions of music not when his words are dissociated from natural objects and specified meanings but when they are liberated from the usual quality of that meaning by transposition into another medium, the imagination.

Sometimes I speak of imagination as a force, an electricity or a medium, a place. It is immaterial which: for whether it is the condition of a place or a dynamization its effect is the same: to free the world of fact from the impositions of 'art' (see Hartley's last chapter[1]) and to liberate the man to act in whatever direction his disposition leads.

The word is not liberated, therefore able to communicate release from the fixities which destroy it until it is accurately tuned to the fact which giving it reality, by its own reality establishes its own freedom from the necessity of a word, thus freeing it and dynamizing it at the same time.

(149–50)

Paul Rosenfeld

'William Carlos Williams', *Port of New York* 1924, 1961

The poems of William Carlos Williams are good biting stuff. Lyric substance has gotten a novel acidulousness of him. Scent bitter like the nasturtium's, and like the nasturtium's fresheningly pungent, mounts off his small spikey forms. The sharp things make gay dangerous

1 Marsden Hartley, *Adventures in the Arts.*

guerilla upon the alkalis coating the brain. Corrosive fluid destroys the properties characteristic of ubiquitous Huyler's; leaves crystals of valuable salt. Poems startle with suddenly brandished cutlery. Poems writhe with the movements of bodies vainly twisting to loose themselves from fixed scorching points. Certain waver indeterminately, blankly, high up in air. Certain murmur faintly, turned in upon themselves. The tone achieves grotesque modulations. It falls unceremoniously from plane to distant unrelated plane; drops out of stars to pinholes; takes queer, off, sour, turns. Words shock with the unexpectedness of their thrusts, scratch voluptuously an instant, sting with soft sudden fangs. Notes are hammered staccato. Queries and ejaculations enter like bird-shot discharged from the muzzle of a Winchester shot-gun. Color-words come; black, yellow, green, white; but what they impart tastes not of fruit-pulps, but of mineral traces in clear spring-water.

Williams's writings are laconic acclamations of the courage to swallow bitter-flavored medicines, to bear unflinchingly the pain of violent cauterizations. They are the forms wherein a poet has given deep sober thanks to the principle by means of which he has managed to maintain his own spirit intact on a steep inclement bank of life, some Greenland on the verge of the Arctic circle. And the homely magic he wishes to hold before men's eyes is light-hearted self-irony, relentless impersonality of regard, sense of the comic and grotesque in his own career, bald matter-of-factness, willingness to stand evil smells and not run from them. Life has tempted this man with the dope of candies; urged glucose on him, cheap substitute for absent sweetnesses. For the world he inhabits is not liberal with satisfactions. It is a world of lowish climaxes and thin releases; whether from premature agedness or retarded youth, one does not know. Monotonous gray of repetition, of usedness, unrolls its scroll day-long across the firmament. At infrequent intervals, slits are cut in the drab-hued curtain. Rose quivers awhile like the ballet of pink slippers with gay pom-poms descending the stairs. A day hops like a yellow bird in April branches. Through the night from afar a sprig of tower-lights hangs against profoundest blue and utters the salutation of joyful cities. Two hours of golden promenade arrive: Columbus's first walk on new-world ground 'among the trees, which was the most beautiful thing which I had ever seen'. The streets end in the sun, and there is

... blue mist
in the distance
with grapevine trellises
with grape clusters
small as strawberries
on the vines
and ditches
running springwater
that continue the gutters
with willows over them.
The reeds begin
like water at a shore
their pointed petals waving
dark green and light.[1]

But the colors are not permanent nor intense enough to change the
aspect of their world. They are merely sufficiently satisfying to keep
the organism in motion. That is all.

Winter is long in this climate
and spring – a matter of a few days
only, – a flower or two picked
from mud or from wet leaves
or at best against treacherous
bitterness of wind, and sky shining
teasingly, then closing in black
and sudden with fierce jaws.[2]

No gradual suns nurse the small hardish buds on the black branches,
melting their green and tight condition, gathering warm color and
sweet flesh until the earth is round and drunk with curving greenery
and clustering juicèd fruits. And when blaze of July strikes them
finally, it arrives upon them with such cruel suddenness that of the
unopened things many shrivel and char upon their stalks, and few
come to radiant maturity. The gray remains; the earth is month-long
scraggly and bare, decked meagerly with a few single separate objects
selected by the poet's subconscious from off the Jersey flats: a shad-
bush on the edge of a clearing, a solitary track of footprints in the

1 *Collected Earlier Poems*, p. 225.   2 p. 43.

snow, a fire in an ash-can, pools left by the tide, the swirl of wind and
the river,

trees
always in the distance, always against
a grey sky?[1]

Truly, a weather-condition which encourages indulgence in dope;
and one very prevalent through these United States, to judge by the
number of institutions devoted within their bounds to the manu-
facture of candies of all kinds. Genius has given Williams a hardier,
cleaner adjustment. This M.D. has developed the stay of esthetic
perception. He finds release in seeing. A certain quantity of perfectly
selfless sympathy is in him. Children exist for him. There are women
in labor. There is a bone-wearied, exasperated woman in bed. There
is a young man with a bad 'pump'. The doctor is the confessor,
today. There is

. . . a band of
young poets that have not learned
the blessedness of warmth
(or have forgotten it).[2]

The first impulse may still be:

You sullen pig of a man
you force me into the mud
with your stinking ash-cart!

Inevitably, the music changes to

Brother!
– if we were rich
we'd stick our chests out
and hold our heads high![3]

Sublimation of brute desires has made the world less fearful. Flash-like
recognition of his proper grotesquerie, dissonance, bondage inside
the persons of others; scenes, rhythms, words, oaths dawning
tantalizingly upon him, have made the circumstances of the poet's
own life less painfully pressing. Capacity for identifying himself with

1 p. 160.   2 p. 43.   3 p. 134.

people in their own terms has made him, on one plane, a successful physician, diagnostician, healer. It is his own health for which he is fighting in other bodies, careless of their cries and cringings. On another, it has made him an artist: turned his existence over to him as stuff for contemplation. For he has found himself lifted onto that plane where men become object to themselves with all the rest of the world. He has viewed himself dispassionately, as though he himself were one of his own cases; placed himself with a not unkindly irony against the remainder of the universe and gotten the exact proportion; applied red-hot irons despite his own fears and outcries to his own gangrened wounds; doused himself with cold water whenever necessary; laughed at his hysterical alarms and abrupt starts; controlled the Madame Bovary inside himself; perceived the effect which he has been having upon those in touch with him as well as the effect they have been having upon himself. He has seen the laws operating in his own life, forcing him to receive the world in certain painful forms. There is no blame laid on time, custom, environment for his leanness, as there is blame in the writings of a poet related to Williams, T. S. Eliot. Williams is aware that if the sum of appeasements in his heart resembles most often the bank-balance of a hand-to-mouth existence: held generally near the two-hundred-dollar mark; occasionally dangerously far below; only rarely up near four hundred dollars, the cause, if there is one, lies in himself. It is

... the madness of the birch leaves opening
cold, one by one[1]

and nothing other.

Because of this singularly mature capacity for insight, Williams's writings have a truthfulness wanting those of certain of his fellows'; wanting, despite the presence of great excellencies, those of T. S. Eliot. His poems give the relationship of things more justly than do those of the émigré's. Williams, for example, does not repeat Bunthorne's lament that 'nothing poetic in the world can dwell', nor represent his spirit as a drowned king. Kings do not appear upon his horizons, or Christs crucified. He does not have to cast a grandiose and egotistical veil over the world; and see in it the Judas to his

1 p. 228.

genius before he can approach it. He can creep close to the lean thing which exists and see it dispassionately. He can give himself, William Carlos Williams, much as he is, without either simple or inverted pride; give himself in his crassness, in his dissonant mixed blood, in absurd melancholy, wild swiftness of temper, man-shyness; Americano, Jerseyite, Rutherfordian; give himself with a frankness, a fearlessness, a scientific impersonality, that is bracing as a shock of needle-spray. The fleeting patterns, the fine breaths, in which destiny manifests itself, contain excitement enough for him. Insight probes

the guts of shadows;

catches subtle acidulous shades, delicate movements of life. Carl Sandburg perceives

. . . an ocean of tomorrows
a sky of tomorrows;

but it takes a maturity as great as Williams's to be able to put the finger on anything as unobvious and fine as the vision contained in *The Nightingales*:

My shoes as I lean
unlacing them
stand out upon
flat worsted flowers.
Nimbly the shadows
of my fingers play
unlacing
over shoes and flowers.[1]

And what exists for him appears in its own tone and color; finds appropriate verbal imagery and rhythmical accent; nicely weds vulgarity with lyricism. A poem begins:

He would enjoy either
like the others
to buy a railroad
or
in his old clothes to

1 p. 224.

chase his wife to
some such outhouse
as they have still on the farms . . .

and we feel lightly the hawk-and-spit of the American mouth. The
crass, unvoluptuous, vitriolic language of *The Great American Novel*
has definitely local color. It is of the American suburbs as *Ulysses* is of
Dublin. And verse and prose both realize the existence of the Sunday-
afternoon family motor drive, of the Pullman plate-glass window in
the parlor wall, and the lump of rock-crystal on the mantelpiece. It
is seen from within. Williams gives the subjective form.

And, in moments of felt power, in moments of conscious toughness
and sharp will, he breaks 'through to the fifty words necessary', and
briskly, laconically, like a man with little time for matters not
absolutely essential to the welfare of the universe, brings into clarity
the relation existing between himself and the things seen by him.
Curious harmonies of bitter and sweet, of harsh and gentle, of sluggish
and swift and sharp and soft in word-color and rhythmical pattern;
nude finely viscous little curves of music in which every line is a
decisive stroke, render the ironic, contained, humorous dance of the
spirit amid the objects of a ramshackle makeshift universe. Life chants
because it can master pain, and move about through disillusionment
like a man going erect and self-contained through mean sites, and
musing and dreaming in

. . . back streets
admiring the houses
of the very poor:
roof out of line with sides
the yards cluttered
with old chicken wire, ashes,
furniture gone wrong;
the fences and outhouses
built of barrel-staves
and parts of boxes, all,
if I am fortunate,
smeared a bluish green . . .[1]

1 p. 121.

Spring dances like Strauss's *Till Eulenspiegel* with mordant buffoonery above the hopeless dullness of things. Intelligence planes sovereign over yards in a fury of lilac-blossoms. Sore, battered, frozen, life outlasts the cold, struggles to its feet despite the weights upon it, lifts itself like the chickory on bitter stems; blossoms like salvia on ash-heaps. It has come finally face to face with some incapacity of its own; but among the wrecks it finds a piquant sprightly music:

If I when my wife is sleeping
and the baby and Kathleen
are sleeping
and the sun is a flame-white disc
in silken mists
above shining trees, –
if I in my north room
dance naked, grotesquely
before my mirror
waving my shirt round my head
and singing softly to myself:
'I am lonely, lonely.
I was born to be lonely.
I am best so!'
If I admire my arms, my face,
my shoulders, flanks, buttocks
against the yellow drawn shades, –

Who shall say I am not
the happy genius of my household?[1]

It knows its power to live in deserts; knows it can make much out of next-to-nothing; hang on by the skin of its teeth:

I bought a dishmop –
having no daughter –
for they had twisted
fine ribbons of shining copper
about white twine
and made a tousled head
of it, fastened it

1 p. 148.

upon a turned ash stick
slender at the neck
straight, tall –
when tied upright
on the brass wallbracket
to be light to me –
and naked
as a girl should seem
to her father.[1]

With pride it feels the return of animal health, the good tickle of the beast-skin:

It is cold. The white moon
is up among her scattered stars –
like the bare thighs of
the Police Sergeant's wife – among
her five children . . .
No answer. Pale shadows lie upon
the frosted grass. One answer:
It is midnight, it is still
and it is cold . . . !
White thighs of the sky! a
new answer out of the depths of
my male belly: In April . . .
in April I shall see again – In April!
the round and perfect thighs
of the Police Sergeant's wife
perfect still after many babies.
Oya![2]

And with joy we receive the reassurance brought by these pieces, take the signal of imminent habitable land they give. The trip from the old to the new world upon which we are all in spite of ourselves embarked has gotten most of us not to a city spreading 'its dark life upon the earth of a new world, rooted there, sensitive to its richest beauty', or about a temple where 'the tribe's deep feeling for a reality that stems back into the permanence of remote origins' has its

1 p. 219.   2 p. 203.

firm hold: achievement of American civilization. It has brought us it seems no further than a low smoky shore looking rather like the Bayonne littoral from the Staten Island ferryboat on a sunless winter's day: a slatey weed-garden of gas-tuns, church-spires, chimneys, gash-like streets, habitations set against ghostly blueless hills. And we have been standing at the rail, how often! undetermined to disembark our baggage; uncertain whether the shore before us is indeed solid earth upon which one can walk and nourish oneself, or merely a fume of strangling smoke; worried by the picture of a silly journey undertaken to a spot which is not firm land, and can never support the whole weight of man. But while we have been standing, somebody excited ashore has sent up some wild signal rockets through the gloom; and we see the scarlet spikey flowers abloom on the cinder-piles, and the little human habitation stand snug and whole in the shadow of vats and chimneys. Life goes on, behind this forbidding wall. The jumbled piles lose their dreadfulness. They have been shown rough customers enough, but beings among whom a sturdy pair of legs can navigate, and a stout brace of lungs breathe up. And we know the journey has led us somewhere, at least, and begin moving up our baggage.

(103–15)

Kenneth Burke

'Subjective History', a review of *In the American Grain*,
New York Herald Tribune Books   14 March 1926

On the jacket of his latest book, his 'modern account of American heroes', William Carlos Williams announces his program as follows:

> In these studies I have sought to re-name the things seen,
> now lost in a chaos of borrowed titles, many of them
> inappropriate, under which the true character lies hidden. In
> letters, in journals, reports of happenings I have recognized
> new contours suggested by old words, so that new names
> were constituted.[1]

1 p. 5.

And these new names, if I understand Williams correctly, are intended merely to be the old names with their original charge restored. They are new, not for the love of novelty, but through piety, through husbandry of tradition; new only in the sense that one might change the label on a bottle from 'Poison' to 'Deadly Poison', employing a modified statement to produce the same effect.

It is Williams's business, then, to see beyond the label, to see the rolling eye and the quivering muscle behind the word 'Poison'; to replace 'Columbus discovered America in 1492' with excerpts from Columbus's diary which show what it was to be approaching America at the turn of that century and to see a continent not as land, but in terms of seaweed, of river birds heard passing in the night, of clouds which, with a glad outcry, are mistaken for islands; to replace Daniel Boone with the image of a man who tramped through Kentucky alone in constant danger of death and, returning, tried to chronicle in dull language that Kentucky was beautiful when, in reality, he meant that Kentucky was beautiful while there was danger of death; to give us, in place of De Soto, a man who advances in a kind of grim nightmare, taking this virgin country as a woman, his life split into a dialogue with an imaginary, non-existent shape, as it is with those poor devils (tabulated by the savants) who under cover of night converse with themselves in two voices, one deep and the other falsetto. Thus Eric the Red is traded in for a sense of fish-blooded butchery by quotation from original documents, witch-craft is restored not only with its gloom, but with its *logic*; and Burr, when made human, is automatically made heroic.

I do not mean to imply that Williams's method always works. It tends toward a maximum of 'interpretation' and a minimum of research; his heroes at times are so busy *living* that they neglect to do anything else, and their inventions, or discoveries, or battles, or policies, become an unimportant by-product. The closing chapter on Lincoln is perhaps his process reduced to its farthest absurdity; Lincoln 'done' in five short paragraphs, and the longest of these devoted to a nearly malapropos digression on Mengelberg, the Philharmonic conductor. His complaints against American women are often puerile, although vigorous and picturesque enough.

They are fit only to be seen in shows, or, in the train of a

launch, on aquaplanes, six at a time, the swift motion only
serving to give the authentic sense of slipperiness, pseudo-
naiads without the necessary wildness and the chill – fit only
to be seen by the box, like Oregon apples, bright and round
but tasteless – wineless, wholesale.[1]

And his respect for brawn and daring has its vicissitudes: on one
page it is a brisk and muscular enthusiasm, and on the next we feel
that no little girl in a convent ever pondered on these things with a
more timid, and a simpler, trust.

The purpose is poetry, not history. Williams seeks bravuras rather
than facts. 'Meaning' in his mind is not to observe, but to cry out.
Ideology, while it is here, is totally secondary; it is never organized, is
low in the evolutionary scale. But splendid wordings turn up continually. I quote from his essay on Raleigh:

Sing, O, muse, and say there is a spirit that is seeking through
America for Raleigh, in the earth, the air, the waters, up and
down, for Raleigh, that lost man, seer who failed, planter
who never planted, poet whose works are questioned, leader
without command, favorite deposed – but one who yet gave
title for his queen, his England, to a coast he never saw but
grazed alone with genius.[2]

Yet the word 'genius', with which this citation closes, suggests to
me that Williams's concern lies elsewhere; at this time, when it is so
prevalent a tendency to look over past lives for the evidences of
genius, Williams shifts the emphasis, he looks for heroes. The
genius is in some way the epitome, the summing-up and concentration point of the forces among which he lives; while in the hero we
emphasize rather his struggle against these forces. The two concepts
are not opposed, they are different; and being so, they may overlap,
separate or totally coincide. In common, however, they possess the
quality of energy, of some internal 'drive' or 'demon'.

There is one attitude of mind which sees this demon, this will, as an
Olympian trait in man: such will as, translated into the diction of
motion-picture titles, becomes the 'lure' or the 'call' of something
or other. But this attitude is continually breaking, and as it does so the

will becomes no longer a beacon shining in advance, no longer an oasis or a harbor just a little way ahead of us, but is rather something which goads us from behind. People of great will are then *ridden* by demons. Their motion is not the answer to a 'call'; it is flight.

Implicit in Williams's book there is something which fluctuates between these two attitudes, an intermingling of their once divided logics, so that we can no longer distinguish, in these pilgrimages of his heroes, between that which is done in aggression and that which is done in defense, between power and starvation, play and malice. (7)

D. H. Lawrence

'American Heroes', a review of *In the American Grain, Nation,* no. 112
14 April 1926 (reprinted in E. D. Macdonald (ed.), *Phoenix,* 1936)

Mr Williams quotes Poe's distinction between 'nationality in letters' and the *local* in literature. Nationality in letters is deplorable, whereas the *local* is essential. All creative art must rise out of a specific soil and flicker with a spirit of place.

The local, of course, in Mr Williams's sense, is the very opposite of the parochial, the parish pump stuff. The local in America is America itself. Not Salem, or Boston, or Philadelphia, or New York, but that of the American subsoil which spouts up in any of those places into the lives of men.

In these studies of 'American' heroes, from Red Eric of Greenland, and Columbus and Cortés and Montezuma, on to Abraham Lincoln, Mr Williams tries to reveal the experience of great men in the Americas since the advent of the whites. History in this book would be a sensuous record of the Americanization of the white men in America, as contrasted with ordinary history, which is a complacent record of the civilization and Europizing (if you can allow the word) of the American continent.

In this record of truly American heroes, then, the author is seeking out not the ideal achievement of great men of the New World but the men themselves, in all the dynamic explosiveness of their energy. This peculiar dynamic energy, this strange yearning and passion and uncanny explosive quality in men derived from Europe, is American, the American element. Seek out *this* American element, O Americans!, is the poet's charge.

All America is now going hundred per cent American. But the only hundred per cent American is the Red Indian, and he can only be canonized when he is finally dead. And not even the most American American can transmogrify into an Indian. Whence, then, the hundred per cent?

It is here that Mr Williams's – and Poe's – distinction between the *national* and the *local* is useful. Most of the hundred per centism is national, and therefore not American at all. The new one hundred per cent literature is all *about* Americans, in the intensest American vernacular. And yet, in vision, in conception, in the very manner, it still remains ninety-nine per cent European. But for *Ulysses* and Marcel Proust and a few other beetling high-brows, where would the modernist hundred per centers of America have been? Alas, where they are now, save for cutting a few capers.

What then? William Carlos Williams tries to bring into his consciousness America itself, the still-unravished bride of silences. The great continent, its bitterness, its brackish quality, its vast glamour, its strange cruelty. Find this, Americans, and get it into your bones. The powerful, unyielding breath of the Americas which Columbus sniffed, even in Europe, and which sent the Conquistadores mad. National America is a gruesome sort of fantasy. But the unravished *local* America still waits vast and virgin as ever, though in process of being murdered.

The author sees the genius of the continent as a woman with exquisite, super-subtle tenderness and recoiling cruelty. It is a myth-woman who will demand of men a sensitive awareness, a supreme sensuous delicacy, and at the same time an infinitely tempered resistance, a power of endurance and of resistance.

To evoke a vision of the essential America is to evoke Americans, bring them into conscious life. To bring a few American citizens into American consciousness – the consciousness at present being all bastardized European – is to form the nucleus of the new race. To have the nucleus of a new race is to have a future: and a true aristocracy. It is to have the germ of an aristocracy in sensitive tenderness and diamond-like resistance.

A man, in America, can only *begin* to be American. After five hundred years there are no *racial* white Americans. They are only national, woebegone or strident. After five hundred years more there may be the developing nucleus of a true American race. If only men, some few, trust the American passion that is in them, and pledge themselves to it.

But the passion is not national. No man who doesn't feel the last anguish of tragedy – *and beyond that* – will ever know America, or begin, even at the beginning's beginning, to be American.

There are two ways of being American: and the chief, says Mr Williams, is by recoiling into individual smallness and insentience, and gutting the great continent in frenzies of mean fear. It is the Puritan way. The other is by *touch*; touch America as she is; dare to touch her! And this is the heroic way.

And this, this sensitive touch upon the unseen America, is to be the really great adventure in the New World. Mr Williams's book contains his adventure; and, therefore, for me, has a fascination. There are very new and profound glimpses into life: the strength of insulated smallness in the New Englanders, the fascination of 'being nothing' in the Negroes, the *spell-bound* quality of men like Columbus, De Soto, Boone. It is a glimpse of what the vast America *wants men to be*, instead of another strident assertion of what men have made, do make, will make, can make, out of the murdered territories of the New World.

It would be easy enough to rise, in critical superiority, as a critic always feels he must, superior to his author, and find fault. The modernist style is sometimes irritating. Was Tenochtitlan really so wonderful? (see Adolf Bandelier's *The Golden Man*). Does not Mr Williams mistake Poe's agony of *destructive penetration*, through all the horrible bastard-European alluvium of his 1840 America, for the positive America itself?

But if an author rouses my deeper sympathy he can have as many faults as he likes, I don't care. And if I disagree with him a bit, heaven save me from feeling superior just because I have a chance to snarl. I am only too thankful that Mr Williams wrote his book.

(334–6)

Marianne Moore

'A Poet of the Quattrocento', *Dial*, vol. 82 1927

It was Ezra Pound's conviction some years ago, that there could be 'an age of awakening in America' which would 'overshadow the quattrocento'. Hopeful for us at that time, 'our opportunity is greater than Leonardo's', said Mr Pound; 'we have more aliment', and never really neglectful of us, he has commended in us, 'Mr Williams's praiseworthy opacity'.

There is distinctness and color (he observed), as was shown in his *Postlude*, in *Des Imagistes*; but there is beyond these qualities the absolute conviction of a man with his feet on the soil, on a soil personally and peculiarly his own. He is rooted. He is at times almost inarticulate, but he is never dry, never without sap in abundance.

This metaphor of the tree seems highly appropriate to William Carlos Williams – who writes of seedling sycamores, of walnuts and willows – who several years ago, himself seemed to W. C. Blum 'by all odds the hardiest specimen in these parts'.[1] In his modestly emphatic respect for America he corroborates Henry James's conviction that young people should 'stick fast and sink up to their necks in everything their own countries and climates can give', and his feeling for the *place* lends poetic authority to an illusion of ours, that sustenance may be found here, which is adapted to artists. Imagination can profit by a journey, acquainting itself with everything pertaining to its wish that it can gather from European sources, Doctor Williams says. But it is apparent to him that 'American plumbing, American bridges, indexing systems, locomotives, printing presses, city buildings, farm implements and a thousand other things' are liked and used, and it is not folly to hope that the very purest works of the imagination may also be found among us. Doctor Williams is in favor of escape from 'strained associations', from 'shallowness', from such substitutes as 'congoleum – building paper with a coating of enamel'. The staying at home principle could not, he is sure, be

1 W. C. Blum, 'American Letter', *Dial*, vol. 70, 1921.

a false one where there is vigorous living force with buoyancy of imagination – as there was apparently in Shakespeare – the artist's excursion being into 'perfection' and 'technical excellence'! 'Such names as Homer, the blind; Scheherazade, who lived under threat – Their compositions have as their excellence, an identity with life since they are as actual, as sappy as the leaf of the tree which never moves from one spot.' He has visited various places and studied various writings and a traveller can as Bacon says, 'prick in some flowers of that he hath learned abroad', In the main, however, Doctor Williams's topics are American – crowds at the movies

with the closeness and
universality of sand,[1]

turkey nests, mushrooms among the fir trees, mist rising from the duck pond, the ball game:

It is summer, it is the solstice
the crowd is

cheering, the crowd is laughing[2]

or

It is spring. Sunshine . . . dumped among factories . . . down a red dirt path to four goats. . . . I approach the smallest goat timidly. . . . It draws away beginning to wind its tie rope around the tree. . . . I back the creature around the tree till it can go no further, the cord all wound up. Gingerly I take it by the ear. It tries to crowd between me and the tree. (I drive it) around the tree again until the rope is entirely unwound. The beast immediately finds new violent green tufts of grass in some black mud half under some old dried water-soaked weedstalks. . . . To the right of the path the other goat comes forward boldly but stops short and sniffs, . . . It ventures closer. Gna-ha-ha-ha-ha! (as in a hat). Very softly. The small goat answers.[3]

1. *Collected Earlier Poems*, p. 267.
2. p. 285.
3. *The Accident*, reprinted in W. Schott (ed.), *Imaginations*, 1970, pp. 305-8.

O spring days, swift
and mutable, wind blowing
four ways, hot and cold.[1]

    Essentially not a 'repeater of things second-hand', Doctor Williams
is in his manner of contemplating with new eyes, old things, shabby
things and other things, a poet. Metre he thinks of as an 'essential
of the work, one of its words'. That which is to some imperceptible,
is to him the 'milligram of radium' that he values. He is rightly
imaginative in not attempting to decide; or rather, in deciding not
to attempt to say how wrong these readers are, who find his poems
unbeautiful or 'positively repellant'. As he had previously asked,
'Where does this downhill turn up again? Driven to the wall you'd
put claws to your toes and make a ladder of smooth bricks.'

    Facts presented to us by him in his prose account of The Destruction
of Tenochtitlan, could not be said to be 'new', but the experience
ever, in encountering that which has been imaginatively assembled,
is exceedingly new. One recalls in reading these pages, the sense
augmented, of 'everything which the world affords', of 'the drive
upward, toward the sun and the stars'; and foremost as poetry, we
have in a bewilderingly great, neatly ordered pageant of magnificence,
Montezuma, 'this American cacique', 'so delicate', 'so full of tinkling
sounds and rhythms, so tireless of invention'.

    One sees nothing terrifying in what Doctor Williams calls a
'modern traditionalism', but to say so is to quibble. Incuriousness,
emptiness, a sleep of the faculties, are an end of beauty; and Doctor
Williams is vivid. Perhaps he is modern. He addresses himself to the
imagination. He is 'keen' and 'compact'. 'At the ship's prow' as he
says the poet should be, he is glad to have his 'imaginary' fellow-
creatures with him. Unless we are very literal, this should be enough.
(213–15)

1. *Collected Earlier Poems,* p. 380.

Gorham B. Munson

'William Carlos Williams, a United States Poet', *Destinations:
A Canvass of American Literature Since 1900* 1928

If one stops to survey the touted American writers of the last fifteen years, one is impressed by the failure of most of them to develop. Take the early books of Carl Sandburg, Vachel Lindsay, Sherwood Anderson, Edgar Lee Masters, Theodore Dreiser, H. L. Mencken, Van Wyck Brooks, many others. What have they done, after all, but repeat their first books? Granting to them an initial blaze, the fire can hardly be said to have increased or brightened or become hotter or consumed fuel of a different character. What I mean is that their early work really contains their later work; I mean that no unpredictable element has entered into their 'progress'.

Waldo Frank is one exception. His first novel, *The Unwelcome Man*, does not point specifically to his third novel, *Rahab*, and in fact something very important to him happened in between. He discovered the Jewish prophets in the Bible: he received a powerful charge from an ancient religious culture, higher in level and more intense in character than any stimulus his own culture gave him, and this charge was a shock to his own development. Something came into his work that was not originally present, and this unpredictable element changed his forms, exalted his attitude, and transformed his materials. A criticism of Frank would deal with a development and therefore would find it convenient and best to take the narrative form, moving from book to book in chronological order.

William Carlos Williams exacts the same tribute. The chronology of his books is insistent, for if Williams has not developed in the sense Waldo Frank has, he has at least *changed*, the changes being due to a frantic effort to develop.

The starting point is a small and scarce book of poetry, *The Tempers*, published in London by Elkin Matthews in 1913. After reading Williams's more accessible works, one digs up this little item and discovers that in it Williams employed rhyme schemes and traditional metrical forms! He used 'classical allusions' freely! He sounds very much like Ezra Pound at that date! The Browning influence (with Pound as its probable carrier) had hit him! There are even translations from the Spanish!

Later on Williams was to make the puerile remark that 'nowadays poets spit upon rhyme and rhetoric': he was to call Pound 'the best enemy United States verse has': he was to become aggressively contemporary and local, thereby chucking outside the classical paraphernalia of names, symbols and associations, and losing all interest in making translations.

But when he was composing the nineteen poems in *The Tempers*, he was, one conjectures, a fellow student of Pound at the University of Pennsylvania. The little book then is to be taken as representing Williams in the Academy, Pound being the teacher. In addition to the teachings, the pupil shows something of his own – a toughness of personality, a talent for emphatic wordings, a genuine poetic sap that is just beginning to run. In the next book this sap will feed surprising foliage, for it will draw on that surrounding soil that Pound deserted and produce a poetry quite dissimilar to Pound's work.

The second poem in *Al Que Quiere* (1917) is a handy illustration, though certainly not among the better poems in that collection.

Pastoral

When I was younger
it was plain to me
I must make something of myself.
Older now
I walk back streets
admiring the houses
of the very poor:
roof out of line with sides
the yards cluttered
with old chicken wire, ashes,
furniture gone wrong;
the fences and outhouses
built of barrel-staves
and parts of boxes, all,
if I am fortunate,
smeared a bluish green
that properly weathered

pleases me best
of all colors.

No one
will believe this
of vast import to the nation.[1]

This poem indicates first of all that Williams has found his subject matter, which is none other than the objects that appear right in front of his eyes, right beneath his nose. Being a practising physician in Rutherford, New Jersey, that means to Williams that his senses tell him of that locality, of the nearby metropolis, New York, and of America at large so far as he touches it. So the choice of subject matter has been definitely settled in *Al Que Quiere*. It is the American background (flora, people, customs, heroes, rigors and scenic atrociousness) from which Williams has never since deviated.

The second choice was between established verse forms and vers libre, and Williams committed himself altogether to the latter. No wonder! Vers libre might have been made to order for this busy literary doctor, writing poems in odd minutes between calls, always liable to be interrupted and always on the jump, day and night. For while vers libre has many difficulties and many possibilities, this also is true of it: a poet with a fair ear and a native feeling for form can trust to improvisation in these respects – rhythm and form – and write good vers libre, provided his attention bears hard and directly upon the individual word. That is why Williams prattles so often and sometimes intelligently about giving freedom to words, the free word, et cetera. For he is himself only concerned in a secondary way with combinations of words: the main thing is a regard for the bite, the weight, the thrust, the individuality of the successive single words he picks out.

By culling a dozen or so quotations from his critical notes, one could construct a disjointed ars poetica by William Carlos Williams, the first article of which would deal with the necessity for cleansing words and putting weight in them and the remaining articles would explain the psychology of his poetic process. Among psychological processes the correspondent to a technical devotion to the 'free word' would be a devotion to the isolated perception, and that is what we

1 *Collected Earlier Poems*, p. 121.

find. To see the thing with great intensity of perception, to see it directly, simply, immediately, and without forethought or after-thought, is the unvarying psychological basis for *Al Que Quiere* and the later books of poems.

Turning back to *Pastoral*, we find what I have been saying. The shabby disorder of the poor quarter of an American village. A simple pattern: the autobiographical statement of a changed attitude, a list of objects to illustrate the attitude, and at the end a generality running out a tangent. A very simple rhythm just to set off the clear stark words. The enumeration of bare perceptions of things seen on a walk. And something more: two qualities.

The first is the national flavor, the much sought for American character in writing. To my mind this is achieved as much by the turn of thinking and phrasing in the opening three lines and in the concluding three lines as it is by the veracity of the scenery, for these lines reveal unmistakably a man who has been pressed upon con-tinuously by American sociology, 'marked up' by it. The other quality – that which makes Williams distinctly a poet – is lyrical. He 'admires' these poor streets: if he is 'fortunate', the outhouses will be colored a bluish green, properly weathered. What is it that gets into the poem by means of these words, that gets into the words 'pleases me best'?

I would say, exhilaration, – the exhilaration that all of us have occasionally felt when we have accidentally made an exact perception of some object, seen an object not hazily as in a dream but with clarity, an exterior thing, apart from us, acting upon us. This feeling of exhilaration at the fact that our senses register vividly, occasional with us, appears to be frequent with Williams, and it saves his compositions from flatness and prosaic demeanor, conferring on them the potentiality of flight. Restraint is beautiful only when the potentiality of escape is present.

The young doctor is dancing with happiness
in the sparkling wind, alone
at the prow of the ferry! He notices
the curdy barnacles and broken ice crusts
left at the slip's base by the low tide
and thinks of summer and green

shell crusted ledges among
      the emerald eel-grass![1]

It is easy to see that there is no principle of selection operative on Williams's subject matter. Given his esthetic of exhilaration induced by sharp and strong perceptions and given his geographical environment as a determinant, he can include everything that affects his sensory equipment – whether it be harebells or children leaping about a dead dog or the winter wind or rusty chicken wire in a backyard. The one gauge is intensity of perception and since the unpleasant has great power of impact upon nostrils, ears, eyes, and so on, it follows that the unpleasant is generously included in Williams's lines, where however it is redeemed by the same exhilaration that a vivid register of the pleasing object also creates. This is the reason for Williams's 'unflinching realism' against which sentimental objections have been lodged.

The problem of an advance after *Al Que Quiere* must have faced Williams quite acutely. He could, of course, go on by refining his instruments of expression and trying for an ever sharper focus, but this would be at best adding to what he had already done or at worst repeating it. Another possibility was to abandon the austerity of bare intense perceptions, without forethought or afterthought, and to make these perceptions work to evoke one emotion or another, one mood or another. This is the ordinary process and Williams himself worked it in a few poems in *Al Que Quiere* such as *In Harbor*. Thus, the usual way was already open for him to incorporate in his later poems a great variety of emotions and perhaps eventually to embody an emotional attitude, all this of course without becoming 'intellectual'.

But Williams chose neither of these possibilities for treatment in *Kora in Hell: Improvisations* (1920): instead he made an unexpected deviation from *Al Que Quiere*.

'The thing that saves your work is opacity, and don't forget it,' Pound had written to Williams, and in reviewing one of the *Others Anthologies* he remarked that 'it also displays Mr Williams's praiseworthy opacity'. Apparently Williams valued the counsel and it was bad, for whereas in *Al Que Quiere* he had written with weight and clarity, in *Kora in Hell* he set out to cultivate opacity and achieved

1 p. 162.

impenetrability. The opaque is simply the strong man's blur and excusable only if it is the maximum luminosity a recalcitrant and profound subject will yield: profundity is scarcely the term to associate with Williams's writing.

The means employed to gain opacity were of the simplest and may be summed up by the phrase – 'association of ideas'. Williams discovered that a group of remote perceptions had surprising points of contact with each other in his mind, so he consolidated these widely divergent glimpses of things for the sake of the personal connection. Then he found that he could state a similar association in another set of terms and relate the two statements to each other as poem and key. Thus

It is still warm enough to slip from the weeds into the lake's edge, your clothes blushing in the grass and three small boys grinning behind the derelict hearth's side. But summer is up among the huckleberries near the path's end and snakes' eggs lie curling in the sun on the lonely summit. But – well – let's wish it were higher after all these years staring at it – deplore the paunched clouds – glimpse the sky's thin counter-crest and plunge into the gulch. Sticky cobwebs tell of feverish midnights. Crack a rock (what's a thousand years!) and send it crashing among the oaks! Wind a pine tree in a grey-worm's net and play it for a trout; oh – but it's the moon does that! No, summer has gone down the other side of the mountain. Carry home what we can. What have you brought off? Ah, here are thimbleberries.

In middle life the mind passes to a variegated October. This is the time youth in its faulty aspirations has set for the achievement of great summits. But having attained the mountain top one is not snatched into a cloud but the descent proffers its blandishments quite as a matter of course. At this the fellow is cast into a great confusion and rather plaintively looks about to see if any has fared better than he.[1]

I select this improvisation because it seems to me much less opaque than the others, and yet it illustrates my point: namely, that since the

1 W. Schott (ed.), *Imaginations*, 1970, pp. 42-3.

'association of ideas' is accidental in the first place and in the second it is personal, private, excessively subjective, therefore whether or not it produces an intended effect upon an intended reader is purely a hit-or-miss proposition. Or, as Kenneth Burke commenting on *Kora in Hell* put it: 'How beautiful the association of the ideas would have been in art if used in one work, by one man, for one page, and for some end other than that of a beautiful association of ideas.'

Williams's own remarks about *Kora in Hell* justify the estimate of it as a detour on which he deviated too far from his path but returned, having learned something from having pushed out so far. On one occasion he was to say: 'Take the improvisations. What the French reader would say is : *Oui, ça; j'ai déjà vu ça; ça c'est de Rimbaud.* Finis.' But why should 'light hearted Williams twirling his November mustachios' mention Rimbaud in this connection? Williams is the child of his mother and he describes her in the *Prologue* to *Kora in Hell.*

My mother is given over to frequent periods of great
depression being as I believe by nature the most light-hearted
thing in the world. But there comes a grotesque turn to her
talk, a macabre anecdote concerning some dream, a passionate
statement about death, which elevates her mood without
marring it, sometimes in a most startling way.

Rimbaud was an altogether different type, a prodigy who came to the end of skepticism and saw no way to make an affirmation: he did not take the name of hell in vain when he wrote a title. Whereas Williams, suffering from the ghastly business of war, could yet try to reconstruct a springtime. On another occasion Williams admits of the improvisations that 'their fault is their dislocation of sense, often complete' and with that we may leave them to return to the straight line that joins *Sour Grapes* (1921) with *Al Que Quiere*, turning over the pages of *Contact* magazine as we go.

That was a curious magazine! The first issue, ten multigraphed sheets stapled between dull orange covers, was dated December, 1920. In January, 1921, there was a larger number, also multigraphed. In February, one supposes that was the date, a printed and illustrated number different in format and paper as well. A little later – who knows just when? – a fourth number came out, printed on only one side of each page. Then a gap until June, 1923, when the fifth and last (?) number was printed.

Contact was edited by Williams in conjunction with a younger man, Robert McAlmon, who has had the peculiar property of being a magical mirror to Williams. Peering at the slovenly scripts of McAlmon, Williams sees there – to everyone's astonishment – the clear hard virtues of his own writing. So that, in writing about McAlmon's work, he comes to write excellent statements of himself.

After the fourth number of *Contact*, McAlmon married an English poet and fortune – a front page story for the American newspapers at the time – and sailed for Europe to continue the publication of the magazine. Something, however, caused him to abandon these plans and instead the Contact Publishing Company was formed in Paris for the purpose of printing books by Marsden Hartley, Mina Loy, McAlmon, Williams and others who by contributing to *Contact* were more or less identified with it.

Besides spawning Robert McAlmon and a publishing company that still publishes, *Contact* set forth to its two hundred readers (if there were that many) a program for American writing. In the first place, beware of the mere acquisition of information as a culture substitute. . . . 'Art may be the supreme hypocrisy of an information – cultured people . . . without CONTACT . . . justifiable perhaps if it becomes at last actually the way sensitive people live . . .' ran the legend on the cover of the first number. *Contact* was founded on the conviction that 'art which attains is indigenous of experience and relations, and that the artist works to express perceptions rather than to attain standards of achievement' and it was carried on by a 'faith in the existence of native artists' of certain specifications 'who receive meager recognition'. But what was meant by contact? The simplest statement was – 'the essential contact between words and the locality which breeds them, in this case America.'

All of this was in the first issue. In the second we read that

in proportion as a man has bestirred himself to become awake to his own locality he will perceive more and more of what is disclosed and find himself in a position to make the necessary translations. The disclosures will then and only then come to him a reality, as joy, as release. For these men communicate with each other and strive to invent new devices. But he who does not know his own world, in whatever confused form it may be, must either stupidly fail to learn from foreign work or stupidly swallow it without knowing how to judge of its essential value. Descending each his own branch man and man reach finally a common trunk of understanding.

And this:

We, Contact, aim to emphasize the local phase of the game of writing. We realize that it is emphasis only which is our business. We want to give all our energy to the setting up of new vigors of artistic perception, invention and expression in the United States. Only by slow growth, consciously fostered to the point of enthusiasm, will American work of the quality of Marianne Moore's best poetry come to the fore of intelligent attention and the ignorance which has made America an artistic desert be somewhat dissipated. We lack interchange of ideas in our country more than we lack foreign percept. Every effort should be made, we feel, to develop among our serious writers a sense of mutual contact first of all. To this also we are devoted.

It remained to broaden the program, as was done in the third issue to mean 'contact with experience'.

contact with experience is essential to good writing or, let us say, literature. We have said this in the conviction that contact always implies a local definition of effort with a consequent taking on of certain colors from the locality by the experience, and these colors or sensual values of whatever sort, are the only realities in writing, or as may be said, the essential quality of literature.'

I take the trouble to make these excavations from the file of *Contact* for several reasons; they make explicit what was already implicit in the working procedure of *Al Que Quiere* and *Kora in Hell*: they constitute an artistic credo to which Williams has adhered with ardor and fidelity: and, best justification of all, Williams has made the program work with a certain measure of success. That is, his writing has inbred local characteristics and it is good writing.

An outstanding feature of the last decade in American letters has been the working of a nationalistic impulse. We see this most blatantly in Vachel Lindsay, most ravenously in Robert J. Coady and his *Soil* magazine, most generalized in the allied phenomena of the group that animated the *Seven Arts*, and most mystically in Alfred Stieglitz. Lindsay's 'new localism', however, is a mere proclamation, scarcely a program: it is simply the expression of a wish that the smaller American communities should be inspired to create their own arts and crafts, that the neighborhood spirit should be directed toward a Campbellite God, a long-skirted Art, and a Wilsonian Democracy. The fruit – that is, Lindsay's verse – has been deplorable. The case of the late Robert J. Coady is much better, but even so it can be summed up as no more than a positive attitude toward a barely differentiated appetite for those phenomena in the environment – works of engineering genius, sports, moving pictures, racy journalism – that seemed flamboyantly national and extraordinarily vigorous in comparison with the official art world with which Coady was disgusted. The *Seven Arts* group had national aspirations but they were thickened by auras of sociology, psychoanalysis and religion until they lost – in most of the individuals concerned – specific direction and definition. Practically nothing survived the *Soil*: not even its attitude crystallized. Whereas the *Seven Arts* group diffused its nationalism in all directions and lost whatever purity it originally had. (An exception must be made for Waldo Frank.) In regard to Alfred Steiglitz, his stresses on thorough workmanship, personal integrity and American qualities have been felt with great force in photography and painting, but, owing to Stieglitz's fumbling grasp of the literary medium, they have been almost inoperative on our letters.

Williams differs from all these in that he has observed the limitations of his program and thereby kept it pure, he has confined himself to the strictly esthetic problems of choice of subject matter and the fashion of perceiving and handling it, and he has borne the fruit proper to the aim of his program – in our next instance that fruit being *Sour Grapes*.

It is hard to hold oneself to the selection of only one poem from this book to show both the continuity with *Al Que Quiere* and the improvement upon it. No poem in the earlier book seems quite so stripped, so weighted and *physical* in its impact as *The Great Figure*. No poem in *Al Que Quiere* seems such a bit of characteristic psychological behavior as *January* in which the poet opposes to the derisive winds the warm comfort of his study – the only thing in the cosmos that apparently at that moment he *knows*. Again, the *Overture to a Dance of Locomotives*[1] could be quoted, for the sake of showing complication in technic and the approach of a philosophic idea[2] without loss of firmness. This very good poem, however, begins to thrust away from the main drive of Williams's writing and is a less revelatory example than *Blizzard*.

Snow:

years of anger following
hours that float idly down –
the blizzard
drifts its weight
deeper and deeper for three days
or sixty years, eh? Then
the sun! a clutter of
yellow and blue flakes –
Hairy looking trees stand out
in long alleys
over a wild solitude.
The man turns and there –
his solitary track stretched out
upon the world.[3]

I am glad to quote from the best criticism of *Sour Grapes* I have seen, that by Kenneth Burke in the *Dial* for February, 1922. 'I should say, therefore, that Williams was engaged in discovering the shortest route between object and subject.' *Blizzard*, it seems to me, is that shortest route between a lonely man staring back at his isolated tracks across a snowfield and the intense feeling of one's impressions of immensity – in short, a highly energized poem on 'the great open spaces' of America. Its power derives principally from the immediacy of the terms and the uttermost compression of words and technic, or, to state it another way, the smallness of the scale intensifies the feeling of vastitude.

1 *Collected Earlier Poems*, p. 194.
2 A feeling for 'eternal recurrence'. This from William Carlos Williams!
3 p. 198.

At this point my description of Williams can stand enlargement of the nature that Burke has made. Burke says:

I take Contact to mean: man without the syllogism, without the parode, without Spinoza's Ethics, man with nothing but the thing and the feeling of that thing. . . . Contact might be said to resolve into the counterpart of Culture, and Williams becomes thereby one of our most distinguished Neanderthal men. His poetry deals with the coercions of nature – and by nature I mean iron rails as well as iron ore – rather than with the laborious structure of ideas man has erected above nature. . . . The Contact writer deals with his desires; the Culture writer must erect his desires into principles and deal with those principles rather than with the desires; the *Urphenomen*, in other words, becomes with the man of Culture of less importance than the delicate and subtle instruments with which he studies it. Williams, however, must go back to the source.'

In a word, Williams is a Primitive and practically all that I have written thus far has been a preparation for that word, has been set down to make it safe to use the word. For observe *The Great American Novel* (1923), his first prose book. He set out, we assume, to write a great American novel. 'If there is progress then there is a novel. Without progress there is nothing. Everything exists from the beginning.' But right there is trouble for him. How can he begin an American novel? What are his own beginnings in the New World? For the rest of the book he keeps trying to start and indicating each time the variety of ignorance or disorder or enormity that blocks progress. In his exasperation he becomes critical or engages in fierce discussion with imaginary opponents: he turns on himself, he sulks, he lunges out desperately. But he never gets the novel under way.

The prose is highly sophisticated. It has similar polarities to those set up in his poetry – one pole being thick and clotted with associa-tions ('Joyce with a difference', Williams calls it) and the other pole (see chapter 17 on the Cumberland mountaineers), a direct emphatic racy simplicity. Between these poles there are many gradations.

But, as we all know, sophistication is not incompatible with primitiveness. Williams couldn't write that novel though he can write a flexible fibrous prose, and the reason is that he is lost in the uncharted American background. He is no master of it: it is not his home: he is trying to become familiar with it. There it is, this huge disorder, this Nuevo Mundo that Columbus's sailors greeted, and he, entranced by its beauty, shaken by its qualities, ferocious or otherwise, but lost in it, utterly lost. To write that novel he feels he must be able to paint the American background: yet he has no pattern for it, only uncoordinated perceptions, impressions, contacts, only a few scattered things that he definitely knows about it. It is the situation of the Primitive. Understanding that, we can understand why Williams sweeps European culture so brusquely aside, even though he is well acquainted with it and responsive to it. Europe is not 'for us', according to Williams, and can give us only sophistication. Williams takes the sophistication, shakes free from it and goes outdoors to discover the new terms that America may present for old or new values.

But no sooner have we tried to encompass Williams with the word – primitive – than this strenuous writer attempts to jump out of the circle. Recall that he began as a poet writing under a freshened academic tradition, then leaped to the straightforward primitivism of *Al Que Quiere*, turned aside for the free association of perceptions in *Kora in Hell*, came back, strengthened, to the primitive contact basis of *Sour Grapes*, and then swerved again into the chaotic prose of *The Great American Novel*. Late in 1923 he fathered *Spring and All*, a collection of twenty-seven poems held apart by chunks of critical, explanatory and proclamatory prose. *Spring and All* is his most recent collection of poems and on the evidence it gives one can say that today Williams is veritably thrashing about on the plane he has hitherto written on. One's feeling is that Williams is determined to fly more swiftly and higher than before and that the difficulties are numerous, unyielding and almost intangible.

All his poetic tenets and achievements 'head up' in this book. What is new is a heavier stress upon novelty and the imagination than he stated in *Kora in Hell*, and a critical stress upon composition: and the poetry produced under these stresses.

The emphasis upon newness – it began in *Kora in Hell* when Williams announced 'nothing is good save the new' and attained capital letters in *Spring and All* when he shouts, 'THE WORLD IS NEW' – is easily associated with his creative mood of exhilaration, for to the receptive person novelty is always exciting. It wakes up the senses and they press out the wine which Williams, the poet, drinks. But we should remember that time either evaporates the beauties of newness or cobwebs them into quaint or wayward conceits or imbeds them in the central traditions of literary experience: in other words, the beauties of newness speedily become beauties of another sort altogether or fade out. So that Williams's enthusiastic quest of novelty continually runs the peril of becoming at best a search for poetic conceits.

As for the imagination, one often wonders what Williams can mean by it. As a psychological faculty, the imagination appears to be superior to reason, feeling and action: a higher development. Its processes occur in a flash, and the word for them is simultaneity. The range of its simultaneous perceptions is not less than the whole of the given field. That is to say, the imagination in a flash takes in the whole of a given object – its origin, its history, its constituents and relations, its uses, and its future: it covers at once all the actualities and possibilities included in what was seen. Poe had a true inkling of it when he stressed harmony as its essence and he propounded the acid question for testing the presence of imagination. But Williams appears to have something else in mind when he refers to 'the imagination'. It is a swift combining faculty, a force, a medium, an electricity, that he talks about, but he does not indicate what he regards to be the laws of combination, as Poe did. Judging by the results of his theory – the majority of the poems in *Spring and All* – the imagination shows its presence by forming unexpected, astonishing, novel combinations, precisely the type of combination that Poe would have named fancy, since it produces the bracing effect of difficulties unexpectedly surmounted.

This is an important point. Williams seeks not to establish a natural harmonious order which covers wholes but an arbitrary composition characterized by *independence*. He is attempting to leap straight from contact (sharp perceptions) to the imagination (order in the highest sense) without working through culture (the attempt to grasp reality practically, emotionally and intellectually). Thus, to my mind his intense effort to expand his primitivism is leading him back to sophistication, the sophistication of a Parisian cubist painter.

As I have said, he stresses composition in *Spring and All* – like a radical modern painter, and it appears to be the so-called abstract or non-representative painting of the day that has given him a notion of composition. He rejects the conception of art as a 'beautiful illusion', a 'lie', and he rejects the copyist formulae – both rightly. Nature 'is not opposed to art but apposed to it', he writes, but his notion of an equal apposition is to purify art by subtracting elements from it for which nature has correspondences. This is not the only alternative: subtraction is merely fancy's method for evading the difficult and tense labor of apposing reality as a whole.

Nevertheless, in spite of the difficulties that a pursuit of novelty, of independent reality, of arbitrary composition has brought down upon Williams there are poems in this book that rank with the very best of his previous work. Poem II, a description upon which Charles Demuth based a painting, is a remarkable union of sensitivity and force. The light and movement of the major portion of the poem seems suddenly to fall, but very quietly, to the center of gravity, the concluding couplet. One might say that before our eyes these flowers reverse the usual process of growth and take root last.

Pink confused with white
flowers and flowers reversed
take and spill the shaded flame
darting it back
into the lamp's horn

petals aslant with mauve

red where in whorls
petal lays its glow upon petal
round flamegreen throats

petals radiant with transpiercing light
contending
         above
the leaves
reaching up their modest green
from the pot's rim

and there wholly dark, the pot
gay with rough moss.[1]

1 *Collected Earlier Poems*, p. 242.

If Williams's latest words as a poet show him trying to transcend primitivism and actually verging toward a sophisticated fancifulness – to repeat, the arbitrary purity of 'independent' compositions, when compared to the organic purity of a complete apprehension of actuality in all its phases and relations (so seldom achieved!), is fancy – his latest writing in prose is a vault back to an intransigent primitivism.

The logic of Williams's position obliged him first to study American history and then to vivify it, particularly its heroes, as he has done in *In the American Grain* (1925). He sets himself against orthodox history – that is stifling and tyrannous to him: on the contrary, 'history must stay open, it is all humanity'. An artist, then, he approaches the American past to rename it and retell it in such a way that its surge and color, its irony and beauty, its own indecisions and suspenses may show themselves. But do not think that the book is a mere exploit in picturesqueness, for Williams is grappling as hard as he can with the difficulties that frustrated his attempt to write the 'great American novel'. The past is made to put its weight directly and heavily upon the present: a vivid sense of historical determinism is constantly awake. In the remarkable conversation with Valéry Larbaud on early Americana which is contained in one of the chapters, Williams exclaims:

It is an extraordinary phenomenon that Americans have lost the sense, being made up as we are, that what we are has its origin in what *the nation* in the past has been; that there is a source IN AMERICA for everything we think or do; that morals affect the food and food the bone, and that, in fine, we have no conception at all of what is meant by moral, since we recognize no ground our own – and that this rudeness rests upon all the unstudied character of our beginnings; and that if we will not pay heed to our own affairs, we are nothing but an unconscious pork yard and oil hole for those, more able, who will fasten themselves upon us.[1]

This preoccupation with the present gives the book its drive, inasmuch as Williams, having realized that he has been formed by

1 *In the American Grain*, p. 121.

history, feels toward history: it is American history with an emotional dimension.

There were three principal factors. First, the New World itself, its geography, flora and fauna, its colossal forces.

The New World, existing in those times beyond the sphere of all things known to history, lay in the fifteenth century as the middle of the desert or the sea lies now and must lie forever, marked with its own dark life which goes on to an immaculate fulfillment in which we have no part. But now, with the maritime successes of that period, the western land could not guard its seclusion longer; a predestined and bitter fruit existing, perversely, before the white flower of its birth, it was laid bare by the miraculous first voyage. . . .
Upon the orchidean beauty of the new world the old rushed inevitably to revenge itself after the Italian's return. . . . They moved out across the seas stirred by instincts, ancient beyond thought as the depths they were crossing, which they obeyed under the names of King or Christ or whatever it might be, while they watched the creative New unfolding itself miraculously before them, before *them*, deafened and blinded.[1]

They came, the Second Factor, the newcomers from Europe. The Spaniards with a large gesture, conquerors, outraging the land. And after the outrages, the destruction of Tenochtitlan and kindred slaughters, the land smiled them on to an ironic defeat: Ponce de Leon shot in the thigh searching for the Fountain of Youth. De Soto alone of the Spaniards married the New World and he was submerged by it in 'one long sweet caress' of the Mississippi. Then the French: Champlain curious, exactly noting every detail, drawing colored maps – a man after Williams's heart. And Père Sebastian Rasles, still more warmed against the writer's bosom, Sebastian Rasles the couragous Jesuit who was supremely interested in the qualities of the new environment. Also the English came, the Puritans that Williams detests.

The Pilgrims were seed of Tudor England's lusty blossoming. The flamboyant force of that zenith, spent, became in them

1 *Collected Earlier Poems.* p. 26.

hard and little. . . . By their very emptiness they were the fiercest element in the battle to establish a European life in the New World. . . . Stripped and little they came resting on no authority but the secret warmth of their tight-locked hearts.[1]

The Third Factor was the Indian, already rooted in what to him was an old world. Williams does not draw the Indian directly, but he repeatedly scores this point: the Indian was 'right', he was the flower of his locality. The settlers were wrong, for they thieved

the problem of the New World was, as every newcomer soon found out, an awkward one, on all sides the same: how to replace from the wild land that which, at home, they had scarcely known the Old World meant to them: through difficulty and even brutal hardship to find a ground to take the place of England. They could not do it. They clung, one way or another, to the old, striving the while to pull off pieces to themselves from the fat of the new bounty.[2]

Almost alone, Daniel Boone, 'by the single logic of his passion', saw the solution. For Americans are not Indians, but

there must be a new wedding. But he (Boone) saw and only saw the prototype of it all, the native savage. To Boone the Indian was his greatest master. Not for himself surely to be an Indian, though they eagerly sought to adopt him into their tribes, but the reverse: to be *himself* in a new world, Indianlike. If the land were to be possessed it must be as the Indian possessed it.[3]

Thus, Daniel Boone for the first time becomes a symbol of esthetic and moral worth for American artists. Sam Houston receives the same honor, his career giving the incentive for an urgent plea to American writers of our day to descend to the ground they stand on – 'It is imperative that we sink.' They must go back to the beginning and come up from under, like Sam Houston.

But the most powerful symbol in the book is Aaron Burr as Williams conceives him. For Burr represents to Williams that for

1 p. 78.   2 p. 145.   3 p. 146.

which the American Revolution was fought and that which was squeezed out and dried up as the new nation consolidated itself. There was

a half-wild colony, young, shooting out green wood.
England? A dry skin to be cast off, an itch, that's all. There
was a deeper matter, a yeast in the sap, an untracked force
that might lead anywhere; it was springtime in a new world
when all things were possible.[1]

That deeper matter was in Burr and he was hounded for it. He was an individual. He stood out for liberty. He gave and received to the full of his instinctive nature. There was purity in his functioning.

What Williams appears to be saying – his psychological reasoning is crude, though sometimes lit by intuitive flashes to the core – is that Burr preserved in his make-up some biological essence, unspoiled by sociological touching, an essence direct and sincere in its action and unwarped and uncomplicated by education. And the axiom is:—he who acts according to his biologic base rather than according to his environmental shell *appears* to be free.

Hence, the 'teaching' of *In the American Grain* comes to this: know your sources, know your ground and your locality, know what has shaped you, in order that you may be 'free', in order that like Burr you may live essentially. It is good psychological doctrine *as far as it goes*, just as Williams's poetry and prose are good up to their limits. But I should like to complete my description of Williams's work before entering on the criticism of it just now implied. It would be slighting as fine prose as any American today has written not to give a few sentences to the splendor and force of the prose in *In the American Grain*.

As the quotations have disclosed, it is prose with a gusto, prose that puts muscle into its stride. And continually the writer of it spades up superb wordings – sentences with a microscopic accuracy of form and movement, apostrophes and descriptions that attain to romantic eloquence. The eloquence, by the way, is a new facet on Williams's style, and frequently resounds with a dignity and firmness akin to some well-written wilderness chronicle. On the other hand, there is a full measure of his more usual broken impatient hammering at the sub-

1 p. 197.

ject and the reader. The important thing is that the whole style never loses its propulsion: it keeps doing things: it is an awakening prose in its effect upon the reader.

Surely Williams's savagery is a unique essence in modern American letters. He has perceived his ground, he has made a beginning, he is riding the forces of his locality. Determinedly, he seeks to be a Daniel Boone in letters, a Sam Houston in method, and an Aaron Burr in personal psychology. What threatens him – be it puritanic pressures or the hard exigencies of combining literature with medicine – he barks at: the dog with a bone in its throat is symbolic of his attitude toward all that might interrupt or diminish his poetic pursuit. He will go on, so his career to date guarantees. But where and how?

Very little space is required to define the range of his achievement. Marathon, we are told, looks upon the sea, but – the mountains look upon Marathon. The senses, the emotions, the intellect look upon objects, but the imagination looks upon these: that is, the imagination overlooks experience. This, according to our description of Williams, he has never done and never tried to do. Nor will he ever succeed in so doing by the descent to the ground, the Sam Houston way, unless the laws of psychology reverse themselves. Not by descent into actualized and fragmentary resources but by ascent into our unrealized potentials does greatness in literature come. Descent gives change and renewal, but ascent gives development, and it is precisely development that we miss in this wholly engaging and very active writer.

He is potent enough to originate a needed school of writing in America, a school that will be vigorous and basic, but only basic. The school itself will require fertilization by elements not in Williams and not peculiar to America, elements to which America has not attained, elements that come out of general consciousness and not from the particular ground-contact, if its writings are to span and act upon the whole experience of the reader, if, in short, its writings are to pass from the category of minor to the category of major in aim, scope and power.

(101–35)

Ezra Pound

'Dr Williams's Position', *Dial*, vol. 85 1928 (reprinted in
T. S. Eliot (ed.), *Essays of Ezra Pound*, 1954)

There is an anecdote told me by his mother, who wished me to understand his character, as follows: The young William Carlos, aged let us
say about seven, arose in the morning, dressed and put on his shoes.
Both shoes buttoned on the left side. He regarded this untoward
phenomenon for a few moments and then carefully removed the
shoes, placed shoe *a* that had been on his left foot, on his right foot, and
shoe *b*, that had been on the right foot, on his left foot; both sets of
buttons again appeared on the left side of the shoes.

This stumped him. With the shoes so buttoned he went to school,
but . . . and here is the significant part of the story, he spent the
day in careful consideration of the matter.

It happens that this type of sensibility, persisting through forty
years, is of extreme, and almost unique, value in a land teeming
with clever people, all capable of competent and almost instantaneous extroversion; during the last twenty of these years it has distinguished Dr Williams from the floral and unconcious minds of the
populace and from the snappy go-getters who'der seen wot wuz
rong in er moment.

It has prevented our author from grabbing ready-made conclusions, and from taking too much for granted.

There are perhaps, or perhaps have been milieux where the
reflective and examining habits would not have conferred, unsup-
ported, a distinction. But chez nous, for as long as I can remember
if an article appeared in Munsey's or McClure's, expressing a noble
passion (civic or other) one could bank (supposing one were exercising editorial or quasi-editorial functions) on seeing the same
article served up again in some fifty lyric expressions within, let us
say, three or four months.

Our national mind hath about it something 'marvellous porous';
an idea or notion dropped into New York harbour emerges in
Santa Fé or Galveston, watered, diluted, but still the same idea or
notion, pale but not wholly denatured; and the time of transit is
very considerably lower, than any 'record' hitherto known. We

have the defects of our qualities, and that very alertness which makes the single American diverting or enlivening in an European assembly often undermines his literary capacity.

For fifteen or eighteen years I have cited Williams as sole known American-dwelling author who could be counted on to oppose some sort of barrier to such penetration; the sole catalectic in whose presence some sort of modification would take place.

Williams has written: 'All I do is to try to understand something in its natural colours and shapes.' There could be no better effort underlying any literary process, or used as preparative for literary process; but it appears, it would seem, almost incomprehensible to men dwelling west of the Atlantic: I don't mean that it appears so in theory, America will swallow anything in theory, all abstract statements are perfectly welcome, given a sufficiently plausible turn. But the concrete example of this literary process, whether by Williams or by that still more unreceived and uncomprehended native hickory Mr Joseph Gould, seems an unrelated and inexplicable incident to our populace and to our 'monde – or whatever it is – littéraire'. We have, of course, distinctly American authors, Mr Frost for example, but there is an infinite gulf between Mr Frost on New England customs, and Mr Gould on race prejudice; Mr Frost having simply taken on, without any apparent self-questioning, a definite type and set of ideas and sensibilities, known and established in his ancestral demesne. That is to say he is 'typical New England'. Gould is no less New England, but parts of his writing could have proceeded equally well from a Russian, a German, or an exceptional Frenchman – the difference between regionalism, or regionalist art and art that has its root in a given locality.

Carlos Williams has been determined to stand or sit as an American. Freud would probably say 'because his father was English' (in fact half English, half Danish). His mother, as ethnologists have before noted, was a mixture of French and Spanish; of late years (the last four or five) Dr Williams has laid claim to a somewhat remote Hebrew connection, possibly a rabbi in Saragossa, at the time of the siege. He claims American birth, but I strongly suspect that he emerged on shipboard just off Bedloe's Island and that his dark and serious eyes gazed up in their first sober contemplation at the Statue and its brazen and monstrous nightshirt.

At any rate he has not in his ancestral endocrines the arid curse of our nation. None of his immediate forebears burnt witches in Salem,[1] or attended assemblies for producing prohibitions. His father was in the rum trade, the rich ichors of the Indes, Hollands, Jamaicas, Goldwasser, Curaçoas provided the infant William with material sustenance. Spanish was not a strange tongue, and the trade profited by discrimination, by dissociations performed with the palate. All of which belongs to an American yesterday, and is as gone as les caves de Mouquin.

From this secure ingle William Carlos was able to look out of his circumjacence and see it as something interesting *but exterior*; and he could not by any possibility resemble any member of the Concord School. He was able to observe national phenomena without necessity for constant vigilance over himself, there was no instinctive fear that if he forgot himself he might be like some really unpleasant Ralph Waldo; neither is he, apparently, filled with any vivid desire to murder the indescribable dastards who betray the work of the national founders, who spread the fish-hooks of bureaucracy in our once, perhaps, pleasant bypaths.

One might accuse him of being, blessedly, the observant foreigner, perceiving American vegetation and landscape quite directly, as something put there for him to look at; and his contemplative habit extends, also blessedly, to the fauna.

When Mr Wanamaker's picture gallery burned in the dead of winter I was able to observe the destruction of faked Van Dykes, etc. *comme spectacle*, the muffler'd lads of the village tearing down gold frames in the light of the conflagration, the onyx-topped tables against the blackness were still more 'tableau' and one could think detachedly of the French Revolution. Mr Wanamaker was nothing to me, he paid his employees badly, and I knew the actual spectacle was all I should ever get out of him. I cannot, on the other hand, observe the nation befouled by Volsteads and Bryans, without anger; I cannot see liberties that have lasted for a century thrown away for nothing, for worse than nothing, for slop; frontiers tied up by an imbecile bureaucracy exceeding 'anything known in Russia under the Czars' without indignation.[2]

1 Note: We didn't burn them, we hanged them. T. S. E.
2 This comparison to Russia is not mine, but comes from a Czarist official who had been stationed in Washington.

And by just this susceptibility on my part Williams, as author, has the no small advantage. If he wants to 'do' anything about what he sees, this desire for action does not rise until he has meditated in full and at leisure. Where I see scoundrels and vandals, he sees a spectacle or an ineluctable process of nature. Where I want to kill at once, he ruminates, and if this rumination leads to anger it is an almost inarticulate anger, that may but lend colour to style, but which stays almost wholly in the realm of his art. I mean it is a qualificative, contemplative, does not drive him to some ultra-artistic or non-artistic activity.

Even recently where one of his characters clearly expresses a dissatisfaction with the American milieu, it is an odium against a condition of mind, not against overt acts or institutions.

The lack of celerity in his process, the unfamiliarity with facile or with established solutions would account for the irritation his earlier prose, as I remember it, caused to sophisticated Britons. 'How any man could go on talking about such things!' and so on. But the results of this sobriety of unhurried contemplation, when apparent in such a book as *In the American Grain*, equally account for the immediate appreciation of Williams by the small number of French critics whose culture is sufficiently wide to permit them to read any modern tongue save their own.

Here, at last, was an America treated with a seriousness and by a process comprehensible to an European.

One might say that Williams has but one fixed idea, as an author; i.e. he starts where an European would start if an European were about to write of America: sic: America is a subject of interest, one must inspect it, analyse it, and treat it as subject. There are plenty of people who think they 'ought' to write 'about' America. This is a wholly different kettle of fish. There are also numerous people who think that the given subject has an inherent interest simply because it is American and that this gives it *ipso facto* a dignity or value above all other possible subjects; Williams may even think he has, or may once have thought he had this angle of attack, but he hasn't.

After a number of years, and apropos of a given incident he has (first quarterly number of *transition*) given a perfectly clear verbal manifestation of his critical attitude. It is that of his most worthy European contemporaries, and of all good critics. It is also symptomatic of New York that his analysis of the so-called criticisms of Antheil's New York concert should appear in Paris, a year after the event, in an amateur periodical.

The main point of his article being that no single one of the critics had made the least attempt at analysis, or had in any way tried to tell the reader what the music consisted of, what were its modes or procedures. And that this was, of course, what the critics were, or would in any civilized country have been, there for. This article is perhaps Williams's most important, or at any rate most apposite, piece of critical writing; failing a wide distribution of the magazine in which it appeared, it should be reprinted in some more widely distributable journal.[1]

It would seem that the illusion of 'progress' is limited, chez nous, to the greater prevalence of erotic adventure, whether developed in quality or merely increased in quantity I have no present means of deciding; the illusion as to any corresponding 'progress' or catching-up in affairs of the intellect, would seem to rise from the fact that in our literary milieux certain things are now known that were not known in 1912; but this does not constitute a change of relation, i.e. does not prove that America is not still fifteen years or twenty years or more 'behind the times'. We must breed a non-Mabie, non-Howells type of author. And of the possible types Williams and Gould serve as our best examples – as distinct from the porous types.

I mean not by this sentence, but by the whole trend of this article: when a creative act occurs in America 'no one' seems aware of what is occurring. In music we have chefs d'orchestre, not composers, and we have something very like it in letters, though the distinction is less obvious.

Following this metaphor; it is undeniable that part of my time, for example, has been put into orchestral directing. Very little of Dr Williams's energy has been so deflected. If he did some Rimbaud forty years late it was nevertheless composition, and I don't think he knew it was Rimbaud until after he finished his operation.

Orchestral directing is 'all right' mais c'est pas la même chose. We are still so generally obsessed by monism and monotheistical backwash,

1 See 'George Antheil and the Cantilene Critics', 1925, Selected Essays, pp. 57-61.

and ideas of orthodoxy that we (and the benighted Britons) can hardly observe a dissociation of ideas without thinking a censure is somehow therein implied.

We are not, of course we are not, free from the errors of post-reformation Europe. The triviality of philosophical writers through the last few centuries is extraordinary, in the extent that is, that they have not profited by modes of thought quite common to biological students; in the extent that they rely on wholly unfounded assumptions, for no more apparent reason than that these assumptions are currently and commonly made. Reputed philosophers will proceed (four volumes at a time) as if the only alternative for monism were dualism; among distinguished literati, si licet, taking personal examples: Mr Joyce will argue for hours as if one's attack on Christianity were an attack on the Roman church in favour of Luther or Calvin or some other half-baked ignoramus and the 'protestant' conventicle. Mr Eliot will reply, even in print, to Mr Babbitt as if some form of Christianity or monotheism were the sole alternative to irreligion; and as if monism or monotheism were anything more than an hypothesis agreeable to certain types of very lazy mind too weak to bear an uncertainty or to remain in 'uncertainty'.

And, again, for such reasons William Williams, and may we say, his Mediterranean equipment, have an importance in relation to his temporal intellectual circumjacence.

Very well, he does not 'conclude'; his work has been 'often form-less', 'incoherent', opaque, obscure, obfuscated, confused, truncated, etc.

I am not going to say: 'form' is a non-literary component shoved on to literature by Aristotle or by some non-litteratus who told Aristotle about it. Major form is not a non-literary component. But it can do us no harm to stop an hour or so and consider the number of very important chunks of world-literature in which form, major form, is remarkable mainly for absence.

There is a corking plot to the *Iliad*, but it is not told us in the poem or at least not in the parts of the poem known to history as the *Iliad*. It would be hard to find a worse justification of the theories of dramatic construction than the *Prometheus* of Aeschylus. It will take a brighter lad than the author of these presents to demonstrate the element of form in Montaigne or in Rabelais; Lope has it, but it is not the 'Aristotelian' beginning, middle and end, it is the quite reprehensible: BEGINNING WHOOP and then any sort of a trail off. *Bouvard and Pécuchet* wasn't even finished by its author. And of all these Lope is the only one we could sacrifice without inestimable loss and impoverishment.

The component of these great works and *the* indispensable component is texture; which Dr Williams indubitably has in the best, and in increasingly frequent, passages of his writing.

In current American fiction that has, often, quite a good deal of merit, and which has apparently been concocted with effort and goodish intentions, the failure to attain first-rateness seems to be mainly of two sorts: The post-Zolas or post-realists deal with subject matter, human types, etc., so simple that one is more entertained by Fabre's insects or Hudson's birds and wild animals. The habits or the reactions of 'an ant' or 'a chaffinch' emerge in a more satisfactory purity or at least in some modus that at least seems to present a more firm and sustaining pabulum to reflection.

Secondly: there are the perfumed writers. They aim, one believes, at olde lavender; but the ultimate aroma lacks freshness. 'Stale meringue', 'last week's custard' and other metaphorical expressions leap to mind when one attempts to give an impression of their quality. One 'ought' perhaps to make a closer analysis and give the receipt for the fadeur; though like all mediocre dilutations it is harder to analyse than the clearer and fresher substance. When I was fourteen, people used to read novels of the same sort, let us say *The House of a Thousand Candles*, etc., of which one may remember a title, but never remembers anything else, and of which the author's name has, at the end of five or ten years, escaped one.

It is perfectly natural that people wholly surrounded by roughnecks, whether in mid-nineteenth century or in The Hesperian present, should want to indicate the desirability of sweetness and refinement, but ... these things belong to a different order of existence, different that is from pity, terror, τὸ καλόν, and those things with which art, plastic or that of the writer, is concerned.

Now in reading Williams, let us say this last book *A Voyage to Pagany* or almost anything else he has written, one may often feel: he is wrong. I didn't mean wrong in idea, but: that is the wrong way to write it. He oughtn't to have said that. But there is a residue of effect. The work is always distinct from writing that one finds merely hopeless and in strict sense irremediable.

There is a difference in kind between it and the mass of current writing, about which there is just nothing to be done, and which no series of re-touches, or cuttings away, would clarify, or leave hard.

Art very possibly *ought* to be supreme achievement, the 'accomplished'; but there is the other satisfactory effect, that of a man hurling himself at an indomitable chaos, and yanking and hauling as much of it as possible into some sort of order (or beauty), aware of it both as chaos and as potential.

Form is, indeed, very tiresome when in reading current novels, we observe the thinning residue of pages, fifty, thirty, and realize that there is now only time (space) for the hero to die a violent death, no other solution being feasible in that number of pages.

To come at it another way: There are books that are clever enough, good enough, well enough done to fool the people who don't know, or to divert one in hours of fatigue. There are other books – and they may be often less clever, and may often show less accomplishment – which, despite their ineptitudes, and lack of accomplishment, or 'form', and finish, contain something for the best minds of the time, a time, any time. If *Pagany* is not Williams's best book, if even on some counts, being his first long work, it is his worst, it indubitably contains pages and passages that are worth any one's while, and that provide mental cud for any ruminant tooth.

And finally, to comply with those requirements for critics which Dr Williams has outlined in his censure of Mr Antheil's critics: The particular book that is occasion for this general discussion of Williams, *A Voyage to Pagany*,[1] has not very much to do with the 'art of novel writing', which Dr Williams has fairly clearly abjured. Its plot-device is the primitive one of 'a journey', frankly avowed. Entire pages could have found place in a simple autobiography of travel.

In the genealogy of writing it stems from *Ulysses*, or rather we would say better: Williams's *The Great American Novel*, eighty pages, Three Mountains Press, 1923, was Williams's first and strongest derivation from *Ulysses*, an 'inner monologue', stronger and more

1 *A Voyage to Pagany*, 1928.

gnarled, or stronger *because* more gnarled at least as I see it, than the *Pagany*.

The other offspring from *Ulysses*, the only other I have seen possessing any value, is John Rodker's *Adolphe*, 1920. The two books are greatly different. *The Great American Novel* is simply the application of Joycean method to the American circumjacence. The *Adolphe*, professedly taking its schema from Benjamin Constant, brings the Joycean methodic inventions into a form; slighter than *Ulysses*, as a rondeau is slighter than a canzone, but indubitably a 'development', a definite step in general progress of writing; having, as have at least two other novels by Rodker, its definite shaped construction. And yet, if one read it often enough, the element of form emerges in *The Great American Novel*, not probably governing the whole, but in the shaping of at least some of the chapters, notably chapter 7, the one beginning 'Nuevo Mundo'.

As to subject or problem, the *Pagany* relates to the Jamesian problem of USA *v.* Europe, the international relation, etc.; the particular equation of the Vienna milieu has had recent treatment 'from the other end on' in Joseph Bard's *Shipwreck in Europe*, more sprightly and probably less deeply concerned with the salvation of the protagonist; I think the continental author mentions as a general and known post-war quantity: the American or Americans who comes or come to Vienna to find out why they can't enjoy life, even after getting a great deal of money.

In the American Grain remains, I imagine, Dr Williams's book having the greater interest for the European reader. In the looseish structure of the *Pagany* I don't quite make out what, unless it be simple vagary of the printer, has caused the omission of 'The Venus' (July *Dial*[1]), pages obviously written to occur somewhere in the longer work, though they do form a whole in themselves, and pose quite clearly the general question, or at least one phase of the question in the *Pagany*.

In all the books cited,[2] the best pages of Williams – at least for the present reviewer – are those where he has made the least effort

1. *Dial*, vol. 85, 1928.
2 *The Tempers*, 1913; *Al Que Quiere*, 1917; *Kora in Hell*, 1920; *Sour Grapes*, 1921; *The Great American Novel*, 1923; *In the American Grain*, 1925; *A Voyage to Pagany*, 1928.

to fit anything into either story, book or (in *In the American Grain*) into an essay. I would almost move from that isolated instance to the generalization that plot, major form or outline should be left to authors who feel some inner need for the same; even let us say a very strong, unusual, unescapable need for these things; and to books where the said form, plot, etc., springs naturally from the matter treated. When put on *ab exteriore*, they probably lead only to dullness, confusion or remplissage or the 'falling between two stools'. I don't mean that Williams 'falls'; he certainly has never loaded on enough shapings to bother one. As to his two dialectical ladies? Of course he may know ladies who argue like that. There may be ladies who so argue, aided by Bacchus. In any case the effect of one human on another is such that Williams may elicit such dialectic from ladies who in presence of a more dialectic or voluble male would be themselves notably less so. No one else now writing would have given us the sharp clarity of the medical chapters.

As to the general value of Carlos Williams's poetry I have nothing to retract from the affirmation of its value that I made ten years ago, nor do I see any particular need of repeating that estimate; I should have to say the same things, and it would be with but a pretence or camouflage of novelty.

When an author preserves, by any means whatsoever, his integrity, I take it we ought to be thankful. We retain a liberty to speculate as to how he might have done better, what paths would conduce to, say, progress in his next opus, etc., to ask whether for example Williams would have done better to have read W. H. Hudson than to have been interested in Joyce. At least there is place for reflection as to whether the method of Hudson's *A Traveller in Little Things* would serve for an author so concerned with his own insides as is Williams; or whether Williams himself isn't at his best – retaining interest in the uncommunicable or the hidden roots of the consciousness of people he meets, but confining his statement to presentation of their objective manifests.

No one but a fantastic impressionist or a fanatic subjectivist or introversionist will try to answer such a question save in relation to a given specific work.

(389–98)

Louis Zukofsky

'William Carlos Williams'   1928 (reprinted in *Prepositions:
The Collected Critical Essays*, 1967)

Writing with a sense of the history and destiny of The United States
– as in the Earlier Discoveries of *In the American Grain* – William
Carlos Williams with *A Voyage to Pagany* impels Americans towards a
Beginning. The curious as to history may find it convenient to draw a
parallel between this later effort of sensitized American intellect and
the earlier effort of Henry Adams in his *Mont St Michel and Chartres*
(1904).

 As there has been no actual contact of subject matter the parallel
can be no more than metaphor. It points the fact that two minds, with
approximately a quarter of a century between them, have reacted as
Americans, along different lines, toward what might be termed the
European unchanging – in the words of Williams, 'the ancient
springs of purity and plenty'.

 Both writers come to Europe: Adams to the cathedrals of France
to see the Virgin; Williams among other places to Paris, 'a stitched-up
woman hunting a lover'.

 'It must be a lover. He must come of machines, he must break
through. Nothing will subdue him.' So they come as lovers, both from
machines. They must break through to get at what they want, since
neither will walk on Nothing. But there is a difference of twenty-four
years.

 Son of his New England family Adams voyaged, a mind replete
with education – the heart as though trip-hammered with its in-
effectualness – to preserve intact the spirit which in the past had preserved his family; in the end a mind surfeited, prodigal to family, the
lover in humility, submitting (perhaps he did not know) to his own
superstructure over French Gothic mind; the spirit mortified, but
somehow complete. In summary he said of it:

Of all the elaborate symbolism which has been suggested for
the Gothic cathedral, the most vital and most perfect may be
that the slender nervure, the springing motion of the broken

arch, the leap downwards of the flying buttress – the visible effort to throw off a visible strain – never let us forget that Faith only supports it, and that, if Faith fails, Heaven is lost.

The new voyage to pagany (pagany meaning Europe) is steered near Adams's original route. Again what was launched is not the machine, but instinct. 'One thing about the man, he never argued with his instincts.' After twenty-four years, it is still the machine which persists. But no need to be mortified. Wary one must be, of course – always the check upon the instincts; America has raised one that way; but one can approach, like the Indian, circle around, and then attack. Attack at least with the precision of the machine become instinct.

The Ancient Beauty, yes. At Santa Croce one is 'purified past the walls of any church', but not subdued: purified for oneself, for one's own Beginning and the Beginning of one's own (*Spring and All*). Europe, Venice of Waters, the Pagan underneath the Christian, Giotto, Cimabue, the world's 'shell of past loveliness', meet it with distrust! Learn, yes, be penetrated, become clear on all levels as with the clarity of Williams's Viennese doctors, but 'close the eyes sharply to, at the height of enjoyment, at the peak of understanding. He had strengthened his understanding of what he had long since discerned. He carried his affirmation away in his pocket – with his timetable.' Like an American. Old Europe may not like it.

What this change means to the writing is clear. The *Mont St Michel and Chartres* of Henry Adams in submission attains an imaginative completeness, a clarity originally foreign and resolves into unity. What might have been a tiresome itinerary becomes a celestial Baedeker, the plan of the book chastened as the nervure of the Gothic arch. What was intended to be impersonal has the element of the personal diffused through design. The struggle of American mind for the ciborium not its own casts the spell of tragedy through the calm of structure.

The recalcitrance of William Carlos Williams in *A Voyage to Pagany* makes for anything but tragedy. What is intended to be a novel becomes in structure an animated itinerary. There is practically no design, since the aim impelling the book is – to move on to the Beginning. There can be no lingering for what is final, for what resolves into unity. Fact – impels from incident to incident, because the Beginning comes only with the finish of what is Past.

Intellectualism is a by-product of this itinerary and teases the imagination. The author of that perfect piece in *Spring and All*, 'The pure products of America go crazy', might have remained on his own ground and implied in a novel of the defeat of those 'pure products', farmers, migrant laborers, substrata of These States, the defeat of intellectualism itself. The poet's nature compelled him otherwise. For one concerned with the Beginning, a portrait of what is closest to oneself to begin with is indispensable; it makes for honesty – the welcome absence of premature sentiment with regard to America's 'peasantry' – rare in recent fiction.

What is good in *A Voyage to Pagany* breaks through – despite the hazards of intellect – sees through incident, surrounds and fathoms objects. The principal character Dev, a constantly impressionable fellow, irritates himself into thought: 'What does anybody find in anybody? Something he can't get except through that somebody'; the words, 'What is it, dear?' making the natural keystone of a perfect love scene; 'Carcassonne, a rock ruined by tears'; 'the tan and grime wrestling the hair stuck together at the ends, growing from the scaly scalps, from poor soil . . .'; the Arno 'river getting broader and going about its business'; 'music a presence which you feel occasionally during the playing'; of Bach's *St Matthew Passion* – 'I heard him agonizing, I saw him *inside*, not cold but he *lived* and I was possessed by his passion.'

Americans might do no better than to emulate the Europeans, and consider the portrait of what is at least their own Beginning – carefully.

(45–7)

Wallace Stevens

Preface to *Collected Poems, 1921–1931* 1934 (reprinted in
Samuel French Morse (ed.), *Opus Posthumus*, 1957)

The slightly tobaccoy odor of autumn is perceptible in these pages.
Williams is past fifty.

There are so many things to say about him. The first is that he
is a romantic poet. This will horrify him. Yet the proof is everywhere. Take the first poem, *All the Fancy Things*. What gives this
its distinction is the image of the woman, once a girl in Puerto Rico
in the Old Spanish days, now solitary and growing old, not knowing
what to do with herself, remembering. Of course, this is romantic
in the accepted sense, and Williams is rarely romantic in the accepted
sense.

The man has spent his life in rejecting the accepted sense of things.
In that, most of all, his romantic temperament appears. But it is not
enough merely to reject: what matters is the reason for rejection.
The reason is that Williams has a romantic of his own. His strong
spirit makes its own demands and delights to try its strength.

It will be observed that the lonely figure in *All the Fancy Things* and
the person addressed in *Brilliant Sad Sun* have been slightly sentimentalized. In order to understand Williams at all, it is necessary to
say at once that he has a sentimental side. Except for that, this book
would not exist and its character would not be what it is. *The Cod
Head* is a bit of pure sentimentalization; so is *The Bull*. Sentiment has
such an abhorrent name that one hesitates. But if what vitalizes
Williams has an abhorrent name, its obviously generative function in
his case may help to change its reputation. What Williams gives, on
the whole, is not sentiment but the reaction from sentiment, or,
rather, a little sentiment, very little, together with acute reaction.

His passion for the anti-poetic is a blood-passion and not a passion
of the inkpot. The anti-poetic is his spirit's cure. He needs it as a
naked man needs shelter or as an animal needs salt. To a man with a
sentimental side the anti-poetic is that truth, that reality to which all
of us are forever fleeing.

The anti-poetic has many aspects. The aspect to which a poet is
addicted is a test of his validity. Its merely rhetorical aspect is valueless.

As an affectation it is a commonplace. As a scourge it has a little more meaning. But as a phase of a man's spirit, as a source of salvation, now, in the midst of a baffled generation, as one looks out of the window at Rutherford or Passaic, or as one walks the streets of New York, the anti-poetic acquires an extraordinary potency, especially if one's nature possesses that side so attractive to the Furies.

Something of the unreal is necessary to fecundate the real; something of the sentimental is necessary to fecundate the anti-poetic. Williams, by nature, is more of a realist than is commonly true in the case of a poet. One might, at this point, set oneself up as the Linnaeus of aesthetics, assigning a female role to the unused tent in *The Attic Which Is Desire*, and a male role to the soda sign; and generally speaking one might run through these pages and point out how often the essential poetry is the result of the conjunction of the unreal and the real, the sentimental and the anti-poetic, the constant interaction of two opposites. This seems to define Williams and his poetry.

All poets are, to some extent, romantic poets. Thus, the poet who least supposes himself to be so is often altogether so. For instance, no one except a *surréaliste* himself would hesitate to characterize that whole school as romantic, dyed through and through with the most authentic purple. What, then, is a romantic poet nowadays? He happens to be one who still dwells in an ivory tower, but who insists that life would be intolerable except for the fact that one has, from the top, such an exceptional view of the public dump and the advertising signs of Snider's Catsup, Ivory Soap and Chevrolet Cars; he is the hermit who dwells alone with the sun and moon, but insists on taking a rotten newspaper. While Williams shares a good deal of this with his contemporaries in the manner and for the reason indicated, the attempt to define him and his work is not to be taken as an attempt to define anyone or anything else.

So defined, Williams looks a bit like that grand old plaster cast, Lessing's Laocoön: the realist struggling to escape from the serpents of the unreal.

He is commonly identified by externals. He includes here specimens of abortive rhythms, words on several levels, ideas without logic, and similar minor matters, which, when all is said, are merely the diversion of the prophet between morning and evening song. It will be found that he has made some veritable additions to the corpus of poetry, which certainly is no more sacred to anyone than to him. His special use of the anti-poetic is an example of this. The ambiguity produced by bareness is another. The implied image, as in *Young Sycamore*, the serpent that leaps up in one's imagination at his prompting, is an addition to imagism, a phase of realism which Williams has always found congenial. In respect to manner he is a virtuoso. He writes of flowers exquisitely. But these things may merely be mentioned. Williams himself, a kind of Diogenes of contemporary poetry, is a much more vital matter. The truth is that, if one had not chanced to regard him as Laocoön, one could have done very well by him as Diogenes.

(254–9)

Marianne Moore

'Things Others Never Notice', a review of *Collected Poems,
1921–1931*, *Poetry*, vol. 44 1934 (reprinted in Marianne Moore
(ed.), *Predilections*, 1955)

Struggle, like the compression which propels the steam-engine, is a main force in William Carlos Williams. He 'looks a bit like that grand old plaster cast, Lessing's Laocoön', Wallace Stevens says in the introduction to this book. And the breathless budding of thought from thought is one of the results and charms of the pressure configured. With an abandon born of inner security, Dr Williams somewhere nicknames the chain of incontrovertibly logical apparent non-sequiturs, rigmarole; and a consciousness of life and intrepidity is characteristically present in *Stop: Go*:

a green truck
dragging a concrete mixer
passes
in the street –
the clatter and true sound
of verse – [1]

[1] *Collected Earlier Poems* p. 59.

Disliking the tawdriness of unnecessary explanation, the detracting compulsory connective, stock speech of any kind, he sets the words down, 'each note secure in its own posture – singularly woven.' 'The senseless unarrangement of wild things' which he imitates makes some kinds of correct writing look rather foolish; and as illustrating that combination of energy and composure which is the expertness of the artist, he has never drawn a clearer self-portrait than *Birds and Flowers*, part 2:

What have I done
to drive you away? It is
winter, true enough, but

this day I love you.
This day
there is no time at all

more than in under
my ribs where anatomists
say the heart is –

And just today you
will not have me. Well,
tomorrow it may be snowing –

I'll keep after you. Your
repulse of me is no more
than a rebuff to the weather –

If we make a desert of
ourselves – we make
a desert . . .[1]

William Carlos Williams objects to urbanity – to sleek and natty effects – and this is a good sign if not always a good thing. Yet usually nothing could better the dashing shrewdness of the pattern as he develops it and cuts it off at the acutely right point.

With the bee's sense of polarity he searches for a flower and that flower is representation. Likenesses here are not reminders of the object, they are likenesses:

And there's the river with thin ice upon it
fanning out half over the black
water, the free middlewater racing under its
ripples that move crosswise on the stream.[1]

He is drugged with romance – 'O unlit candle with the soft white plume' – but like the bee, is neither a waif nor a fool. Argus-eyed, energetic, insatiate, compassionate, undeceived, he says in *Immortal* (in *The Tempers*), 'Yes, there is one thing braver than all flowers, . . . And thy name, lovely One, is Ignorance.' Wide-eyed resignation of this kind helps some to be cynical but it makes Dr Williams considerate; sorry for the tethered bull, the circus sea-elephant, for the organ-grinder 'sourfaced', for the dead man 'needing a shave –'

the dog won't have to
sleep on his potatoes
any more to keep them
from freezing –[2]

He ponders 'the justice of poverty its shame its dirt' and pities the artist's prohibited energy as it patiently does for the common weal what it ought to do, and the poem read by critics who have no inkling of what it's about. But the pathos is incidental. The 'ability to be drunk with a sudden realization of value in things others never notice' can metamorphose our detestable reasonableness and offset a whole planetary system of deadness. 'The burning liquor of the moonlight' makes provable things mild by comparison. Art, that is to say, has its effect on the artist and also on the patron; and in Dr Williams we have an example of art that disregards crochets and specifications. The poem often is about nothing that we wish to give our attention to, but if it is something he wishes our attention for, what is urgent for him becomes urgent for us. His uncompromising conscientiousness sometimes seems misplaced; he is at times almost insultingly specific but there is in him – and this must be our consolation – that dissatisfied expanding energy, the emotion, the cock-spur of the medieval dialectician, the 'therefore' that is the distinguishing mark of the artist.

Various poems that are not here, again suggest the bee – and a too eclectic disposing of the honey.

1 p. 291.   2 p. 78.

Dr Williams does not compromise, and Wallace Stevens is another resister whose way of saying is as important as what is said. Mr Stevens's presentation of the book refreshes a grievance – the scarcity of prose about verse from one of the few persons who should have something to say. But poetry in America has not died, so long as these two 'young sycamores' are able to stand the winters that we have, and the inhabitants.

(136–9)

William Carlos Williams

from a letter to Marianne Moore   2 May 1934 (reprinted in J. C. Thirlwall (ed.), *Selected Letters*, 1957)

The thing that I like best about your review of my book[1] is that you have looked at what I have done through my own eyes. I assure you that this is so. Had it not been so you would not have noticed the 'inner security' nor the significance of some of the detail – which nobody seems to value as I have valued it.

The inner security though is an overwhelmingly important observation. I'm glad to have had you bring it up. Not that anyone will notice it. It is something which occurred once when I was about twenty, a sudden resignation to existence, a despair – if you wish to call it that, but a despair which made everything a unit and at the same time a part of myself. I suppose it might be called a sort of nameless religious experience. I resigned, I gave up. I decided there was nothing else in life for me but to work. It is the explanation for the calumny that is heaped on my head by women and men alike once they know me long enough. I won't follow causes. I can't. The reason is that it seems so much more important to me that I *am*. Where shall one go? What shall one do? Things have no names for me and places have no significance. As a reward for this anonymity I feel as much a part of things as trees and stones. Heaven seems frankly impossible. I am damned as I succeed. I have no particular hope save to repair, to rescue, to complete. . . .

(147)

1 *Collected Poems: 1921–1931.*

Alfred Kazin

'White Mule', *New York Times Book Review*   20 June 1937

Poets who turn to the novel face a problem that rarely troubles other members of the guild. There is such a thing as poetic insight. Most of us hover around it like sleepwalkers, respond to it with some common appreciation of its suggestiveness. The poet uses it with a reflex motion. When he turns to dramatic realism he cannot forego the pleasure of seeing men as creatures of light. By seeing the general in every particular, he is oppressed by the pathos or tragedy of the norm. By assuming that all men are eaten by the same worm, he hears the threnody of the world in the pulse of behavior.

At its worst this means the lyric novel, wherein farmers talk like angels and machinists sing too, too prettily at work. At its most thoughtful – and *White Mule* is a superb example – the common material of the novel is given a new texture. The superficially lyric mind distends everything. The genuine poet has a more perceptive feeling for detail, and there, since the novel is built on the odds and ends of temporality, he finds his mission. Open Dr Williams's book and you are in a new world of sound. Accents cling to the air. The harmony is the rough, gravely ironic rhythm of public speech. Like James Joyce, whose blindness has sharpened his extraordinary musical ear, Dr Williams has his characters talk with such a native freshness that the sound is never obtrusive. It is a pure speech because it is so richly characteristic, and its utter realism is therefore deeper, more meaningful than the violent accuracy of naturalism.

The quotation marks have been dropped to bring us closer to every moment in the drama, which is fashioned, after all, by accumulation. In another book the novelist would use quotation marks to tell us that the characters are talking, but here motion is blended with every nuance. We see precisely because we hear. The action evokes so many of the sights and sounds of life that we are stirred at every point by remembrance, but the associations are neither drearily commonplace nor dreamy. The story of Joe Stecher and his wife, Gurlie, may or may not be a parable, but since they are both immigrants, since both are at once restive with nostalgia and determined to follow the promise of a new life, the American dream is part of their story. They may look with scorn at the uncouth aborigine, but they are afraid of him. They, too, want to belong, but the act of adoption costs them something – in pride, in security, in tenderness.

They know that they cannot go back. Their responsibilities have enclosed them. The novel opens, portentously enough, on the birth of their second daughter, a sickly, troublesome child. Joe is frugal, industrious, scrupulously careful to make things go; but his foreman's job at a printing plant does not satisfy Gurlie. The World War is many years away. Expansion is in the blood. Joe was once the co-worker of Samuel Gompers, but when the men in his plant go out on strike, he fights them bitterly. He belongs nowhere. He despises the American workmen, but he hates his own employer. Gurlie's ambition depresses him. The child's delicacy forces them to move from one place to another and prompts a further need of money.

Within this frame of domesticity, Joe and Gurlie try to meet the bleak, hostile scene that is America to them. Joe leaves his employers to start a new business. Gurlie, proud and ironic but not without her moments of deep feeling, is forced to keep special watch over the baby. There are family dinners, a walk in the park, some genial drinking between old friends. Time is measured by the growth of their baby, the increase of their income, the search for old roots. America is a loud stranger, but they would like to know him better. America is not all dollar sign, they see, but some external confusion repels them. Too much noise, heat; too much American laziness. Life for Joe has been an unceasing struggle. He enjoys sweating for his bread. That is the moral law he knows, for from it he gleans purpose and order and the dignity that makes him tick the way he does. But at a Fourth of July double-header he sits thinking about the new business and the crowd heckles McGraw and screams for Mathewson.

Like the millions they live with, Joe and Gurlie would like some sense of citizenship. Their world moves in an orbit around a job, an ill child, a house, a raise. They are too tired, too human, to think of the rest. And so their world, the only one they know, a world of flicker and appearance, encompasses and misleads them. The vague memory of the European past may be solace, but in the end it is an excuse for irony. Joe has to work too hard and too long to make declarations or ask the spiritual question. But he lives before us as most men do in real life: as a gleam in the darkness. He moves in a cycle of sleep, work and dinner: there is a quarrel with Gurlie, many a headshaking over the child, a curse for the enemy of the moment. It is his wry speech that sets the tone, the shiver in his voice that declaims the crisis of his own humanity. But in reality there is no declamation; there is only stasis and the ebb and flow around it, the particular given to us with so much honesty, so much understanding, that what we hear is the echo of a communal whisper.

(7)

Philip Rahv

'Torrents of Spring', *Nation*, no. 144   26 June 1937

It is a fine thing that Dr Williams's *White Mule* has at last been brought out in book form. Dr Williams, though among the most bracing and original talents in American letters, has never received the recognition so frequently accorded to those who denature and conventionalize the new attitudes and techniques launched by people like himself. That he is detached from all efforts at popular appeal goes without saying. Kenneth Burke once said of Williams that he was engaged in 'discovering the shortest route between subject and object', but the reader, unfortunately, having become accustomed to the fatigue induced by long detours, has come to regard the short cut as an aberration of literary faddists.

Williams is too hardy a frontiersman of the word to permit himself the idle luxuries of aestheticism. There are too many things to be seen and touched, too many cadences of living speech to be listened to and recorded; and his novel is as busy doing that as his poetry. What happens on the most ordinary level of American living is the theme of this narrative of a man, his wife and their two children. Like the spokes of a wheel all the episodes in the book radiate from the first chapter, called To Be, which describes the birth of the second child and the first few days in the world. As in a microcosm the author's creative credo is embodied in this chapter, so instinct with natural piety and pure in its virile tenderness, so alive with sensory detail recreated in language that is swift, bare, tonic, and elated by its closeness to the object. Such plain and humble subject matter is characteristic of Williams, who has a passion for the anti-poetic, which he sees as the solvent of the unreal in art. Moreover, it is this very quality which causes his elements to move with such simple grace and which releases in him a sensibility of springtime that in itself becomes the source of a new poetics. In this sense, if a good deal of modernist writing represents a vision of the end of the world, Williams's distinct strength lies, conversely, in calling forth a vision of its beginnings. And this would explain why he has been able to work within the modernist medium without sharing its decadence.

The novel as a whole, however, is not content with the perception of facts and the feeling of them. There are certain problems, obviously, that the aesthetics of neo-primitivism cannot encompass. Continuing in a different vein the intense search for America that marked his prose work *In the American Grain*, Williams employs his characters as instruments to register with unwonted sensitiveness the peculiarities of the American scene. Joe Stecher, the foreman of a printshop, is an Alsatian who came to America in early youth, and his wife, Gurlie, is Norwegian. As foreigners, they are acutely aware of the contrast between the old world and the new and singularly perceptive of American qualities. Gurlie is so rife with the natural humors of a wife that she emerges as a veritable goddess of the home, but since it is an American home she is constantly urging her husband to get into the game, beat the other fellow, and make money. Joe's principal motivation, however, is his pride of workmanship; he is the pure artisan, the man who has not yet been alienated from the product of his labor and who thinks of money as the reward of labor and nothing else. Hence he takes a middle position between employer and worker. He is assailed by vexatious questions, such as are the unions merely businesses or do they represent a higher principle of social justice? Yet essentially he regards both sides in the struggle as interfering with the efficiency of production. Ambition stirs him, and despite himself he gradually becomes more and more involved with the employers. As this is only the first book in what promises to be a series, it is premature to predict the eventual resolution of Joe's beliefs.

It is interesting to observe that Williams too, like most American writers, has not escaped the political baptism of our decade. Patently, there is a correspondence between Joe Stecher and himself. Joe's philosophy of workmanship also defines the relation of Williams, a writer who is primarily a craftsman, to the literary trends of recent years. It is not difficult to see how to him the conflict of classes in literature might seem to be interfering, and perhaps gratuitously so, with the clean functioning of the written word. He would naturally be affronted by the automatism with which the phrase springs to the lips of the political fanatic. Hence, not the least of the tasks he has set himself in his work is the discovery of an attitude toward society that will prove compatible with his creative methods as a writer. (733)

R. P. Blackmur

from 'John Wheelwright and Mr Williams', a review of
Complete Collected Poems, 1906–1938   1939 (reprinted in
Language as Gesture, 1954)

We are concerned here merely with the facts of poetic character. There is, to begin with, the fact that Dr Williams writes exclusively in free verse of an extraordinary solid and flexible species. Further he despises traditional English meters; the sonnet he thinks good only for doggerel, subverts most intelligences, and has as a word a definitely fascistic meaning. I do not doubt that he may be right for himself; which goes to show only that his intellect is in him so badly proportioned that it interferes with the operation of his sensibility. He needs to work, as it were, under cover; needs to find his work seemingly already done for him when he takes it up. The depth and rightness of his instinct for himself is shown by the mastery in at least twenty poems of varying length of a form adequate in every respect to his poetic purpose. Yvor Winters says that this is the form of free verse, and that it scans, has outer rules and an inner scheme. I refer the reader to Winters's *Primitivism and Decadence* where the technique of Dr Williams's free verse is fully discussed; I cannot follow the discussion myself, preferring to believe (until I can follow it) that Dr Williams's astonishing success comes from the combination of a good ear for speech cadence and for the balance of meaning and sound, plus a facility for the double effect of weight and speed. When Mr

Winters (in the *Kenyon Review*, January 1939) compares Dr Williams to Herrick as equally indestructible, the justice of his comparison, if there be any, must lie in the comparison of incongruities; for the older poet spent his life refining his sensibility in terms of his medium, precisely as the younger has evidently insisted on his sensibility at the *expense* of his medium.

However that may be, what remains of Dr Williams's medium has been so successful for himself, that many have thought it would be successful for anybody. We are accustomed to think of him as a fertile poet – as fruitful in poems for other poets to read. The pages of the poetry journals every now and then show the results; curiously, the imitation is almost always of the poorer or more crotchety poems. The fact is, it seems to me, that Dr Williams is a product of fertility. All the signs and recognitions of fertility in his work point backward. He is almost a reduction not a product, a reduction to a highly personalized style to express personal matters – a remarkable, but sterile, sport. You can imitate him, as you can imitate anything; but you cannot incorporate him. In short, his work adds to the sentiments but not to the sensibility.

One reason is that almost everything in Dr Williams's poetry, including the rendering, is unexpanded notation. He isolates and calls attention to what we are already presently in possession of. Observation of which any good novelist must be constantly capable, here makes a solo appearance: the advantage is the strength of isolation as an attention-caller to the terrible persistence of the obvious, the unrelenting significance of the banal. Dr Williams perhaps tries to write as the average man – that man who even less than the normal man hardly exists but is immanent. The conviction which attaches to such fine poems as *The Widow's Lament in Springtime*, *Youth and Beauty*, or the first section of *Spring and All*, perhaps has its source, its rationale, in our instinctive willingness to find ourselves immanently average; just as, perhaps, the conviction attaching to tragic poetry is connected with our fascinated dread of seeing ourselves as normal. Dr Williams has no perception of the normal; no perspective, no finality – for these involve, for imaginative expression, both the intellect which he distrusts and the imposed form which he cannot understand. What he does provide is a constant freshness and purity of language which infects with its own qualities an otherwise gratui-

tous exhibition of the sense and sentiment of humanity run-down –
averaged – without a trace of significance or a vestige of fate in the
fresh familiar face. . . .
(348–50)

William Carlos Williams

Author's Introduction to *The Wedge* 1944 (reprinted in
Collected Later Poems, 1950)

The war is the first and only thing in the world today.

The arts generally are not, nor is this writing a diversion from that
for relief, a turning away. It is the war or part of it, merely a different
sector of the field.

Critics of rather better than average standing have said in recent
years that after socialism has been achieved it's likely there will be no
further use for poetry, that it will disappear. This comes from nothing
else than a faulty definition of poetry – and the arts generally. I don't
hear anyone say that mathematics is likely to be outmoded, to disappear shortly. Then why poetry?

It is an error attributable to the Freudian concept of the thing, that
the arts are a resort from frustration, a misconception still entertained
in many minds.

They speak as though action itself in all its phases were not compatible with frustration. All action the same. But Richard Coeur de Lion
wrote at least one of the finest lyrics of his day. Take Don Juan for
instance. Who isn't frustrated and does not prove it by his actions –
if you want to say so?

But through art the psychologically maimed may become the
most distinguished man of his age. Take Freud for instance.

The making of poetry is no more an evidence of frustration than
is the work of Henry Kaiser or Timoshenko. It's the war, the driving
forward of desire to a complex end. And when that shall have been
achieved, mathematics and the arts will turn elsewhere – beyond the
atom if necessary for their reward and let's all be frustrated together.

A man isn't a block that remains stationary though the psychologists
treat him so – and most take an insane pride in believing it. Consist-

ency! He varies; Hamlet today, Caesar tomorrow; here, there, somewhere – if he is to retain his sanity, and why not?

The arts have a complex relation to society. The poet isn't a fixed phenomenon, no more is his work. That might be a note on current affairs, a diagnosis, a plan for procedure, a retrospect – all in its own peculiarly enduring form. There need be nothing limited or frustrated about that. It may be a throw-off from the most violent and successful action or run parallel to it, a saga. It may be the picking out of an essential detail for memory, something to be set aside for further study, a sort of shorthand of emotional significances for later reference.

Let the metaphysical take care of itself, the arts have nothing to do with it. They will concern themselves with it if they please, among other things.

To make two bald statements: There's nothing sentimental about a machine, and: A poem is a small (or large) machine made of words. When I say there's nothing sentimental about a poem I mean that there can be no part, as in any other machine, that is redundant.

Prose may carry a load of ill-defined matters like a ship. But poetry is the machine which drives it, pruned to a perfect economy. As in all machines its movement is intrinsic, undulant, a physical more than a literary character. In a poem this movement is distinguished in each case by the character of the speech from which it arises.

Therefore each speech having its own character the poetry it engenders will be peculiar to that speech also in its own intrinsic form. The effect is beauty, what in a single object resolves our complex feelings of propriety. One doesn't seek beauty. All that an artist or a Sperry can do is to drive toward his purpose, in the nature of his materials; not to take gold where Babbitt metal is called for; to make: make clear the complexity of his perceptions in the medium given to him by inheritance, chance, accident or whatever it may be to work with according to his talents and the will that drives them. Don't talk about frustration fathering the arts. The bastardization of words is too widespread for that today.

My own interest in the arts has been extracurricula. Up from the gutter, so to speak. Of necessity. Each age and place to its own. But in the US the necessity for recognizing this intrinsic character has been largely ignored by the various English Departments of the academies. When a man makes a poem, makes it, mind you, he takes words

142 R. P. Blackmur

as he finds them interrelated about him and composes them – without distortion which would mar their exact significances – into an intense expression of his perceptions and ardors that they may constitute a revelation in the speech that he uses. It isn't what he says that counts as a work of art, it's what he makes, with such intensity of perception that it lives with an intrinsic movement of its own to verify its authenticity. Your attention is called now and then to some beautiful line or sonnet-sequence because of what is said there. So be it. To me all sonnets say the same thing of no importance. What does it matter what the line 'says'?

There is no poetry of distinction without formal invention, for it is in the intimate form that works of art achieve their exact meaning, in which they most resemble the machine, to give language its highest dignity, its illumination in the environment to which it is native. Such war, as the arts live and breathe by, is continuous.

It may be that my interests as expressed here are pre-art. If so I look for a development along these lines and will be satisfied with nothing else.

(3–5)

R. P. Blackmur

from 'Notes on Seven Poets', a review of The Wedge   1945
(reprinted in Language as Gesture, 1954)

Williams takes a great, but unredeemed, care for the underlying modes that inhabit the language itself; the modes that give magnani-mous reality to the *report* of a conversation; but it is a spoiling care, it lets the modes do as far as possible all the work; and what it spoils is the chance of that high level of performance which is possible, apparently, only to purposive and convicted minds, with just so much of a felt need of order as makes anarchy actual. Williams ignores the sense of order that goes with the long history of the craft of verse by transposing it to the belief that each poem has an intimate order of its own, which it is the business of the poet to make out of the ardor of his direct perceptions. There is no reason why he should not be right for himself, in his own relation to his verse; he can, as he does, find the sonnet as dead as dead; but he is wrong for his readers in their relations to his poems, because his readers, finding the relations (not the substance) of the verses uncontrolled, cannot tell whether or not they are in intelligent contact with the intimate form of the verse. To the reader it seems no more likely that a piece of verse has an intimate form *de novo* than a woman has, and if either did it would not excite him. The most intimate form underlies common flesh. Some of Williams's poems know this for themselves even if their maker did not. Here is one:

Liquor and love
when the mind is dull
focus the wit
on a world of form

The eye awakes
perfumes are defined
inflections
ride the quick ear

Liquor and love
rescue the cloudy sense
banish its despair
give it a home.[1]

Here, as you might say, intimate form and common form are indentical, and are so because of the uniting force, the warming relish, of an old convention about love and drunkenness. There is something a little more in the third quatrain of *The A, B and C of It*. The first quatrain says 'Love's very fleas are mine', and the second says the fleas recoiled from the odors of the lover.

Take me then, Spirit of Loneliness
insatiable Spirit of Love
and let be – for Time without
odor is Time without me.[2]

The little more is in certain musical and rhetorical conventions like those in the dead sonnet; that is to say, conventions or habits of

1 *Collected Later Poems*, p. 20.
2 p. 45.

perception itself. Form is a way of thinking. It may be observed, too, for what it is worth, that to the accustomed ear Williams's four lines tend to rearrange themselves as three iambic pentameters, with the second and third rhyming. What it suggests is that the poetic mind gets ahead somewhat by counting . . . .
(353-55)

Part Two The Debate on *Paterson*

Introduction

Williams's shorter poems frequently mime for us the hesitancies of a mind feeling its way. The uncertainties on which they draw are made part of the aesthetic effect of cadence and of tone. In this sense the writer, as Williams says, 'thinks with his poem'. In the larger form of *Paterson*, the hesitancies acquire more explicitness: they are embodied in self-questionings and in the use of quoted letters – from a neurotic woman writer, C., from Edward Dahlberg and also from Ezra Pound. *Paterson* thus contains within itself the critical debate concerning its own success and the poet's right to his subject matter. Williams even heeds the voice of his wife, complaining, 'What I miss . . . is the poetry, the pure poem of the first parts'.[1] Unless this procedure is handled with tact (Eliot brings off something like it in *Four Quartets*), the result can seem intractably self-conscious. Joseph Bennett's *The Lyre and the Sledgehammer* (see p. 175), complains that, in the life versus literature issue, introduced by C.'s letters, Williams '[indicates] a split attitude on this question'. The trouble is, I think, that C. is a bore and so are her letters. Williams's toleration and display of them at length do seem to show – since they are directed at *him* – a curiously priggish self-regard as much as any concern for C. Of all the critical letters incorporated into *Paterson*, the most radical and interesting is Dahlberg's,[2] which presses the charge of a basic coldness, to be expanded by Dahlberg in *Alms for Oblivion* (see p. 198). Perhaps this 'coldness' is the reverse side of a certain sexual sentimentality one finds elsewhere in Williams and which erupts most noticeably in *Paterson*, Book Five.

Paterson transfers the concerns of *In the American Grain* to a single locality, the New Jersey industrial town of that name, lying in a valley under the Passaic Falls. Lawrence described Williams's earlier book as trying to bring into his consciousness 'America itself, the still-unravished bride of silences . . . the consciousness at present being all bastardized European . . .' (see p. 90). In this long

1 *Paterson*, Books One to Five, 1964, p. 202. 2 p. 40.

poem, Williams seeks to express Lawrence's 'spirit of place' both in terms of Paterson's contemporary industrial squalor and of the geographic and historic presences that underlie the city. The form of his poem offers, at the same time, a challenge to the 'bastardized European' consciousness which prevailed in previous literary handling of the *Paterson* area. The debate on *Paterson*, to translate it into Williams's terms – i.e. what are the adequate forms in which the Passaic region can be made articulate? – really begins with Washington Irving's poem, *On the Passaic Falls* of 1806. There, Irving, as Williams might have said, failing to 'think with his poem', and ignoring the resistance of subject for 'an easy lateral sliding', decorously tidies away his experience into conventions of the English picturesque. More ambitiously, Thomas Ward of Newark (like Williams a doctor) published in 1842 under the pseudonym of Flaccus, *Passaic, A Group of Poems Touching that River*. Here, both Sam Patch and Mrs Cumming, characters in Williams's own poem, first appear. The river in Ward's poem flows in time with the Thames of Sir John Denham's *Cooper's Hill*, but he breaks the even tenor of his form by introducing a series of lyrics. This, at any rate, was a movement in the direction of Williams's discontinuous approach, the ruffled surfaces of Ward's text indicating something of the recalcitrance of his theme.

Williams made the Passaic river his subject early on, 'the fascination of what's difficult' exercising his mind, over the years, in discovering a form to 'define the traditional in terms of my own world'.[1] Thus, there was a critical rightness in the fact that Conrad Aiken in *Modern American Poets* (1922) should have introduced English readers to Williams by printing whole his *Rococo Study, The Wanderer* centring on the Passaic – 'my first "long" poem', as Williams was to describe it, 'which in turn led to *Paterson*. It was the "line" that was the key – a study in the line itself, which challenged me'.[2] In *The Wanderer*, Williams,

[1] *I Wanted to Write a Poem*, p. 84.   [2] *Autobiography*, pp. 60–61.

rejecting the Keatsian procedures of the long narrative work which he tells us he burned, carries out, over a poem of some length, his first tentative experiments with 'the line itself', which were to issue in the three ply cadences of *Paterson*, Book Two (see p. 162), and the structural basis for his later verse (see A. Kingsley Weatherhead, 'William Carlos Williams: Prose, Form and Measure', p. 318).

For Williams the primary debate on *Paterson* begins with the struggle to shape his collected materials. Of this we gain glimpses in his remarks to various correspondents, beginning with Ezra Pound in 1936 (see *Selected Letters*, letter to Ezra Pound, 6 November 1936; letters to Horace Gregory, 1 January 1945, 8 February 1945; letter to Norman Macleod, 25 July 1945). The sifting and shaping process was of long duration and there exist various shots at the subject in verse which pre-date *Paterson* itself (see *Collected Earlier Poems*, pp. 233–5, 438–42; *Collected Later Poems*, pp. 10–11). In the first of these, published in 1927, the basic conceit of the poem, the identification of man and city, has already been established. Perhaps the idea for the poem's formal arrangement even goes back to Williams's college days when, as he tells us, 'Together with Hilda Doolittle ("H.D.") I discovered . . . the wonders of *Aucassin and Nicolette*, the prose and verse alternating'.[1]

The immediate result of the appearance of *Paterson* was, for Williams, the gain of recognition. *Paterson*, Book One, came out in 1946. The early forties had been a period when Williams had received least critical notice, a fact due perhaps variously to the dominance of the New Criticism, of Eliot as poet and source of criteria, and even to the wartime paper shortage (the important volume, *The Wedge*, came out not from New Directions, but in a tiny edition and from a tiny press). Williams had to make his way against indifference and adverse feeling (as documented by R. L. Beum in 'The Neglect of Williams',[2] but one of the cheering

1 p. 52. 2 *Poetry*, vol. 80, August 1952, pp. 291–3.

aspects about the reception of *Paterson* is that indifference had not
changed to the inert critical approval which has characterized much
recent Williams criticism. Thus Leslie Fiedler[1] recognizing the
achievements of Book Two of the poem, speaks of 'the lack of a
felt necessity in its transitions and conjunctions' and 'the masculine
soupiness under the hardboiled surfaces' in Williams's work.
Again Edwin Honig ('The Paterson Impasse' – see p. 168) could
salute *Paterson*, Book Two, while querying the use of letters and
'the obtrusive autobiographic turn which . . . begins to disrupt the
objective symbolic relationships set up in Book One.' Vivienne
Koch, whose modest and pioneering *William Carlos Williams*
(1950) was the first full scale study, could remark[2] on the contagion
from Pound's Cantos in *Paterson*, Book Four, though qualifying
with 'The object hasn't been in view long enough and we must
look at it some more to become accustomed to its strangeness.'
Sister Bernetta Quinn, in her account of *Paterson* in *The
Metamorphic Tradition in Modern Poetry* (1955) confines herself,
after the manner of Miss Koch's book, more to exploration than
evaluation. This is something that is to characterize much – too
much – criticism of *Paterson*, whether it is brilliantly done, as by
Hugh Kenner (should not his review of *Paterson*, Book Five,[3]
have contained *some* mention of the sentimentality of the poem's
view of prostitution?) or lumpishly, as by John C. Thirlwall,[4] or
with scholarly adequacy as by Louis L. Martz.[5] A good example
of the way an intelligent critic, Walter Sutton, dodges the necessity
for evaluation shows in his 'Williams's *Paterson* and the Quest for

1 'Some Uses and Failures of Feeling', *Partisan Review*, vol. 15, August 1948,
pp. 924–31.
2 'The Man and the Poet', *Kenyon Review*, vol. 14, Summer 1952, pp. 502–10.
3 'To Measure is All We Know', *Poetry*, vol. 94, May 1959, pp. 127–32.
4 'William Carlos Williams's *Paterson*: The Search for the Redeeming
Language', *New Directions 17*, 1961, pp. 252–310.
5 'The Unicorn in *Paterson*', *Thought*, vol. 36, Winter 1960, pp. 537–54.

Form'.[1] The refusal to dodge marks J. M. Brinnin's dealings with the poem in his pamphlet, *William Carlos Williams* (1963), though he, too, is silent when it comes to weighing up the *degree* of success in *Paterson*, Book Five, in three paragraphs tacked on to his conclusion. Brinnin gives a hint of why it is easy to bring off the sleight of hand of Sutton's essay when he writes that *Paterson* has 'an all-of-a-piece consistency on an intellectual level, but on an emotive level the poem is vastly uneven . . .' Thus Sutton confines himself to the consistency of Williams's 'blueprint' – the 'intellectual level'.

The recognition accorded by Randall Jarrell in his 1946 *Partisan Review* notice to *Paterson*, Book One (see p. 151), seemed to put Williams in touch with a younger generation. Although Jarrell was to change his mind about the success of *Paterson* once Books One to Four were complete, and a coolness ensued (see the tone of Williams's remarks to Edith Heal in *I Wanted to Write a Poem*, pp. 91–2), the relationship which followed his early review gave rise to Jarrell's introducing the *Selected Poems* of 1949[2] in an edition of four thousand copies, and this book set the pattern of Williams's achievement for younger readers for some years to come. It also, together with *Paterson*, Books One and Two, won the National Book Award for Poetry in 1950. Robert Lowell's review of Book One, following closely Jarrell's lead, brought Williams another new relationship which, on the evidence of the letters, meant a good deal to him. 'I particularly appreciate,' Williams wrote to Lowell, 'your observation that, "It is a defect perhaps that human beings exist almost entirely in the prose passages." That's something to think about.'[3] Is the park sequence in Book Two a result of Williams having thought? Five years later (11 March 1952) Williams acknowledged 'a very discerning and friendly letter'

1 *Criticism*, vol. 2, Summer 1960, pp. 242–59.
2 New Directions.
3 *Selected Letters*, pp. 259–60.

from Lowell, which 'has changed my attitude towards Eliot more than anything I have ever read of him.'

The final word can be left to two very different poets, Charles Olson and Robert Creeley, through whose work and partly through their association with Black Mountain College, Williams's influence was to spread. *Paterson* has been compared with the Cantos of Ezra Pound – see, for example, the Introduction, p. 23, to Geoffrey Moore's *Penguin Book of American Verse* (1954) – but Olson points out in *Mayan Letters* (1953), 'Pat is exact opposite ... Bill HAS an emotional system which is capable of extensions and comprehensions the ego-system (the Old Deal, Ez as Canto Man, here dates) is not.' This placing of the Cantos as ultimately an 'ego-system', is glossed by Robert Creeley, introducing *Selected Writings of Charles Olson* (1966), pp. 5–6, when he writes:

Olson feels that Williams offers an *emotional* system, which does not limit the context of writing to an assumption of *understanding* – or, better, it attains a way of writing that *feels* as it goes as well as *sees*. This allows the experience of writing to be more sensitive than the ego alone can admit.

Perhaps one might add that Williams too remains in some ways a very egocentric poet, but that his poetry, at its best, eludes his own conception of himself. The unevenness of *Paterson* often comes down to Williams's failure to do just that. The lesson Olson and Creeley draw from Williams belongs to that part of the history to be related in the final section of this book, when, in the early fifties, different attitudes to poetry, based to some extent on Williams's example, were making themselves felt in America.

Randall Jarrell

from 'The Poet and his Public', *Partisan Review*, vol. 13   1946

Paterson (Book One) seems to me the best thing William Carlos Williams has ever written; I read it seven or eight times, and ended up lost in delight. It seems a shame to write a little review of it, instead of going over it page by page, explaining and admiring. And one hates to quote much, since the beauty, delicacy and intelligence of the best parts depend so much upon their organization in the whole; quoting from it is like humming a theme and expecting the hearer to guess from that its effect upon its third repetition in a movement. I have used this simile deliberately, because – over and above the organization of argument or exposition – the organization of *Paterson* is musical to an almost unprecedented degree: Mr Williams introduces a theme that stands for an idea, repeats it over and over in varied forms, develops it side by side with two or three more themes that are being developed, recurs to it time and time again throughout the poem, and echoes it for ironic or grotesque effects in thoroughly incongruous contexts. Sometimes this is done with the greatest complications and delicacy; he wants to introduce a red-bird whose call will stand for the clear speech of nature, in the midst of all the confusion and ugliness in which men could not exist except for 'imagined beauty where there is none': so he says in disgust, 'Stale as a whale's breath: breath! | Breath!' and ten lines later (during which three themes have been repeated and two of them joined at last in a 'silent, uncommunicative', and satisfying resolution) he says that he has

Only of late, late! begun to know, to
know clearly (as through clear ice) whence
I draw my breath or how to employ it
clearly – if not well:

          Clearly!
speaks the red-breast his behest. Clearly!
clearly!

(I, ii, p. 31)

These double exclamations have so prepared for the bird's call that it strikes you, when you are reading the poem, like the blow which dissolves an enchantment. And really the preparation has been even more complicated: two pages before there was the line 'divorce! divorce!' and half a page before the birds and weeds by the river were introduced by

> White, in
> the shadows among the blue-flowered
> pickerel-weed, in summer, summer! if it should
> ever come, . . .
> (1, ii, p. 30)

If you want to write a long poem which doesn't stick to one subject, but which unifies a dozen, you can learn a great deal from *Paterson*. But I do not know how important these details of structure will seem to an age which regards as a triumph of organization that throwing-out-of-blocks-upon-the-nursery-floor which concludes *The Waste Land*, and which explains its admiration by the humorless literalness of believing that a poet represents fragments by eliminating metre, connectives, and logic from the verses which describe the fragments.

The subject of *Paterson* is: How can you tell the truth about things? – that is, how can you find a language so close to the world that the world can be represented and understood in it?

> Paterson lies in the valley under the Passaic Falls
> its spent waters forming the outline of his back. He
> lies on his right side, head near the thunder
> of the water filling his dreams! Eternally asleep,
> his dreams walk about the city where he persists
> incognito. Butterflies settle on his stone ear.
> (1, i, p. 14)

How can he – this city that is man – find the language for what he dreams and sees and is, the language without which true knowledge is impossible? He starts with the particulars ('Say it! No ideas but in things.') which stream to him like the river, 'rolling up out of chaos, | a nine months' wonder'; with the interpenetration of everything with everything, 'the drunk the sober; the illustrious | the gross; one';

> It is the ignorant sun
> rising in the slot of
> hollow suns risen, so that never in this
> world will a man live well in his body
> save dying – and not know himself
> dying; . . .
>
> (I, Preface, p. 12)

The water falls and then rises in 'floating mists, to be rained down and | regathered into a river that flows | and encircles:'; the water, in its time, is 'combed into straight lines | from that rafter of a rock's | lip.' and attains clarity; but the people are like flowers that the bee misses, they fail and die and 'Life is sweet, they say' – but their speech has failed them, 'they do not know the words | or have not | the courage to use them', and they hear only 'a false language pouring – a | language (misunderstood) pouring (misinterpreted) without | dignity, without minister, crashing upon a stone ear.' And the language available to them, the language of scholarship and science and the universities, is

> a bud forever green
> tight-curled, upon the pavement, perfect
> in juice and substance but divorced, divorced
> from its fellows, fallen low –
>   Divorce is
> the sign of knowledge in our time,
> divorce! divorce!
>
> (I, ii, p. 28)

Girls walk by the river at Easter and one, bearing a willow twig in her hand as Artemis bore the moon's crescent bow,

> holds it, the gathered spray,
> upright in the air, the pouring air,
> strokes the soft fur –
>
>   Ain't they beautiful!
>
> (I, ii, p. 29)

(How could words show better than these last three the touching half-success, half-failure of their language?) And Sam Patch, the drunken frontier hero who jumped over the Falls with his pet bear, could *say* only: 'Some things can be done as well as others'; and Mrs Cumming, the minister's wife, shrieked unheard and fell unseen from the brink; and the two were only

: a body found next spring
frozen in an ice-cake; or a body
fished next day from the muddy swirl –

both silent, uncommunicative
(I, ii, p. 31)

The speech of sexual understanding, of natural love, is represented by three beautifully developed themes: a photograph of the nine wives of a Negro chief; a tree standing on the brink of the waterfall; and two lovers talking by the river:

We sit and talk and the
silence speaks of the giants
who have died in the past and have
returned to those scenes unsatisfied
and who is not unsatisfied; the
silent, Singac the rock-shoulder
emerging from the rocks – and the giants
live again in your silence and
unacknowledged desire –
(I, ii, p. 36)

But now the air by the river 'brings in the rumors of separate worlds', and the poem is dragged from its highest point in the natural world, from the early, fresh and green years of the city, into the slums of Paterson, into the collapse of this natural language, into 'a delirium of solutions', into the back streets of that 'great belly | that no longer laughs but mourns | with its expressionless black navel love's | deceit.' Here is the whole failure of Paterson's ideas and speech, and he is forced to begin all over; Part Two of the poem ends with the ominous 'No ideas but | in the facts.'

Part Three opens with this beautiful and unexpected passage:

How strange you are, you idiot!
So you think because the rose

is red that you shall have the mastery?
The rose is green and will bloom,
overtopping you, green, livid
green when you shall no more speak, or
taste, or even be. My whole life
has hung too long upon a partial victory.
(I, iii, p. 41)

The underlying green of the facts always cancels out the red in which
we had found our partial, temporary, aesthetic victory; and the poem
now introduces the livid green of the obstinate and compensating
lives, the lifeless perversions of the industrial city: here are the slums
and the adjoining estate with its acre hothouse and weedlike orchids
and French maid whose sole duty is to 'groom | the pet Pomeranians –
who sleep'; here is the university with its clerks

spitted on fixed concepts like
roasting hogs, sputtering, their drip sizzling
in the fire

Something else, something else the same.
(I, iii, p. 44)

Then (in one of the fine prose quotations – much altered by the poet
surely – with which the verse is interspersed) people drain the lake
there, all day and all night long kill the eels and fish with sticks, carry
them away in baskets; there is nothing left but the mud. The sleeping
Paterson, 'moveless', envies the men who could run off 'toward the
peripheries – to other centers, direct' for some 'loveliness and |
authority in the world', who could leap like Sam Patch and be found
'the following spring, frozen in | an ice cake'. But he goes on thinking
to the very bitter end, reproduces all the ignorance and brutality of
the city; and he understands its pathos and horror:

And silk spins from the hot drums to a music
of pathetic souvenirs, a comb and nail-file
in an imitation leather case – to
remind him, to remind him! and
a photograph-holder with pictures of himself
between the two children, all returned

weeping, weeping – in the back room
of the widow who married again, a vile tongue
but laborious ways, driving a drunken
husband . . .
(I, iii, p. 49)

Yet he contrasts his own real mystery, the mystery of people's actual
lives, with the mystery that 'the convent of the Little Sister of | St Ann
pretends'; and he understands the people 'wiping the nose on sleeves,
come here | to dream'; he understands that

Things, things unmentionable
the sink with the waste farina in it and
lumps of rancid meat, milk-bottle-tops: have
here a still tranquillity and loveliness
(I, iii, p. 51)

Then Paterson 'shifts his change', and an earthquake and a 'remarkable rumbling noise' frighten but do not damage the city – this is told
in the prose of an old newspaper account; and, at the end of the poem,
he stands in the flickering green of the cavern under the waterfall (the
dark, skulled world of consciousness), hedged in by the pouring
torrent whose thunder drowns out any language; 'the myth | that
holds up the rock, | that holds up the water thrives there – | in that
cavern, that profound cleft'; and the readers of the poem are shown,
in the last words of the poem,

standing, shrouded there, in that din,
Earth, the chatterer, father of all
speech . . .
(I, iii, p. 52)

It takes several readings to work out the poem's argument (it is a
poem that *must* be read over and over), and it seemed to me that I
could do most for its readers by roughly summarizing that argument.
There are hundreds of things in the poem that deserve specific
mention. The poem is weakest in the middle of Part Three – I'd
give page numbers if good old New Directions had remembered to
put in any – but this is understandable and almost inevitable. Everything in the poem is inter-woven with everything else, just as the

strands of the Falls interlace: how wonderful and unlikely that this extraordinary mixture of the most delicate lyricism of perception and feeling with the hardest and homeliest actuality should ever have come into being! There has never been a poem more American (though the only influence one sees in it is that of the river scene from *Finnegans Wake*); if the next three books are as good as this one, which introduces 'the elemental character of the place', the whole poem will be far and away the best long poem any American has written.

(493–8)

Parker Tyler

from 'The Poet of *Paterson* Book One', *Briarcliff Quarterly*, vol. 3 1946

In practice, Williams reversed the orientation of Mr Eliot's objective-correlative by trying to piece together, in an inspired 'jig-saw' fashion, the picture of the material out of which American poets should write their poetry. If addressed by the criticism of the Eliotian objective-correlative, Dr Williams could only defend this view by saying:

My theory of poetry was that it arises from
immediate environment, and in the case of *my*
environment, America, the poetic formulas for familiar
(or 'objective-correlative') emotions did not exist. Why
not? Because the emotions themselves, and the very
imagery of their implicit situations, were elusive and
unformed.

This theory is the inevitability of Dr Williams's *style*. This style was a radical effort to establish the concrete elements from which feelings arise, in the sense that a cry arises from a person in one specific situation and in no other. If the situation is not self-evident, the 'cry' is hollow: musical in the limited, abstract sense. The Swinburnian 'voice' in poetry is the effeteness of the objective-correlative; nothing but the 'cry', the typical epithet and the closed vocabulary, emerges. Twentieth-century poetry, not only here but also in France and England, was a reaction against the Swinburnian voice, authentic in itself but inapplicable to human development.

(169)

Robert Lowell

from 'Thomas, Bishop and Williams', *Sewanee Review*, vol. 55 1947

When it is completed, *Paterson* will run to over a hundred pages, and be in four parts. As only Part One has been published, the critic is faced with many uncertainties, and forced to make many conjectures.[1] Williams's own rather breathless and incoherent introductory note will, perhaps, be of little help. 'A man in himself is a city, beginning, seeking, achieving and concluding his life in the ways which the various aspects of the city may embody – if imaginatively conceived – any city, all the details of which may be made to voice his most intimate convictions.' The poet begins with a slightly different statement of this purpose: 'Rigor of beauty is the quest. But how will you find beauty when it is locked in the mind past all remonstrance?' The answer is 'to make a start out of particulars . . . no ideas but in things'. This may appear crude and vague, but Williams has nothing in common with the coarse, oratorical sentimentalists, most favorably represented by Carl Sandburg, who have written about cities and the people. More than any of his contemporaries, he resembles Wordsworth in his aims and values; and in its maturity, experience, and sympathy, *Paterson* appears to me to be comparable to the *Prelude* and the opening of the *Excursion*.

I am not sure that I can say very clearly why, or even how it is that Williams's methods are successful. By personifying Paterson, and by 'Patersonizing' himself, he is in possession of all the materials that he can use. First the City is his: all its aspects, its past, its present, its natural features, its population and its activities are available for him to interrelate and make dramatic. But also he can use his whole

1 As the poem stands, it has many insufficiently related odds and ends. It is a defect perhaps that human beings exist almost entirely in the prose passages.

life in the City – every detail is an experience, a memory, or a symbol. Taken together, Paterson is Williams's life, and Williams is what makes Paterson alive.

For Williams, a man is what he experiences, and in his shorter lyrics he has perfected a technique of observation and of empathy. He can move from man outward:

The year plunges into night
and the heart plunges
lower than night
to an empty, windswept place
without sun, stars or moon
but a peculiar light as of thought
that spins a dark fire. . . .[1]

Or the observed is personified:

Lifeless in appearance, sluggish
dazed spring approaches –
They enter the new world naked,
cold, uncertain of all
save that they enter.[2]

Which end he starts from matters little. Williams triumphs in his sense of motion, his ability to observe, and to fit his observations to the right rhythms.

But if the short poems show Williams as an excellent stylist, there is nothing in them to indicate that their thematic structure could be extended to a long poem. How this has been done and how *Paterson's* various themes are stated, developed, repeated, opposed, broken, and mingled, has been demonstrated at some length by Jarrell in *Partisan Review*. Here I shall confine myself to quoting passages in which the principal themes are expressed and to pointing out a few of their more important connections and meanings. The theme on which all the others depend is threefold: a city – Paterson, New Jersey –, a mountain, and a river that flows from the mountain into Paterson – a man, a woman, and the man's thought. First the city:

1 *Collected Earlier Poems*, p. 433.
2 p. 241.

Paterson lies in the valley under the Passaic Falls
its spent waters forming the outline of his back. He
lies on his right side, head near the thunder
of the waters filling his dreams! Eternally asleep
his dreams walk about the city where he persists
incognito. Butterflies settle on his stone ear.
Immortal he neither moves nor rouses and is seldom
seen, though he breathes and the subtleties of his machinations
drawing their substance from the noise of the pouring river
animate a thousand automatons.
(I, i, p. 14)

The mountain is introduced in a parallel passage:

And there, against him, stretches the low mountain.
The Park's her head, carved above the Falls, by the quiet
river; Colored crystals the secret of those rocks;
farms and ponds, laurel, and the temperate wild cactus,
yellow flowered . . . facing him, his
arm supporting her, by the *Valley of the Rocks*, asleep.
Pearls at her ankles, her monstrous hair
spangled with apple-blossoms is scattered about into
the back country, waking their dreams – where the deer run
and the wood-duck nests protecting his gallant plumage.
(I, i, p. 17)

The passage introducing the river is too long to quote in full.

Jostled as are the waters approaching
the brink, his thoughts
interlace, repel and cut under,
rise rock-thwarted and turn aside
but forever strain forward – or strike
an eddy and whirl, marked by a
leaf or curdy spume, seeming
to forget. . . .
(I, i, p. 16)

The Man-City and the Woman-Mountain are easier to understand
than the river which symbolizes thought. It is the elemental thought

that lacks a language, the source of life and motion. It is described again and again, always with such powerful precision that one is in no doubt of its grimness and strength. It is intercourse between Paterson and the mountain, and above all, it is Paterson's thoughts, his population – the primal vitality behind their lives and speech. The two lovers later meet under its falls, and in the prose records that are interspersed with the poetry, one reads of the men and women who were drowned in it, and the pearls and fish that were taken out of it. This three-fold main-theme is repeated in smaller themes, such as the African chief with his seven wives on a log, and 'the lightnings that stab at the mystery of a man from both ends'. It is broken up in the two divorces: the university,

> a bud forever green,
> tight-curled, upon the pavement, perfect
> in juice and substance but divorced, divorced
> from its fellows, fallen low –
> (I, ii, p. 28)

and the

> girls from
> families that have decayed and
> taken to the hills. . . .
> Life is sweet
> they say: the language!
> – the language
> is divorced from their minds.

'In ignorance a certain knowledge and knowledge, undispersed, its own undoing.'

This is the tragedy of Paterson, what the poem is really about. It is the divorce of modern life, of intellect and sensibility, spirit and matter, and of the other stock categories that come to mind. His 'quest for beauty' is a search for the whole man, whose faculties are harmonious, and whose language corresponds with the particulars and mystery of reality. Williams is liberal, anti-orthodox, and a descendant of Emerson and Whitman. But if a man is intense and honest enough, the half-truth of any extreme position will in time absorb much of its opposite. Williams has much in common with

Catholic, aristocratic and Agrarian writers. For all his sympathy with his people, he makes one feel that the sword of Damocles hangs over Paterson, the modern city and world. As with Yeats, 'things fall apart'. The educated lack connection, and the ignorant are filled with speechless passion.

Williams has had much to say about Ezra Pound, one whom he may have envied for being able to 'run off toward the peripheries to find loveliness and authority in the world – a sort of springtime toward which his mind aspired.' Some of his pronouncements seemed unfair and hysterical, but in *Paterson* his position has paid off, when compared with Pound's. It is a sort of anti-Cantos rooted in America, in one city, and in what Williams has known long and seen often. Not only are its details enriched and verified by experience, but the whole has a unity that is analogous to the dramatic unities of time, place, and action.

Paterson resembles *The Bridge*; but Hart Crane's poem, for all its splendor in its best moments, will not stand up to the comparison. It seems relatively inexperienced, chaotic and verbal. Even as a rhetorician Williams is much superior. It would be fruitless to compare *Paterson* with the best writing of Eliot, Stevens, Tate or Auden, for the ways of writing very well are various; but for experience and observation, it has, along with a few poems of Frost, a richness that makes almost all other contemporary poetry look a little secondhand. If Parts Two, Three and Four are as good as Part One, *Paterson* will be the most successful really long poem since *The Prelude*. (500–503)

William Carlos Williams

from *I Wanted to Write a Poem* 1958, 1967

Paterson, Book Two is a milestone for me. One of the most successful things in it is a passage in section three of the poem which brought about – without realizing it at the time of writing – my final conception of what my own poetry should be; a passage which, sometime later, brought all my thinking about free verse to a head. I think it should be included here so that you can see the pattern.

The descent beckons
          as the ascent beckoned
                    Memory is a kind
of accomplishment
      a sort of renewal .
               even
an initiation, since the spaces it opens are new
places
          inhabited by hordes
               heretofore unrealized,
of new kinds –   .
          since their movements
               are towards new objectives
(even though formerly they were abandoned)

No defeat is made up entirely of defeat – since
the world it opens is always a place
          formerly
               unsuspected. A
world lost,
          a world unsuspected
               beckons to new places
and no whiteness (lost) is so white as the memory
of whiteness .

With evening, love wakens
          though its shadows
               which are alive by reason
of the sun shining –
      grow sleepy now and drop away
                  from desire .

Love without shadows stirs now
          beginning to waken
               as night
advances.

The descent
          made up of despairs
               and without accomplishment

realizes a new awakening :
                              which is a reversal
of despair.
              For what we cannot accomplish, what
is denied to love,
          what we have lost in the anticipation –
                                a descent follows,
endless and indestructible   .
(II, iii, p. 96)

Several years afterward in looking over the thing I realized I had hit
upon a device (that is the practical focus of a device) which I could
not name when I wrote it. My dissatisfaction with free verse came to
a head in that I always wanted a verse that was ordered, so it came to
me that the concept of the foot itself would have to be altered in our
new relativistic world. It took me several years to get the concept
clear. I had a feeling that there was somewhere an exact way to define
it; the task was to find the word to describe it, to give it an epitaph,
and I finally hit upon it. The foot not being fixed is only to be described
as variable. If the foot itself is variable it allows order in so-called
free verse. Thus the verse becomes not free at all but just simply
variable, as all things in life properly are. From the time I hit on this
I knew what I was going to have to do.

I have told you before that my two leading forces were trying to
know life and trying to find a technique of verse. Now I had it – a sea
change. The verse must be coldly, intellectually considered. Not the
emotion, the heat of the life dominating, but the intellectual concept
of the thing itself.
(84–6)

William Carlos Williams

from a letter to Babette Deutsch 28 July 1947 (reprinted in
J. C. Thirlwall (ed.), *Selected Letters*, 1957)

In Part or Book Two, soon to appear (this fall, I think), there will be
... much more relating to the economic distress occasioned by human
greed and blindness – aided, as always, by the church, all churches
in the broadest sense of that designation – but still, there will be little
treating directly of the rise of labor as a named force. I am not a
Marxian.

(259)

Robert Lowell

from 'Paterson, Book Two', *Nation*, no. 166   19 June 1948

Paterson, Book Two, is an interior monologue. A man spends Sunday
in the park at Paterson, New Jersey. He thinks and looks about him;
his mind contemplates, describes, comments, associates, stops, stutters
and shifts like a firefly, bound only by its milieu. The man is Williams,
anyone living in Paterson, the American, the masculine principle – a
sort of Everyman. His monologue is interrupted by chunks of prose:
paragraphs from old newspapers, textbooks and the letters of a
lacerated and lacerating poetess. This material is merely selected by
the author. That the poetry is able to digest it in the raw is a measure
of power and daring – the daring of simplicity; for only a taut style
with worlds of experience behind it could so resign, and give way to
the anthologist. The didactic chapters in *Moby Dick* have a similar
function, and are the rock that supports the struggle of Captain Ahab.

The Park is Everywoman, any woman, the feminine principle,
America. The water roaring down the falls from the park to Paterson
is the principle of life. The rock is death, negation, the *nul*; carved and
given form, it stands for the imagination, 'like a red basalt grasshopper, boot-long with window-eyes'. The symbols are not allegori-
cal, but loose, intuitive, and Protean.

Paterson like Hart Crane's *Marriage of Faustus and Helen*, is about marriage. 'Rigor of beauty is the quest.' Everything in the poem is masculine or feminine, everything strains toward marriage, but the marriages never come off, except in the imagination, and there, attenuated, fragmentary and uncertain. 'Divorce is the sign of knowledge in our time.' The people 'reflect no beauty but gross . . . unless it is beauty to be, anywhere, so flagrant in desire.' 'The ugly legs of the young girls, pistons without delicacy'; 'not undignified'; 'among the working classes *some* sort of breakdown has occurred.' The preacher in the second section, attended by the 'iron smiles' of his three middle-aged disciples, by 'benches on which a few children have been propped by the others against their running off,' 'bends at the knees and straightens himself up violently with the force of his emphasis – like Beethoven getting a crescendo out of an orchestra' – ineffective, pathetic and a little phony. He has given up, or says he has given up, a fortune for the infinite riches of our Lord Jesus Christ. Interspersed through his sermon, as an ironic counter-theme, is Alexander Hamilton, whose fertile imagination devised the national debt and envisioned Paterson as a great manufacturing centre. Nobody wins. 'The church spires still spend their wits against the sky.' 'The rock-table is scratched by the picnickers' boot-nails, more than by the glacier.' The great industrialists are 'those guilty bastards . . . trying to undermine us'. The legislators are 'under the garbage, uninstructed, incapable of self-instruction'. 'An orchestral dulness overlays their world.' 'The language, tongue-tied . . . words without style!'

This is the harsh view. Against it is the humorous, the dogs, the children; lovely fragments of natural description; the author's sense of the human and sympathetic in his people.

Williams is noted as an imagist, a photographic eye; in Book One he has written 'no ideas but in the facts'. This is misleading. His symbolic man and woman are Hegel's *thesis* and *antithesis*. They struggle toward *synthesis* – marriage. But fulness, if it exists at all, only exists in simple things, trees and animals; so Williams, like other Platonists, is thrown back on the 'idea'. 'And no whiteness (lost) is so white as the memory of whiteness.' 'The stone lives, the flesh dies.' The idea, Beauty, must be realized by the poet where he lives, in Paterson. 'Be reconciled, Poet, with your world, it is the only truth,' though 'love' for it 'is no comforter, rather a nail in the skull.'

Paterson is an attempt to write the American Poem. It depends on the American myth, a myth that is seldom absent from our literature – part of our power, and part of our hubris and deformity. At its grossest the myth is propaganda, puffing and grimacing: Size, Strength, Vitality, the Common Man, the New World, Vital Speech, the Machine; the hideous neo-Roman personae; Democracy, Freedom, Liberty, the Corn, the Land. How hollow, windy and inert this would have seemed to an imaginative man of another culture! But the myth is a serious matter. It is assumed by Emerson, Whitman and Hart Crane; by Henry Adams and Henry James. For good or for evil, America *is* something immense, crass and Roman. We must unavoidably place ourselves in our geography, history, civilization, institutions and future.

The subjects of great poetry have usually been characters and the passions, a moral struggle that calls a man's whole person into play. One thinks of the wrath of Achilles, Macbeth and his conscience, Aeneas debating whether he will leave Dido, whether he will kill Turnus. But in the best long American poems – *Leaves of Grass, The Cantos, The Waste Land, Four Quartets, The Bridge* and *Paterson* – no characters take on sufficient form to arrive at a crisis. The people melt into voices. In a recent essay Eliot has given his reasons why a writer should, perhaps, read Milton; Williams has answered with an essay that gives reasons why a writer should *not* read Milton – Eliot and Williams might learn something from *Paradise Lost* and *Samson Agonistes*, how Milton populated his desert.

Until Books Three and Four are published, it is safer to compare *Paterson* with poems that resemble it; not with *The Bridge*, that wonderful monster, so unequal, so inexperienced – dazzling in its rhetoric at times in the way that Keats is dazzling; but with a book in which its admirers profess to find everything, *Leaves of Grass*. Whitman is a considerable poet, and a considerable myth. I can never quite disentangle the one from the other. I would say that Whitman's language has less variety, sureness, and nerve than Williams's; that his imagination is relatively soft, formless, monotonous and vague. Both poets are strong on compassion and enthusiasm, but these qualities in Whitman are *simpliste* and blurred.

Paterson is Whitman's America, grown pathetic and tragic, brutalized by inequality, disorganized by industrial chaos, and faced with annihilation. No poet has written of it with such a combination of brilliance, sympathy and experience, with such alertness and energy. Because he has tried to understand rather than excoriate, and because in his maturity he has been occupied with the 'raw' and the universal, his *Paterson* is not the tragedy of the outcast but the tragedy of our civilization. It is a book in which the best readers, as well as the simple reader, are likely to find *everything*.

(692–94)

Edwin Honig

'The Paterson Impasse', a review of *Paterson*, Book Two, and *The Clouds, Aigeltinger, Russia, etc., Poetry*, vol. 74   April 1949

In Book Two of *Paterson*, Dr Williams's long poem-in-progress, the character of the work as testament and confession becomes more pronounced. The subtitle, *Sunday in the Park*, indicates its subject: a series of episodic shots, composed like a montage drawing, of a day of life in a Paterson park. This is 'the narrative thread' which runs through the three sections of the book. The role of Paterson-as-man-and-observer, delineated in Book One, is further personalized in Book Two to include Paterson-as-poet-and-actor. Dr Williams is trying to merge the contemporary physical being of a city (Paterson) and relevant bits of its history with his own personal existence and history as a poet. In the lineaments of this conception we find the micro-macrocosmic myth basic to the functioning of a master work. This is not to say that *Paterson* is a master work, but to indicate that the prescription for one is inherent in it.

What Dr Williams is saying about himself, he is also saying by implication about all of us. Writing for poets and critics, he is showing presumably why he cannot write for everyone else, though he tries to write *about* the others. The reason is principally a matter of divorce between knowledge and feeling. It concerns the technical difficulty of escaping from the staleness of old forms, old language, old styles. And it concerns the moral impossibility of putting into words, however beautiful and accurate, anything that finally does not underestimate, pervert or elude the reality of what is physically and essentially ever-new, ever-recreated about us. Dedicated to the word, the verbal invention, the poetic expression, the poet is divorced from the concretions which he means to express. Thus he becomes devitalized, incapable of satisfying human relationships, and is cast off by the culture in which he is born. Not only the poet, but the culture itself is divided by the same great divorce. The people of Paterson have been codified, because distrusted and feared ('a great beast', said Hamilton), in terms of economic potentials by the legislators, the industrialists, the textbook writers of history, the statisticians, the law-enforcers. Thus the poet identifies himself with the poor, those most palpably exploited by the mythical divorce: those who, lacking words, create beauty, for whom pleasure is a drunken love, an aborted dance, an ecstatic but neglected confession, a lazy Sunday afternoon sleep in the park. By this vicarious identification, the poet is 'accepted' among the rejected: he finds his place as artist and human being with those who have never found their place as human beings.

The poetry in Book Two is overshadowed by long prose excerpts from a letter which seems actually to have been written to the poet (thinly anonymized as 'Dr P.') by a woman writer with whom he has broken relations. Agonizedly personal, self-conscious and painfully recriminative, the document seems to throttle the poet and the poetry both, as well as to serve as 'a replica' of the divorce theme in its most ambivalent sense. The use of documentary material taken bodily from various unnamed texts to provide historical analogues to the poem (a kind of selective system of footnoting loosely fitted into the poetry) is a practice continued here from Book One. But whereas one inclines to accept their relationship to the poetry (and to recognize in the invented and poeticized 'document' of the revivalist preacher in Book Two a further organic connection) one finds oneself after a second or third reading gliding over the prose and concentrating on the poetry. In all cases, that is, but in the case of the rejected woman poet's letter. Dominated and drawn by its prominence in the book, the reader returns to it again and again till gradually its depressive weight obliterates the poetry itself, even as a refuge from the harrowing complaint of the anonymous woman writer.

Thus it seems that the obtrusive autobiographic turn which *Paterson* takes in Book Two (represented by the letter) begins to disrupt the objective symbolic relationships set up in Book One. Such a weakness points, on the one hand, to the structural limitations of the poem's method, and, on the other, to the theoretical uncertainty of its conception.

It is not that a long poem based, as *Paterson* is, on a Heraclitean view of the world cannot be successfully done. Lucretius did it in *De Rerum Natura*. The point about Dr Williams's failure to do it thus far is this. He accepts a basically scientific view of the world, a world in flux, always changing into significantly new and identifiable relationships; and he accepts the state of things in such a world, as Lucretius did, without the guidance of a supernatural ideal. But like Lucretius and all the pagans, new and old, he must nevertheless find some ideal island, some place of rest. Lucretius found it in the symbol of Venus the procreator, the repository of all earthly beauty. Williams finds it in beauty, too, but in a more difficult and artistically compromising kind – the beauty of honesty. Through such an ideal the dual identity of the poet is revealed: first as an objective visualizer of undiscovered phenomenal relationships, and then as a romantically displaced, culturally rejected and underprivileged citizen. As such, the poet who remakes the world, as Williams proposes, in the mythical image of a man–city relationship, continually succumbs to the belief that the whole of his myth-made universe is conditioned not by the fortuitious and objective relationships according to which he has molded his aesthetic, but by a personally determined impasse, the mirror of his own dislocations. To enforce the ideal of honesty, the concept of man-as-city is altered to poet-as-city, a role so specialized as to limit seriously the universal relevance of the original identification.

In this sense, honesty becomes a nostalgic talisman, like Stephen Daedelus's ashplant, rather than the kingly scepter which one recognizes, without having to have it pointed out, because it is more the symbol of active power than of ornamental disuse. Instead of signifying truthful detachment, the acceptance of things as they are believed to be, honesty becomes a license for the poet's anarchic resentment of things as they are and a valve for emitting steam concerning things as they should be, or used to be.

One may not feel that a consistent philosophic view is necessary in order to write a long, serious poem. But if it is clear, as I believe it is in Williams, that the poet implies his acceptance of a definite philosophic point of view, in his short poems as well as in *Paterson*, then his failure to be consistent in it is related to a deficiency in the poetry itself.

In a passage of self-commiseration toward the end of Book Two, Williams points to the inadequacy of the whole mythic concept upon which *Paterson* is built. He is speaking of 'Faitoute' or 'Paterson' or 'Dr P' – himself, the poet:

> that the poet,
> in disgrace, should borrow from erudition (to
> unslave the mind): railing at the vocabulary
> (borrowing from those he hates, to his own
> disenfranchisement)   .
> – discounting his failures   .
> seeks to induce his bones to rise into a scene,
> his dry bones, above the scene, (they will not)
> illuminating it within itself, out of itself
> to form the colors, in the terms of some
> back street, so that the history may escape
> the panders
> . .   accomplish the inevitable
> poor, the invisible, thrashing, breeding
> .   debased city
> (II, iii, p. 99)

And again, in his poem to the rebel mathematician Aigeltinger, in Williams's new collection of poems, he applauds the man's 'profundity' on the basis of Aigeltinger's rejection by society:

> But where is profundity, Aigeltinger
> mathematical genius
> dragged drunk from some cheap bar to serve
> their petty purposes?
>
> Aigeltinger, you were profound[1]

And in his poem *Russia* the poet 'call(s) upon folly to save us,' appealing to Russia to avoid the title 'idiot of the world' by returning to the old 'home of my dream, Russia', to the days when Mayakovsky was alive.

1 *Collected Later Poems*, p. 65.

There are always at least two poets in William Carlos Williams: the lounging, dispassionate re-creator of the everyday world of the senses, the exquisite miniaturist, and the besieged expositor of poetic values, striking out at a devaluating world. In him we observe the impasse created by the conception of the artist as both 'fabulous artificer' and declassed human being 'trying to communicate' with other human beings in a world constantly goaded to conflict between dehumanized categories. It is a situation sufficiently dramatized in all of Dr Williams's work – and to a supreme degree in *Paterson* – to constitute a major achievement in contemporary literature. But one wonders, because one still hopes for something more and greater, whether the master work of our age should not derive from a sensibility historically enfranchised from that typical impasse, and thus capable of writing in the highest artistic terms not only about but *for* all the mythically divorced citizens in a world of Patersons. (37–41)

Randall Jarrell

from 'A View of Three Poets', *Partisan Review*, vol. 18   1951

Paterson (Book One) seemed to me a wonderful poem; I should not have supposed beforehand that William Carlos Williams could do the organizing and criticizing and selecting that a work of this length requires. Of course, Book One is not organized quite so well as a long poem *ought* to be, but this is almost a defining characteristic of long poems – and I do not see how anyone could do better using only those rather mosaic organizational techniques that Dr Williams employs, and neglecting as much as he does narrative, drama, logic and sustained movement, the primary organizers of long poems. I waited for the next three books of *Paterson* more or less as you wait for someone who has gone to break the bank at Monte Carlo for the second, third and fourth times; I was afraid that I knew what was going to happen, but I kept wishing as hard as I could that it wouldn't.

Now that Book Four has been printed, one can come to some conclusions about *Paterson* as a whole. My first conclusion is this: it doesn't seem to *be* a whole; my second: *Paterson* has been getting rather steadily worse. Most of Book Four is much worse than Two and Three, and neither of them even begins to compare with Book One. Book Four is so disappointing that I do not want to write about it at any length: it would not satisfactorily conclude even a quite mediocre poem. Both form and content often seem a parody of those of the 'real' *Paterson*; many sections have a scrappy inconsequence, an arbitrary irrelevance, that is extraordinary; poetry of the quality of that in Book One is almost completely lacking – though the forty lines about a new Odysseus coming in from the sea are particularly good, and there are other fits and starts of excellence. There are in Part Three long sections of a measure that sounds exactly like the stuff you produce when you are demonstrating to a class that any prose whatsoever can be converted into four-stress accentual verse simply by inserting line-endings every four stresses. These sections *look* like blank verse, but are flatter than the flattest blank verse I have ever read – for instance:

Branching trees and ample gardens gave
the village streets a delightful charm and
the narrow old-fashioned brick walls added
a dignity to the shading trees. It was a fair
resort for summer sojourners on their way
to the Falls, the main object of interest.
(IV, iii, p. 228)

This passage suggests that the guidebook of today is the epic of tomorrow; and a more awing possibility, the telephone book put into accentual verse, weighs upon one's spirit.

Books Two and Three are much better than this, of course: Book Two is decidedly what people call 'a solid piece of work', but most of the magic is gone. And one begins to be very doubtful about the organization: should there be so much of the evangelist and his sermon? Should so much of this book consist of what are – the reader is forced to conclude – real letters from a real woman? One reads these letters with involved, embarrassed pity, quite as if she had walked into the room and handed them to one. What has been done to them to make it possible for us to respond to them as art and not as raw reality? to make them part of the poem *Paterson*? I can think of no answer except: *They have been copied out on the typewriter.* Anyone can object, *But the context makes them part of the poem*; and anyone can reply to this objection, *It takes a lot of context to make somebody else's eight-page letter the conclusion to a book of a poem.*

Book Two introduces – how one's heart sinks! – Credit and Usury, those enemies of man, God, and contemporary long poems. Dr Williams has always put up a sturdy resistance to Pound when Pound has recommended to him St Sophia or the Parthenon, rhyme or metre, European things like that; yet he takes Credit and Usury over from Pound and gives them a good home and maintains them in practically the style to which they have been accustomed – his motto seems to be, *I'll adopt your child if only he's ugly enough.* It is interesting to see how much some later parts of *Paterson* resemble in their structure some middle and later parts of the *Cantos*: the Organization of Irrelevance (or, perhaps, the Irrelevance of Organization) suggests itself as a name for this category of structure. Such organization is *ex post facto* organization: if something is somewhere, one can always find Some Good Reason for its being there, but if it had not been there would one reader have missed it? if it had been put somewhere else, would one reader have guessed where it should have 'really' gone? Sometimes these anecdotes, political remarks, random comments seem to be where they are for one reason: because Dr Williams chose – happened to choose – for them to be there. One is reminded of that other world in which Milton found Chance 'sole arbiter'.

Book Three is helped very much by the inclusion of 'Beautiful Thing', that long, extremely effective lyric that was always intended for *Paterson*; and Book Three, though neither so homogeneous nor so close to Book One, is in some respects superior to Book Two. But all three later books are worse organized, more eccentric and idiosyncratic, more self-indulgent, than the first. And yet that is not the point, the real point: the *poetry*, the lyric rightness, the queer wit, the improbable and dazzling perfection of so much of Book One have disappeared – or at least, reappear only fitfully. Early in Book Four, while talking to his son, Dr Williams quotes this to him: 'What I miss, said your mother, is the poetry, the pure poem of the first parts.' She is right.

I have written (sometimes in *Partisan Review*) a good deal about Dr Williams's unusual virtues, so I will take it for granted that I don't need to try to demonstrate, all over again, that he is one of the best poets alive. He was the last of the good poets of his generation to become properly appreciated; and some of his appreciators, in the blush of conversion, rather overvalue him now. When one reads that no 'living American poet has written anything better and more ambitious' than *Paterson*, and that Dr Williams is a poet who gives us 'just about everything', one feels that the writer has in some sense missed the whole point of William Carlos Williams. He is a *very* good but *very* limited poet, particularly in vertical range. He is a notably unreasoning, intuitive writer – is not, of course, an intellectual at all, in either the best or the worst sense of the word; and he has further limited himself by volunteering for and organizing a long dreary imaginary war in which America and the Present are fighting against Europe and the Past. But go a few hundred years back inside the most American American and it is Europe: Dr Williams is just as much Darkest Europe as any of us, way down there in the middle of his past.

In his long one-sided war with Eliot Dr Williams seems to me to come off surprising badly – particularly so when we compare the whole of *Paterson* with the *Four Quartets*. When we read the *Four Quartets* we are reading the long poem of a poet so temperamentally isolated that he does not even put another character, another human being treated at length, into the whole poem; and yet the poem (probably the best since the *Duino Elegies*) impresses us not with its limitations but with its range and elevation, with how much it knows not simply about men but about Man – not simply about one city or one country but about the West, that West of which America is no more than the last part.

(691–700)

Joseph Bennett

from 'The Lyre and the Sledgehammer', *Hudson Review*, vol. 5   1952

The gift was, to begin with, purely lyric. It was small and clear, pure and true. It was there; and it flashes through occasionally in the later poetry. It was a single string, delicate and sure, matched with a fine

ear and watched with a discriminating eye. The villain was the vice
of grandeur, the attempt to forge out of a single metal string a
sledgehammer which could beat against the major anvils. . . .
(295–6)

As a poet, Williams is intensely self-preoccupied, entranced with
the image of his own ego. This preoccupation has its roots in his
Romanticism, as does the concept of the self as hero – I pick the hair
from her eyes|and watch her misery|with compassion – *he is always*
pitying someone. It reaches its characteristic development in the
sentiment of self-righteousness. The *persona* of the neurotic poetess
who appears so persistently throughout *Paterson* exhorts him to

take all your own literature and everyone else's and toss it
into one of those big garbage trucks of the Sanitation Depart-
ment, so long as the people with the top-cream minds and the
'finer' sensibilities use those minds and sensibilities not to
make themselves more humane human beings than the average
person, but merely as means of ducking responsibility toward
a better understanding of their fellow men . . .
(II, iii, p. 101)

That is to say, the criterion of value of a literary work is a biographical
one, determined by a study of the author's personal life to decide
whether he is a more 'humane human being' than the average.
Some sort of a norm of average 'humane human' behavior would
have to be established, and then the moral life of the author in question
weighed to determine whether it falls short of, or exceeds this norm.
The exhortation – an unusually cantankerous display of priggishness,
of moral superiority – is made against himself through a *persona*,
indicating a split attitude on this question.

Implicit throughout much of Williams's work, and part of his
priggishness, is the self-congratulatory feeling that he is more sensitive
to moral values than the general run of writers. Self-pity is naturally
associated with this attitude, and the theme of the poet as a sacrificial
victim of society grows until it becomes one of the major obsessions
of his work. This incestuous preoccupation with the pathos of the
existence of poets – a preoccupation Romantic in origin – adds to the
inwardness of his work. The duties, the destinies, the miseries of
poets – the poetry breeds upon itself for subject matter.

The Romanticism which is the mainspring of Williams's compulsions manifests itself in the most obvious ways – zest for the Gothically gruesome; fascination with the natural functions of defecation, and, to an incredible degree, of urination; the loud anti-intelligence harangues. Such phrases as 'But who are You?' are likely to occur at random, in any of the poems, and then disappear in a mass of blurred, foggy images, confused ideas, turgid rhetoric, pathetic fallacy and sentimentality of a moaning, sobbing type. He poses in Shelleyan attitudes, echoes Swinburne, and, Delphically inspired, prophesies like Elizabeth Barrett Browning.

The Strawberry Hill Gothic is presented with such zest, in all the gruesome details and incidents of the shorter poems and *Paterson*, and in such quantity, that it lends a determining strain of its own to Williams's Romanticism:

Or better, a brain without a
skull. I remember once a guy in
our anatomy class dropped one
from the third floor window on
an organ grinder in Pine street.

What aesthetic effect is secured, what dramatic point is made, what emotion is expressed or underlined, escapes me. I cannot see in such writings as 'Twenty feet of|guts on the black sands of Iwo' any care or any patience, anything but a childish pleasure in the gruesome for gruesomeness' sake.

The obverse face of the gruesomeness is the sentimentality; an age which takes pleasure in gruesomeness is generally a sentimental age. In Williams's work, there is a maudlin quality which is not exceeded by any other writer of our time:

I can't be half gentle enough,
half tender enough
toward you, toward you,
inarticulate, not half loving enough
BRIGHT en
the cor
ner
where   you   are!
(III, ii, p. 154)

The sentimental is often directly mixed in with the gruesome, and in one interesting case, both are combined with the mail carrier's motto. Occasionally, the indulgence in raw emotion reaches the point of hysteria:

Your face! Give me your face, Yang Kue Fei!
your hands, your lips to drink!
Give me your wrists to drink –
I drag you, I am drowned in you, you
overwhelm me! Drink!
Save me!

More often it is at the level of the maudlin, incessant repetitions of the 'Beautiful Thing' motto in *Paterson*, or in the constant emphasis throughout his work on the passive suffering of helpless victims, the pathos of tortured creatures who cannot fight back and who do not provide a subject for dramatic development.

Williams continually uses the word 'love' as a slogan or a label, but it remains a *word* only – it is never achieved in the context of the poem. It does not arise as the supreme unifying crux of a train of symbolism, of a series of carefully conceived images, or of a dramatic action. The word is merely tossed in at random – whenever there is a slow spot – whenever, as in *Paterson*, the ramble of language, the adventitious succession of images, the babble of opinions and moralizing hits a slow spot and will no longer flow. Coagulated, choked with detritus, the thing grinds to a halt of its own inanity, and the word 'love' is tossed up into it. The use of the term is so paltry and disfiguring that the ear is dulled to it; it becomes a dead word, a killed word, four letters merely of black print on the page, as harsh and stuffless as any of the verbal counters knocked about in commercial advertising that once were part of the living language.

Williams's anti-intellectual attitude is puerile in its implications. 'Let the metaphysical take care of itself, the arts have nothing to do with it,' he warns in his 1944 Introduction, and proceeds to his old whipping boy, the university. The dreary, repeated attack on the university throughout his work amounts to a phobia in *Paterson*, with the hammering repetition of its motto 'No ideas but in things'. It reveals a pompous, bigoted mind, not merely anti-intellectual in attitude, but dedicated to the principle of non-intelligence. Note again that these attacks occur without relation to their context in the work itself.

In the long discordant babble of *Paterson*, a Whitmanesque celebration of the Self occurs –

What shall it become,

Snot nose, that I have
    not been?
I enclose it and
    persist, go on.

Let it rot, at my center.
    Whose center?
I stand and surpass
    youth's leanness.

My surface is myself.
(i, iii, p. 43)

This celebration is interrupted, without relevance, by a typical harangue against the university – that which opposes the Self in its divine non-intellectual compulsions. The university is made up of

                    clerks
got out of hand forgetting for the most part
to whom they are beholden.
(i, iii, p. 44)

This harangue, the Self versus the lowly clerks, is in turn interrupted by a prose sequence in which a doctor examines a specimen of a patient's urine. There had been no hint of a medical theme in the forty-four pages of *Paterson* preceding. This is immediately followed by a scene in which a young naked colored woman proposes copulation. The copulation sequence is cut short by a Technicolored picturization of luxury life, with political overtones. This hackneyed bit of poster art is then superseded by a prose inventory, by items, of a small estate left in 1803, to contrast with the luxury. And so on, for the two hundred and twenty-eight pages of *Paterson*.

Williams's use of repetition is perhaps his most pronounced anti-intellectual device. Such passages as

Level it down
for him to build a house

on to build a
house on to build a house on
to build a house
to build a house on to . . .
(Sic. End of poem)

babbling away senselessly, are in their inanity an affront to the intellect. The overwhelming repetition of sententious phrases – *I believe*;
So be it; *Beautiful Thing* – especially marked in *Paterson*, has an effect
of sledgehammering the mind into eclipse so that it functions as a
sensory organ only.

The use of onomatopoeia – *Cha cha, chacha, cha!* – seems an extension of this technique, as do the various devices employed to give an
air of pseudo-profundity to simple-minded statements:

I warn you, the sea is *not* our home.
> the sea is not our home.

The sea *is* our home whither all rivers
(wither) run
> the nostalgic sea
sopped with our cries
> Thalassa! Thalassa!
calling us home

I say to you, Put wax rather in your
ears against the hungry sea
> it is not our home!
(IV, ii, p. 235)

The passage[1] is from *Paterson* and illustrates Williams's habit of trying
for an air of 'profundity' by making a pompous statement and then
reversing it – *the sea is* not *our home; the sea is* our *home*. Elsewhere in
the same poem, the Furies are dropped in here and there, as with an
eye-dropper, and splattered irrelevantly over the page:

1 Note the imitation of Joyce – whither (wither), and the 'borrowing' of the
Anna Livia theme. Also the open lift from the *Cantos* – *Put wax rather in your
ears*, and the *Thalassa!* echoes.

foreign 12,868 of whom 237 were French, 1,420 German,
3,343 English – (Mr Lambert who later built the Castle among
them), 5,124 Irish, 879 Scotch, 1,360 Hollanders and 170 Swiss –

Around the falling waters the Furies hurl!
Violence gathers, spins in their head summoning
them:

The twaalft, or striped bass was also abundant, and even
sturgeon, of a huge bigness, were frequently caught: – On
Sunday, August 31, 1817, one seven feet six inches long and
weighing 126 pounds,
(i, i, p. 19)

Williams is quick to pick up and transmit echoes of the important
writers of his time. He depends heavily on surrealist techniques;
there is much in *Paterson* that resembles a bad reading of Cocteau or
Apollinaire. Joyce, Eliot and especially Pound reverberate off and on
throughout his work, and Marianne Moore will find some of her
fish turning among Williams's 'undulant seaweed'. Joyce provides
him with the portmanteau word and Anna Livia's river, but without
the intellectual force and concision which made them vivid. Eliot
is alternately attacked, parodied and imitated – almost every style of
Eliot's long career is copied in parts of Williams's verse.

Pound's influence is extensive. There are a number of direct references, and there is the full page letter from Pound which constitutes
all of page 165 of *Paterson*. Occasionally Williams utilizes typical
rhythms of the *Cantos* – page 65 of *Paterson* derives rhythmically
direct from the *Usura* canto. The technique of Williams's page set-up
is now and then like that of the *Cantos* and there are a number of
passages in *Paterson* which are, stylistically, close imitations. The
extended section on money and credit theories in *Paterson*[1] is heavily
influenced by the *Cantos* in page set-up, rhythm and style. Another
letter from Pound is quoted briefly, and the credit theories, which are
hysterically presented, are essentially the same ones which Pound
has attempted to popularize in the *Cantos* and elsewhere. Unfortunately, their presentation lacks the vivacity and clarity of presentation
that Pound was able, earlier, to give the same material.

1 Part Two of Book Four.

No doubt Williams had the *Cantos* in mind in making up his own long poem, *Paterson*, with the ambition of producing a work as inclusive and powerful. But in the *Cantos*, even in the Inferno sections, it is seldom that there is a lapse of intelligence. The material is always organized with an aesthetic, or narrative, or ideological intent, and the less glamorous, even the repellent, sections of the *Cantos* remain passable and negotiable, to become eventually rewarding. The splendor and accuracy of the *Cantos* do not justify their occasional failures and their eccentricities of composition. But the splendor and accuracy do tend to mitigate these faults. The point is, that in Williams there is little splendor and little accuracy; and there is not the eccentricity of an intelligent, cunning artisan, but merely incoherence.

Space prevents a detailed formal analysis of *Paterson*. The poem, clearly establishes Williams's descent from Whitman and Sandburg. It purports to take a city – Paterson – as a type of the world-city, and incorporates this city in various *personae* – a man, Paterson; his daughter, Phyllis; a river at the Falls; a neurotic poetess; a neurotic young male poet; and a myriad set of lesser *personae*. The poetess and the poet correspond at great length – apparently with Mr Williams – discussing their personal neuroses. The poetess is the most exasperating of these correspondents – one of her letters, covering pages 105–13 of *Paterson* continuously, is nearly nine pages long. At times Wagnerian, at times folksy, the poem flows on, shifting confusingly from one of these *personae* to another, and introducing at haphazard, wholesale prose sections of local history, about 40 per cent of which have a gruesome slant. Inexplicably, the poem returns constantly to the voice of Mr Williams himself, apparently *not* as one of the *personae* incorporating the world-city of Paterson, and we get both self-pity and Whitman-esque paeans of the Self; as well as cantankerous opinions and harangues on banking and credit, labor relations, the atom bomb and theories of literary composition.

There is nothing wrong with the idea of taking one city as the world's city, and developing its character in the direction of universals through *personae*. It could, if intelligently developed, be a fruitful and original theme. But to put this stamp on the formless morass of *Paterson* and claim that it describes some rational plan behind the non-sequential babble is impossible.

Much of it is purely capricious – there is the 'slant' page, where each line of type is slanted at a different angle on the page, and another full page of the poem is devoted to the drilling log of an artesian well. As an example of all that is worst in Williams, take the Madame Curie-Atom Bomb sequence in Part Two of Book Four of *Paterson*. This ridiculous *mélange* is openly derived from the Hollywood extravaganza, starring Greer Garson, on Madame Curie –

Curie (the movie queen) upon
>   the stage at the Sorbonne
a half mile across! walking solitary
>   as tho' in a forest, the silence
of a great forest (of ideas)
>   before the assembly (the
little Polish baby-nurse) receives
>   international acclaim (a
drug)
(IV, ii, p. 202)

It goes on for ten or twelve pages, a curious mixture of popular science and sentimentality, sprouted in a movie-house, and interspersed throughout the section with harangues on labor relations and banking, and a full-page circular on credit theory presumably provided to Williams for insertion in *Paterson* by one 'August Walters, Newark, NJ'. Also to be found between the Greer Garson-Madame Curie episodes is a long letter from the young neurotic male poet, continuing for three pages; passages from St Luke and Chaucer; references to Sappho, Sophocles, Woodrow Wilson, Carrie Nation, Artemis, Liberia, the Abbess Hildegarde, Tate, the Spanish Civil War, Phideas, Reuther and Ben Shahn; part of a Pound letter; a diarrheal case history in prose concerning 'a stool submitted by the nurse for the usual monthly examination'; and a prose account of an early explorer's landing on the shores of what is presumably New Jersey.

The question arises as to whether Williams' intent is poetic – that is, is he attempting, fundamentally, to write poetry:

When a man had gone up in Russia from a small town to the
University he returned a hero – people bowed down to him
– his ego, nourished by this, mounted to notable works. Here
in the streets the kids say Hello Pete! to me – What can one

be or imagine? Nothing is reverenced, nothing looked up to. What can come of that sort of disrespect for the understanding?

This is a short poem of the late Forties, *The Unfrocked Priest*, written out without any line breaks. Read as prose, the lines are a limply-phrased statement of comparison of the social attitudes towards university graduates in Russia and the United States, with definite overtones of self-pity. Try it as a 'poem';

1

When a man had gone
up
in Russia from a small
town
to the University
he
returned a hero –
people
bowed down to him –
his
ego, nourished by this,
mount-
ed to notable works.

2

Here
in the streets the kids
say
Hello Pete! to me –
What
can one be or
imagine?
Nothing is reverenced
nothing
looked up to. What
can
come of that sort of
dis-
respect for the under
standing? [1]

[1] *Collected Later Poems*, p. 148.

Or is the arrangement of the words into broken lines a hoax; that is, is the arrangement purely adventitious, casting prose – and pretty bad prose, at that – into the 'form' of poetry, but not altering its structure? Here is another one:

By constantly tormenting them with reminders of the lice in their children's hair, the School Physician first brought their hatred down on him. But by this familiarity they grew used to him, and so, at last took him for their friend and adviser.

If the reader wishes to see how this statement is converted into 'poetry', he should consult page 206 of Williams's collection.[1]

I think that Williams avoids poetry, for the most part, sidestepping it, and substituting for it sentimentality, pathos, self-revelation, self-pity, surrealism, raw emotion, gruesome anecdotes, and hammering repetition of grand-sounding phrases. In *Paterson* this is especially marked. His 'poems' are headless and footless. Cut them anywhere, excise their middles, slit them in half, and like amoebas, the jelly flows back together and the animal is the same. Cut off their heads, take off their tails, put their elbows down where their knees should be – no harm is done because the animal is formless, plastic; it all flows together, and any part of *Paterson* can be taken out and put elsewhere in the poem. The poem can be started at any point in its text, run around its entire circle and brought to a conclusion at the starting-point; and no harm is done.
(298–305)

Hugh Kenner

'With the Bare Hands', *Poetry*, vol. 80   August 1952
(reprinted in *Gnomon*, 1958)

What should be new is intent upon one thing, the metaphor – the metaphor is the poem. There is for them only one metaphor: Europe – the past. All metaphor for them, inevitably so, is the past: that is the poem. That is what they think a poem is: metaphor.

1 *Collected Earlier Poems.*

In the five years during which Parts One to Four of *Paterson* were appearing, the fact contained in these words of Dr Williams rendered the appreciative unusually inarticulate. The poem was respectfully, enthusiastically received, and in unexpected quarters. But it isn't a metaphor, it isn't 'about' *something else* (Europe – the past); so it seems undiscussable, except via 'the inadequacy of Imagism' or some such trodden detour.

Neither does some familiar modus of meaning inform the novel materials of *Paterson*, nor is it the poet-physician's 'view of life' that we are to listen for as we turn its pages. This is writing that by a Jacob's wrestle with words *gets down what happens* –

> they coalesce now
> glass-smooth with their swiftness,
> quiet or seem to quiet as at the close
> they leap to the conclusion and
> fall, fall in air! as if
> floating, relieved of their weight,
> split apart, ribbons; dazed, drunk
> with the catastrophe of the descent
> floating unsupported
> to hit the rocks: to a thunder,
> as if lightning had struck
> (I, i, p. 16)

– the language never reaching out of its proper dimension, level and solid as ice a foot thick, but buoyed up by the whole depth and weight of the profound reality with which it is in contact, and whose contours it holds fast. This note of reality, this sense of the poem being in touch with something dense, not something that the writer has densified by mixing quick-drying ideas with it, is everywhere in the book:

> a bud forever green
> tight-curled, upon the pavement, perfect
> in juice and substance but divorced, divorced
> from its fellows, fallen low –
>
> Divorce is
> the sign of knowledge in our time,

divorce! divorce!
(I, ii, p. 28)

        While in the tall
buildings (sliding up and down) is where
the money's made
           up and down
                directed missiles
in the greased shafts of the tall buildings   .
They stand in torpid cages, in violent motion
unmoved
      but alert!
           predatory minds, unaffected
      UNINCONVENIENCED
        unsexed, up
and down (without wing motion) This is how
the money's made .   using such plugs
(IV, i, p. 195)

  Williams tells the story of a lady who wanted to know 'What is all that down in this left hand lower corner' of a picture she admired and was thinking of buying. The curator replied, 'That, madam, is paint.' 'This story marks the exact point in the transition that took place, in the world of that time, from the appreciation of a work of art as a copying of nature to the thought of it as the imitation of nature, spoken of by Aristotle in his *Poetics* . . . misinterpreted for over two thousand years and more. The objective . . . is to imitate nature, which involved active invention, the active work of the imagination.'

          without invention
nothing lies under the witch-hazel
bush, the alder does not grow from among
the hummocks margining the all
but spent channel of the old swale,
the small foot-prints
of the mice under the overhanging
tufts of the bunch-grass will not
appear: without invention the line
will never again take on its ancient

divisions when the word, a supple word,
lived in it, crumbled now to chalk.
(II, i, p. 65)

The invention that arranges the 'paint' is fed by preoccupation
with dense fact. Williams has spent some forty years listening to
people talk, respecting them, becoming them:

Who are these people (how complex
the mathematic) among whom I see myself
in the regularly ordered plateglass of
his thoughts, glimmering before shoes and bicycles?
They walk incommunicado, the
equation is beyond solution, yet
its sense is clear – that they may live
his thought is listed in the Telephone
Directory –
(I, i, p. 18)

He has a sense of that unique thing, the American community, a
community built upon no past or fragments of a past, permeated by
a dielectric that all but baffles communication, united by symbols
held unexpectedly in common, parodying itself in its every printed
word; not the remnants of former order the best modern poetry
has learned to express by using shards of older forms, the 'unreal
city' of *The Waste Land* or the spezzato paradise of *The Cantos*, not
a great order smashed but a new one so far voiceless.

How to begin to find a shape – to begin to begin
again,
turning the inside out: to find one phrase that will
lie married beside another for delight . ?
– seems beyond attainment .

American poetry is a very easy subject to discuss for the simple
reason that it does not exist
(III, iii, p. 167)

– of this, make it of *this*, this
this, this, this, this .
(III, iii, p. 168)

– in a hundred years, perhaps –
the syllables

       (with genius)

             or perhaps

two lifetimes

Sometimes it takes longer   .
(III, iii, p. 171)

Europe seems *there*, comprehended, more graspable than America because it has a literature, a provincial literature as well as the literature of the Great Record that extends from Homer. American literature has been with insignificant exceptions a provincialized pastiche of the provincialisms of Europe: Europe's puritanism (New England), Europe's mildewed grandeur (the South). Even Whitman, the democracy snob, was an enlarged Byron, welcoming all men as fellow-aristocrats in the *Song of Myself* and shaking the dust of the past from his feet.

Hart Crane was another spiritual alien. Frost's sense of community is rudimentary. Dr Williams is the first American writer to discover, not the phases of America that reflect what was in Europe, but the core of America that is itself, new, and so far unvocal. His sense of community is neither sociological nor sentimental. Paterson, NJ, provides him neither with cases for scrutiny nor with a background for lyrical performance. One cannot, in a given passage, zone out the compassion and the astringency. They fuse to lead the reader, clue-like, into the unique 'feel' of the material. 'A reply to Greek and Latin with the bare hands,' the author notes in an epigraph:

To make a start,
out of particulars
and make them general, rolling
up the sum, by defective means –
(Preface, p. 11)

  and the craft,
subverted by thought, rolling up, let
him beware lest he turn to no more than
the writing of stale poems . . .

Minds like beds always made up,
                    (more stony than a shore)
unwilling or unable.
(Preface, p. 13)

Because he is content to have devoted a lifetime to making a start, he
gets the start made. *Paterson* expresses much more than its author's
clinical individuality. From beneath the fractured words, the vio-
lences, the voiceless impasse of the mill-town citizen –

Blocked.
            (Make a song out of that: concretely)
By whom?
(II, i, p. 78)

– comes straining the ache of the mind, what the numb gestures
would mean and the null words would express, straining to transcend
the febrile 'self-expression' that the citizen has become convinced he
ought to want to intend:

.   in the pitchblende
the radiant gist   .

   Dr Williams writes in his *Autobiography* (p. 359)

Day in day out, when the inarticulate patient struggles to lay
himself bare for you ... so caught off balance that he reveals
some secret twist of a whole community's pathetic way of
thought, a man is suddenly seized again with a desire to speak
of the underground stream which for a moment has come up
just under surface. ... We begin to see that the underlying
meaning of all that they want to tell us and have always
failed to communicate is the poem, the poem which their
lives are being lived to realize. No one will believe it. And it
is the actual words, as we hear them spoken under all
circumstances, which contain it. It is actually there, in the life
before us, every minute that we are listening, a rarest element
– not in our imaginations but there, there in fact.

From the words that are going in at our ears 'we must recover
underlying meaning as realistically as we recover metal out of ore.'

The radiant gist: hence the long section of Book Four devoted to the heroism of the Curies

A dissonance
in the valence of Uranium
led to the discovery

Dissonance
(if you are interested)
leads to discovery
(IV, ii, p. 207)

The poem that is beneath the words doesn't localize, it inheres in the design of the whole. Its controlling image is the roar of the Paterson waterfall:

A false language. A true. A false language pouring – a
language (misunderstood) pouring (misinterpreted)
        without
dignity, without minister, crashing upon a stone ear.
(I, i, p. 24)

These terrible things they reflect:
the snow falling into the water,
part upon the rock, part in the dry weeds
and part into the water where it
vanishes – its form no longer what it was: . . .

the whole din of fracturing thought
as it falls tinnily to nothing upon the streets
(I, ii, p. 33)

        The language   .   words
without style! whose scholars (there are none)
.   or dangling, about whom
the water weaves its strands encasing them
in a sort of thick lacquer, lodged
under its flow   .
(III, iii, p. 100)

The scholars dangle; but there are other lives. A bewildered woman plummeted in; Sam Patch in the 1820s dove repeatedly into chasms, master of the technique of communion, until the day of the exhibition jump when technique failed: 'But instead of descending with a plummet-like fall his body wavered in the air – Speech had failed him. He was confused. The word had been drained of its meaning. . . .'

Patch leaped but Mrs Cumming shrieked
and fell – unseen (though
she had been standing there beside her husband half
an hour or more twenty feet from the edge).

:a body found next spring
frozen in an ice-cake; or a body
fished next day from the muddy swirl –

both silent, uncommunicative
(I, ii, p. 31)

   This roar, this speech to which Dr Williams listens that he may make a replica –

           I must
find my meaning and lay it, white
beside the sliding water: myself –
comb out the language – or succumb
(III, iii, p. 173)

– is modern cousin to the murmur that fills books:

          A cool of books
will sometimes lead the mind to libraries
of a hot afternoon, if books can be found
cool to the sense to lead the mind away.

For there is a wind or ghost of a wind
in all books echoing the life
there, a high wind that fills the tubes
of the ear until we think we hear a wind,
actual   .

               to lead the mind away
(III, i, p. 118)

They murmur and draw us down the wind, while the falls roar; or they may lead us back to the present, not quite to the falls but to the roar of the stream in our own minds:

> a reverberation
> not of the falls but of its rumor
> unabated

(III, i, p. 119)

Eliot goes unforgiven by Dr Williams for giving poetry back to 'literature' ('Europe – the past') – the wind of books and the rumor of the falls in the mind – just when the breakthrough to direct perception of the present, the actual falls in the stream, had seemed possible. The burning of the library in Book Three is a complex image; it is part impatience with books, part purgation of them, part an image of live reading, a lending of blood and heat to the past (no longer 'cool to the sense') as Pound, in parable of his own translator's activities, portrayed Odysseus serving blood to the ghosts in Canto I.

> Awake, he dozes in a fever heat,
> cheeks burning   .   .   loaning blood
> to the past, amazed   .   risking life.

>   The pitiful dead
> cry back to us from the fire, cold in
> the fire, crying out – wanting to be chaffed
> and cherished
>   those who have written books

> We read: not the flames
> but the ruin left
> by the conflagration

> Not the enormous burning
> but the dead (the books
> remaining). Let us read   .

> and digest: the surface
> glistens, only the surface.
> Dig in – and you have

> a nothing, surrounded by
> a surface, an inverted
> bell resounding, a

white-hot man become
a book, the emptiness of
a cavern resounding.
(III, ii, p.148)

Here we have the metaphoric clue to Williams's celebrated
'opacity', his eschewal of sonorities and reverberations, of words
exploited for the sake of their 'tentacular roots'. A poem is a solid
surface, hollow, ringing; 'depth' is an illusion. The most startlingly
successful imaginative leap in *Paterson* is the page-long tabular
record of specimens found in the boring of an artesian well, ending
with the attempt abandoned,

the water being altogether unfit for ordinary use. . . . The
fact that the rock salt of England, and of some of the other
salt mines of Europe, is found in rocks of the same age as this,
raises the question whether it may not also be found here.
(III, iii, p. 166)

This is in the section about finding language; perhaps we were wrong
to look for water; perhaps there is rock salt under the Passaic; the
European analogy raises a possibility, not a prescription. In the next
book, however, comes an interpolation in the unmistakable idiom of
an old friend of the poet's:

.   just because they ain't no water fit to drink in that spot (or
you ain't found none) don't mean there ain't no fresh water to
be had NOWHERE . .
(IV, ii, p. 215)

The table of well-bore specimens carries all this thematic weight by
not seeking to be more than itself, by not being cramped into a metaphor. 'Reverberation' will arise of itself from a bell with a hard
enough surface; the surface is the poet's level of concern. Synthetic
plangency is an illusion, a tampering with the reader's responses.
Such incantations 'lead the mind away' from the dissonant actual
roar. They would introduce into Williams's poem a past not his
past, or impose a rhythm which he does not hear but which the
tranquil (conventional) mind would prefer to find.

As Carrie Nation
          to Artemis
                    so is our life today   .

They took her out West on a photographing
expedition
        to study chiaroscuro
                to Denver, I think.
Somewhere around there   .
              the marriage
was annulled. When she returned
            with the baby
                 openly
taking it to her girls' parties, they
            were shocked
– and the Abbess Hildegard, at her own
funeral, Rupertsberg, 1179
had enjoined them to sing the choral, all
women, she had written for the occasion
and it was done, the peasants kneeling
in the background   .   as you may see
(IV, ii, p. 211)

This is from Book Four; by so late in the poem, Dr Williams has so
thoroughly presented the actual Paterson world that he can afford
to insert one measuring point from the European past without
sentimental nostalgia. Similarly the unrhymed quatrains near the
end of Book Three ('On this most voluptuous night of the year')
are presented not as a climax but as a powerful undertow, the easy
way out of a poetic dilemma:

> Be reconciled, poet, with your world, it is
> the only truth!
>
> Ha!
> – the language is worn out.
>
> And She –
>   You have abandoned me!
>
> – at the magic sound of the stream
> she threw herself upon the bed –
> a pitiful gesture! lost among the words:
> Invent (if you can) discover or

> nothing is clear – will surmount
> the drumming in your head. There will be
> nothing clear, nothing clear
>
> He fled pursued by the roar.

(II, iii, p. 103)

Hence we find him in his bewilderment

> –saying over to himself a song written
> previously   .   inclines to believe
> he sees, in the structure, something
>   of interest:

> On this most voluptuous night of the year
> the term of the moon is yellow with no light
> the air's soft, the night bird has
> only one note, the cherry tree in bloom
>
> makes a blur on the woods, its perfume
> no more than half guessed moves in the mind.

(II, iii, p. 105)

Replying, in the pioneer fashion, 'to Greek and Latin with the bare hands', he must invent rhythms, a measure, images, the whole articulation of a comprehensive poem; it is the struggle to do this that the poem dramatizes, and in dramatizing succeeds in doing. Everyone struggles, the roar is in everyone's ears, everyone in Paterson must either strive as the poet does, or merge himself with the stream in some direct despairing way like Patch and Mrs Cumming, or remain 'blocked'.

'With the bare hands' is to some extent overstated. If there are 'no ideas but in things', yet 'Stones invent nothing, only a man invents.' Williams draws on other inventors: Pound who in cutting *The Waste Land* and building *The Cantos* revised our concept of poetic structure, Joyce who fused a man and a city and spent his life in astringent, compassionate cataloguing of banalities so as to set them down and force them to utter the poetry they ordinarily short-circuit. The very title is a Joycean pun: Paterson is a city, a man (sometimes a doctor), and Pater-son, the molecule of generative succession.

Generative succession carries the poem forward from the elemental male and female forms of the opening through the days when

>   the breathing
> spot of the village was the triangle square
> bounded by Park Street (now lower Main Street)
> and Bank Street

to the day ('October 10, 1950') when the twentieth-century poet contemplates the running-out of his particular experience to the sea:

> Yet you will come to it, come to it! The
> song is in your ears, to Oceanus
> where the day drowns   .
>
>   No! it is not our home.
>
> You will come to it, the blood dark sea
> of praise. You must come to it. Seed
> of Venus, you will return   .   to
> a girl standing upon a tilted shell, rose
> pink   .
>   Listen!
>
> Thalassa! Thalassa!
>   Drink of it, be drunk!
>   Thalassa
> immaculata: our home, our nostalgic
> mother in the dead, enwombed again
> cry out to us to return   .
>   the blood dark sea!
> nicked by the light alone, diamonded
> by the light   .   from which the sun
> alone lifts undamped his wings
>   of fire!

(IV, iii, p. 236)

The penultimate image is not a merging and death, but a dryly circumstantial rebirth; a man who emerges from bathing, slides 'his shirt on overhand (the | sleeves were still rolled up)' and heads inland, followed by his dog. The finale to Book Four with fine inclusive irony gathers up Sam Patch, Mrs Cumming, the violent who have recurrently illustrated 'a poverty of resource', the fade-out of an American movie, the end of *The Hollow Men* (Fawkes on the scaffold, 'not with a bang'), and for better or worse (*'La Vertue | est toute dans l'effort'*) the enterprise of the poem itself:

John Johnson, from Liverpool, England, was convicted after
20 minutes conference by the Jury. On April 30th, 1850, he
was hung in full view of thousands who had gathered on
Garret Mountain and adjacent house tops to witness the spectacle.

This is the blast
the eternal close
the spiral
the final somersault
    the end.
(IV, iii, p. 238)

An image which Dr Williams doesn't use in the poem but which his whole career as physician and poet urges on the attention, recommends itself as the most adequate basis for summary and praise: the obstetrician devoting in a few critical moments his every wile, his concentration, so far as his capacity allows, of the entire tradition of medical science since Hippocrates, to the deliverance, with his bare hands, into independent life of something he did not make, the identity of which he unshakeably respects, and which but for his ministrations would die voiceless.
(276–80)

Edward Dahlberg

'Word-Sick and Place-Crazy', *Alms for Oblivion* 1964

Books are wild beasts or brackish water or dead ravines. It is hard now to find a book that one can depend upon, and in which branch is bough, bird is bird, and apple talks like apple. Books are more mixed and dirty than ever, and though there is rot and swinepen in every poet, the old Levitical differences between fungused places and unclean froggish things and the arbute and gillyflower are gone. There is so much lion and jackal mischief in our morals, and man at best, as Hamlet says, is indifferent honest, that the poet is no longer homely and plain about simple and plain things. He is like William Carlos Williams, the Paterson rock poet, who gives us skill and invention in the place of the Cana marriage wine. His original books are Medusa's, likely to turn the heads of a generation into stone, and *Paterson* and *The Later Collected Poems* are lawless art. *Paterson*, which he says is the pride of locality, is a word-manual for the journeyman poet, and its hard river words will yield much pleasure to the reader. Socrates once said that the misuse of words induces evil in the soul, and this remarkable observation is very close to the problem of the Paterson poem; Williams had a martial passion for the sentence – his phrases have the firing-power of an automatic revolver. Bleak mountain skill, or what we call poetic invention, can slay the spirit. Originality is often a stepmother Muse that gives her breast to the hawk and the mountain, and is the greatest curse in our literature; there is a surfeit of originality in *Paterson*.

Williams was a congealed river-and-rock man who wrote a very remarkable hot book, *In the American Grain*. But our most gifted writers have too much seawater in their heads, and all of them were cold men. Let it be enough here just to mention Thoreau's *Walden* and *A Week on the Concord and Merrimack Rivers*, for the titles of these wonderful volumes are ample proof of their contents. Melville's *Moby-Dick* is an astonishing but inhuman masterpiece. Shale and river books are not wisdom literature. Hawthorne, who had as polar a soul as Thoreau, cried out against his boreal nature. In *The Christmas Banquet* Hawthorne writes that to be cold is the most wretched plague of the heart; yet the debile, sinning husband of Hester Prynne in *The Scarlet Letter* is Chillingworth.

The early Greek thinkers believed that where there was too much moisture there was injustice, saying that man at first was a seagoing shark; correct science or not, this is an unusual truth about people. Take heed, then, of those wild, watery men in literature, and remember that Odysseus is miserable until his hapless water-journey is ended, and that he pines not so much for Penelope as for Ithaca, his swine, sheep and fruits.

A poet ought to be one, to have a single deity that wills and purposes for his whole nature. We imagine a writer to be both Diogenes and Hercules, blunt speaking and a moral force. Without Hercules's lion's skin and club, philosophy and poetry and science are deceitful, profligate and willess. We look in vain for moral volition in *Paterson* and *The Later Poems*, for the rocks that simulate fortitude are inhumanities and the water is death. Heraclitus said that too much moisture is death to the soul. It is true that poets have more unstable water in them than other thinkers; Plutarch is more reliable than Shakespeare. There is no mistaking the riggish vices of such caitiffs as Antony and Cleopatra in Plutarch, but there is enough anarchy in the great English poet to confuse the reader, and these wantons are plumaged peacocks with astonishing Asiatic lusts, which Shakespeare forces us to admire. However, Iago had one nature, reechy Goneril is single, and Timon is of one stuff.

The American poet is double, his character chameleon, and he has double moral hands, unlike the philosopher Charles S. Peirce who wrote out his questions with one hand and answered them with the other. As for Williams, it is impossible to know what his affections or his morals are; he so constantly changes his shape that he is like that ever-changing debtor in the comedy of Epicharmos who refuses to pay his creditor because he says he is no longer the same person who borrowed the money. We cannot be in moral debt to Williams because we do not know what he owes us either in negations or in a straight honest yes. In art, as Dostoyevsky has written, two plus two equals five, and this provides for the underground nihilism in modern man; but in morals two and two are always four. The distinction between art and ethics cannot be so considerable as to make it almost impossible to know the difference between the false and the true, between Acheron and the tender, growing earth. Either we are to get health from a poet or else all this sick water-verse will drive us mad.

We cannot put upon a poet a creed or religion, but he must have one character or we will have the most dreary pluralistic morals, a moral for every new occasion. The shabbiest cynics at Athens had a few lentil, lupin and thyme rules by which they lived and were recognized. One finds this hardy fare of customs and morals in Homer and in those philosophical dogs who slept and cohabited in the public porches and were as houseless, unblanketed and unroofed as the Paterson poem, and one of whom offered the following recipe for his pupils: 'Set aside ten minas for a chef, a drachma for the doctor, five talents for a flatterer, a talent for a whore, three obols for a philosopher.' It is this kind of receipt that we call style or form in a poet or thinker, and whether it is reckoned good or not, it is clear. We blame man less for a principle we may not agree with, and reject, than for his confusion, which we may not comprehend and accept; confusion is the begetter of the greatest evil in the soul.

It is impossible to know whether Williams is a man-hater or not, for though he employs a people's language, the bare hummocks, the 'treeless knoll', and the waterworks in the poems are nomadic nihilism. 'The water married to the stone' is not pioneer hardihood but supine pessimism and dingy misanthropy. He is homeless and parentless, begotten by January ravines, and always *outside* among 'humped roots', 'calcined husks', with 'rock, bole and fangs'; his affections, moreover, are so *natured* that he can neither house, kitchen, nor table man or earth. The words 'stone' and 'rock' appear seventy-eight times, and 'falls' nineteen times; besides these, 'river' and 'stream' occur perhaps even more often than the stones, and 'gorge', 'ledge', 'precipice' and 'cataract' are also reiterated. Toward the end of the long poem divided into four parts, Williams gives us a log which tells the amount of shale and red sandstone that are at the various depths of a well. 'Fanged-toothed rock', 'grasshopper of red basalt' and 'gulls upon the ice-strewn river' look at first like force and stoicism – we often mistake what is raw and primitive for innocence and primal strength – but are really cold, wet verse.

It is the letters in *Paterson* that are the sun and the blood, the human cry and the conscience absent in the shale and pickerel-weed. The most rancorous epistles are written by an anonymous woman bitterly chiding this man who has become place, for place can be a liar and devour us. The woman writes that the poet has metamorphosed her faculties into some 'impenetrable congealed substance', 'rough ice'. An Egyptian osier burial basket has more human warmth than those feral, cold nature poems.

To use Platonic language, what is in the world must have its counterpart in universals, that is, horse as a particular of the world must be represented by universal horseness, and a chair must have its ideal chairness. In *Don Quixote* the barber's basin is also the helmet of Mambrino; if the one is not also the other, we have either common matter as it is precisely uttered by Williams, or inhuman abstractions, and one without the other is confusion and madness. Melville writes in *Moby-Dick*, 'Be thou in the world, but not of it,' which counsels a man to be familiar with Polonius and Hamlet, Christ and Barabbas, and to be able to know one from the other. Williams tells the reader of the *Later Poems* to be reconciled with the world, advice that is likely to beget a charlatan, a busybody and a liar, and that is what the world has been to every real poet, including Jesus who cries out, 'O I have overcome the world!'

Both Thoreau and Williams relish a tawny sentence; *The Concord and Merrimack* and *In the American Grain* are American canonical geography; Williams has submitted to Greenland and to savage territory as much as he dares. He wrote with deep understanding of the pilgrims that came to conquer a vast wilderness continent and were possessed by it. Take the following phrases out of these two authors' volumes and judge whether they belong to Thoreau or to Williams: 'eels and a moon', 'rock, bole and fangs', 'sweet-barked sassafras', 'treeless knoll', 'pumice-covered', 'calcined husks', 'file-sharp grass', 'flint arrow head', 'old swale'. Do not think this American literary geology is of trifling value, not to be remembered. Homer also has his catalogues of ships, of names, and of towns, and they are poems. There was a writer of Greek comedies by the name of Mermippus who in 429 BC drew up a list of imports which are edible verses, for the mind eats what it perceives, and it must thrive and not sicken upon its food: 'Hides and vegetable relish from Cyprus; grains and meat from Italy; pork and cheese from Syracuse; sails and papyrus from Egypt . . .' One cannot feed too long on the bogs of Thoreau or on the ravished gravel and grubby river Paterson; those that fall in love with this wild, malignant beauty will be sorely wounded by it. Thoreau and Williams are frontier minds, with an acute wind-and-bramble logic of the physical ground, but all earth is not suitable habitation for the imagination. I can't talk to rocks and trees, says Socrates.

Look at this poet William Carlos Williams: he is primitive and native, and his roots are in raw forest and violent places; he is word-sick and place-crazy. He admires strength, but for what? Violence! This is the cult of the frontier mind. 'The hungry animal underlying all other power.' He has succumbed to the frontier ground no less than Crèvecoeur, Fenimore Cooper, Twain and Parkman. But who wants to read these American anchorites on bleak ravines and desolate scrub-pines just to be more inhuman than one already is by nature? What Shakespeare truth or Jeremiah vision is there in these cankered mists and gulches?

Paterson is a homeless, desperado poem; it's all outdoors. 'Hypaethral' is the word Thoreau uses. The Paterson Falls is icy nihilism. The poet longs to leap from the ledge into the fatal ice flood, but he has the minister's wife and a tight-rope walker fall into the February river, and when it is dredged the bodies are found, ice-caked. 'Rather the ice than their way.' But this is fearful ice-sickness, which is the dread of human touch and being involved with people. That's all there is to those cataracts, the waterworks, and the rapids; he knows it but as animal skin has knowledge. Melville was also a lawless cold writer; he wrote *Mardi* to heat his blood. *In the American Grain* is Williams's one hot book, with tropical Aztec and Florida Indian names, and reptile and alligator sexuality, with 'sugar cane from the Canaries', 'the oil of walnuts . . . drawn like olive oil', 'Chicaca . . . stocked with maize' and 'loaves made of pulp of plums'. The jasper floor of Montezuma's palace is as asiatic as Menelaus's dwelling. There is a lovely chant to Raleigh where Williams writes, 'the true form escapes in the wind, sing O Muse . . . of the pursuit of beauty and the husk that remains . . . sing O Muse.' But Williams, understanding the tabu fear of touch of the American returns in *Paterson* and in the *Later Collected Poems* to the 'hard, repressive pioneer soil of the mind'. The poet desires to be place, 'the gap between touch and thing'. But can locality judge the heart, the liver and the affections? Like Melville who succumbed to the Pacific, Williams says goodbye to Montezuma, Joppa, Nineveh and disappears in the Paterson River. He is just homeless, without parent, or man or woman to be near; a prey of the fiercest elements. There is no creative metamorphosis but brutish submission and the cowering animal feeding upon its own paws.

The writing Ishmael bothered Williams. He had a fine imaginative faculty but distrusted books. He made some observations about Dante, Isaiah and the Aztecans. Like all pioneers Williams hated the old world, and took his revenge upon the old European culture. He thought that the ancient civilizations could not be seeded here, which is a frontier perversion. Melville turned to Job and Lear, Thoreau to the *Bhagavad-Gita*, and Charles S. Peirce used Duns Scotus. Woe be to him who lets any of his higher faculties remain unexplored, wrote Thoreau.

No people require maxims so much as the American. The reason is obvious: the country is so vast, the people always going somewhere, from Oregon apple valley to boreal New England, that we do not know whether to be temperate orchards or sterile climate. Great cultures come out of small Homeric or Hebraic lands; our bigness has given us such humbug size that we are too big for pity or sorrow or for others. Is a man given a talent to use it for himself alone? What our genius lacks most is being simple. If that is clear a poet won't reject his head, as Williams did, because it will smell, according to the Upanishads, like a raven's nest. He will not, like Williams, take up violence in his arms as a bride.

When a poet has some abiding morals in him he can make whatever images he likes, for it will be clear to him that books are the lilies and birds that are more than raiment and meat.

We must return to *In the American Grain*, the genius of the wild and the savage flower in Williams. He tells us a dark parable, and he was the first to gather up American history as a fabulist. He relates how the discoverers came to plant the old European soul here, and though they killed and subdued everything, it was they who were enslaved by primitive river and mountain. The planters were fierce ice men, Red Eric, Hudson, La Salle, Cartier, De Soto, Raleigh. We think Christian non-resistance archaic Asian wisdom, and do not understand how old in lore was brave Montezuma, who submitted to Cortes and a miserable small band, giving him rubies, gold, emeralds, knowing what has always been Indian knowledge, that the conqueror will be the slave. Even the Aztecan names – Napateca, Caliquen, Paraxcoxi – are ancient volcanic gods which enter us as we kill them.

We are still discoverers, new-world logicians, mistaking the Pharaoh cliffs of New Mexico and Arizona and that Egyptian Nile peninsula, Florida, for the ancient epical civilization. There is a terrible truth in this American fable; every discoverer we have had has been a wild homesteader among the seers of the world. Melville, Thoreau, Parkman, Prescott and Williams are all river and sea and plateau geniuses, ranging a continent for a house, and all of them outdoors.
(20–27)

Part Three The 1950s and 1960s

Introduction

The news that MacGibbon & Kee were to bring out an English edition of Williams's poems reached America two days after his death which occurred on 4 March 1963. The final decade of his life had seen the publication of *The Desert Music* (1954), *Journey to Love* (1955) and *Pictures from Brueghel* (1962), and it was with a composite edition of these, under the title of the last named, that Williams's poetry first became generally obtainable in Britain. In the fifties, the publisher, Peter Owen, had imported copies of *Paterson*, Books One and Two, but the message did not travel far. And even as late as 1965 it was possible to read in *The Times*: 'Paterson is an imaginary town in New Jersey which Williams created as his symbol of America, and the poem is a mosaic of lyrical and narrative fragments about the people of this town, interspersed with fascinating newspaper clippings and letters.'[1]

The spread of Williams's reputation here came first of all through the little magazines (as chronicled by Michael Weaver[2]), transmitting, from the start of the fifties on, America's own belated awareness of its poet. In the war years Williams read, often to small audiences, on various American campuses. This was the first stage of a gradual breakthrough in the universities. An honorary degree from Buffalo in 1948 gives an indication of how far he had come, and in the next few years, not only was there a monograph (Vivienne Koch's *William Carlos Williams*, 1950), and an increasing body of articles on him in the literary quarterlies, but one could even read about him in the middle-brow *Saturday Review of Literature* (Richard Eberhart, 'Prose, Poetry and the Love of Life', ibid., vol. 37, 20 November 1954, p. 70; William Bittner, 'William Carlos Williams: Muse or Patron Saint', ibid., vol. 40, 7 September 1957, pp. 13–14, 37; John Ciardi, 'The Epic of Place', ibid., vol. 41, 11 October 1958, pp. 37–9).

By the close of the fifties the rumble of the Williams's industry was

1 'American Poetry's Casual Look', *The Times*, 7 January 1965, p. 13.
2 'Measure and its Propaganda', *Cambridge Opinion*, no. 41, October 1965.

not far off in America. In Britain the process worked more slowly.
One might almost call it parsimonious. 'Williams is damned in
London (in the *New Statesman* and *Nation* by G. S. Fraser), as
Charles Olson complained, 'for his "neologisms" and
"barbarisms".'[1] Later on, when *Pictures from Brueghel* came out,
Donald Davie was to write, 'I agree with G. S. Fraser that British
readers cannot *hear* Williams's rhythms . . .' – no reflections made
on British ears – and: 'I do not find myself sorry or indignant that
British readers, by and large, hold on to their misgivings. . . .'[2]
Davie intelligently goes on to discriminate, as Williams's American
critics had mostly refused to do, but perhaps he is over-indulgent to
those 'British readers'. After all, too little of Williams's work had
been available here to put them (granting their existence) in a
position to have either misgivings or anything else short of plain
prejudice.

In addition, there had been little real critical guidance. The
fluctuations of view can be seen from the pages of *The Times
Literary Supplement*. In the issue for 17 September 1954, 'American
Writing Today: Its Independence and Vigour' excludes any
mention of Williams from its section (covering the period 1913–51),
'Opinions at the Time: The Books Reviewed'. Both Edith Sitwell and
W. H. Auden pass over Williams in their account of American
poetry in this issue, though he turns up in 'Poetic Background:
A Period of Consolidation', a 'remarkable talent', seen in dignified
retrospect among 'the older experimentalists'. 'The Vanishing
Avant-Garde' salutes him in passing. A poem, *The Ivy Crown*, also
appears, but he gets most marks for his short stories in 'The Art of
the Short Story: Principles and Practice in the United States'. In
the issue of the *TLS* for 6 November 1959, containing 'The
American Imagination; Its Strength and Scope', Williams is listed
among a heterogeneous 'profusion of talents as yet unnoticed'

1 *Black Mountain Review*, Spring 1955, p. 55.
2 'Two Ways out of Whitman', *Review*, no. 14, December 1964.

(these include Ring Lardner, Thurber, Salinger and Lowell). But in another article Williams's stock is clearly falling: 'We have passed the period of aggressive nativeness in American poetry, the sort of thing illustrated so determinedly (and for British readers so bewilderingly) in the poetry of William Carlos Williams.' This, in 'Eternal Verities: Howlers and Those Who Hear Ancestral Voices', is preluded by a quotation by Richard Wilbur – one which illustrates his cosmopolitan ease – his poetic presence a sign that American verse can now relax. It is curious that Wilbur, for a time, was presented here as *the* significant talent of the American fifties and that his own *Poems, 1943–56* should have preceded Williams's publication by so long.

'It is interesting to note that English readers never "get" Williams, though he is one of our greatest living writers. He is so American in sensibility that the English simply cannot understand what he is saying.' This was James Laughlin replying on the subject of whether there was such a thing as 'a typically American poetry' in *Focus 5: Modern American Poetry* (1950) edited by B. Rajan. Williams's own lengthy answer to the same questionnaire (pp. 187–90) marked his first appearance in England as theorist and polemicist ('Eliot's work stopped the development of American poetry for over twenty years by the tremendous popular success of its mannerisms.'). Williams's verse also received a fair showing – ten page's worth. In contrast with the other principal poets represented, there was no accompanying study on him, presumably – to judge from the editor's apology – because no one could be found on hand to write it.

In 1954 both Marcus Cunliffe's *The Literature of the United States* and Geoffrey Moore's *Penguin Book of Modern American Verse* made room for Williams. The first of these found 'his choppy lines and muttered diction . . . hard for a non-American to understand', conceding, 'he is a good poet, with a wide vision', but critically did not get far beyond the kind of thing typified by 'This has a glistening, child's eye immediacy, and its structure is artfully artless.' Geoffrey Moore presented a sensible though short selection of Williams's verse, a useful bibliography and some fair if apologetic comment: '... it must not be assumed that Dr Williams is unintelligent or quite so much of a barbarian as some of his critics have thought.' Poor Williams! James Southworth's *Some More American Poets*, of the same year, included an elementary essay on Williams. Irvin Ehrenpreis argued convincingly on behalf of Williams in *Departure*,[1] contrasting his buoyant secularism with contemporary British poetry and its tendency 'toward the hesitant, the pathetically ironic, the self-pitying, the desperate.' But it was probably Denis Donoghue's article (extracted in a revised version, p. 383), 'For a Redeeming Language',[2] that represented the first piece of real criticism to appear on Williams in a significant English review, followed a year later by Donald Davie's 'The Legacy of Fenimore Cooper',[3] an assessment of *In the American Grain*. The mimeographed *Migrant*, sent free of charge to those who wanted it by its editor, Gael Turnbull, was simultaneously urging on us not only Williams but poets like Ed Dorn and Robert Creeley who followed him. Hugh Kenner's perceptive 'The Drama of Utterance' appeared in the seventh number in July 1960. The *Review*[4], in a Black Mountain issue, charted the course of American poetry from Williams to Olson, Creeley, Duncan, Levertov. Its editor, Ian Hamilton, in thanking the guest editor, entered a characteristic English proviso with, 'The editorial motive of the *Review* in this project has been documentary rather than, necessarily, a critical one. We believe that the movement ought at least to be known about.' But Williams, at any rate, had been launched by the appearance of *Pictures from Brueghel* the previous year and critics began to write

1 Vol. 4, no. 11, January 1957, pp. 5–10.
2 *Twentieth Century*, vol. 163, no. 976, June 1958, pp. 532–42.
3 *Essays in Criticism*, vol. 9, no. 3, July 1959.
4 No. 10, January 1964.

about him. In *Stratford-upon-Avon Studies* (1965), *American Poetry*, edited by Irvin Ehrenpreis, he emerges as 'perhaps the most successful employer of a diction and an idiom that we can confidently identify as American in the twentieth century'.[1] Tony Tanner's *The Reign of Wonder* (1965) went on to relate Williams to previous American currents, seeing the links between Transcendentalism and Imagism. Geoffrey Moore's *American Literature: A Representative Anthology of American Writing from Colonial Times to the Present*, entering into its second edition in 1966 (it had first appeared two years before) grants Williams 'a Lawrencian acuity of perception' and now finds him, in matters of allusion, 'less akin to Pound than to Wallace Stevens' (why, in particular, Stevens?). Thom Gunn quoted 'an influential English critic, (who was *he*, one wonders) who ten years ago could talk about 'William Carlos Williams's poetry of red brick houses, suburban wives, cheerful standardized interiors'.[2] *Agenda*[3] brought out a Williams number; so did *Cambridge Opinion*.[4]

But enough has been said to indicate the changed atmosphere in England. In the States, with the waters rising throughout the fifties, by the mid to late sixties the dykes were down. Williams's name was made – perhaps a triumph of advertisement as much as one of criticism. The Muse was often appealed to – sometimes with excruciating results – as in Berryman's *An Elegy for W.C.W., the Lovely Man* from *His Toy, His Dream, His Rest*:

Henry in Ireland to Bill underground:
rest well, who worked so hard, who made a good sound
constantly, for so many years:
your high-jinks delighted the continents and our ears:

1 David Ferry 'The Diction of American Poetry', *American Poetry*, 1965, p. 135.
2 'William Carlos Williams', *Encounter*, vol. 25, 25 July 1965, pp. 67–74.
3 Vol. 3, no. 2, October–November 1963.
4 No. 41, October 1965.

you had so many girls your life was a triumph
and you loved your one wife.

Pound had made the classic statement years before in verse
in Canto 78:

and as for the solidity of the white oxen in all this
        perhaps only Dr Williams (Bill Carlos)
                will understand its importance,
    its benediction. He wd | have put in the cart.

A wide range of articles, often good, mostly dull, now
appeared everywhere from the very little magazines to
Publications of the Modern Language Association of America
(some very stolid ones here). Linda Wagner's unexcitingly
competent *The Poetry of William Carlos Williams* (1963) was
the first of a number of studies in a similar, not highly
vivacious idiom. Perhaps the best of these is James Guimond's
*The Art of William Carlos Williams, a Discovery and
Possession of America* (1968), but it remains largely wanting
in discrimination (see for example its solemn treatment of
Williams's plays). On a purely scholarly level must be
mentioned Linda Wagner's 'A Decade of Discovery,
1953–63: Check List of Criticism, William Carlos Williams's
Poetry',[1] and Emily Mitchell Wallace's *A Bibliography of
William Carlos Williams* (1968), a model of fullness and
accuracy with an interesting 'Introductory Note' on
Williams's work. Beside these, there is Hans Galinsky's
indispensable study of Williams's European reception,
'William Carlos Williams: Eine vergleichende Studie zur
Aufnahme seines Werkes in Deutschland, England und
Italien (1912–65)'.[2]

1 *Twentieth-Century Literature*, vol. 10, January 1965, pp. 166–9.
2 *Jahrbuch für Amerikastudien*, vol. 11, 1966, pp. 96–175, and vol. 12, 1967,
pp. 167–205.

At the beginning of Williams criticism we have Rosenfeld's vision of his replacing the other-worldliness of Albert P. Ryder. In later writing on Williams there is one often penetrating account (see p. 373) that does something very similar: this is chapter seven of J. Hillis Miller's *Poets of Reality* (1966) – his excellent volume in the Twentieth-Century Views series, *William Carlos Williams*, came out in the same year. According to Miller, 'If the disappearance of God is presupposed by much Victorian poetry, the death of God is the starting point for many twentieth-century writers.' And so his framework for Williams is 'the journey beyond nihilism toward a poetry of reality'. With the appearance in the twentieth century of 'the new art', things appear to be taking a turn for the better: 'The new art which gradually emerges in the work of Yeats, Eliot, Thomas and Stevens reaches full development in the poetry of William Carlos Williams.'[1] It is not so much a question of value judgements on individual poems – indeed, Miller seems oddly shy about making them and he rarely follows out the entire course of a Williams poem; it is rather that Williams receives his honours for the role he plays in a new myth of re-association of sensibility ('beyond subjectivism and dualism') that puts right the old one, derived from Eliot, about dissociation. Miller quotes Williams's 'The light | for all time shall outspeed | the thunder crack' (*Asphodel*), and concludes with: 'This radiant promise is the climax of Williams's writing, and the climax too of the development so far of twentieth-century poetry.' This seems an absurd way of looking at art, not least because it ignores the uniqueness of talents very different from Williams. In the first of two talks delivered at the University of Parma in March 1969[2] Jerome Mazzaro

1 p. 1.
2 Both reprinted in *Intrepid* (Buffalo), no. 17, 1970.

argues intelligently against Miller, in terms different from my own, urging that he presents Williams as holding to a given and static position far more philosophically than in fact he does.

Poetry itself – as distinct from literary tributes to 'the lovely man' – showed the clear impact of Williams's example with the emergence of those writers who are associated with Black Mountain College, in the intense hesitancies of Robert Creeley's early pamphlets (first brought together in *The Whip* of 1957), and in the more eloquent verse of Robert Duncan, whose poem, *Essay At War*, takes its central figure, of poetry as a state of war, from Williams's preface to *The Wedge* (see p. 140). The title poem of Denise Levertov's *Overland to the Islands* (1958) reads almost like a manifesto for this asymmetrical type of poetry with a movement that is 'intently haphazard', the intentness rectifying the apparent casualness:

Let's go – much as that dog goes,
intently haphazard. The
Mexican light on a day that
'smells like autumn in Connecticut'
makes iris ripples on his
black gleaming fur – and that too
is as one would desire – a radiance
consorting with the dance.
              Under his feet
rocks and mud, his imagination, sniffing,
engaged in its perceptions – dancing
edgeways, there's nothing
the dog disdains on his way,
nevertheless he
keeps moving, changing

I saw the Figure 5 in Gold, painting by Charles Demuth.

An Apple, a Boulder, a Mountain, photograph by Edward Steichen.

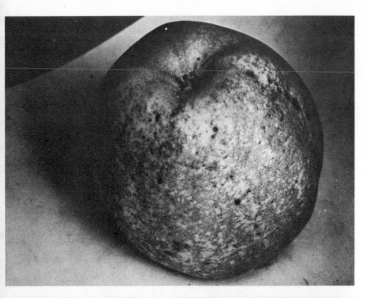

After Sir Christopher Wren, painting by Charles Demuth.

Left. *Flowers, Cyclamen,* painting by Charles Demuth.

Bucks County Barn, painting by Charles Sheeler.

Classic Landscape, painting by Charles Sheeler.

pace and approach but
not direction – 'every step an arrival'.

Behind these three writers stands the late Charles Olson as
well as Williams. His essay, 'Projective Verse' (1950), was a
basic document for them (as it was for Williams who
reprinted part of it in chapter fifty of his *Autobiography*).
'Projective Verse' looks for the writer who will 'put himself
in the open', composing verse 'as though not the eye but
the ear was to be its measurer ... the ear, which is so close
to the mind that it is the mind's, that it has the mind's
speech'. Williams's frequent and perhaps abortive attempts
to define 'measure' (see p. 313) concern this point, and with
his three-ply verse, based on a 'variable foot', he hoped he
had solved the matter. But, as Donald Wesling has it, 'it is
more likely that it is the nature of this measure to be elusive,
requiring that each poetic utterance authenticate its form as
it proceeds'.[1] The extent of Williams's poetic influence
leaves room for a book in itself (M. L. Rosenthal's *The New
Poets* (1967) prepares the ground), and the influence shows up
in writers as distinct as James Laughlin, Robert Lowell –
particularly in *Life Studies* (1959) recalling Williams's poems
about his parents, *Adam* and *Eve* – and George Oppen whose
The Materials (1962), *This In Which* (1965), *Of Being
Numerous* (1969) resume a poetic career mysteriously
interrupted after *Discrete Series* (1934), a volume that itself
owes a still earlier debt to Williams. Laughlin (as Lowell
acknowledges – see p. 367) was also an early transmitter –
his *A Small Book of Poems* (1948) is dedicated to Williams –
and the poem, *Easter in Pittsburgh* (in *Some Natural Things*,
1945), develops out of Williams a method of dealing with
the American upper class family milieu that perhaps

1 'The Inevitable Ear', *English Literary History*, vol. 36, no. 3, September 1969.

influenced Lowell's own *Life Studies*. Williamsite procedures have, of course, changed the tone of most of the poetry magazines both in England and America. The results are often as abysmal as the Audenesque and the Eliotese that preceded them. If Williams is to be of real use to the poet at this time, it will not come about from that attitude of a new chauvinism (consorting oddly, or perhaps not so oddly, with the politics of the New Left) that seems to be seeping through American literary life, but from a genuine appreciation of how his best work has found new measures for 'the mind's speech'.

Spring and All

Neil Myers

'William Carlos Williams's *Spring and All*', *Modern Language Quarterly*, vol. 26, no. 2   1965

Spring and All, published in 1923, is William Carlos Williams's first major achievement and 'one of the most important volumes of modern poetry' of the twenties, 'a veritable "book of examples" of the principles (implicit and explicit) that governed the making of it. . . .' The book is an intensely stylized set of exercises in reduction, often intentionally confusing and difficult; in it Williams perfected a technique of ordering objects into 'a still life of a special kind . . . in which progress is clearly seen either in spatial and temporal movement or in symbolic pattern'.[1] But to call this poetry 'still life', even 'of a special kind', is misleading; it is anything but still. It consists of consciously formal, almost geometrical, arrangements of hard-edged things, but it is also full of powerful inward tension, of strongly contrasting elements put together in coherent, graceful patterns under great stress. It suggests energy meeting forms which remain facile and elegant while being barely able to hold their content.

The basic importance of *Spring and All* is that it is Williams's first major study of the relation of formal art to the various forms of human and natural energy that he would explore for the rest of his career. The book makes particularly explicit Williams's fascination with forms of violence – age, inarticulate pain, frustration, exploitation, urban disintegration, death – that the pastoral mood of earlier poems half concealed. The real change is that what Williams now poses against violence is no longer largely a matter of reported images – the grace of 'Wu Kee; young, agile, clear-eyed | And clean-limbed, his muscles ripple | Under the thin blue shirt' (*The*

1 Frederick J. Hoffman, 'Williams and His Muses', *Poetry*, no. 84, 1954, pp. 23–4.

Young Laundryman) – or of outright ecstatic pronouncements of 'Joy! Joy!' (*Complaint*).[1] Williams still draws on the vitality of commonplace men and things, but they are made almost elemental by his strenuous forms. The lines of a rose, a piece of jazz, the order and disorder of a downtown wilderness are all isolated from their full natural background, cut through and viewed in heightened sections, so that bits of words, phrases, objects and complex scenes are drawn into a bewildering but dynamic whole. In large part, Williams's effort is to fight stock response by the cubist technique of exploding things into hard, fascinating, independently viable pieces, and rearranging them into 'spatial and temporal' patterns whose first recognizable quality is an utterly new rhythm and coherence. The end, even in the most despairing poems of the book, *To an Old Jaundiced Woman* and *To Elsie* pp. 268, 270,[2] is a mood of exuberance, of sudden enthusiastic delight over the imagination's ability to master violence.

Throughout *Spring and All*, Williams is interested in the kinds of violence that work on his immediate world. Violence can mean 'J.P.M.' (in *At the Faucet of June*, p. 251), raping a native Persephone with his quick robber-baron solutions, his alien art, 'A Veronese or | perhaps a Rubens –' and his 'cars ... about | the finest on | the market today –.' It can mean failing to see things as they are, and so not coping with actual fragmentation and destruction – the 'Black winds' that

> from the north
> enter black hearts. Barred from
> seclusion in lilies they strike
> to destroy –

the stock response that is dangerous in any form because it cannot handle the real source of energy, the 'strident voices, heat | quickened, built of waves | Drunk with goats or pavements' (*The Black Winds*, p. 245). It can mean a surrealistic moon world horribly resembling the world of daylight but sucked of 'juice | and pulp . . . where peaches hang | recalling death's | long-promised symphony' (*Rigamarole*, p. 278). It can mean the chaos implicit wherever 'energy

1 *Sour Grapes*, in *Collected Earlier Poems*, pp. 204, 199.
2 The page references are to *Spring and All* in *Collected Earlier Poems*.

in vacuo' occurs, especially in cities – in the anarchic subway-poster collages of *Rapid Transit*:

Somebody dies every four minutes
in New York State –

behind them the innate violence of nature, the threat of absurdity:

To hell with you and your poetry –
You will rot and be blown
through the next solar system
with the rest of the gases –

AXIOMS

Don't get killed

Careful Crossings Campaign
Cross Crossings Cautiously
(p. 282)

It can mean normal death (*To an Old Jaundiced Woman*) which, in one stark, terrible vision of natural process, is at the center of the book:

I can't die

– moaned the old
jaundiced woman
rolling her
saffron eyeballs

I can't die
I can't die
(p. 268)

Everywhere in *Spring and All* Williams assumes that 'destruction and creation | are simultaneous'. The fundamental material of all life is always unpredictable and dangerous, like 'the crowd . . . alive, venomous', the 'dynamic mob' for whom movies, ball games, anti-Semitism, 'the Inquisition, the | Revolution' alike are art (*Light Becomes Darkness*, p. 266, and *At the Ball Game*, p. 284). Human fertility can appear in pagan 'drivers for grocers or taxi-drivers' who become

satyrs in the spring, 'horned lilac blossoms | in their caps – or over
one ear | . . . Dirty . . . | vulgarity raised to the last power', destructive,

> They have stolen them
> broken the bushes apart
> with a curse for the owner –

> sneering and delightful:

> adorned with blossoms

> Out of their sweet heads
> dark kisses – rough faces
> (*Horned Purple*, p. 273)

Or, without control (in *To Elsie*), it can become barren, grotesque,
a 'numbed terror | under some hedge of choke-cherry | or viburnum',
part of a social collapse that leaves only a nameless sexual idiocy, a
woman 'expressing with broken | brain the truth about us | . . . as if
the earth under our feet | were | an excrement of some sky'; so that
imagination, art, the ability to respond to nature are meaningless.
There is 'something | . . . only in isolate flecks' and an industrialized
insanity –

> Somehow
> it seems to destroy us

> No one
> to witness
> and adjust, no one to drive the car
> (p. 270)

Even the introductory *Spring and All* centers around a birth that is
only deceptively limited to the small things of a 'dazed spring',
'lifeless . . . sluggish' and trivial in a world of 'waste', of 'broad,
muddy fields | brown with dried weeds' (p. 241). Williams always
finds birth awesome and irresistible; later, in *Catastrophic Birth* (*The
Wedge*, 1944), he equates it with the eruption of Mount Pelée. In the
context of the whole book, spring's 'stark dignity of entrance', the
rooting and awakening that quietly impinge on the observer, setting
off the static, deadly 'contagious hospital' and creating constant
'clarity, outline of leaf' (p. 241), implies a power that anyone interest-

ed in unity and grace must both follow and resist. *Spring and All* is a
carefully chosen title; it means energy that demands an equivalent
human response. *The Farmer* must cope with it by becoming an
'artist figure | . . . composing | – antagonist', a dramatic hero 'pacing
through the rain | among his blank fields . . . | in his head | the harvest
already planted', imposing order when the dynamic world around
him is ready for it:

On all sides
the world rolls coldly away:
black orchards
darkened by the March clouds –
leaving room for thought.
(p. 243)

The problem is to establish control, to find things, to order them and
one's reaction to them, to resist 'the old mode' and 'cling firmly to
the advance' (*The Black Winds*). Like the farmer 'artist . . . antagonist',
one must come up against the truth which is always present, always
new, the bare 'dashes of cold rain', and thereby *plan*.

The critical danger is stock response, which *Spring and All* attacks
by attempting to formalize the energy of things wherever it occurs.
Imagist, objectivist, cubist, whatever one calls his techniques, Williams
sees them as essential to recognize and deal with the energy we live in
and represent. We can choose between 'writings' 'clean' art or stock
response and death:

Wrigley's, appendicitis, John Marin:
skyscraper soup –

Either that or a bullet!
(*Young Love*, p. 253)

Thus in every poem here, the ordered vitality which means art is made
to appear where normal dulled response would take something for
granted as trivial or static. A line beginning at a rose petal penetrates
'the Milky Way' (*The Rose*, p. 250); the ordinary skyline of the city
becomes

     a crown for her head with
castles upon it, skyscrapers

filled with nut-chocolates

        dovetame winds –

stars of tinsel
(*Flight to the City*, p. 244)

and a casual 'nameless spectacle' on a nameless road takes on 'supreme importance' (*The Right of Way*, p. 258). This is the real source of the internal event that marks Williams's best poetry. In the famous, extremely reduced *Red Wheelbarrow*, an inconspicuous scene is brought to expression by focusing on relationships: on the barrow 'glazed with rain | water', asserting itself at the heart of the scene and pulling everything together; and on an outright introductory statement of significance, 'so much depends', which, in view of the trivial objects, barrow and chickens, seems firmly impertinent (p. 277). The process is clearest in the later *Between Walls*, in which 'the broken | pieces of a green | bottle' are brought to life by a central verb, made to 'shine' amid conventional death, the cinders of

the back wings
of the

hospital where
nothing

will grow. . . .
(p. 343)

In such reduced poetry the image, centered clearly in precise architectural arrangements of objects, means self-expression which reveals real order; like the 'bridge stanchions' of *The Agonized Spires*, it can finally 'knit peace' and bring meaning and 'rest' to an 'untamed' world (p. 262). To isolate centers of life in words and things is to restore their original force, despite the conventionality that threatens to make them meaningless. Similarly, later in his short stories, Williams's point would be the assertion of life against the most grotesque conditions of slum life, in a tough, starved, six-month-old infant or in an adolescent *Girl with the Pimply Face*. In the last poems it would be the expression of the artist's own vitality in the face of death.

The best poems of *Spring and All* attack stock response through sharply dramatic internal movement. In *Death the Barber* the process literally means a momentary defeat of death. Most of the poem summarizes death in a way that makes it inhuman and macabre. Death is like a barber, a barber tells Williams, 'cutting my | life with | sleep to trim | my hair'; it's 'just | a moment'; we 'die | every night', when we are apart from our usual selves; death means second childhood, baldness, 'old men | with third | sets of teeth', etc. But the unpredictable reality suddenly appears as Williams is talking,

to the cue

of an old man
who said
at the door –
Sunshine today!

for which
death shaves
him twice
a week
(p. 264)

Typically, the brief quiet scene and the strongest of the terse two-beat lines – 'Sunshine today!' – turn the poem upside down. The old man approaching death is a reality, not a distant curiosity; he carries 'Joy!' as certain as the gold needle of the sun which the ministering doctor sees against the winter 'misery' and 'vomiting' of the earlier *Complaint* (p. 199). The *fact* of the old man's delight humanizes everything by forcing attention on concrete life; it makes the barber himself seem a sentimentalist, genuinely like 'death'. The last stanza is openly ironic: death remains strange and frightening, but it is no longer a game for complacent metaphor-makers.

To Have Done Nothing suggests the basis of Williams's attempt to subvert stock response in *Spring and All*. The poem is an elegant, formalized wordplay which changes the value of ordinary words; like the 1915 *Portrait of a Lady*, it describes *not* doing something, in this case directly doing 'nothing'. At most, doing 'nothing' means death; at least, the lack of commitment to ordinary virtues. Williams makes it a tangible, precisely ordered, rhythmic act. His images are sentence parts, fragmented over the lines, so that each part takes on a weight far beyond its normal stress:

No that is not it
nothing that I have done
nothing
I have done

is made up of
nothing
and the diphthong

ae

together with
the first person
singular
indicative

of the auxiliary
verb
to have

everything
I have done
is the same. . . .

The poem begins with a sudden outright denial and goes on to talk about its lack of content; but content lies in the actual concentration of negatives. The basic words and phrases become meaningful by isolation, by continued, almost hypnotic rhythmic stress and repetition: with the title, 'nothing' occurs four times in seven brief lines, and 'I have done' twice in four lines; at every repetition, context and color of word and phrase shift, emphasis becomes stronger. The 'ae', at once a phonetic sign and a cry, rises both naturally and unexpectedly out of the sentence rhythm and syntax; because it occupies a whole stanza, it adds emotional stress to the general feeling of undefined but powerful intention. Gradually, the word 'nothing' becomes as substantial as any visual image; against it, a conventional definition of 'everything', which is 'the same' and from the beginning 'not it',

involving the
moral
physical
and religious

codes

seems slack, stock and banal. What Williams wants is not to define a
word but, like Gertrude Stein, to make it hard, colored, particular
and expressive in its literal, grammatical context, by means of
ordered rhythmic play – like a fragment of a sign, a newspaper or
the hands of a clock, on a Braque canvas. Forms which fail to do this,
to give things their concreteness, to make them alive – even seemingly
abstract units of ordinary sentences – forms which remain just 'codes',
lead to chaos:

for everything
and nothing
are synonymous
when

energy *in vacuo*
has the power
of confusion

while to ignore 'everything', 'to | have done nothing' in the face of
official pressures, simply to avoid stock response – to respond to
sunshine, watch a wheelbarrow or play with language – is a crucial
step away from 'confusion' and toward art:

which only to
have done nothing
can make
perfect
(p. 247)

In *The Right of Way*, Williams develops an experience of idleness,
of the delight of doing nothing. Nothing literally happens; Williams
drives along

passing with my mind
on nothing in the world

but the right of way
I enjoy on the road by

virtue of the law –

But the 'law' means not restriction but the right to exploit rather
than suffer normal experience. Williams sees a brief 'nameless
spectacle':

an elderly man who
smiled and looked away

to the north past a house –
a woman in blue

who was laughing and
leaning forward to look up

into the man's half
averted face

and a boy of eight who was
looking at the middle of

the man's belly
at a watchchain –

Like *The Red Wheelbarrow*, the poem ties together seemingly dis-
parate objects; it has a similar enigmatic ascription of 'supreme
importance', and a similar sense of a luminous event reduced to
essentials, incomplete but final and expressive. The point is partly
the freedom to observe, to draw art and order from the most basic,
seemingly trivial and capricious fragments. Partly it is the discovery
of relationships, of nameless, almost unindividual people stripped to
the essence of a common concrete act, committed to each other,
concentrating, 'laughing' in a perfect moment of delight. When the
whole process is repeated at the end, it becomes a response to a
conventional problem of value:

Why bother where I went?
for I went spinning on the

four wheels of my car
along the wet road until

I saw a girl with one leg
over the rail of a balcony
(p. 258)

Like a period, the still watching girl balances and ends the poet's
movement. The 'supreme importance' of the whole 'nameless
spectacle' is that, if approached without preconception and with an
eye for their full assertion, things fit into an equilibrium that absorbs
the chaos of life and constitutes the basis of art.

Meaning resides in equilibrium; it can be established even where
the material is most fragmented, conventionally hopeless. Several
poems of *Spring and All* study a world emphatically broken up; they
suggest a strenuous conflict between the artist-antagonist and
equally antagonistic materials. In *The Eyeglasses* it is simply a matter
of visual garbage strewn about,

                    the candy
with melon flowers that open

about the edge of refuse
proclaiming without accent
the quality of the farmer's

shoulders and his daughter's
accidental skin,

Against it are 'eyeglasses' that can interpret with a 'favourable |
distortion . . . | that see everything and remain | related to mathe-
matics'. Artificial and commonplace, 'in the most practical frame
of | brown celluloid made to | represent tortoiseshell', they discover
the means of art:

A letter from the man who
wants to start a new magazine
made of linen

They lie amid a repose of ordinary forms ready for organization,
emblems of quiet depth, of potentiality for compelling violence,
'tranquilly Titicaca' (p. 256).

In other poems, the process is less tranquil. In *The Agonized Spires*
it is a problem of painfully making sense out of an urban explosion in

which everything is tormented and flowing, caught in 'thrusts of the sea | Waves of steel | from swarming backstreets'. The poem alternates images of roughly textured disorder with equally violent images of insane urban conglomeration, like a neon sign flashing on and off:

Lights
speckle
El Greco
lakes
in renaissance
twilight
with triphammers

which pulverize
nitrogen
of old pastures
to dodge
motorcars
with arms and legs –

The order that rises out of this chaos is, like the rest of the poem, harsh and linear, a strong vertical thrust upward out of the 'aggregate | . . . untamed'. The 'but | of agonized spires' suddenly appears pitted against and channelling the 'encapsulating | irritants' below, and, in the masculine, forward movement of the poem, 'knits peace'

where bridge stanchions
rest
certainly
piercing
left ventricles
with long
sunburnt fingers
(p. 262)

The imagery still describes pain and tension, but the 'stanchions' hold the collage together as they hold a suspension bridge, at once at 'rest' and under enormous tension, enigmatically pointing somewhere else, in difficult dynamic repose.

The difficulty of forging such equilibrium, of bringing living things under formal rhythmic control that preserves their full liveliness, is the real problem of *Spring and All*. The artist is an 'antagonist' basically because he is caught in a struggle both to keep from being overwhelmed by natural energy, and to keep art from deadening it: hence Williams's constant references to the traditional materials of art and to artists, from El Greco, Veronese, Rubens, Juan Gris, John Marin, Tolstoy, Pound's *Song of the Bowmen of Shu*, to movie houses, passion plays and 'the cave of | *Les Trois Frères*' (*The Avenue of Poplars*, p. 281). The artist's most explicit appearance is as the jazz musician of *Shoot it Jimmy!* – a poem put immediately after *To an Old Jaundiced Woman* like an alternative, his enthusiastic vitality opposed to her lust for death. The poem is an assertion of eagerness, of the sheer joy of self-expression; it rejects any stock response, any 'sheet stuff', and moves constantly forward with intense syncopated rhythms and a slang sense that catches up all clichés in an easy metaphorical language of its own:

Our orchestra
is the cat's nuts –

Banjo jazz
with a nickelplated

amplifier to
soothe

the savage beast –

Here, in the center of the book, chaos is given speech, measure, caught unobtrusively and fully up in the momentum of language. To 'Get the rhythm' is to 'soothe | the savage beast'. The jazzman has the artist's natural equilibrium: his talk is that of violence contained. Like the farmer, he is riding the flow of energy that threatens to overwhelm other poems:

Man
gimme the key

and lemme loose –
I make 'em crazy

with my harmonies –
Shoot it Jimmy

Through the ability of art to use 'nothing', to put fragments together and improvise on them, to 'imitate' and control chaos, the jazzman emerges as unique, individual and *found*:

Nobody
Nobody else

but me –
They can't copy it
(p. 269)

Equally suggestive of an explicit conception of art are the flower poems that appear in the book. Like the collage poems *Composition* and *The Eyeglasses*, they are clearly painterly, especially the abstract, meditative *The Rose*, written in imitation of a Juan Gris etching – an anticipation of the great 1930 *Crimson Cyclamen*, a memorial to Charles Demuth. The poem studies a rose petal's natural lines, clean and dynamic enough to restrain and order violence. It begins with a statement about stock response, like an apparent surrender: 'The rose is obsolete'; it ends as

The fragility of the flower
unbruised
penetrates space

and calmly masters the absurd 'solar system' into which, in *Rapid Transit*, poet and poetry will 'be blown . . . | with the rest of the gases'. The flower's 'edge' is like an artifact which 'cuts without cutting', and Williams immediately relates it to human artifacts, its 'double facet | cementing the grooved | columns of air' like a classical design. It 'renews | itself in metal or porcelain'; as it becomes 'Sharper, neater, more cutting', it is 'figured in majolica – | the broken plate | glazed with a rose'; then it suggests 'copper roses | steel roses', like the product of an effortless craftsman:

Crisp, worked to defeat
laboredness – fragile
plucked, moist, half-raised
cold, precise, touching

Like a mathematical design, the poem moves continually forward, neatly cutting, circling, and doubling on itself. Stanza form and language emphasize constant stopping, self-questioning; the line ends abruptly 'somewhere', then quietly reappears, always firmer and wider in scope. 'The edge | . . . renews'

itself in metal or porcelain –

whither? It ends –

But if it ends
the start is begun
so that to engage roses
becomes a geometry – . . .

From the petal's edge a line starts
that being of steel
infinitely fine, infinitely
rigid penetrates
the Milky Way
without contact – lifting
from it – neither hanging
nor pushing

This forward, comprehensive movement is part of an attempt to identify the nature of the power of art, at once a craftsman's principle of 'geometry', the

favorable
distortion of eyeglasses
that see everything and remain
related to mathematics –
(p. 256)

and 'love', which appears suddenly at the center of the poem, an expression of a final harmonious 'end', of controlled, ordered strength which brings everything relevant together:

The rose carried weight of love
but love is at an end – of roses
It is at the edge of the
petal that love waits
(*The Rose*, p. 249)

Even in the slight final poem of the book, *The Wildflower*, the theme
is implicitly the same: the 'Black eyed susan | rich orange | round
the purple core' is more powerful than the 'Crowds' of white daisies
because it expresses violence turned by natural art into harmony and
strength. Typically, Williams's imagery is at once social, sexual and
a description of art: 'the white daisy | is not enough':

Crowds are white
as farmers
who live poorly

But you
are rich
in savagery –

Arab
Indian
dark woman.
(p. 287)

Many of the poems of *Spring and All* are slight, and in many ways
they seem to come close to the dehumanization frequently ascribed
to Williams.[1] The artist as active, subjective, personal presence does
not dominate the book, but the *creating* artist certainly does, sometimes explicitly, always implicitly. *Spring and All* may be impersonal,
but it is not dehumanized; it is simply neither romantic nor expression-
istic. The point about a poem like *To an Old Jaundiced Woman* is not
that it is lacking in pity, but that it evokes ordered art out of a
commonplace scene which, if left to stock response, would be
genuinely oppressive. To hear 'I can't die' or 'Shoot it Jimmy!' is to
face, through Williams's stylization, strong feelings of horror or
delight before a human reality.

Williams's intention in *Spring and All* is to develop an art that can
draw not just 'meaning' but 'Joy!' from the energy of commonplace
events. This is why he attempts to imitate rigorously the effort of
cubist painters to break up old patterns and reorder them – something
prefigured by Sterne but never accomplished successfully before this

1 See William Van O'Connor, *Sense and Sensibilty in Modern Poetry*, 1963,
p. 64.

by a poet writing in English. This is the reason *Spring and All* is Williams's most stylized, reduced work; never again would he be so intent on reproducing the structure of painting throughout a single book, although he would continue to use painterly themes. After *Spring and All*, Williams moves toward both maintaining the clear rhythmic eternality he had achieved here and developing 'measured' looseness and flow of structure and intense emotionality of theme – in long, expansive poems like *An Elegy for D. H. Lawrence*, *Two Pendants: for the Ears*, *The Desert Music*; or in sudden brief visions of life, reduced to essentials and deeply inward, like the beautiful *Young Woman at a Window* of *Adam and Eve and the City* or *The Wood-thrush* of *Pictures from Brueghel*. *Spring and All* establishes the central themes for most of this poetry. It does away with the vague sentimentality of the earlier books and establishes the identity of art, love, and the dance and their struggle with universal violence. The struggle is brought to a climax in *Paterson*, where Faitoute dies without 'the language', the ability to

Burst it asunder
break through to the fifty words
necessary –
(*Flight to the City*, p. 244)

and where, in the great last *Paterson*, Book Five,

> the Jew
> in the pit
>
> among his fellows
> when the indifferent chap
> with the machine gun
> was spraying the heap

can use 'necessary' words as an expression of consummate love, a final defiance of chaos:

he had not yet been hit
but smiled
comforting his companions
(v, ii, p. 260)

His act is treated as a full expression of the dance of art, of the cubist effort to 'shatter' the 'tyranny of the image' and build new 'designs'. *Spring and All* is Williams's first full description of those designs, forty years earlier, and it is full of sunlight.

(285–301)

In the American Grain

Donald Davie

from 'The Legacy of Fenimore Cooper', *Essays in Criticism*,
vol. 9, no. 3   1959

In the American Grain, by William Carlos Williams, had a *succès d'estime* when it first appeared in 1925, but in common with Williams's poetry attracted few readers until after the last war; in the last few years the concerted effort in America to do belated justice to Williams has resulted in this book getting the classic status of a paperback edition. (This is quite unironical; the discrimination shown by the paperback publishers is extraordinary and impressive.) It cannot be long before the current American vogue for Williams produces British reverberations; and already, in fact, there has been a laudatory essay in *The Twentieth Century* by Denis Donoghue. Better late than never; and a British edition of *In the American Grain* cannot be deferred much longer. . . .
(222)

The *genre* may be defined as 'impressionistic history'; a bastard kind, of which the only examples we are likely to recall belong to sub-literature. The reader may be forgiven for fearing, on the one hand, self-consciously 'fine-writing', on the other, as in the historical novel, fact eked out by fiction, and imagination in difficulties sinking groggily to rest on antiquarian fact. As for the first charge, self-consciously poetical writing can be found in Williams, in for instance the section 'De Soto and the New World', where the personification of the American earth as a woman seems to be, here as in Hart Crane's *The Bridge*, an irresistible temptation to roseate muddles of both thought and language (like the Irish Cathleen-na-Houlihan); but this is only a temporary lapse by Williams. . . .
(223)

Anyone who asks suspiciously how much of Williams is historical fact, how much is interpretive fiction, will come up with the unexpected answer that far more is fact than he had supposed, and fact of the irrefragable kind; unacknowledged wholesale quotation or minimal adaptation from sources. Williams says exultantly of his chapter given to John Paul Jones, 'Battle Between the Bon Homme Richard and the Serapis', 'no word is my own'. This whole section, in fact, is a scissors-and-paste job on Jones's own dispatches; and the same is true in only slightly less degree of many of the other sections, for instance those on Cotton Mather and Benjamin Franklin (see *Selected Letters* of Williams, p. 187). . . .
(223–4)

In Williams's case, the closeness to authentic documents immediately determines the quality of the style. As Williams says of *In the American Grain,*

The book is as much a study in styles of writing as anything
else. I tried to write each chapter in the style most germane to
its sources, or at least the style which seemed to me appropriate
to the material. To this end, where possible, I copied and
used the original writings. . . . I did this with malice aforethought
to prove the truth of the book, since the originals fitted into
it without effort on my part, perfectly, leaving not a seam.[1]

In other words, the governing principle of the style is delicate *pastiche*; and here once again is an instructive parallel with Pound's *Cantos*, where the medley of styles and the pervasiveness of pastiche as stylistic principle – so far from proving, as they are taken to prove, Pound's dilettantism – prove his determination to hew to the contours of his subject, to 'prove the truth' of his book. . . . One is reminded of those American history *Cantos* of Pound which are similarly a catena of snippets from Jefferson, Benton and the Adamses; and of Williams, as of Pound, it is more rational to complain that the historical fact is reproduced unlicked and unmodulated than that it is 'fictionalized' out of usefulness. . . .
(224)

1 *Selected Letters*, p. 187.

As for *genre*, if the historical romance has come down in the world since *Waverley*, we need not suppose that this represents any scruples on the part of the public about a confounding of the roles of poet and historiographer. In fact, at a time when the layman seems to see the academic historiographer leaving less and less margin for imaginative interpretation of the material he presents, it may well seem that the historical romance and the historical novel are due for a revival. But in any case novels are not what we are confronted with; and if the genre of impressionistic history appears to be a peculiarly American form, there are interesting reasons why this should be so. It makes some sense to say that if Williams confounds the roles of poet and historian, he does so in the interest of the larger synthesis of *myth*. That too of course is a word of ill-omen: where 'the American myth' doesn't mean bluntly 'the American self-deception', it may seem to promise nothing better than yeasty heavings from the Jungian unconscious. But some fears may be allayed if we take 'myth' to mean, for present purposes, no more than what Lawrence sought to uncover in his *Studies in Classic American Literature*. What Lawrence seems to have recognized is that, just because American history begins after the invention of print, printed literature has played a part in the forming of the national self-consciousness such as in older cultures has been played by folklore and legend. It is not hard to see that this is so. It isn't necessary, for instance, to share the Lawrencian mystique, or to adopt the Lawrencian rhetoric (of racial blood-flows, and the rest of it), in order to agree with and make use of his perception, in his essay on Cooper, that the fate of the red man is an unhealed and perhaps unhealable wound in the white-American psyche. Even this language may be thought too figurative for comfort. If so, consider merely Albert Keiser's *The Indian in American Literature*, a 'standard work' of painstaking diligence but strikingly inept in whatever approaches critical judgement. Keiser lists painstakingly all the even minimally serious treatments of the Indian question in American literature from Captain John Smith to Edna Ferber; and nothing is so remarkable as the all but unanimity with which writers before and after Cooper have taken the part of the red man. Of one of the books that Keiser considers, Helen Hunt Jackson's *Ramona* (1884), Carey McWilliams remarks in his *Southern California Country* (1946):

What is astonishing is the presence in the legend of an
element of masochism, with the Americans, who
manufactured the legend, taking upon themselves full
responsibility for the criminal mistreatment of the Indian and
completely exonerating the Franciscans.[1]

What is here said in relation to the California mission Indians seems
equally true, in the light of Keiser's book, of the white man's attitude
to all Indians elsewhere, at least as represented in the white man's
literature. 'Masochism' is probably inaccurate, certainly over-
emphatic; what there is, however, is a sense of guilt, or a need to have
such a sense. And the evidence for this is so overwhelming that, so
far as literature is concerned, the question doesn't arise whether the
guilt is justified; justified or not, the feeling apparently exists, and so
persistently that one can only suppose it satisfies a profound imaginative demand. The myth exists, and is infinitely more powerful than
the reality (which anyway there is now no way of knowing, and
perhaps there never was – for how could a white man know the
reality of the red man's life before the white man knew him?);
therefore any writer on the Indians, which is to say any writer on
American history, has to come to terms with Fenimore Cooper's
Indian, has to take him on Cooper's terms. It is far too late to try to
explode the myth – at least in imaginative writing. The American
imagination has invested too much in Chingachgook; and its need
to do so can never be allayed or met by a writer who refuses to
acknowledge the investment. We need mean no more than this when
we speak of the myth of the Indian, and applaud Lawrence as the
first to decipher it.

There is no better index of the sophistication of American criticism,
and of the worth of that sophistication at its best, than the ability of
American critics to incorporate and utilize Lawrence's insights, so
'prophetic', so intransigent as they are. One suspects that British
criticism, placed in the same or an analogous situation, would not
have coped so well. I take almost at random a formulation from the
Preface to the thoroughly hard-headed *Virgin Land* of Henry Nash
Smith, which has the subtitle, 'The American West as Symbol and
Myth':

The terms 'myth' and 'symbol' occur so often in the following pages that the reader deserves some warning about them. I use the words to designate larger or smaller units of the same kind of thing, namely, an intellectual construction that fuses concept and emotion into an image. The myths and symbols with which I deal have the further characteristic of being collective representations rather than the work of a single mind. I do not mean to raise the question whether such products of the imagination accurately reflect empirical fact. They exist on a different plane. But ... they sometimes exert a decided influence on practical affairs.

Smith's work is one of several examples that could be cited to justify Richard Chase in his recent book, *The American Novel and its Tradition* (itself a distinguished example of the usefulness of the 'mythic' attitude), when he writes:

Lawrence's approach to American literature, which may be described variously as historical, cultural or mythic, has been congenial to those modern critics who have not devoted themselves merely to textual analysis. The recent critical effort has responded to the tone of the times, and the times have been all in favour of the reassessment of the American past and a consolidation of knowledge and opinions about it. ... History has fully justified the critics involved in this first period of reassessment and consolidation.

This is pertinent to any consideration of *In the American Grain* and/or Janet Lewis's *The Invasion*, because they can equally well be regarded as works of critical 'reassessment and consolidation'; and as themselves supplements to the myth of American history. In particular Williams in part, and Janet Lewis almost entirely, are concerned with that part of the myth which has to do with the fate of the Redskin.

Williams's debt to Lawrence is obvious, though I don't know that it has ever been acknowledged. It extends much further than the similarity of style illustrated from 'The Founding of Quebec'. The long section, 'Père Sebastian Rasles', which begins with magnificent gusto and audacity among the expatriates of Paris of the twenties and then proceeds, through a conversation with Valéry Larbaud, into a comparison between the French Catholic missions in Arcadia and the Protestants in New England in the seventeenth century, is the place where the Lawrencian note is struck and sustained in content as well as in manner:

He would not suffer the contrite Indians to lay their hands upon him, as the Catholic fathers in the north had done, but drew back and told them to address themselves to God alone. Ah, very fine, you say. But it is very ugly – and it is *that* which has persisted: afraid to touch! But being forced to it every day by passion, by necessity – a devil of duplicity has taken possession of us.[1]

It is hard to think of another instance in which the Lawrencian vocabulary, along with a centrally Lawrencian idea, has been taken over to other than calamitous effect. The 'touching', the readiness to risk that intimacy, is made the basis of all that Williams claims for Rasles:

He was a great MAN. Reading his letters, it is a river that brings sweet water to us. THIS is a moral source not reckoned with, peculiarly sensitive and daring in its close embrace of native things. His sensitive mind. For everything his fine sense, blossoming, thriving, opening, reviving – not shutting out – was tuned. He speaks of his struggles with their language, its peculiar beauties, '*je ne sais quoi d'énergique*', he cited its tempo, the form of its genius with gusto, with admiration, with generosity. Already the flower is turning up its petals. It is *this* to be *moral*: to be *positive*, to be peculiar, to be sure, generous, brave – TO MARRY, to *touch* – to *give* because one HAS, not because one has nothing. And to give to him who HAS, who will join, who will make, who will fertilize, who will be like you yourself: to create, to hybridize, to crosspollenize – not to sterilize, to draw back, to fear, to dry up, to rot. It is the sun. In Rasles one feels THE INDIAN emerging from within the pod of his isolation from eastern understanding he is released AN

1 p. 130.

INDIAN. He exists, he is – it is an AFFIRMATION, it
is alive. Père Rasles, often suffering the tortures of the
damned as the result of an early accident – fracture of both
thighs, badly mended – lived with his village – alone,
absorbed in them, LOST in them, swallowed, a hard
yeast –

English prose has never got nearer than this to approximating to the
rhythms and contours of excited speech. Lawrence, I think, even in
Studies in Classic American Literature, never went so far. And it may
be thought that the recourse to italics and capitalizations betrays that
already this is to go too far, that the style fails of its effect because we
feel it to be not excited but excitable, that it protests too much. In
context, as the climax of a train of thought itself arising from a
dramatic situation, I think the manner is justified, and a remarkable
if eccentric achievement. . . .
(230–34)

Alan Holder

'*In the American Grain*: William Carlos Williams on the
American Past', *American Quarterly*, vol. 19, no. 3 1967

Acknowledging that his memory might have deceived him, William
Carlos Williams distinctly recalled that while en route to Europe
from America in 1924, he occupied himself with a treatment of the
most famous voyage ever made in the opposite direction.[1] His
version of Columbus's discovery of the New World was eventually
to be included in his book *In the American Grain* (1925), a study of
various figures out of the American past. Touring a Europe that drew
so many of our literati abroad in the 1920s, Williams kept part of
his attention reserved for the band left temporarily behind, as he
continued to work on the book. In so doing he was, in effect,
declaring his distance from the expatriate temper of that period.

One of the chapters of *In the American Grain* opens with a sketch of
contemporary Paris, a Paris that had collected Pablo Picasso, Gertrude

1 *Selected Letters*, pp. 185–8.

Stein, James Joyce and Ezra Pound, among others. It is in this same chapter that Williams declares:

> what we [Americans] are has its origin in what *the nation* in
> the past has been. . . . there is a source IN AMERICA for
> everything we think or do. . . . unless everything that is,
> proclaim a ground on which it stand, it has no worth;
> and . . . what has been morally, aesthetically worth while in
> America has rested upon peculiar and discoverable ground.[1]

The shifting away from the exiles gathered in a foreign capital to the 'peculiar' ground of America nicely dramatized Williams's belief that art must grow out of 'local conditions'.[2] During a career pursued in conscious opposition to the way taken by Ezra Pound and T. S. Eliot, he repeatedly asserted that the artist must steep himself in the multiple particulars of his native milieu.[3] A culture, Williams claimed, has to be where it arises, or everything related to the life there ceases. . . . It is the realization of the qualities of a place in relation to the life which occupies it; embracing everything involved, climate, geographic position, relative size, history, other cultures. . . .[4] *In the American Grain* may be said to represent Williams's attempt to embrace the history of the place in which he found himself.

> Of mixed ancestry, I felt from earliest childhood that
> America was the only home I could ever possibly call my
> own. I felt that it was expressly founded for me, personally,
> and that it must be my first business in life to possess it; that
> only by making it my own from the beginning to my own
> day, in detail, should I ever have a basis for knowing where
> I stood.[5]

The work resulting from his ambition to 'possess' his country, make its history a portable acquisition of his mind, turned out to be at once wider and narrower in scope than this statement would suggest. The 'America' of *In the American Grain* came to include both Canada

1 *In the American Grain*, p. 121.
2 *Autobiography*, 1951, p. 146.
3 See, e.g. *Autobiography*, pp. 174–5, and *Selected Letters*, pp. 224–7.
4 *Selected Essays*, 1954, p. 157.
5 *Selected Letters*, p. 185.

and Mexico; however, Williams's treatment of history *per se* ultimately got no closer to his 'own day' than the period of the Civil War.[1]

He conceived of his enterprise not merely as an artist's private act of self-education, but as a public gesture, one which would break through the insulation from its past that America, in his view, had built up. Accusing our historians of being imperceptive,[2] he adopted the strategy of going directly to the historical documents themselves (e.g. the journal of Columbus, the dispatches of Cortez), in his effort to discover the essential nature of the America that had been, and thereby illuminate the America that had come to be. What he produced is not simply a sourcebook; it is, rather, a highly selective, impressionistic account of our history, the product of his imagination playing over the documents.[3] As might be expected of such a work, it is not committed to a single, monolithic thesis, but has several central concerns: a stressing of the place of the tragic in human endeavor so as to correct our country's tendency to deny it; a displaying of a number of heroes from out of the past as models to be used by the present; an attack on the persistence of Puritanism in our culture; and a celebration of the Indian linking him to the spirit of the American earth.

In part, Williams's study of the past resulted, at least implicitly, in the desire to fill a large gap in the usual American conception of life's possibilities. At one point in the book he complains: 'We have no feeling for the tragic. Let the sucker who fails get his. What's tragic in that? That's funny! To hell with him. He didn't make good, that's all' (p. 185). Whether or not Williams *consciously* intended to demonstrate the inadequacy of this characteristic American response, his

1 Originally he had hoped to do a second volume, beginning with Jefferson and coming up to 'the present day to end with Pancho Villa' (*Autobiography*, p. 237). But the poor sales of *In the American Grain* caused him to cancel his plans.

2 *Autobiography*, pp. 178, 179, 188.

3 Even when Williams is supposedly presenting the sources themselves, he sometimes does so in a way that historians would find very dubious. On occasion he will excise or combine material from his documents without acknowledging that he is doing so, interpolate details that are not in the original, cite as a fact something that is a matter of conjecture, or get a date or place name incorrect.

selection and treatment of a number of figures out of the past reveal a strain in our history that might be called the American failure story. It is hard to believe that he did not have the dramatization of such a strain in mind when he chose to open his book by focusing on Eric the Red rather than Eric's son, Leif Erickson, who is more closely associated with the discovery of the American continent, and who would therefore seem a more appropriate figure with which to begin (Leif plays only a secondary role in the 'Red Eric' chapter). But Leif was fortune's darling; indeed, he was called Leif the Lucky. This appellation only heightens, by contrast, the sense of frustration and defeat that is evoked in Williams's treatment of Red Eric, who feels displaced by the coming of Christianity to Greenland. Eric's unhappiness over the unwelcome appearance of Christian priests, his sense of homelessness in the Greenland he discovered, is further heightened by Williams's having converted the neutral, third-person narrative of the original sagas into a brooding dramatic monologue, giving much more space than do the sources to Eric's rejection of Christianity.[1] Thus, the first personage to greet us in Williams's recreation of the American past is one isolated and embittered, defiant, but hopelessly so.

The succeeding figure, Columbus, would appear to be a supreme instance of magnificent success not only in American history but in the history of the world. Yet, in noting the marvelous feat of his first voyage to America, Williams says 'it is as the achievement of a flower, pure, white, waxlike and fragrant, that Columbus's infatuated course must be depicted, especially when compared with the acrid and poisonous apple which was later by him to be proved' (p. 26). So Williams has no sooner recognized Columbus's achievement than he leaps forward in time, anticipating at the start the difficulties and ingratitude that Columbus will encounter despite his success. While the Columbus section ends on a triumphant note, with the text reverting to the first days of discovery (even fitting the events of

1 Williams spoke of having used *The Long Island Book* as his source (*Autobiography*, p. 178). There is no book by that title so far as I have been able to determine. Williams undoubtedly meant the *Flateyarbok*, or *Flat Island Book*. He appears to have read as well the *Saga of Eric the Red*. Both of these works can be found, in translation, in the first volume of *Original Narratives of Early American History*, 1906, a series that seems to have supplied Williams with several of his sources.

several days into two presumably to intensify the sense of Columbus's pleasure at what he saw), much of the chapter's materials have been chosen in such a way as to give us not a triumphant voyager so much as a terribly put-upon man, intrigued against, vilified, ruined. Williams calls him America's 'first victim' (p. 29).

The next four chapters extend the portrait gallery of defeat and failure. It is Montezuma, as head of the doomed Aztec civilization, who dominates 'The Destruction of Tenochtitlan'. Ponce de Leon, old, sorrowing over the death of his beloved dog, meets an abrupt, mocking end to his quest for the Fountain of Youth: 'The Yamasses put an arrow into his thigh at the first landing – and let out his fountain. They flocked to the beach, jeered him as he was lifted to the shoulders of his men and carried away. Dead' (p. 60). De Soto, moving through Indian territories, falls ill and dies without having discovered the gold he sought. Williams incorporates that portion of his source (*The Narrative of the Expedition of Hernando De Soto, by the Gentleman of Elvas*) which says of Dè Soto, 'He was advanced by fortune, in the way she is wont to lead others, that he might fall the greater depth' (p. 72) – the path of the tragic hero. His property, Williams's version of the account tells us, was found to consist of 'two male and three female slaves, three horses and seven hundred swine. From that time forward most of the people owned and raised hogs' (p. 73). In the original source, we are informed what each slave, horse and hog was sold for. Williams's exclusion of this information produces a compression that comments sardonically on the career's end of one of the great conquistadores.

As we move, in the next chapter, from the Spanish to the English, the pattern of failure or incompletion persists. Sir Walter Raleigh is presented as an instance of many-sided defeat. Williams calls him 'that lost man: seer who failed, planter who never planted, poet whose works are questioned, leader without command, favorite deposed . . .' (p. 76). Among other things, Williams was undoubtedly thinking of Raleigh's difficult and fruitless expeditions to Guiana in search of El Dorado.

In presenting these figures (as well as that of Aaron Burr), Williams appears to be trying to make his fellow Americans perceive that failure is as much a part of existence as success, trying to rid them of the innocence that proclaims otherwise (in varying ways, such of his contemporaries as Frost, Hemingway, Fitzgerald and Faulkner also made this attempt). He describes the America Columbus was to discover as 'a predestined and bitter fruit' (p. 26), Columbus's enemies as 'natural and as much a part of the scheme as any other' (p. 29).

Williams's concern with examples from our history that do not fit into the American success pattern may derive not only from his 'feeling for the tragic', but from his apparent belief that failure, or non-achievement, can breed valuable characteristics. It is such characteristics that the American Negro embodies according to the presentation of him in the short chapter 'Advent of the Slaves'. The Negro, 'NOBODY' in America, is possessed of a poise 'in a world where [he has] no authority . . .' (p. 212). Paradoxically, Williams seems to see the Negroes' lack of status as the source of tenderness *and* ferocity in them, both of which he finds attractive. Rather than responding to the Negro as an example of victimization, Williams regards him as adding a 'delightful' quality to the American scene.

Complementing this depiction of the Negro as the American nobody is Williams's handling of such prominent success stories as those of Washington and Franklin. He suggests in both cases that success came at too high a cost, the repression of a valuable, anarchic passion within in the case of Washington, the shutting out of the wild spirit of the American continent in the case of Franklin.[1] One use of the past for Williams, then, would appear to be the undermining of characteristic American assumptions about success and failure, the enlarging and complicating of our notions of life's possibilities and values.

A further examination of the way in which Williams attempts to bring the past to bear on the present reveals in him two opposing

---

1 Williams's attack on Franklin's values is an explicit one, but it may be that he was undercutting him implicitly by following the Franklin chapter with John Paul Jones's account of the battle between the *Bon Homme Richard* and the *Serapis*. For even though Jones's account is, technically, that of a victory, it seems much more a tale of confusion, ineptitude and treachery, with his own ship ending up in worse condition than the *Serapis*. Placing the Jones chapter where he does, Williams may be advancing an implicit commentary on Franklin's image of a world in which the determined, energetic self cannot but meet with a successful ending, a world that is not intrinsically flawed. Such an interpretation of the juxtaposition of the two chapters is particularly suggested by the fact that Jones's ship was named after Franklin's Poor Richard.

conceptions of our history. In the first of these, he appears to regard the American past as a repository of heroes,[1] men who can serve as models or inspiration for those living in the present. It is his job to serve as a medium for putting us in contact with those men who have unfortunately been allowed to turn ghostly; through such contact their exemplary force will be released. His heroes include so well-known a figure as Daniel Boone, and the relatively obscure French Jesuit, Père Sebastian Rasles. Boone, we are told, is 'Far from dead . . . but full of a rich regenerative violence he remains, when his history will be carefully reported, for us who have come after to call upon him' (p. 140). His life remains 'still loaded with power . . .' (p. 145). Père Rasles, in his dealings with the Indians, displayed a generosity of spirit that is a 'moral source . . . one of the sources that has shaped America and must be recognized' (p. 133). Rejecting the widely-held notion of Aaron Burr as an unscrupulous adventurer, Williams finds in him, among other things, an admirable love of freedom and disregard for public opinion. Such historical figures exist for Williams in a state of potential resurrection, our secular saviors if we would only recognize them as such.

But if the American past is capable of kindling in him a passionate admiration and a desire to see it embodied in the life of the present, it can just as frequently provoke him to radical rejection and rage. The prime villain is the spirit of Puritanism, which Williams sees as a force of the greatest importance both in its impact on early America, and in its effect on his own time as well. (The intense hostility of *In the American Grain* toward Puritanism makes it very much a book of the 1920s.) He finds that this spirit has manifested itself both in Franklin's fear of the wilderness and in the shame our women are made to feel about their sexual desires. The Puritan temper has become 'a malfeasant ghost that dominates us all' (p. 80). While Cotton Mather's books are not read, 'what is in them lives and there hides, as in a lair from whence it sallies now and then to strike terror through the land' (p. 127). Williams's language here may strike us as extravagant, but it is appropriate to the intensity of his hatred. In presenting the Puritans he would appear to assume the role of psychiatrist to a culture, his patient the American mind, its malady a crippling inhibition that affects our sexuality, makes us avoid real

[1] See also *Autobiography*, p. 178.

relationships with others, and prevents us from opening ourselves to the spirit of the American earth. Operating on an assumption parallel to that once made by actual psychoanalysis, namely, that bringing to consciousness the source of a mental disorder will result in the purgation of that disorder, Williams speaks of his wish 'to drag that THING [Puritanism] out by itself to annihilate it' (p. 126). 'I wish to disentangle the obscurities that oppress me, to track them to the root and to uproot them –' (p. 128).

Thus, the American past can draw forth both love and hatred from Williams. The two responses are closely related to each other in that at least some of his heroes, men he loves, possess in common a quality that sets them against the Puritanism he detests. In one instance, he makes this crucial antagonism explicit when he says 'All that will be new in America will be anti-Puritan. It will be of another root. It will be more from the heart of Rasles, in the north [i.e. Canada]' (p. 131). 'Puritan' in this context means a blindness to the American earth, the wilderness, the Indian, a blindness bred out of fear of the new and the vast. His eye cocked on Eternity, the Puritan had 'nothing of curiosity, no wonder, for the new World ...' (p. 124). He 'was precluded from SEEING the Indian. They never realized the Indian in the least save as an unformed PURITAN' (p. 125). Such inability or unwillingness to apprehend the newness of the New World persists. 'Our resistance to the wilderness has been too strong. ... As a violent "puritanism" it breathes still' (p. 127). Rasles, on the other hand, applied himself diligently to studying the language of the Indians, saying that it had 'its real beauties, and a certain indescribable energy in the turn and manner of expression.'[1] His capacity for appreciation, exemplified in this statement, his knowledge of the habits and mentality of the Indians, his living among them, eating what they ate, sharing their strenuous life – all these greatly endear Rasles to Williams.[2]

1 From a letter written by Rasles, reproduced in an English translation in the Rev. William Ingraham Kip's *The Early Jesuit Missions in North America*, Wiley, 1845, p. 28. See also *In the American Grain*, p. 134.
2 Rasles tells of using snowshoes for the first time, thinking he would never be able to walk with such machines; 'but when I made the attempt, I found myself immediately an expert, that the Indians could not believe it was the first time I had used them' (p. 24). On another occasion, he saved himself from drowning

Openness to the Indian, a readiness to regard him as companion or
model, is the link connecting Rasles to other figures in the book who
are treated by Williams with obvious affection. There is Thomas
Morton, who consorted with the Massachusetts Indians, his establishment at Merrymount an affront to 'the Puritans of the Plymouth
colony. . . .' (p. 90). Helping him erect the famous Maypole, the
Indians were present at the ensuing revels. To Daniel Boone, 'the
Indian was his greatest master' (p. 146). He chose an Indian for
companion 'even out of preference to his own sons . . .' (p. 148).
Sam Houston ran away to live with the Indians when still very
young, returned to them after the break-up of his first marriage, and
took an Indian woman for his wife – it is these facts that Williams
chooses to focus on in his chapter about the Texan, treating his
famous victory at San Jacinto and all his ensuing career in less than a
paragraph. That this emphasis on Houston's relationship with the
Indians may be in part misleading, even when he is considered as a
private man rather than a public figure, is indicated by Robert Penn
Warren's remarks on him. Warren points out that Houston is not to
be thought of 'as a simple hunter and woodsman, a white runaway
gone Indian. His head was full of the ambition to read Homer. He
carried into the wilderness a copy of Pope's translation of the *Iliad*.'
During his retreat in the Texas campaign, he read Caesar's *Com-
mentaries* and *Gulliver's Travels*.[1] Houston himself said he read the
Pope translation so consistently he could 'repeat it almost entire from
beginning to end.'[2] Williams never points to this appearance of
European culture in Houston's life. He gives us a Houston who is a
Redskin, purged of that which made him a Paleface as well. This
concern with Houston and the Indian can certainly be justified by the
evidence (there is, in addition to the man's personal relationships with
the Indians, his repeated attempts to defend their rights against the
greed and dishonesty of the whites), but its one-sidedness can also be
taken as an expression of Williams's own preoccupations in *In the
American Grain*.

by following the example of his Indian companions, leaping from one block
of ice to another to get across a river. Williams was unquestionably entranced
by such items as these.

1 Warren, *How Texas Won Her Freedom: The Story of Sam Houston & The
Battle of San Jacinto*, San Jacinto, 1959, pp. 2, 12.
2 *The Autobiography of Sam Houston*, University of Oklahoma Press, 1954, p. 5.

Set against these men who reached out to the Indian – Rasles, Morton, Boone, Houston – there stands, at least by implication, Benjamin Franklin. At the end of his hostile chapter on the creator of Poor Richard, Williams speaks bitterly of 'the suppression of the superb corn dance of the Chippewas ...' (p. 165). Earlier in the chapter, he says 'There has not yet appeared in the New World any one with sufficient strength for the open assertion. . . . Nowhere the open, free assertion save in the Indian. . . . Franklin is the full development of the timidity. . . . He was the dike keeper, keeping out the wilderness with his wits' (p. 162). It can be stated that the response made to the Indian serves Williams as a touchstone in his judgements on the men of the American past.

Several of the 'original records' Williams apparently consulted could have contributed to his sense of the Indians as a precious product of the New World, maligned by the reports of the early New England settlers. Thomas Morton spoke of the Massachusetts Indians as being 'more full of humanity then [sic] the Christians.'[1] Père Rasles noted both the Indian's skill as a warrior, and his tenderness toward children. Boone also spoke of these qualities, as well as of the Indian's '"attachment for that land to which [he] belong[s], unknown to the inhabitants of any other country"'. The hunter did not hesitate to declare to the day of his death that the manners and habits of the Indians were 'far more agreeable to him than those of a more civilized and refined race.'[2] Houston, telling of his sojourn among the Indians as a boy, said he had preferred 'the wild liberty of the Redmen ... [to] the tyranny of my own brothers.'[3]

But in Williams's sources there are materials that convey a very different response to the American native. Champlain, who is the subject of Williams's eighth chapter, was of the opinion that the Indians 'are all in fact of no great worth'.[4] Perhaps this was not a significant evaluation to Williams, who describes Champlain as failing to perceive the essential otherness of the wilderness, and believing that it could be turned into an extension of French civiliza-

1 *New English Canaan*, Prince Society Publications, 1883, p. 256.
2 *Life and Adventures of Colonel Daniel Boone*, Wilder, 1823, p. 37.
3 *Autobiography of Sam Houston*, p. 6.
4 *Voyages of Samuel de Champlain 1604–18*, ed. W. L. Grant, Scribner, 1907, p. 73.

tion. But even in Boone, whose attraction to the Indian Williams so stresses, we can find the description of an occasion on which the Indians, conducting a forced march of captives, tomahawked those who were weak and faint, including women and children.[1]

Turning to the dispatches of Cortez (which Williams used as the basis for his chapter on that explorer), we find awful accounts of human sacrifices by the Indians of Mexico. According to Cortez, the victims, sometimes children, had their breasts cut open while still alive, their hearts and entrails removed and offered to the idols. 'It is the most terrible and frightful thing that has ever been seen.'[2] Indians who had allied themselves with Cortez against Montezuma showed the inhabitants of the beleaguered Tenochtitlan 'their country-men cut in pieces, telling them they would sup off them that night and breakfast off them next morning, as in fact they did.'[3] They rejoiced greatly at the Spaniard's decision to level the city, and Cortez claims to have had 'more trouble preventing our allies from killing and torturing than we had in fighting those Indians, for no such inhuman cruelty as the natives of these parts practice was ever seen among any people'.[4] That a conquistador should have been provoked to such a comment is terrible tribute indeed to the Indian's capacity for cruelty.

Francis Parkman's *The Jesuits in North America in the Seventeenth Century* (a book Williams quotes from) made evident the hideous cruelty the North-American Indian could display, not merely toward the white man but toward the members of other tribes. To spare our sensibilities, Parkman sometimes cuts short his descriptions of Indian tortures, and most readers will rest content with the details he does give, of living victims having strips of flesh torn from them, fingers cut or bitten off, bodies burned piecemeal, agonies protracted for hours.

Williams's Indians, northern or southern, are simply not portrayed in this way. When he mentions the practice of human sacrifice, he does so briefly or condoningly, his intention at one point being to

---

1 John Filson, *The Discovery, Settlement and Present State of Kentucky*, Corinth, 1962, pp. 71–2.
2 *Conquest: Dispatches of Cortes from the New World*, eds. Irwin Blacker and Harry Lowen, 1962, p. 17.
3 p. 125.   4 p. 142.

condemn the white man's 'sacrifices' of the witches at Salem rather than Indian behavior (p. 82). Following a long American literary tradition, Williams pictures the Indian simply as victim, the conquistador or colonist his oppressor. In so doing, he tends to convert men who have been unjustly treated into total innocents. He is determined to have his savages noble, despite their ignoble savagery. Comparison with Parkman's account of the Indian immediately points up the lack of balance in Williams's book. Parkman is ready to admire the Indian's ability to face with courage and endurance the truly arduous circumstances of his life. But Parkman is also ready to exhibit his less attractive qualities.[1]

It is not, however, so much a question of one-sidedness in Williams's image of the Red Man that renders that image suspect. More crucial is the fact that a book making so much of the Indian, holding him up as a model of right, organic relationship to the New World, should be so unwilling (or unable) to portray him in any but the sketchiest manner. In the chapter on Rasles, cast in the form of a discussion between the author and Valéry Larbaud,[2] Williams offers himself the opportunity to discourse on the Indian by having Larbaud ask him 'Who were these Indians of whom you speak? What sort of men were they? What were their qualities?' He responds by offering instances of victimization of the Indian by the white man, and the story of a Protestant minister refusing to allow Indians to touch him, in contrast with 'the Catholic fathers in the north . . .' (p. 130). We then get some remarks on Puritan repressiveness, and praise of Rasles. Several pages go by before Williams offers a direct reply to Larbaud's questions, and then only a very short one. We are told that through Rasles, the Indian 'stands out strangely revealed as a child, a passionate friend, a resourceful man and – a genius in attack, another music than the single horror of his war-whoop terrifying the invader' (p. 135). This minuscule description is simply not enough to sustain the burden of significance assigned to the Indian by the book. He ultimately figures in it only as a teasing presence, flitting through its

1 Moreover, in direct contrast to Williams's contention that in the Indian we find 'open, free assertion', Parkman speaks of the Indian's 'dread of public opinion. . . .' Parkman, *The Jesuits in North America in the Seventeenth Century*, 1875, p. xlix. See also p. 256.

2 This is apparently based on an actual conversation Williams had with Larbaud (Williams, *Selected Letters*, p. 60).

pages, but staying just beyond our range of vision. Parkman, contemplating the disappearance of the Algonquin tribes, spoke of them as undergoing 'that process of extermination, absorption or expatriation, which, as there is reason to believe, had for many generations formed the gloomy and meaningless history of the greater part of this continent.'[1] Williams does much too little to challenge this conception of the history of the Indian, whose near-disappearance he so laments.

The Indian is precious to Williams as 'the flower of his world', a 'natural expression' of the American continent (p. 146). The reaction to him by the French, Spanish, English, and their American-born descendants is for Williams a synechdoche of the white man's response to the New World. To dramatize that response, Williams personifies the American earth as a woman, linking this image to a recurrent metaphor of sexual union or marriage which represents the kind of love and acceptance of the New World that he constantly looks for in his exploration of our past.

The most explicit and extended occurrence of the earth-woman personification is to be found in the chapter on De Soto, where it takes the form of a series of speeches or responses by a 'She', alternating with sections of narrative relating the exploits of the Spaniard. It is possible that Williams's use of this technique was inspired by his source,[2] in which we find a series of messages or addresses composed by various Indian chieftains and directed to De Soto. These always begin in a most respectful way and are positively feminine in their submissiveness. One was actually composed by a female chieftain. She, however, after being put under guard, tricked her captors and escaped. Williams's 'She' combines in her being this same mixture of submissiveness and elusiveness, of yielding and defiance. 'She' describes herself as beautiful, seductive, alternately victorious over and defeated by De Soto. Victory for her appears to consist of his turning 'native', though the exact content of this is not clear. It may refer to De Soto's treachery in killing several natives ('She' says to this: '"Well done, Spaniard! like an Indian"'), or to his acceptance of two Indian wives, the gifts of a chief. Early in the chapter, 'She'

1 Parkman, p. 246.
2 *The Narrative of the Expedition of Hernando De Soto by the Gentleman of Elvas in Spanish Explorers in the Southern United States 1528–43*, Scribner, 1907.

promises De Soto that he will receive nothing of her 'save one long caress as of a great river passing forever upon your sweet corse' (p. 61). The meaning of this becomes clear at the end of the section when we are told of De Soto's corpse being consigned to the Mississippi river, and only if we have knowledge of Williams's *The Great American Novel* (1923). In that work, he says this of De Soto:

The best he had done was to locate a river running across his
path, the greatest he had ever seen or heard of, greater than
the Nile, greater than the Euphrates, no less indeed than any.
Here he had confronted the New World in all its mighty
significance and something had penetrated his soul so that in
the hour of need he had turned to this Mighty River rather
than to any other thing. . . . Out of the tangle around him,
out of the mess of his own past the river alone could give him
rest. Should he die his body should be given to this last resting
place. Into it Europe should pass as into a new world . . .
there at the edge of that mighty river he had seen those little
fish who would soon be eating him, he, De Soto the mighty
explorer – He smiled quietly to himself with a curious satisfaction.[1]

This passage provides a clue to what was in Williams's mind when, in his *American Grain* account of De Soto's river burial, he included a description of various kinds of fish. The description *is* found in his source, but there it occurs at a point prior to De Soto's death and is given in reference to a *lake* rather than the Mississippi. In transposing it, Williams apparently wished to suggest that only in death, eaten by the fish of the New World, was De Soto's relationship to that world consummated (perhaps because only such consummation was possible to the essentially violent relationship of De Soto to America). Williams dramatizes that relationship largely in sexual terms, not only through his use of 'She', who addresses De Soto as a lover, speaking of caresses (see pp. 61, 64, 66), and of his having 'straddled' her (p. 68), but through his reference to De Soto's descending corpse as a 'solitary sperm . . .' (p. 73).

The beginning of the chapter that follows the one on De Soto, Williams's account of Sir Walter Raleigh, sustains the use of sexual

1 Williams, *The Great American Novel*; reprinted in W. Schott (ed.) *Imaginations*, 1970, p. 204.

metaphor, as it speaks of Raleigh 'plunging his lust into the body of a new world, ...' According to Williams's image of him, Raleigh's interest in the western hemisphere appears as a release from or substitute for his unhappy, unstable relationship with Queen Elizabeth, though 'it turned out to be a voyage on the body of his Queen: England, Elizabeth – Virginia' (p. 75). (The reference appears to be to Raleigh's having given the name Virginia to land discovered by an expedition to America that he had sent out).[1] Williams's language is in keeping with a metaphor Raleigh himself employed in his *Discovery of Guiana*, where he said, '"Guiana is a country that hath yet her maidenhead."'[2] Perhaps because Raleigh never actually saw North America, and because his voyages to Guiana were unsuccessful, his relationship to the New World appears to figure in Williams's chapter as a kind of *coitus interruptus*. How greatly to be regretted, Williams seems to be saying, is the fact that Raleigh was never able to put his talents to work in America, not because he disdained or feared this continent, but only because of unfortunate circumstances.

In playing off Thomas Morton against the repressive Puritans, Williams employs no metaphor but he does present materials that are closely linked to the sexual imagery I have been pointing to. He offers Morton's 'consorting with the Indian girls' as one cause for the 'Puritan disgust' with him, considers the question of whether or not Indian women had a notion of chastity, and juxtaposes Morton's taking such women to bed with the Puritans' fear of touching the 'bounties' of the New World (p. 95). A restrained sexuality is here equated to or at least connected with a refusal to accept the nature of the land. That Morton did accept it is attested to by his *New English Canaan*, where he repeatedly compares Old England to the New, favoring the latter.

Daniel Boone, sexless in the popular imagination, is introduced to us by Williams as 'a great voluptuary ...' (p. 140). The chapter in

1 Williams's conception of Raleigh as desperately in love with Elizabeth may seem strained, particularly to those who regard Raleigh's letter to Sir Robert Cecil, saying his heart was broken because imprisonment in the Tower had separated him from the Queen, not as a sincere expression of love but as a ploy to restore him to Elizabeth's favor by appealing to her vanity. See *Sir Walter Raleigh and His Colony in America*, ed. the Rev. Increase N. Tarbox, Prince Society Publications, 1865, p. 47.

2 p. 54.

question proceeds to convert this unorthodox characterization into a metaphor, as we are told that 'the beauty of a lavish, primitive embrace in savage, wild beast and forest ... possessed him wholly,' that Boone 'sought only with primal lust to grow close' to the New World's beauty (p. 146). He saw that 'there must be a new wedding', i.e. of the self and the American earth, the prototype of such a wedding to be found in the Indian's continuity with his environment. Wedding and sexual (or at least generative) metaphors are also to be found in the chapter on Père Rasles, advanced in such a way so as not to seem incongruous with the Jesuit's celibacy. Of Rasles's interested, admiring response to the Indian language, Williams says: 'It is *this* to be *moral* ... TO MARRY, to *touch – to give* ... to create, to hybridize, to crosspollenize ...' (p. 132).

We are reminded of the chapter on Boone, not only by the portrait of Rasles, but by that of Franklin as well, with the latter again serving as a counterfigure to the other two, as he had in the matter of responses to the Indian. Franklin, we are told, possessed a '*voluptuous* energy' which he had borrowed from his surroundings 'without recognition ...' (p. 161 – italics mine). Impelling him was fear of the wilderness, of 'the dance' – presumably the fertility dance of the Indians (p. 165). He wished only to 'touch' whatever he put his hand to (p. 164), 'touch' here carrying the very opposite meaning of what it has in the chapter on Rasles, representing in Franklin's case only superficial contact.

The precise significance in the book of sexual and matrimonial metaphor used in conjunction with acceptance or rejection of the New World, personified as a woman, is a difficult thing to pin down. In some instances, e.g. that of Rasles, the metaphor remains metaphor, and is used to suggest the *intensity* with which America was lovingly responded to, or should have been responded to. But in the book there is also a tendency for the metaphoric to slide into the literal, and to involve actual sexuality or, rather, its denial. In the case of the Puritans, Williams explicitly presents us not only with a group blind to the beauty and uniqueness of the land they had come to, but also sexually repressed. The two qualities appear together again in that spiritual descendant of the Puritans, Franklin. For, after telling us of the tremendous inner restraint operating on Franklin's voluptuous energy, his mode of merely touching, Williams notes that he had 'tentatively loosed himself once to love, to curiosity perhaps, which was the birth of his first son. But the terror of that dare must have frightened the soul out of him' (p. 164). Fear of the New World in general and fear of sexuality in particular are here clearly joined. A closely related, if not identical pattern can be seen in Williams's description of Washington, when we consider it together with the chapter on Franklin which it immediately precedes. Washington is viewed as a man of great sexual attractiveness and a strong sexual drive, the latter part of a tremendous passionate potential, 'a mad hell inside that might rise, might one day do something perhaps brilliant, perhaps joyously abandoned – but not to be thought of' (p. 50). Franklin and Washington would appear to be linked together in Williams's mind when he says 'the character they had (our pioneer statesmen, etc.) was that of giving their fine energy, as they must have done, to the smaller, narrower protective thing and not to the great, New World' (p. 164). In all these instances, there is a connection made between a refused commitment to that world and the repression of sexual energy.

If the wedding and marriage metaphors of the book tend to approach the literal, a similar process occurs with the underlying personification of the American earth as woman. Presumably originating as a device for showing the depth of love or fear occasioned by the New World, the earth-woman comes to be ranged alongside the actual American woman, sisters in rejection. Denial of the New World stands joined by Williams to denial of woman's sexuality.[1] The latter has resulted in our not having had true women in America 'since pioneer Katies . . .' (p. 184). Made by our Puritanism to regard their desires as evil, American women have evolved into beings 'fit only to be seen by the box, like Oregon apples, bright and round but tasteless – wineless, wholesale' (p. 188). The wife of Houston is a case study. Williams speculates that the cause of Houston's breakup with his white bride was 'a disproportion between them; a man of primitive vigors loosed upon her in private, she was overborne by him in some manner, or she refused to be overborne' (p. 215).

'There are no women – Houston's bride is frightened off . . .' (p. 162). (Houston's happy marriage to another white woman is

1 M. L. Rosenthal has spoken of Williams's 'special interest in women' as one of the 'overriding preoccupations relevant to all of [his] work'. See *The William Carlos Williams Reader*, ed. M. L. Rosenthal, New Directions, 1966, pp. x–xi.

completely ignored.) Williams's view of the status of the American woman explains the stress he places on Aaron Burr as a man who took women seriously. Burr was to the American woman what Boone was to the American earth – an appreciative lover. Burr's contemporaries regarded women as 'necessary but not noble, not the highest, not deliciously a free thing, apart, *feminine*, a heaven; – afraid to delve in it save like so much dough. Burr found the spirit living there, free and equal, independent, springing with life' (p. 208).[1] That his appreciation of them included the sexual is pointed up by Williams's statement that the 'obscene flesh in which we dig for all our good, man and woman alike, Burr knew and trusted. Here he lived, giving and receiving to the full of his instinctive nature' (p. 210). *In the American Grain* values loving recognition of the American woman as well as of the American earth.

There are two women in the book whose presence suggests that for Williams the ideal female possesses robustness and bold assertiveness, and that possessing these, she is an expression of the American earth. About a third of the chapter on Eric the Red is given over to Eric's daughter, Freydis. Pregnant, and confronted by the hostile Skrellings, she 'stripped down her shirt and slapped her breast with her bare sword' (p. 24). The Skrellings retreat in terror from this spectacle. Freydis's ability to operate effectively in a violent role is again shown in her calling for an axe to kill the women belonging to a household against which she has brought unjust accusations. This Nordic Clytemnestra, at once admirable and terrible, may be said to anticipate a woman presented for our approval later in the book. At the end of the chapter given over to Williams's meditation on the nature of the American female, we are told of a Sachem of mixed blood, Jacataqua, scarcely eighteen years old, being attracted to the young Aaron Burr, then fighting in the French and Indian War. She opens a conversation with him thusly: '"These," with a wave of her brown hand toward Howard [an American captain] and the group of officers, "these want meat. You hunt with me? I win."' Williams tells us that on this occasion Burr was at a loss before a woman for the first and last time in his life.

1 Williams's image of Burr was probably shaped, at least in part, by Burr's letters to his beloved daughter, Theodosia. These show him as continually occupied with her education and development.

That Williams shows himself drawn to such formidable figures as Freydis and Jacataqua is of a piece with his conception of the genius of the American continent. The Aztecs' practice of human sacrifice displayed he says, 'the realization of their primal and continuous identity with the ground itself ... [of] the mysterious secret of existence whose cruel beauty they, the living, inherited from the dead' (p. 49). Cruel beauty is what the 'She' in the De Soto chapter exhibits, being at once lavish in her gifts and punishments: 'every arrow has upon its barbs a kiss from my lips' (p. 64). Traversing the wilderness alone, Boone, according to Williams's image of him, experiences both an ordeal and an ecstasy. Later, Indians will offer him companionship, but they will also kill his son. Boone accepts both. Such acceptance of the dual nature of the American continent, its beauty and its terror, is what the book as a whole is urging.

The historian, Williams complains, is too ready to portray men 'in generic patterns', determined by environment or circumstance. He asks: 'Are lives to be twisted forcibly about events, the mere accidents of geography and climate?' He answers that it is 'an obscenity which few escape – save at the hands of the stylist, literature, in which alone humanity is protected against tyrannous designs' (p. 193). What Williams is saying, I believe, both here and through the method of his book taken as a whole, is that studies of the past should preserve the contours of the individual, be responsive to his particular style, and allow him some measure of autonomy,[1] that history is best treated as biography (when it resists being treated as such, when, e.g. Williams finds the Pilgrims functioning as a group with no individual leader discernible, he is contemptuous). American history for him is not a matter of mass movements, political and economic developments, sectional conflicts, institutions – it is primarily a matter of the individual. This is why his book repeatedly focuses on a particular man, and why it adopts a different form or style for each of its chapters

---

1 It may be his desire to stress the autonomy of a particular kind of man, the artist that accounts for the book's paradoxical chapter on Poe. For after telling us that in Poe, the local, the genius of the American place, found its first great expression, he pictures Poe as desiring to be connected with no particular place, and makes the 'local' an expression of Poe's own soul. Williams's contradictory treatment may have been the result of a reluctance to see the good artist's work as simply an 'accident of a geography and climate' even while he desired the American artist to be responsive to his surroundings.

(sometimes letting the subject speak for himself through his own writing).[1] We move from the intense, bitten-off sentences of Red Eric, to the swooning speech of De Soto's 'She', to the stately narrative describing Montezuma's civilization. *In the American Grain* proposes to restore our history to us through vivid renderings of the personalities, tensions, miseries and delights of individual men. In his prefatory note, Williams says, 'Everywhere I have tried to separate out from the original records some flavor of an actual peculiarity the character denoting shape which the unique force has given.' The syntax here is a little gnarled, but the interest in individual particularity is clear enough. To be sure, Williams does not treat the past purely as an array of discrete, unrelated entities; he does not conceive of himself as simply making a series of separate antiquarian excursions. His mind is by no means completely free of assumptions that would encourage the use of the historian's generic patterns, and he does look for certain designs within history which are relevant to his own day. But the book is so composed as to call our attention to particular men in their relationship to particular times and places.

Williams's personification of the American earth as a woman, that turning of historical materials into myth, is admittedly a nebulous affair and may well make historians squirm. It suggests at times a sexual interpretation of our past without an explicit commitment to a consistent, overall theory of cause and effect. At the same time, this personification allows Williams to focus attention on something the historian might neglect, the sense of the American place as it has impinged on various individuals during the course of our history. The personification reinforces the use of the different styles in helping create a sense of the inner being of Williams's historical figures, transforming public effigies into private persons. Williams strives simultaneously to keep his eye on the public world and on the single, separate self, setting in motion an interaction between the two that engages the deepest, most intimate aspects of the self, its personality. Concern with the structure of the past and with large developments is subordinated to a concern for the texture of private experience. As such, the book furnishes a desirable complement to the historian's characteristic focus on the public aspect of the past. (499–515)

[1] See Williams, *Autobiography*, p. 184.

The Parisian Aspect

Kenneth Rexroth

from 'The Influence of French Poetry on American', *Assays* 1958

He was partly educated in France. He has lived there for extended
periods. He knows personally most of the heroic generation of post-
First World War poets and has translated a novel of Soupault's. He
was a friend of Valéry Larbaud and the American editor of *Com-
merce*. Intensely personal, local, antiliterary, absolutely devoted to the
achievement of a truly American vision, he is none the less the one
American poet who ranks with the best of his French contemporaries,
who speaks to them as an equal in a language they can understand. I
would say too that the ordinary French reader today could get more
out of him than from any other American poet except Whitman. It is
the true autochthones who circulate most freely in all lands. Williams
could be said to belong in the Cubist tradition – Imagism, Objectivism, the dissociation and rearrangement of the elements of
concrete reality, rather than rhetoric or free association. But where
Reverdy, Apollinaire, Salmon, Cendrars, Cocteau and Jacob are all
urban, even megalopolitan, poets of that Paris which is the international market of objects of *vertu*, vice and art, Williams has confined
himself in single strictness to the life before his eyes – the life of a
physician in a small town twenty miles from New York. In so doing,
his localism has become international and timeless. His long quest for a
completely defenseless simplicity of personal speech produces an
idiom identical with that which is the end product of centuries of
polish, refinement, tradition and revolution.
(160)

Harold Rosenberg

from 'French Silence and American Poetry', *The Tradition of the New* 1961

The best French poetry since Baudelaire has been enlisted in a siege against the cliché. This has not been by any means merely a question of taste. It has been more a matter of life and death.

Any educated Frenchman can make up a poem, just as any American can improvise a new 'popular' tune. The French language is heavy with old literature, as the American air is loaded with ta ta, ta tá tá.

A word over there, as soon as it enters the mind, begins rolling down into a fine ready-made phrase. No leaf can fall except into an endless series of poetic mirrors of autumn. To get a glimpse of his mistress, the Frenchman has to invent ways of singling her out in a bath house full of literary twins.

The Frenchman has so much tradition he can easily say anything except what he wants to say.

To be conscious of his own feelings, to see with his own eyes, he must restore freshness to his language. This is a magical undertaking that can only be carried on by poetry, and which marks certain non-versified writings as indubitably poetry. . . .

(87)

Lifting up a word and putting a space around it has been the conscious enterprise of serious French poetry since Baudelaire and Rimbaud. With this 'alchemy' poetry dissolves traditional preconceptions and brings one face to face with existence and with inspiration as a fact. Or it re-makes the preconceptions and changes the known world.

A French poet refers to the 'fragility' of the commonplace. Of course. The commonplace is the effect of a perspective to which the observer is held by a web of vocabulary. It turns to dust when the acid of poetry burns each word away from the old links.

Poetry as verbal alchemy is a way of experiencing, never the expression or illustration of a 'philosophy'. It neither begins with ideas nor ends with them. Its magic consists in getting along without the guidance of generalizations, which is the most difficult thing in the world. . . .

French poetry has a lot to say about silence. The poet feels a tremendous need to turn off the belt-line of rhetoric that keeps automatically pounding away in his brain twenty-four hours a day. Before any poetic event can happen the cultural clatter must be stopped.

The silence of the French poet arises on the opposite side of the globe from the silence of the Kansas farmhand.

With the latter silence just is, an emptiness coming from American space and time.

The Frenchman has to will his silence, he struggles for it, in it he purifies himself of the past, makes himself ready for a new word, a round word, that can be his own and which will open to him a continent of *things*.

When he succeeds he is in the same position as the Kansas farmhand: sitting on a rail and waiting for something to show up. Whatever it is, it will be something totally real.

Mallarmé and Valéry tried to extricate the word that is a thing from the old poetry. That gives them the look of classicists or traditionalists. They seem direct opponents of the radical Dadaists or Surrealists, whose method is to pick up in the streets a word that had never been in a poem before. Certainly, different kinds of poems will result from beginning inside of poetry to restore words to innocence than from beginning outside of it to find innocent words.

But when Mallarmé and Valéry cut the word 'palm' out of the old poetry in order to make it into a finger touching a new experience, isn't their motive the same as that of the Dadaist who invites into poetry 'sardine can' which is nothing else than experience? . . .
(88)

Keeping in mind the silence of the farmhand and the inevitable non-rhetoric of the word that breaks it, we can understand why the French were the first to appreciate the American tongue. About twenty-five years ago René Taupin pointed out that poets in America were lucky in having a lingo that hadn't yet settled into a literary language.

The revival of American poetry around the First World War and the twenties depended on an awareness of this luck, an awareness in which the French consciousness played a leading part. The poets who spoke American best – Williams, Cummings, Stein, Pound, Moore, Eliot, Stevens – had all been enthusiastically frenchified. They learned from Paris what it meant to find a word that was free of poetry or that stuck out of it at an angle. Whitman alone had been unable to teach them this. They needed to see it in the French reflection.

'Call the roller of big cigars,' sang Stevens, the most conventional of them in form. With cigars and ice cream, billboards and wheelbarrows, American poetry became the poet's act of making his existence real to him, an act not 'assimilable' to any previous poetry.

Then a depressing series of events took place.

First, a new generation of American poets started out to invent themselves and found they had a philosophy, Marxism. With this doctrine it made no difference what the poet experienced, so long as he expressed the doctrine. The best expression would be the one most useful in getting the Marxian message to readers. This meant using traditional verse forms and familiar poetic language. The language most easily recognized in America as poetry is *English*.

The cliché was restored to a premium. In time this led the Marxist poets to Hollywood, which is America's version of literary tradition, its treasury of poetic platitudes.

American poetry might have wiggled out of Marxism without too much damage, or even done something with it, as one or two European surrealists did. But having forgotten its French lesson regarding the space around words necessary for consciousness, it began hunting for speech in the poetic tradition. The turn toward tradition was too much for it.

Beyond Hollywood, tradition can mean only one thing for Americans – back to England. In the past twenty years American poetry has become English again.

To be a radical or fascist ideologist, an American must turn to the ideas of the Continent. To be respectable he need only learn to love Merrie Olde Englande. The foreign relations of American poetry were divided between Ezra Pound and T. S. Eliot.

(89–90)

American poetry has never been deeper than it is today in English schoolbooks. Unfortunately, though, not so far in as to reach the Elizabethans.

The Elizabethans are not tradition. They, too, *think* in their poetry and don't know where they will come out. They gather up every novelty and run an open bazaar of language, putting space around their words. A tradition must make itself superior to such acts of consciousness – that is its whole point, to make thinking unnecessary or, at least, safe.

Like a philosophy, tradition asserts that the important thinking has been done before the poet started to write his poem. The poem is thus an entertainment, or an illustration of the traditional conviction. The new traditionalists have done their best to compress the Elizabethans into their Order or to show the 'heresy' of their thought.

Convinced by Marxism, by psychoanalysis, by sociology, in a word, by 'science', that the truth was already in existence elsewhere than in the poem, the Americans were softened up for Anglicanization. Once this had taken place, it did not matter if some also added Catholicism.

For American poetry, France meant experiment, risk, perception, conversion of the everyday; England means a poetry of comments that sound like poetry.

The chief Pied Piper to *The Oxford Book of English Verse* was, of course, Eliot. He had learned to think his feelings by way of French symbolism. But his own thinking was not enough for him; sometimes he gave the impression that it made him sick. He needed other thoughts – those of Maurras and the French reaction. Finally, he needed the thoughts of The Church.

The combination in Eliot of poet and academician, word specialist and snob, made him destructive in the moment of America's decline in poetic and individual independence. With his famous formula of the supremacy of tradition over individual talent, he succeeded in making poetry appear as a thing with a life of its own, to which a certain caste had given itself as to a minor trade or cult.

On this premise, the French concept of the not-to-be-duplicated word emerging from the unknown was perverted into the petty guild of 'precision', which enabled Eliot to stamp REJECT on the keenness of Blake and the brightness of Shelley, and which let loose on poetry a mob of professors determined to make their logic the last word regarding the meaning of an image. In this triumph he was aided by the disconcerting triviality of the semanticists and the 'scientific' criticism.

In his own verse, Eliot continued to preserve silence as a source – though a silence protected by dogma. For those, however, who accepted his 'classicism' as the term for their refusal to test their own powers, it was left only to keep busy.

With poetry separated from the act of discovery, the poet as a maker of verses could circulate at will from terminus to terminus of the Moscow-Hollywood-Rome axis. By simply redefining 'tradition' he could drop an offering, one after another, in all three repositories of authority, usefulness and the delivered audience.

Whoever speaks the American language is forced into romanticism. His strictest discipline is itself a spiritual oddity and gives birth to an oddity – witness *The Scarlet Letter*, Emily Dickinson, the early gas engine. The American landscape is not easily mistaken for an endless wallpaper of nymphs and fountains – in the American language it takes hard application to achieve academic deadness. Precisely the fact that it gives them something to do and keeps them out of trouble is perhaps what makes the filing cabinets of tradition so desirable to the morally insecure.

Homeopathy apart, the American poetic impulse in this century has been given its most intimate hints toward self-knowledge by the French poetry of immediate presences, through which Poe's psychic experiments, Whitman's vocabulary of objects and the strange American fact have been growing steadily more speakable.

(91–5)

Williams and Painting

Ruth Grogan

'The Influence of Painting on William Carlos Williams'   1969

Contacts with Painting: 1913 to 1923

Williams once enjoined his reader to 'remember I had a strong inclination all my life to be a painter', and added: 'Under different circumstances I would rather have been a painter than to bother with these godamn words.'[1] The reminder is worth taking. Williams's predilection for paint finds more than a superficial reflection in his poetry; it is an essential clue to understanding the mysterious energies and structures under his apparently artless poetic surfaces. Though his interests were not confined to twentieth-century art, modern painting is especially important in establishing these characteristics and tracing his relationship with other writers. According to Williams, 'it was the work of the painters following Cézanne and the Impressionists that, critically, opened up the age of Stein, Joyce and a good many others.'[2] Instead of linking Williams during those *anni mirabiles* simply to the Imagists and his literary acquaintances, as is usually done, his development from the publication of *The Tempers* in 1913 to the crucial *Spring and All* of 1923 can be fruitfully traced in terms of painting and painters.

The years 1905 to 1925, revolutionary in American painting as in European painting, saw on both continents a peculiarly close association between painters and writers. In London in 1914 Pound was planning a College of Arts for the 'inter-stimulus and inter-enlightenment' of painters, sculptors and writers; in Paris Apollinaire and Picasso were utilizing techniques of more than one art; inspired by the Cubist painters, Gertrude Stein was inventing a 'Cubist prose', which became in some ways representative of American writing for a whole period. In New York Walter Arensberg, the wealthy poet, buyer of

1 *I Wanted to Write a Poem*, p. 41.   2 *Autobiography*, p. 380.

paintings and exponent of the Baconian authorship of Shakespeare's works, played a social role similar to Gertrude Stein's in Paris, bringing together in his living-room a whole galaxy of poets and painters, and providing opportunity for excited inter-disciplinary discussions. Williams participated actively in the turmoil. In fact, Constance Rourke has seen the friendship between Williams and the painter-photographer Charles Sheeler as representative of this entire era of cooperation among the American arts.[1]

The ferment began, if the origins of such movements can be located with any precision, in February 1913 at the opening of the sensational Armory Show. Its impact on Williams can be gauged partially by the difference between *The Tempers* of 1913, still lingering in the wake of Ezra Pound, and the mature poems, many of them obviously composed by a painterly eye, of his next volume, *Al Que Quiere* of 1917. The greatest excitement was caused, predictably, by the more experimental work of both Europeans and Americans. Of the Americans, Sheeler was included, as well as the abstractionists Macdonald-Wright and Morgan Russell. Visitors also saw a generous number of paintings by Gauguin, Van Gogh, Cézanne, Matisse, as well as the Cubist works of Picasso, Braque, Léger, de la Fresnaye, Gleizes, Picabia and Duchamp.[2] Public reaction was contemptuous and hostile to a sometimes psychopathic degree, and the initial nose-thumbing at the great American bourgeoisie by small groups of artists, and later on their loneliness after the first reckless spirit had worn off, was much more than a Bohemian pose. For a few years, however, the Show generated among young artists and writers a buoyant optimism. In 1913 and 1914 several new galleries for modern art opened in New York, including the Daniel Gallery directed by a friend of Williams, Alanson Hartpence. Williams was also a frequent visitor at Stieglitz's gallery, '291'; though established in 1905 as a photography gallery, it had soon opened its doors to painters, and its list of exhibitions until its closing in 1917 (including Matisse, Toulouse-Lautrec, Rousseau, Picasso, Brancusi, as well as many American painters) is an astonishing tribute to the sophistication of at

1 *Charles Sheeler, Artist in the American Tradition*, 1938, p. 50.
2 See Barbara Rose, *American Art Since 1900: A Critical History*, Thames and Hudson, 1967, and Milton W. Brown *American Painting from the Armory Show to the Depression*, Princeton University Press, 1955.

least some of the New York art public, and an index to what Williams probably saw. Collectors like Arensberg and John Quinn, advised by young experimental artists, began to buy modern paintings. The exhilarating sense of liberation from academic tastes and imitative techniques, and the determination to push their advantage, finds typical expression in Williams's recollections of the time:

Here was my chance, that was all I knew. There had been a break somewhere, we were streaming through, each thinking his own thoughts, driving his own designs towards his self's objectives.[1]

One special focus of the artistic activity resulting from the Armory Show was Walter Arensberg. The gatherings in his studio often included Marcel Duchamp, Picabia, Man Ray, Marsden Hartley, Joseph Stella, Charles Demuth and Sheeler, along with an assorted group of writers including Williams, Wallace Stevens, Alfred Kreymborg, Donald Evans, and Allen and Louise Norton. After Duchamp's arrival on the New York scene in 1915 Arensberg's living-room became the centre of Dadaist activity. Both Williams and Stevens mention, on different occasions, being lunched or dined by Arensberg, and afterwards taken back to his studio for a view of the Duchamps in progress. Stevens admits that he made very little out of them, just as Williams confessed some trepidation before Cubist paintings: 'It disturbed and fascinated me. I confess I was slow to come up with any answers.'[2] Guests at Arensberg's parties could meet Duchamp, an habitué, and look at Cézanne's *Woman Bathers* or a number of other modern paintings in his collection, by Gleizes, Matisse, de la Fresnaye and Picasso. Williams recalls heated discussions of Cubism, and a concurrent interest in the structure of poetry, though the fruit of these discussions as he remembers it – omitting rhyme or the capitals at the head of each line[3] – indicates no great penetration, at that point, of the deeper structural implications of Cubism.

Nevertheless, it was these deeper structural implications and their transmutation into literature that Williams would attempt to unravel. In this respect he differs from Wallace Stevens, whose appropriations from painting, as Robert Buttel has implied in his study of Stevens's

1 *Autobiography*, p. 138.   2 p. 136.   3 p. 136.

early development, are generally speaking visual (colour and light) and symbolical rather than structural.[1] It is nicely significant that, in writing to Williams about his recently published *Al Que Quiere*, Stevens should have recommended Renoir as a model: 'One has to keep looking for poetry as Renoir looked for colours in old walls, woodwork and so on.'[2] Williams was more taken by the counter genius of Cézanne, Juan Gris and Sheeler.

The spirit of the first poem in *Al Que Quiere*, *Sub Terra*,[3] written within a year of the Armory Show, epitomizes the artistic stirrings of a whole generation. Much later Williams was to remember in connection with this poem that:

I thought of myself as being under the earth, buried in other words, but as any plant is buried, retaining the power to come again. The poem is spring, the earth giving birth to a new crop of poets, showing that I thought I would some day take my place among them, telling them that I was coming pretty soon. See how earnest and passionate about the idea I was?[4]

The Imagist movement presides over the poems of this book; *Metric Figure*,[5] for instance, with its image of fish, would fit comfortably into a volume of almost any one of the Imagists. Several poems, however, without departing from Imagist practice, are frank transcriptions of real or imagined paintings, as for instance *Winter Sunset*,[6] *A Portrait in Greys*,[7] *To a Solitary Disciple*,[8] *Conquest*[9] and parts of *January Morning*,[10] all of them employing primary colour words as though bold, flat patches in a painting. At least two poems, *Tree*[11] and *Virtue*,[12] seem to have adopted the Fauvist frenzy:

Now? why –
whirlpools of
orange and purple flame
feather twists of chrome
on a green ground

1 *Wallace Stevens, The Making of Harmonium*, Princeton University Press, 1967, ch. 6.
2 *Selected Essays*, pp. 12–13. 3 *Collected Earlier Poems*, p. 117.
4 *I Wanted to Write a Poem*, p. 32. 5 *Collected Earlier Poems*, p. 123.
6 p. 127. 7 p. 160. 8 p. 167. 9 p. 172. 10 p. 162.
11 p. 142. 12 p. 152.

funneling down upon
the steaming phallus-head
of the mad sun himself –
blackened crimson!

One poem in particular, *Spring Strains*,[1] seems a venture in transcribing pictorial structure into a poem:

In a tissue-thin monotone of blue-grey buds
crowned erect with desire against the sky
     tense blue-grey twigs
slenderly anchoring them down, drawing
them in –

     two blue-grey birds chasing
a third struggle in circles, angles,
swift convergings to a point that bursts
instantly!

     Vibrant bowing limbs
pull downward, sucking in the sky
that bulges from behind, plastering itself
against them in packed rifts, rock blue
and dirty orange!
                             But –
(Hold hard, rigid jointed trees!)
the blinding and red-edged sun-blur –
creeping energy, concentrated
counterforce – welds sky, buds, trees,
rivets them in one puckering hold!
Sticks through! Pulls the whole
counter-pulling mass upward, to the right
locks even the opaque, not yet defined
ground in a terrific drag that is
loosening the very tap-roots!

On a tissue-thin monotone of blue-grey buds
two blue-grey birds, chasing a third,
at full cry! Now they are
flung outward and up – disappearing suddenly!

1 p. 159.

The poem represents a shallow, two-dimensional landscape in a limited palette, Williams's favourite colours of that period, oranges and blues. A 'tissue-thin monotone of blue-grey buds' could only be made of paint, for in tangible actuality even the frailest and tiniest of buds are more substantial than tissue. The 'circles, angles, | swift convergings to a point that bursts | instantly' of the birds' flight is the verbal presentation of lines on a plane; none of the words draws the eye inward, into depth. In the poem the sun is dragging the massive earth 'upward, to the right', whereas in normal perception the sun moves from the distant horizon gradually upward, over and down again, a movement through three dimensions, not two. The limbs of the trees are 'sucking in the sky | that bulges from behind, plastering itself | against them in packed rifts', as though the sky were pressed solidly right up against the branches, as in low relief sculpture. At the end of the poem the birds 'are | flung outward and up – disappearing suddenly', where else but off the edge of the canvas? Consciously or not, Williams's sense of the limitations or 'edges' of a poem has fused with the frame and shallow space of the paintings he has been viewing and discussing. It had been part of the Cubist programme to renounce the illusion of infinite distance, and to exploit the formal potentialities inherent in the medium, that is, the flat pictorial plane and area restricted by a frame. The effect of *Spring Strains* is in some measure due to the obscure tension between the burgeoning spring energies of birds, buds and sun, and the physically constricting two-dimensional pictorial plane.

Williams's next publication, *Kora in Hell* (1920), with its frontispiece by Stuart Davis, is again a volume illuminated by its context in painting. Among the painters Williams knew, painting had become at this period predominantly abstract or Dadaist. The Forum Exhibition of 1916, showing the work of young American artists associated with Stieglitz and Daniel, tended toward abstraction, and the painters' short statements of intentions published in the catalogue, were almost unanimously in defence of a non-representational art based on artistic personality and inner feeling. In the following year the Independents' Exhibition impressed itself on Williams's memory chiefly by its rejection of Duchamp's entry, a urinal signed R. Mutt.[1] It was probably at this exhibition that Williams read his two poems,

1 *Selected Essays*, p. 6.

Overture to a Dance of Locomotives and *Portrait of a Woman in Bed*.[1] The Prologue to *Kora in Hell*,[2] with its several references to Duchamp, including the controversy over his *Fontaine*, is in some respects Williams's own version of a Dadaist manifesto. 'I didn't originate Dadaism,' he said later, 'but I had it in my soul to write it.'[3] Like the Dadaists, Williams proclaims the dissolution of boundaries between art and non-art and the supremacy of accident, caprice and novelty. He recounts with amused approbation Duchamp's venture into a hardware shop to buy the first object that caught his eye as his 'construction' for the day; the artist ought to be able to lift to the imagination the pick-axe Duchamp came out with, or any other of those things 'which lie under the direct scrutiny of the senses, close to the nose.'[4] The speed and brokenness of the writing in *Kora* has the proper Dadaist intention of breaking down rigidified categories; 'it is to loosen the attention, my attention since I occupy part of the field, that I write these improvisations.'[5] The 'hey-ding-ding touch', which H. D. deplored in one of his poems and which Williams defends in his Prologue as essential to the improvisations, corresponds to Dadaist whimsy and cynicism in its derisive somersaulting of all sober virtues and conventional patterns of perception and behaviour. *Kora* belongs with the highly conscious and perverse playing with objects and disruptions of associations that characterize Duchamp's aesthetic rather than with the semi-mystical pursuit of the subconscious in symbolist or surrealist literature, though of course there is a point at which they are difficult to distinguish. Williams's efforts to loosen the attention resemble in some respect Rimbaud's programme of 'le dérèglement de tous les sens'; Williams's motive, however, unlike Rimbaud's, was a firmer foothold in commonplace external reality.

To see only the Dadaist colouring of *Kora*, of course, would be a distortion. It is also, ambiguously, a confrontation with human

---

1 *Collected Earlier Poems*, pp. 194 and 150. In *I Wanted to Write a Poem* (p. 46) and his *Autobiography* (p. 136) Williams mentions reading these poems at the Armory Show; but since, as far as I know, there were no poetry readings at the Armory Show, and since Williams's memory also plays him false in locating Duchamp's *Fontaine* at the Armory Show (*Autobiography*, p. 134), I think it more likely that this reading took place at a later date.

2 *Selected Essays*, pp. 3–26.   3 *I Wanted to Write a Poem*, p. 60.

4 *Selected Essays*, p. 11.   5 p. 11.

suffering. Williams was by temperament too restrained, awkward and compassionate for Dadaist flamboyance, and in this resembled other American artists of the time who were unwilling to follow French logic to its extreme.

The poems of Sour Grapes, written between 1917 and 1921, reveal few specific debts to painting. On the whole these are subdued winter poems, of drily fluttering leaves, stubborn resistance to winds, and cold, reduced and solitary satisfactions, reflecting in mood the approach of the poet's fortieth year, and his consciousness of the slow pace of his own intellect and growth. 'I am late at my singing', he says in the first poem of the volume. In his autobiography, after recalling a humiliation dealt him by the self-assured Duchamp, he remarks: 'I bumped through these periods like a yokel, narrow-eyed, feeling my own inadequacies, but burning with the lust to write.'[1] The mood of these poems reflects too the gradual subsidence of the first burst of enthusiasm after the Armory Show. America had entered the war, and, in the narrower realm of the arts, the magazine Others had collapsed, '291' had been forced to close in 1917, and many American painters, whose understanding of Cubism and abstraction had been dubious at best, were returning to a more realistic expression.

The prose sections of the next volume, Spring and All (1923), Williams was to describe later on as 'a mixture of philosophy and nonsense. It made sense to me, at least to my disturbed mind – because it was disturbed at that time – but I doubt if it made any sense to anyone else.'[2] His perplexity is due, at least partly, to his new efforts to come to grips with the implications of modern painting, particularly Cubism. Cubism was, after all, a foreign importation, suddenly and telescopically thrust upon imaginations unprepared, as the French were, by the direct implications of the preceding half century of art. As Barbara Rose says in her American Art Since 1900, 'to be an American Cubist was by definition to be an imitator';[3]

for the majority of Americans who called themselves Cubists, Cubism meant little more than sharp lines and acute angles. Cubism was seen, not as a new attitude of mind, but in terms of its surface effects. Thus, many blithely set about

1 p. 137.   2 I Wanted to Write a Poem, p. 48.   3 p. 86.

super-imposing directional lines and fragmented shapes on
top of essentially realistic compositions.[1]

Perhaps, as she suggests, the intellectual analysis and the composure
of classical Cubism were basically at odds with the more restless,
dynamic American temperament. Of the Americans, only Marsden
Hartley (a friend of Williams) and Man Ray produced genuinely
Cubist canvases, and by 1920 Hartley had renounced abstraction
while Man Ray became a permanent exile in Paris. Two of Williams's
closest friends, Demuth and Sheeler (to whom I shall return in
another context), were among the few Americans who managed to
assimilate the foreign style and evolve a valid fusion of French
Cubism and American realism. Along with all the enthusiasm and
courage emanating from the Armory Show, Williams too seems to
have felt from the first some uncertainty about the new painting.
His fury at being snubbed by Duchamp on the occasion I have
already mentioned, and his realization 'then and there that there
wasn't a possibility of my ever saying anything to anyone in that
gang from that moment to eternity'[2] reflects his ambiguous feelings
about French painting and the mental Atlantic Ocean between
French and American art.

Adding to the pressure for an authentic assimilation of French art
was the growing demand by critics such as Van Wyck Brooks to
turn toward America, a summons that Williams was soon to answer
with his *In the American Grain* essays. Everything conspired at this
period to provoke a more rigorous questioning of Cubism and its
possible implications for verbal and native purposes. Though *Al Que
Quiere* had used the more obvious elements of a painterly style, and
though the Prologue to *Kora in Hell* had adopted Dadaist allusions
and tone, I would argue that *Spring and All* is unprecedented in its
poetic encounter with the basic structural tenets of Cubism, and an
advance in Williams's understanding of his own creativity.

The tenets of Cubism, as set forth by Barbara Rose, are:

the preservation of the integrity of the picture plane, the
analysis of both the structure of objects and the means by
which objects are perceived, the assertion of the independent,
self-referential reality of the work of art.[3]

1 p. 85.   2 *Autobiography*, p. 137.   3 p. 87.

The prose passages of *Spring and All* hurried and spontaneous as they appear, accommodate all these principles in what might be called 'an aesthetic of energies'. First the 'independent self-referential reality of the work of art': for Williams this was the perception at the source of modernity. There is a 'cleavage', he thought, between on the one hand the old (nineteenth-century) idea of art as 'prose painting representative [representational?] work, clever as may be in revealing new phases of emotional research presented on the surface', and on the other hand self-referential art, such as that of Cézanne, Juan Gris and certain of the primitives.

Here, of course, we confront the perennial stumbling-block in discussions of the parallels between modern poetry and modern painting, the fact that words are simply not self-referential; they insist on reminding us of some 'reality' beyond their own black marks or vocal vibrations. Literature that aims at confining words exclusively to a visual aesthetic of black hieroglyphics on white background or to auditory noises – 'concrete poetry', for example – inevitably violates one of the other Cubist premises: that art should work within, accept and exploit the potentialities and limitations of its own medium (thus a painting should insist on its own flat surface and limited area; a sculpture should look like stone, not wood or flesh; and poetry should be reconciled to the transparency of language).

Williams, however, saw the self-referential independence of a painting in terms that could include a poem's mode of independence; in the modern conception, he thought, a 'work of the imagination [is] not "like" anything but transfused with the same forces which transfuse the earth – at least one small part of them'.[1] Thus, to choose a simple example from his own work, the poem *Dawn*[2] is structured or organized as a mounting crescendo of energy, a small part of the forces transfusing the universe.

This formulation protects poetry and painting from the compulsion to go totally abstract. Juan Gris, for instance, 'marking more clearly than any I have seen what the modern trend is'[3] paints recognizable things:

things with which he is familiar, simple things – at the same time to detach them from ordinary experience to the

1 *Imaginations*, p. 121.   2 *Collected Earlier Poems*, p. 138.
3 *Imaginations*, p. 107.

imagination. Thus they are still 'real', they are the same
things they would be if photographed or painted by Monet,
they are recognizable as the things touched by the hands
during the day, but in this painting they are seen to be in
some peculiar way – detached.[1]

A tree or wheelbarrow in Williams's poetry, like a bunch of grapes
in Juan Gris's painting, share in the forces of the universe, but at the
same time they live in the poem by virtue of the kind of energies and
proprieties imposed upon them by the medium.

The transfer into poetry of the Cubist 'analysis of both the structure
of objects and the means by which objects are perceived' is again
paralleled in Williams's aesthetic of energies. If the 'structure' of an
object or situation is conceived in terms of forces seeking equilibrium in and around objects, then the artist perceives these forces
by an empathy deriving from awareness of his own interior tensions
and forces, from the sympathetic ability, as Williams says, 'to feel
every form which he sees moving within himself'.[2] Williams's
rather abstruse dictum that 'the inevitable flux of the seeing eye
toward measuring itself by the world it inhabits can only result in
crushing humiliation unless the individual raise himself to some
approximate co-extension with the universe'.[3] I take to mean as
follows: that the seeing eye of the individual will be confused and
overwhelmed by external reality, will find no coherence or measure
either in himself or in reality, unless these sympathies flow between
mind and object, and he feels the forces, or at least a part of them,
transfusing the earth. Williams continues: 'This is possible by aid of
the imagination. Only through the agency of this force can a man
feel himself moved largely with sympathetic pulses at work.'[4]

The imagination is capable of these perceptions because it shares in
the nature of what it is observing: 'the imagination is an actual force

1 *Collected Earlier Poems,* p. 110. Williams goes on to describe the painting he
has in hand: 'Here is a shutter, a bunch of grapes, a sheet of music, a picture
of sea and mountains. . . . One thing laps over on the other, the cloud laps
over on the shutter, the bunch of grapes is part of the handle of the guitar, the
mountain and sea are obviously not "the mountain and sea", but a picture of
the mountain and the sea.' It is clearly a reproduction of one of a series called
The Open Window which Juan Gris worked on in 1921.
2 p. 105.   3 p. 105.   4 p. 105.

comparable to electricity or steam, it is not a plaything but a power that has been used from the first to raise the understanding of – . . . ' [1]
'Prose has to do with the fact of an emotion; poetry has to do with the dynamization of emotion into a separate form. This is the force of imagination.' [2]

Williams's conversion of the third Cubist tenet, 'the preservation of the integrity of the picture plane', I have already touched on. It corresponds, I think, to a resignation to ordinary language and a renunciation of the effort to capture mystical or non-linguistic intuitions in the linguistic net, the kind of effort which made Eliot complain of language as 'shabby equipment always deteriorating'.

The dedication of the poems of *Spring and All* to Charles Demuth and their apparently casual references to Hartley, Marin, El Greco and prehistoric paintings are no accident. They continue to expose the congruity of object, structural framework and modes of perception. In *The Rose*, [3] for instance, perception of roses involves the structure of mathematics:

so that to engage roses
becomes a geometry –

In *The Eyeglasses* [4] the innate structure of eyesight discloses and composes 'the universality of things'. If in Cubist painting a bottle or guitar suffices to reveal the mechanism of seeing, here a flower growing at the edge of a refuse heap performs the same function:

. . . It is
this that engages the favorable

distortion of eyeglasses
that see everything and remain
related to mathematics –

Similarly, in *Composition* [5] a red paper box serving a variety of purposes, to hold pins, glue and gummed labels, becomes a kind of universal symbol:

for this eternity
through its
dial we discover

1 p. 120. 2 p. 133. 3 *Collected Earlier Poems*, p. 249.
4 p. 256. 5 p. 260.

– not eternal metaphysical verities – but more of the furniture of this world, tissue on a spool or luggage labels. Even though the aesthetic skeleton is too rawly exposed in these last two poems, they serve as a gauge of Williams's concerns at the time.

Under such pressure to lay bare the reciprocity of perception and objective structure Williams's world seems on occasion to have collapsed; or to put it in other words, the intuition that reality depends upon our own modes of perception spawns a radical scepticism about the coherence of both. Thus *Spring and All* contains several poems of extreme fragmentation, such as *Young Love*, *Rapid Transit* and *The Agonized Spires*,[1] uncharacteristic of Williams's basic faith in the coherence of objects and language. At the opposite pole of possible responses to Cubist analysis, however, is the untroubled, amoral lucidity of *The Avenue of Poplars*,[2] corresponding to the paintings of Cézanne and Juan Gris in its lack of egotistic turmoil:

The leaves embrace
in the trees

it is a wordless
world

without personality
I do not

seek a path
I am still

. . . .

I ascend

through
a canopy of leaves

and at the same time
I descend

for I do nothing
unusual –

I ride in my car
I think about

1 pp. 253, 282, 262.   2 p. 280.

prehistoric caves
in the Pyrenees –

the cave of
Les Trois Frères

Although narrowly analytical concerns are left to the 'object' poems, some of the poems about people in this volume are still, obliquely, concerned with poetic composition. A farmer walking thoughtfully through his bare March field becomes the generic figure of the poet-painter, simultaneously struggling ('antagonist') and cooperating with ('composing') a blank but potentially fruitful nature:

The farmer in deep thought
is pacing through the rain
among his blank fields, with
hands in pockets,
in his head
the harvest already planted.

. . . .

Down past the brushwood
bristling by
the rainsluiced wagonroad
looms the artist figure of
the farmer – composing
– antagonist[1]

Affinities with Photographers

In the never-ending debate of those years about what it meant to be American, the painters and critics whom Williams knew agreed almost without a dissenting voice that Americanism involved a devotion to the 'object' rather than the 'subject'. It is this aesthetic of the 'object' conceived in a painterly or photographic manner that links Williams most unambiguously to a group which began with Stieglitz's Photo-Secession Gallery and always included photographers; and it is this aesthetic that most clearly distinguishes him from contemporary

1 p. 243.

writers, both expatriate and stay-at-home. The intellectual and psychological structure in which Americanism, photography and the 'object' were key concepts was best articulated in Paul Rosenfeld's *Port of New York* (1924).[1] Briefly, the creed advocates a reconciliation between the American artist and his own environment, a doctrine which merges with the conviction that the 'self' can only be discovered by fidelity to the objective world; the outer world is full of forms awaiting discovery, and these forms, if faithfully responded to, express and reveal the inner truth of the 'I'. These premises sprout easily into, on the one hand, a primitivistic myth of the soil and sexuality, and on the other hand, a challenge to adapt to the modern urban and industrial environment. Williams deeply admired Rosenfeld,[2] and the admiration was fully returned, for the centre of *Port of New York*, as epitome of the whole aesthetic, is an essay on Williams.

If Williams's poetry embodied the aesthetic in verbal form, Alfred Stieglitz's photography embodied it, for Rosenfeld, in visual form; and the final and definitive essay in the book is on Stieglitz. No more heart-sick trips to Europe. The camera for Stieglitz seems to have been what poetry was for Williams, an instrument for perceiving and coming to terms with his own environment, demanding a close perusal of the object combined with a selective imagination in the artist:

There is no matter in all the world so homely, trite, and
humble that through it this man of the black box and
chemical bath cannot express himself entire. A tree, a barn,
a bone, a cloud, have released the spirit in Stieglitz.

Capacity for instantaneous crystallization, for dazzling flashlike
selections of the unconscious mind from among the welter of
materials present to his senses, is a principle of Stieglitz's
psyche.[3]

Williams, of course, had little patience for talk of the psyche and the unconscious, but his poetry reveals the same process – the seizing of the outer object in all its ugliness and particularity as a full embodiment

1 Reprinted by the University of Illinois Press, 1961.
2 *Autobiography*, p. 271.
3 Rosenfeld, pp. 237, 243.

of an inner state. The dual role of camera and camera-man easily transposes itself to the realm of poetry:

The photographer can synthesize feelings gotten from many objects in the object present before the dead eye of the machine; and he has the power of intelligent control over the filter and bath of developers to assist in the process of selection made by his emotion from among the range of materials before him. All forms exist in nature. The artists have merely assembled them. The Italian primitives are written over the face of Umbria and Tuscany. But the photographer whose emotion has failed to make the significant selection and simplification, and who gums and fuzzies and diffuses his plates and introduces the human hand into the process of photography is not living as his medium demands he live.[1]

Williams's refusal to go to school to poets of earlier centuries is echoed in Stieglitz:

It has never interested him to analyse the old painters. He has merely been trying to do justice to his feelings about the matters before him. And yet the same dramatic oppositions and double-pulls of form, the same interplay of angles and curves present in the paintings of the old men are to be found in all the later photographs of the New Yorker; Stieglitz's form of proof that the masters, too, sat before nature, and were moved by a passion to represent what they saw.[2]

Describing some of his later exhibitions, Rosenfeld remarks that 'the Stieglitz photographs lie at that point where the objective world and the subjective world coincide. They are true alike to fact and to the inner sense of life.'[3]

A similar conception of art appears in another member of the Stieglitz group, the photographer Edward Steichen, with whom Williams had a close friendship.[4] Steichen's ideas on the function of photography parallel Stieglitz's, and involve several of Williams's

1 p. 248.   2 p. 250.   3 p. 270.
4 *Autobiography*, p. 322.

favourite images. Looking for discipline in post-impressionist art, Steichen reports:

> I set out to try to understand nature's discipline. I decided to make a study of the ratio of plant growth and structure. For many years, I had been impressed by the beauty of the spiral shell on the snails so abundant in our garden. . . . I found some form of the spiral in most succulent plants and in certain flowers, particularly in the seed pods of the sunflower, of which I had made so many photographic studies.

The sense of constriction that he, like Rosenfeld and Williams, felt in those early years, found release in his studies of natural organic structure.

> As I worked on the Golden Measure or Golden Section, I discovered that everything growing outdoors had become exceptionally alive to me. . . . I experienced a sense of freedom. . . . I believe it came from the knowledge that I was doing something based on nature's laws. The inexorable discipline gave me a new kind of freedom.[1]

Steichen's photographs of flowers and plants convey the rhythm, power and strength of natural things, as well as their sinister, ugly qualities. Some of his enlarged photographs of apples and pears, where the fruit, unglamorously pocked and gritty, swells out almost beyond the confines of the frame, might be used as illustrations of William's poetry.

> Still, ripe, heavy,
> spherical and close,
> they mark the hillside.
> It is a formal grandeur,
>
> a stateliness,
> a signal of finality
> and perfect ease.[2]

1 Edward Steichen, *A Life in Photography*, W. H. Allen, 1963, no pagination. All quotations are from ch. 5.
2 *Collected Earlier Poems*, p. 88.

Steichen at one point 'was particularly interested in a method of representing volume, scale and a sense of weight', and his fruit photographs were experiments in this direction. The title itself of one of his photographs of an apple conveys a sense of weight and immensity – it is called *An Apple, a Boulder, a Mountain* (plate 2). Perhaps it was with Steichen's plant photographs in mind that Carl Rakosi, a fellow Objectivist in poetry, noted in Williams's poems:

an isolation of detail (largely linear) that resembles a
photographic magnification of the plant parts . . . . The
surface sketchiness and accuracies . . . are a function of the
author's naturalness and the product of focusing and
concentration. When the light has been sharply caught and
the objective adjusted to the optimum distance the material
suddenly appears clear and natural, the surface a little plainer,
as if a dark pencil (or a stylus, as in *At the Faucet of June*)
assisted the eye.[1]

Affinities with Cézanne, Demuth and Sheeler

Williams had his favourites among painters – first among them Cézanne, an acknowledged 'god',[2] and source in Williams's view of literary as well as artistic modernism, and next his two close friends, Charles Demuth and Charles Sheeler.[3]

1 'William Carlos Williams', *Symposium*, vol. 4, October, 1933, pp. 441–2.
2 *Autobiography*, p. 322.
3 In a late poem Williams remembers

> You know how we treasured
>   the few paintings
> we still cling to
>   especially the one
>   by the dead
> Charlie Demuth,

(*Pictures from Brueghel*, p. 168). Williams owned a tempera painting by Demuth called *End of the Parade: Coatsville, Pa.* (1920, see A. C. Ritchie, *Charles Demuth*, 1950, p. 70, for illustration); also two Demuth watercolours, one called *The Gossips* (1914, mentioned in Ritchie, p. 89), and the other called *Tuberoses* (1922, illustrated in Ritchie, p. 79). Demuth's painting *I saw the Figure 5 in Gold* (1928, plate 1) is a tribute to Williams, referring to his poem *The Great Figure* (*Collected Earlier Poems*, p. 230). Gorham Munson (*Destinations*, Folcroft, 1928, p. 126)

There was plenty of opportunity to see Cézanne canvases – at the Armory Show, in Arensberg's studio, at a 1915 exhibition at Knoedler's Gallery[1] and in Paris galleries during his 1924 trip to Europe. Much later in life he was to publish a poem on Cézanne:

No pretense no more than the
French painters of
the early years of the nineteenth century

to scant the truth
of the light itself as
it was reflected from

a ballerina's thigh this Ginsberg
of *Kaddish* falls apart
violently to a peal of laughter or to

wrenched imprecation from a
man's head nothing can
stop the truth of it art is all we

can say to reverse
the chain of events and make a pileup
of passion to match the stars

No choice but between
a certain variation
hard to perceive in a shade of blue.[2]

One poem exceptionally reminiscent in tone and structure of Cézanne, though there is no reason to posit direct influence, is *Wild Orchard*:

It is a broken country,
the rugged land is
green from end to end;
the autumn has not come.

---

tells us that Demuth based a painting on poem 2 in *Spring and All* (*Earlier Collected Poems*, p. 242). Williams also owned a *Still Life* by Sheeler (1922, mentioned in the catalogue of *Charles Sheeler*, intro. by William Carlos Williams, 1939).

1 *Selected Letters*, p. 30.
2 Uncollected; published in the *Nation*, vol. 92, 13 May 1961, p. 416.

Embanked above the orchard
the hillside is a wall
of motionless green trees,
the grass is green and red.

Five days the bare sky
has stood there day and night.
No bird, no sound.
Between the trees

stillness
and the early morning light.
the apple trees
are laden down with fruit.

Among blue leaves
the apples green and red
upon one tree stand out
most enshrined.

Still, ripe, heavy,
spherical and close,
they mark the hillside.
It is a formal grandeur,

a stateliness,
a signal of finality
and perfect ease.
Among the savage

aristocracy of rocks
one, risen as a tree,
has turned
from his repose.[1]

As in Cézanne's Provençal landscapes, the perspective is flat and
two-dimensional: 'the hillside is a wall'; the picture is constructed
line by line and plane by plane, of grass, orchard, rocks, hillside and
sky; all is motionless, heavy; there is no sentiment, no philosophy
and no incident. In the earlier *Spring Strains* the energies of spring

1 *Collected Earlier Poems*, p. 88.

were structured and contained within the painterly conventions of flat area and frame; in this less mannered and more impressive poem, the painterly flatness and limitations of area are more compatible with the subject. The energies in this landscape need no artificial confinement, but have been caught at a moment of inherent, late-summer poise and culmination. Such obviously painterly land-scapes are, of course, rare in Williams's work, since the technique is unamenable to most poetic subjects; narrative, movement, verbal abstraction, indeed most of the resources of poetry, burst through the limiting illusion of a frame and shallow space.

Louis Zukofsky's remark on Williams's poetic architecture: 'In Williams, the advance in the use of image has been from word structure paralleling French painting (Cézanne) to the same structure in movement',[1] suggests even further that the slow word-for-word integrity of Williams's syntax is similar to Cézanne's sober, unadorned analysis, element by element, of a landscape. This is not clearly discernible, however, until we see Cézanne's influence refracted through the work of Charles Demuth, whose work at an early stage (like Sheeler's) was a worshipful imitation of the French painter.

The *Spring and All* disturbance in Williams's poetic growth had been anticipated and partly caused by a question he had posed in *Contact*, 1921: 'How then are we to love France?' with its accompanying answer:

In proportion as a man has bestirred himself to become awake to his own locality he will perceive more and more of what is disclosed and find himself in a position to make the necessary translations. . . . But he who does not know his own world, in whatever confused form it may be, must either stupidly fail to learn from foreign work or stupidly swallow it without knowing how to judge of its essential value.[2]

Demuth and Sheeler, almost alone among American painters of the

1 'American Poetry, 1920-30', *Symposium*, vol. 2, January 1931, p. 73. Zukofsky adds later in his article that *The Pure Products of America Go Crazy* 'could perhaps be realized only by one who has vicariously written, rather than painted as he has always wished to do' (p. 84).
2 *Selected Essays*, p. 27.

time, were able to make these 'necessary translations' in their painting, from Cézanne and French Cubism into a native American style
(baptized Cubist-Realism by art historians). This is why, among other
reasons, the affinities are strongest and most particular between their
painting and Williams's poetry.

Demuth's water-colours, with their wide margins, their scraps of
unpainted canvas, their unerased pencil lines visible under the
colour, and their brilliant fragile fruits and flowers like tissue paper
pasted on white background (plate 3) are, for all their distinction,
direct descendants from Cézanne; and the 'incompleteness' of
Cézanne's or Demuth's paintings can be compared to the silences in
Williams's poems (pauses at line ends, dashes, spaces between couplets
or triplets, wide margins), 'leaving room for thought' as he says in
one poem.[1] The bareness of both painting and poetry suggests not the
volatility of reality but the essential structure to be grasped by a
patient eye behind the volatility. That the parallel is conscious and
deliberate is revealed in the poem Williams dedicated to Demuth
after his death in 1935, *The Crimson Cyclamen*.[2] The poem assumes a
congruence of painting and poetry. The painted flower, like a poem,
is

an abstraction
playfully following
centripetal
devices, as of pure thought –
the edge tying by
convergent, crazy rays
with the center –

Both Demuth's leaves and Williams's words are

freakish, of the air
as thought is, of roots
dark, complex from
subterranean revolutions
and rank odors
waiting for the moon –

1 *Collected Earlier Poems*, p. 243.
2 p. 397.

When Williams says of the flowers, 'silence holds them – | in that space', the identity of silent intervals in poetry and empty canvas in painting is made explicit; the flowers are supported by the almost tangible space around them the way words hang in a pregnant silence.

> And
> color has been construed
> from emptiness
> to waken there –

the poem continues, applying to colour a term normally used of language; colour is 'construed from emptiness' the way a word is construed from silence to give shape to a hitherto vague, almost non-existent mental stirring.

Like so many recent critical and artistic concerns, our present bewitchery by space – poetic, musical, pictorial and geographic – was anticipated in the early years of this century. In 1912 *Camera Work* was publishing analyses by Sadakichi Hartmann, in which the effects of Mallarmé's innovatory blank space in the midst of his verses are compared with Debussy's use of silence in music. In 1910 the Cubist poet and painter, Max Weber, wrote an article for the same magazine in which he describes his 'consciousness of a great and overwhelming sense of space, magnitude in all directions at one time, . . . the space that envelopes a tree, a tower, a mountain or any solid.' Corollary to this perception, 'a form at its extremity still continues reaching out into space if it is imbued with intensity or energy'.[1] As in these articles and in so much modern sculpture and painting, space in Williams's poetry takes on a peculiarly positive existence, so that silence in the voice, space on the page and the air-filled space in which objects are located must be defined in terms of latency or potentiality. Space or emptiness takes on a presence, a thingness, an intangible weight. Williams's poem, *The Sun*,[2] plays on the 'isness' of what is normally felt as negative, pressureless or non-existent. 'Cloud and sea | weigh upon the | unwaiting air,' the silence is 'hasteless'. The children playing are

1 'The Fourth Dimension from a Plastic Point of View', *Camera Work*, no. 29, July, 1910, p. 25.
2 *Collected Earlier Poems*, p. 412.

logged
in the penetrable
nothingness

whose heavy body
opens
to their leaps
without a wound –

'Unwaiting air', 'penetrable nothingness', 'an ample silence',[1] 'that gentleness that harbours all violence',[2] 'the complicated innocent'[3] – this series of phrases opens up some of the related aspects of Williams's sensibility, which can perhaps best be summarized as a sensuous awareness of potentiality.

   The Crimson Cyclamen unites all these inquiries into space. After equating empty gaps in painting with silence in poetry, it goes on to what we have seen as the complement of this notion – that the emptiness and silence are really invisibly full and potent. The flower, like the 'argument' of a poem, breaks off and disappears at its edge

where the under and the over
meet and disappear
and the air alone begins
to go from them –
the conclusion left still
blunt, floating

The apparently empty air contains the unspoken (or unpainted) conclusion which the wary and scrupulous artist hesitates to articulate.

   Not all of Charles Demuth's paintings are of wavy-edged tissue-thin flowers and fruits. In his adaptation of Cubism, he made severe architectural compositions out of the geometrical lines and surfaces of his home town churches and streets. His frequent studies of a Wren-like church near his own home are preoccupied with the way, as Weber put it, 'a form at its extremity still continues reaching out into space if it is imbued with intensity or energy'. In this case the lines and planes of a church steeple are retained in the air and elongated beyond the actual physical edge (plate 4). Williams's poem, *To*

1 *Collected Later Poems*, p. 73.   2 p. 29.
3 *Many Loves and Other Plays*, p. 13.

A Solitary Disciple,[1] though its date precedes these Demuth studies, describes similarly converging lines of a steeple, which meet at the pinnacle, then escape upwards, forming a kind of ghostly flower in the air.

Rather grasp
how the dark
converging lines
of the steeple
meet at the pinnacle –
perceive how
its little ornament
tries to stop them –

See how it fails!
See how the converging lines
of the hexagonal spire
escape upward –
receding, dividing!
– sepals
that guard and contain
the flower!

A similar spatial awareness finds more mature expression in the airy dynamics of *The Rose*,[2] symbol of poetry in general:

From the petal's edge a line starts
that being of steel
infinitely fine, infinitely
rigid penetrates
the Milky Way
without contact – lifting
from it – neither hanging
nor pushing

The fragility of the flower
unbruised
penetrates space.

1 *Collected Earlier Poems*, p. 167.
2 p. 249.

Charles Sheeler is the other American painter to whom Williams pays special tribute. In an introduction he wrote for a Sheeler exhibition catalogue Williams notes his precision and objectivity; in his *Autobiography*[1] he recalls their long and intimate friendship, the integrity of Sheeler's search for American values, and the symbolic poignancy of Sheeler's own small cottage, which was all that remained of a wilfully destroyed Hudson River estate, and represented for Williams, like Sheeler's art and his own poetry, the hidden, reduced, but still living seed of what is valuable in the American past. Like Demuth, Sheeler was a photographer as well as a painter; early in his career he made a living by photographing newly finished houses for their architects, thus developing an eye for architectural mass, texture and function. He painted first under the influence of Cézanne, and, after the Armory Show, under the influence of Cubism, using both to advance his basic, classical search for objective form and organization. In a 1920 exhibition Sheeler had begun to fuse foreign and local, Cubism and his American environment, in a series with titles like *Barn Red* and *Barn Contrasts*, paintings partly abstract and partly based on the barns of his own Bucks County, hard-edged flat patterns formed by the oblongs, squares and cylinders of rambling farm outbuildings (plate 5).

Sheeler was seeking, not the American 'subject', painted with such facility by numerous artists of the twenties and thirties, but an essentially American 'form', growing with recognizable consistency through American history. It was present, he felt, in American architecture: in New England frame farmhouses and barns, stone cottages of Maryland and one-room slave houses in Louisiana. Sheeler saw in these constructions an undistracted means to an end, uncorrupted by foreign styles, unornamented, beautiful by virtue only of their surfaces, line and well-wrought structure. The same severe beauty he found in Shaker craftsmanship, in their tables, pots and houses, all of which appear again and again in his paintings and photographs.

A simple juxtaposition of Williams's and Sheeler's works, regardless of dates and sources, is illuminating. Compare, for instance, Williams's *Classic Scene*[2] with some of Sheeler's industrial paintings and photographs (plate 6). In 1927 Sheeler had been commissioned

1 pp. 320–22, 322–4. 2 *Collected Earlier Poems*, p. 407.

to photograph the Ford Plant at River Rouge, Detroit. These photographs he followed with several oils, dated variously 1928, 1930, 1931, and entitled *Industrial Plan, Smoke Stacks, River Rouge Plant, Classic Landscape* and *American Landscape*. Williams's poem, published in 1938, is almost certainly a reference to one or several of his friend's paintings.

A power-house
in the shape of
a red brick chair
90 feet high

on the seat of which
sit the figures
of two metal
stacks – aluminum –

commanding an area
of squalid shacks
side by side –
from one of which

buff smoke
streams while under
a grey sky
the other remains

passive today –

Similar are the clarity and simplification of shapes (a 'power-house | in the shape of | a red brick chair), the sense of space (the stacks are 'commanding an area'), the emphasis on sky, and the imperturbability, remarkable among contemporary invectives against the machine, with which both accept the industrial scene. *Classical Scene* is instructive, however, not simply for its resemblances to Sheeler paintings and photographs, but also for its successful injection of strictly poetic or metaphoric dynamics into the scene – the relationship of parts implied in the word 'commanding' and the electric anticipation of tomorrow in the ultimate line.

Both poet and painter savour texture and surface. Williams enjoys freshly-painted stairs with white risers and mahogany treads, the unmoving blue of the sky, coloured whorls of petals, and bare beams and darkened panes of an attic; and Sheeler expresses a similar delight in wood, stone and plaster:

Contrasting surfaces may contribute much to a picture, not merely to create interesting variations but for the actual design. A given texture, as of rough stone, may hold the attention by its rich complications and so give emphasis or depth which could not otherwise exist. A smooth texture may bring about a quickened tempo which may be essential to the whole. . . .[1]

The visual play of texture – sky, smokestacks, river, weathered blistering wood, grainy stone – is indeed a major element in Sheeler's art. In a poem, of course, such exclusive dependence on texture is apt to yield only inertness. The first of *The Descent of Winter* series,[2] with its visual contrast (a celluloid disc stamped with the number two, tacked against white enamelled woodwork by two bright nails) but verbal limpness, shows how Williams was occasionally misled by his painter's eye.

The composed precision of Sheeler's urban and industrial pictures is close to more than one of Williams's poems, for instance, to the shabby stability of the monastery in *The Semblables*:[3]

The red brick monastery in
the suburbs over against the dust-
hung acreage of the unfinished
and all but subterranean

munitions plant:. . .

. . . .

that trinity of slate gables
the unembellished windows piling
up, the chapel with its round
window between the dormitories

peaked by the bronze belfry
peaked in turn by the cross,
verdegris – . . .

1 Quoted in *Charles Sheeler*, p. 98, by Constance Rourke, to whom I am indebted for much of my information about Sheeler.
2 *Collected Earlier Poems*, p. 287.   3 *Collected Later Poems*, p. 244.

Besides barns and factories, Sheeler painted and photographed old houses, Shaker homes and colonial mansions. An oil by Sheeler called *Governor's Palace, Williamsburg*, showing a dignified, moderate-sized, white frame house, represents what he admired in the 'good old style', and might easily have served as a model for Williams's *The Old House*.[1] The symmetry of its gables, its simplicity, its fulfilment of desire and necessity, correspond to Sheeler's values; his implied criticism of an age which could decline into sham, weakness, and disrelatedness is made explicit in Williams's poem. Williams probably had in mind an actual house in Rutherford, but his eye and taste were undoubtedly in debt to Sheeler's more professional study of architecture.

Even when no exact visual counterpart is offered, Sheeler's values disclose the deeper qualities of feeling in the artless surface of some of Williams's poems. In *The Stone Crock*,[2] for instance, the glazed surface, rounded line and intense colour interrupted only by a small decoration, is like a Sheeler tea pot or saucepan, and the shift from the crock to the gentle persistence of the unnamed friend suggests the values Williams located in such surfaces – gentleness, endurance, craftsmanship and homeliness.

It is only by realizing Williams's relationship with painting and the function of his painter's eye that the moral and psychological meaning, the 'complicated innocence', adhering to his lines, masses and surfaces, can be properly understood. An early poem, *March*,[3] is an evocation of the cold creative fury of spring, the desperate poet seeking thin warmth in Babylonian enamels and a Fra Angelico Annunciation. Both pictures seize a moment of climactic tension, in one a king with drawn bow confronting lions, in the other the angel's eyes holding Mary's 'as a snake's hold a bird's'. The Fra Angelico was painted on plaster, the Babylonian picture done on enamelled walls; both media have a flat translucent clarity of colour, a mosaic-like stylization and distinction of detail, which contrast with their emotionally intense subjects. It was this fusion of emotional storm and cold control which appealed to the 'lean and frozen' poet of March winds. In another poem figuring a small print of Leonardo's *Last Supper* his attention has been caught by the background, a flat surface and simple lines,

1 p. 116.   2 *Pictures from Brueghel*, p. 28.
3 *Collected Earlier Poems*, p. 43.

reticent, quietly independent yet dedicated to something other than
itself; his 'keen eyes'

> . . . . noticed
> this famous picture not because
> of the subject matter but because
> of the severity and simplicity
> of the background! Oh there was
> the passion of the scene, of course,
> generally. But particularly,
> ignoring the subject, I fell upon
> the perpendiculars of the paneled
> woodwork standing there, submissive,
> in exaggerated perspective.
>
> There you have it. It's that background
> from which my dreams have sprung. . . .[1]

Pictures from Brueghel

Pictures from Brueghel (1962), Williams's salute across four centuries
to a kindred spirit, makes, in its union of both formal and humane
concerns, a vigorous climax to Williams's career and a convenient
epilogue to this discussion of his debt to painting. Williams probably
saw his first Brueghel canvases during his 1924 visit to Vienna, but
one of his most delightful poems, *The Dance*, published in 1944,
testifies that their impression did not fade during the intervening years:

> In Brueghel's great picture, The Kermess,
> the dancers go round, they go round and
> around, the squeal and the blare and the
> tweedle of bagpipes, a bugle and fiddles
> tipping their bellies (round as the thick-
> sided glasses whose wash they impound)
> their hips and their bellies off balance
> to turn them. Kicking and rolling about
> the Fair Grounds, swinging their butts, those
> shanks must be sound to bear up under such
> rollicking measures, prance as they dance
> in Brueghel's great picture, The Kermess.[2]

1 *Collected Later Poems*, p. 93.   2 *Collected Later Poems*, p. 11.

What appealed to Williams was the crowded gusto and humour of Brueghel's canvases, his Flemish peasantry caught at their unidealized daily activities:

men with scythes tumbling
the wheat in
rows[1]

a riotously gay rabble of
peasants and their

ample-bottomed doxies[2]

little girls
whirling their skirts about
until they stand out flat[3]

Even Brueghel's religious and mythological scenes are of this world; Aldous Huxley has remarked that Brueghel painted Calvary

as it would have appeared to any casual spectator on the road
to Golgotha on a certain spring morning in the year A.D. 33.
Other artists have pretended to be angels, painting the scene
with a knowledge of its significance. But Brueghel resolutely
remains a human onlooker.'[4]

Though Williams does not include this Calvary scene in his repertory of poems, Huxley's observation applies equally well to the poems about Icarus and the Nativity. Williams notices how the Icarus painting focuses on 'the whole pageantry' of spring; everything is 'concerned with itself' and quite undistracted by the irrelevancies of mythology:

unsignificantly
off the coast
there was

a splash quite unnoticed
this was
Icarus drowning[5]

1 *Pictures from Brueghel*, p. 8.   2 p. 10.   3 p. 13.
4 'Brueghel', *On Art and Artists*, ed. M. Philipson, 1960, p. 212.
5 *Pictures from Brueghel*, p. 4.

When painting the Nativity Brueghel's alert mind was

... dissatisfied with
what it is asked to
and cannot do

that is, to assume an angel's superhuman knowledge, and he instead

... painted
it in the brilliant
colors of the chronicler[1]

seeing it as an event purely human, though worthy in the imagination of 'profound worship'.

The Brueghel poems are concerned with the artist's organizing mind and artistic form as well as with boisterous or poignant humanity. *The Hunters in the Snow*[2] takes on its own poetic shape as Williams's eye moves over its corresponding picture. Beginning with a reference to 'the over-all picture', it ends with 'a winter-struck bush ... to | complete the picture', thus opening and closing with a reminder that we are looking not at a real scene but at a work of art. Background and foreground, the margins of both painting and poem, refer to icy, motionless things – 'icy mountains' and the 'winter-struck bush' – enclosing and controlling the activity around the inn-yard fire of the central stanzas.

The opening poem of the Brueghel series, a *Self-Portrait*, with, significantly, no counterpart among Brueghel's works, hints at a growing self-consciousness and complexity in Williams's attitudes to art during his last years, especially evident in his remarks on portrait painting. In 1951 Williams sat for his portrait by Emanuel Romano, and was inspired to write an essay in which portrait painting – 'of all paintings ... the most complex, and the most satisfying' – embodies his concern in those years for the nature of human communion.[3] Imaginative understanding between one person and another is something like that between 'the painter and the sitter. It is a world of unrealized proportions. It is a drawing together such as that between Van Gogh and the "Potato Eaters" – a man facing

1 p. 6.   2 p. 5.
3 See 'Emanuel Romano' (1951), *Form*, no. 2, September 1966.

other men and representing on the canvas himself as modified by those others so inexplicably placed before him evoking his distress, his disappointments, his love. It is that that he must paint ... the internal contours of that other face ... facing his own.' 'The artist is always and forever painting only one thing: a self portrait', but self and portrait discover or create each other, for 'it is his own face in the terms of another face'. In the Brueghel poems Williams touches only lightly on the painter himself:

... the mind the resourceful mind
that governed the whole[1]

But this meditation on the portrait, on 'how the artist and the sitter combine', elucidates the impersonal introspection of the majority of his late poems.

In the later poems (collected under the inclusive title *Pictures From Brueghel*) painters are mentioned frequently, and Williams's sympathies are, if anything, more catholic than ever before. Besides Brueghel, one comes across Bosch, Dürer, Daumier, Gauguin, Van Gogh, Klee, Picasso, Juan Gris, Japanese pictures, a tapestry, even a coloured photograph on a calendar. Their functions are as various as the poems – it is the satire in Daumier that appealed to him, the friendship between Gauguin and Van Gogh, the withdrawn expression in a Picasso portrait, the grotesqueness of Bosch creatures, and so on. The fifth part of *Paterson* is dedicated to an old favourite, Toulouse-Lautrec, and American painters such as Jackson Pollock and Ben Shahn appear in it. Williams is willing to appreciate whatever a painter offers. His later poems are, on the whole, less self-consciously painterly; there are none like *Wild Orchard* or *To A Solitary Disciple*. As he relaxed his strictly 'objectivist' principles, his painter's eye, though still keen, surrendered its supremacy to the 'dance of the mind'; he came, as he admits in *Tribute to the Painters*[2] to

the knowledge of
the tyranny of the image
and how

men

1 *Pictures from Brueghel*, p. 6.
2 p. 135.

in their designs
        have learned
                to shatter it
whatever it may be,
        that the trouble
             in their minds
shall be quieted,
        put to bed
            again.

How Some of the Poems Work

Albert Cook

from 'Modern Verse: Diffusion as a Principle of Composition',
Kenyon Review, vol. 21, no. 2   1959

The poet in our time begins with urgent fragments, a phrase in the head, a persistent burst of rhythm, even a quotation. If the particularity of the world has its own inscape, it may take Hopkins as long to put together a dappled thing from his notebook entries as to make the decision that poetry is permissible to the Jesuit (two versions of the same process, perhaps).

Others take the way of Valéry and early Rilke, the poem hermetically sealed around an interpretation of a single object profoundly meditated: but the severe singleness of concern gives away the violence with which this has been wrested from a bewildering flux: Valéry was silent twenty years, and Rilke, pondering about as long, to break forth jubilantly at the end of this time into a new, diffuse style.

Even the 'ordered' style need not keep strictly to its object. Yeats holds to his wild swans, but in *Le Cygne* Baudelaire remembers, diffusely, a bird escaped from a cage seen once when he crossed a new bridge in Paris. He reminds himself of the inexorably changing city, the Louvre, the old Carrousel, his melancholy, and a negress far from Africa; but first of a legendary Trojan woman (possibly – the rhythms lend credence – filtered diffusely through Racine):

Andromaque je pense à vous! Ce petit fleuve
Pauvre et triste miroir où jadis resplendit
L'immense majesté de vos douleurs de veuve,
Ce Simoïs menteur qui par vos pleurs grandit,

A fécondé soudain ma mémoire fertile,
Comme je traversais le nouveau Carrousel.
Le vieux Paris n'est plus (la forme d'une ville
Change plus vite, hélas! que le coeur d'un mortel) . . .

And he gets to his swan only after two more such masterfully diffuse stanzas. So that the swan is not his subject, though it furnishes the title of the poem; it is not even a centrally exfoliating symbol, but merely a central point of organization for the cognitive experience attached to it. . . .
(199–200)

Diffusion by its nature is a principle of composition; it must be so in its function of putting parts of a poem together (and apart). For this reason it has to do with the unity of a poem, and this is very close to what a poem is finally about. . . .
(202)

The rhythms of *The Poor* by Williams[1] follow the contours of speech, the abstracted near chaos of the actual voice, and avoid the canons of rhythm:

It's the anarchy of poverty
delights me, the old
yellow wooden house indented
among the new brick tenements

Or a cast-iron balcony
with panels showing oak branches
in full leaf. It fits
the dress of the children

reflecting every stage and
custom of necessity –
Chimneys, roofs, fences of
wood and metal in an unfenced

age and enclosing next to
nothing at all: the old man
in a sweater and soft black
hat who sweeps the sidewalk –

his own ten feet of it –
in a wind that fitfully
turning his corner has
overwhelmed the entire city

1 *Collected Earlier Poems*, p. 415.

Through the years Williams has argued against using the classical rhythms of English, and the emphasis of that American voice appears throughout in the stresses of this poem. 'It's the ánarchy of poverty', and so on. The poem might almost be said to build itself loosely within these four line stanzas in order to set up a portable concert room for each cadence of meandering voice. . . .
(208–9)

Williams in his poem is approaching personally and genially a human condition, poverty, which is fundamental and hard-pressed, fundamental because hard-pressed. But Williams is not interested, or delighted, in the sentiments which the word's overtones may carry (that is, these overtones are there but he does not develop them). He attends to the effects of poverty on what the eye can see, human beings leaving their anarchic mark on a nature which other poems of Williams express as being equally anarchic.

When a man makes a poem (Williams says) makes it, mind
you, he takes words as he finds them interrelated about him
and composes them – without distortion which would mar
their exact significances – into an intense expression of his
perceptions and ardors.

In each of these stanzas we are presented with one or more human beings on the one hand and on the other with one or more man-made objects in a landscape. In the first stanza the human being is Williams, the objects an old yellow house 'indented' – like the beginning of a paragraph – among new, *the* new brick tenements. The article gives extra finality to the 'new' but is less demonstrative than 'those' would be; Williams wishes the words to make the tenement sound inevitable without giving this image special prominence. In the second stanza the object comes first, an instance of anarchy. *Die Natur can hinzutreten*[1] only in the form of a cast iron oak branch on a balcony. The branch is in full leaf, at a perpetual height, like the children whose dress therefore 'it fits' (the antecedent of 'it' is ambiguous, being also anarchy, not to say also the general situation of the poem). In this stanza the human beings are these children, and their dress is continued on into the third stanza with the poem's fullest

[1] The phrase is from a poem by Benn discussed elsewhere in this article. [Ed.]

set of abstractions, clothing their innocence as it were by giving compass bearings on their anarchy:

> It fits
> the dress of the children
>
> reflecting every stage and
> custom of necessity –
> Chimneys, roofs, fences of
> wood and metal

'It fits' for the reason that scene, anarchy and dress, all reflect every stage and custom of necessity. Note that Williams as he says 'the' tenements uses the participle, 'reflecting', and not 'because it reflects', or 'in order to reflect', or any other schema for the abstractions which then stand in their inviolable paratactic equality as an anatomy of anarchy: stage and custom of necessity. Custom may include stage, stage may include custom, by necessity so to speak, but again we have a simple copula, 'stage and custom'. The genitive 'of necessity' goes equally with both; and it is both objective and subjective genitive at once, or rather is so primal in its presentation as to be strictly neither.

Only a dash can cover the distance to the next perception – a dash of the sort dear to modern poets from Emily Dickinson on. The dash bridges the gap from abstractions to diffuse objects. For the humanity of the children in this third stanza, our objects are the protective parts of houses, those that let out smoke and keep off rain and keep out intruders, 'chimneys, roofs, fences'. But the anarchic weather is too penetrating to be kept off; behind the fences in the fourth stanza which enclose next to nothing at all, we have an old man, a single person while the children were plural, whose dress is concrete while theirs was abstract, 'a sweater and soft black | hat'. The man is 'old', as was the yellow wooden house (Williams somewhere remarks that one must always have justification for repeating a word in a poem). Here, as in the poetry of Rilke, normally mature human beings, except for the poet's persona, are absent. We have only those so innocent or so old and beyond caring as to be completely attuned to anarchy. The black of the old man's hat is still a more abstract color than the yellow of the wooden house; and he is absorbed in the rather abstract act of doing homage to anarchy by a ritual of order, sweeping his own ten feet of sidewalk, as tiny a space as Benn's 'drei Meter'. He sweeps on into the fifth, final stanza, where the visible object balancing his humanity is not tenements or balcony or fence, but no less than the entire city the wind has overwhelmed. He has stature enough in his very subservience to the petty needs of life to master anarchy as the poem is doing.

For consider: on which side of the fence is the old man sweeping? Syntax has him inside the fence, 'enclosing next to nothing at all: the old man'. But sense tells us that he is outside the fence, where sidewalks usually are: it is probably not the private sidewalk that leads to the door, or Williams would not have said 'his own ten feet of it'. He cannot be both inside and outside, but in an 'unfenced age' it depends on your point of view. He is enclosed but outside, which makes sense only when you perceive that spatial anarchy is a kind of order. 'Say it | no ideas but in things' Williams asserts, meaning thereby not that there are no ideas, but that ideas are in things, here one idea in a group of diffuse things. Williams through these diffuse images has created an idea, an apperception which is painterly – a city quarter of indefinite length with yellow, black, cast iron, red brick, variegations of dress – ; and at the same time this apperception is intellectual, defining anarchy, custom, necessity, stage, as interwoven with the eye and the heart. . . .

For the flux of the self, as of nature, Baudelaire also provides key terms. He says in *Mon Coeur Mis à Nu*, 'De la vaporisation et de la centralization du *Moi* Tout est là'. The vaporization and the centralization of the Ego. Everything is there.

Vaporization and centralization constitute poles of the same *Moi*. So poets who vaporize with diffusion of images, and poets who centralize through strict control over a single image, are approaching the same problem from two different directions. It is because of their centralization in the midst of a consciously resisted flux that the modern poem of severe control and exclusive statement seems far more airtight than its romantic or classic prototypes.

(209–12)

Winifred Nowottny

from 'Language in "Artificial" Forms', *The Language Poets Use* 1962

The poem I have chosen to illustrate one effect of sustained contrivance at the level of lineation is *The Red Wheelbarrow*:

so much depends
upon

a red wheel
barrow

glazed with rain
water

beside the white
chickens.[1]

This poem tries to present the power of art to make us see things in a non-utilitarian way, making us dwell on properties of ordinary objects usually passed over in our ordinary dealings with such things. Nowhere in the poem does the poet explicitly say that art emphasizes the intrinsic qualities of an object; instead of saying this he tries to do it – to make words achieve the condition of pictorial art so that we see visual properties in their individual particularity. The method he adopts is the eccentric placing of line-endings, so that they cut compound words into their separate elements ('rain | water', 'wheel | barrow'), elements as it were separately perceived. Stanza divisions are used to separate the qualifying phrase from what it qualifies ('barrow' | 'glazed with rain'). The poem attempts to make words do what a painting can do: to make us see not a vaguely-generalized barrow in vaguely-generalized rain but redness and wheel and glaze and rain and water. Spatial relations too are emphasized: 'upon' gets a line to itself and is followed by a break between stanzas. Similarly colour-relation has a line to itself ('beside the white'). It appears too that we are meant to treat the poem as though it were a picture, by moving about inside it and seeing different groupings in turn, since

1 *Collected Earlier Poems*, p. 277.

the link in sense and the separation by line and stanza endings pull us in different ways. If the line and stanza endings were nullified by reading out the poem, to someone who had never seen it on the page, as though it were continuous prose, the poem would lose its point. To say this, is to point out the paucity of formal relations in the poem, not to condemn the particular use made of such relations as there are. The paucity was perhaps unavoidable; the conflict between the lineation and our tendency to read continuously, automatically practising grammatical subordination, and abstraction, as we go, has to be decided by a very strong stress on the peculiarity of the lineation – a stress achieved by keeping out of the poem other relations which might interfere with it. A particularly unfortunate result of this technique is that the word 'red' and the word 'white' are not given qualitative immediacy; they remain almost as inert and general as in ordinary contexts, since there is nothing in the poem to fill in the mere conceptual outline they afford.

Because this poem confines its exploitation of verse form to one main kind of formal relation – the relation between certain words and the incidence of the lineation – it simplifies some of the problems of discussing the bearing of formal relations upon meaning. For instance, reference to this example makes it clear that though the relations between particular words and the incidence of the lineation can be stated (e.g. line splits compound word, preposition stands alone, etc.), it is a long way from such a statement to the inferences I made in my comments on the pictorial character of the poem. To describe a relationship is not the same as saying what it does to the meaning – that is, what construction it causes us to put upon the words it involves.

(119–21)

Hugh Kenner

'Syntax in Rutherford', from 'Ghosts and Benedictions',
Poetry, vol. 113, no. 2   1968

Any word at all:

cat.

A 'noun'. And what happens if we affix the article is highly mysterious:

the cat –

for the grammarians' distinction – definite article for the particular,
indefinite for the general – is meant to operate between speakers, live
persons in a real place who already know, because they are talking
about it, which cat is 'the cat': 'Have you put out the cat?' But typed
on a sheet of paper, as if to designate some one cat though we cannot
identify him, the article performs in pure abstraction a gesture of
as-if-specifying: something operative not in the kitchen or the garden
but in a language field, where on an invisible string a knot has been
tied.[1] (A poem is a machine made out of words.) The invisible string
is the infinity of cats; the knot, *the* cat.

  Tense the string:

As the cat

– an exact structure, empty but located, as asymptotes locate a hyperbola. Empty but torqued: the spine braces against an anticipated
swing: there will be two actions, two doings, parallel and related;
hence two verbs, the first to be expected immediately.

As the cat
climbed over
the top of
the jamcloset
first . . .

1 This knot, like the surfer in a later paragraph, is borrowed from the discourse
of Buckminster Fuller, who plays a prominent role elsewhere in *The Pound Era*,
Kenner's projected book.

– we are braced, now for the second verb; but the sentence has other business, and we are given instead a distinction:

first the right
forefoot

– a clarification, but the verb is still deferred; meanwhile 'first' has generated a new substructure for the sentence to complete. First, hence second; do we next encounter 'second' or some surrogate? No, we encounter

carefully

– an adverb as precariously placed as the cat's forefoot. And at last, a structure is acknowledged; 'first' receives its answer:

then

'First the right forefoot, then' – the left?

then the hind

Though our local foreseeings are inaccurate, we remain attentive, and at last comes the verb we have long anticipated, even as the cat once embarked on this expedition has anticipated, movement by movement, responsive solidities:

first the right
forefoot

carefully
then the hind
stepped down

into

This ideal cat, this verbal cat, this cat of linguistic torsions has (though 'carefully') stepped down not onto but 'into' –

into the pit of

worse and worse –

the empty

– ?

flowerpot

Verbal flowerpots are as hollow and frangible as verbal cats are agile. There is no more: we have examined two steps in slow motion, and if the front foot has been where the hind foot goes, we can feel as secure in the paradigm as we can in the knowledge that two subjects are competent to govern one verb. This structure of twenty-seven words commenced off balance – 'As' – and closes on a resolution of achievement and precariousness – 'flowerpot'. It is one sinuous suspended sentence, feeling its way and never fumbling. Its gestures raise anticipatory tensions, its economy dislodges nothing. The cat is as much an emblem of the sentence as the sentence is of the cat. It is headed *Poem*.[1]

'Of course it must be understood that writing deals with words and words only and that all discussions of it deal with single words and their associations in groups.' – Williams in *Spring and All*, 1923. 'Either to write or to comprehend poetry the words must be recognized to be moving in a direction separate from the jostling or lack of it which occurs within the piece.'

The surfer planes obliquely down a hill that renews itself at just the rate of his descent. But for encountering the beach he could glide eternally, leftward and inward and always as if downward, but never further down: always hung midway on the face of the wave. He shifts, precarious, through innumerable moments of equilibrium. And the wave bears him and there is no moving wave: the molecules of water move not forward at all but only up and down, their forward movement a pattern not a displacement, as his downward movement is no displacement but a pattern: on and on, self-renewing. So through mere words, renewed by every reader, the cat walks safely forever. Williams had achieved *Poem* by 1931: its wave decades later is undisplaced, unspent: the poem thrown decisively into the language.

Though Williams seems to have discovered it for himself, the principle of *Poem* is as old as, say, Ibycus:

Ἦρι μὲν ἅι τε Κυδώνιαι ...
... though it's in spring that the quinces and ...

A 'men' clause promises a 'de' clause ('on the one hand', 'on the other hand'); 'Eri men' offers to relate spring happenings to other

1 *Collected Earlier Poems*, p. 340.

sorts (though quince-time is spring, love assails me at all seasons). And a 'te' foretells a second 'te', paired members; 'te Kydoniai', producing the quinces, engages to produce comparable details (quinces bloom, and vine-shoots bristle). Such a poem fulfils a syntactic undertaking, purely in a verbal field, as a picture realizes potentialities of design purely within the flat picture plane: which is not the world but a place with its own laws, as a sentence is a governed system of energies, not the world's but its own. And cats, verbal cats, stalk through poems, verbal quinces bloom, flowerpots receive delicate steps, Thracian winds blow: all verbal. As a knot is not rope but a pattern the rope makes visible, so the poem is not consequent on the cat but precedent to the cat, not a pattern proffered and conceivable as pure syntax, but a pattern which the cat renders substantial. And renders meaningful: the sentence's poised 'carefully' corresponds to, is substantiated by, the careful precision of a walking cat. But for the poem, no cat upon the page; and instead of asking what the poem is all about we may quite as sensibly ask what an exploring cat is all about, and answer that it is about the poem.

For consider the two of them as analogous patterns. This, directed by mental options unimaginable in their intricacy but limited by the availabilities within a language system, patterns language which exists only in human minds, and does not dislodge words. That, directed by neural feedback of intricacy equally unimaginable, but limited by gravitation, equipoise and material impenetrability, patterns space, apperceived by minds, and does not dislodge clay pots. Is either prior? As some cat walked before *Poem* was composed – and maybe only in Williams's imagination – so other cats walk after. We can no more imagine what it is like to be a cat than we can imagine what it is like to be a sentence. We think words, we think cats; and though God can imagine, we cannot imagine cats before cats were named, and detached by being named from the 'big, blooming, buzzing confusion' Henry James's brother was at pains to stipulate.

Which did the child learn first? Did he learn first to isolate
'mama' [sc. 'cat'] from the confusion of his sensory world
and thereby to think mama first or did he learn the word
mama first? The question appears quite impossible to answer.
If anything, the word came first and the concept after. Only

the word was not really a word until the concept
accompanied it. Previously it was just a sound. . . .'[1]

And:

Language gives the infant access to hundreds of thousands of
years of human experience – millions of man-hours
previously spent – developing the concepts with which
language furnishes him. It is at least questionable whether
anyone would have an effective incentive to think in the
absence of a going language, access to the world of sound,
and older persons eager to initiate him into the linguistic
world. Even if he did have an incentive, he might well never
really get his thinking drives off the ground. Instead of
forming the concept of mama or man as he is in fact so
urgently coached into doing, he might waste his time
forming fruitless and relatively unreal categories. He might
group together, for example, all upright, brown, smoothish
things – chair legs, tree trunks, brown painted oars leaning
against houses, and so on. Or he might form a concept
grouping all small fuzzy yellow things: dandelions, certain
caterpillars (but only certain ones), pieces of fluff from two
of his mother's dresses, and other miscellanea.[2]

And a cat inherits none of this. But thanks to our access to millenia
of human experience we can enter the shared world our language
creates in our co-lingualists, and draw out of it like needles from a
haystack certain trim words to make a mental structure with:

As the cat
climbed over
the . . .

Williams drew, he said, on 'the speech of Polish mothers'.

Though *Poem*, the language-disposing faculty behaving cat-wise, is
unique in its neat suavity, its principle of syntactic leverage is discover-

1 Walter J. Ong, *The Presence of the Word*, 1963, Yale University Press, p. 143.
2 p. 144.

able everywhere in Williams's work of the twenties. At the top of a sheet he types

Young Sycamore

then

I must tell you
this young tree
whose round and firm trunk
between the wet

pavement and the gutter
(where water
is trickling) rises
bodily

into the air with
one undulant
thrust half its height –
and then

– half the poem. It is an effort to stop transcribing, because each phrase reaches forward. From line three to line seven we are drawn past unit after unit of attention by the promise of a verb to fulfil 'whose trunk'; then granted that verb but still waiting for the structure initiated by 'this young tree' to declare itself, we press on, alerted (by 'into the air with') that the dependent clause continues. 'And then', a major structural node, undertakes yet a further dependent verb; the poem rushes on –

and then

dividing and waning
sending out
young branches on
all sides –

hung with cocoons –
it thins
till nothing is left of it
but two

eccentric knotted
twigs
bending forward
hornlike at the top[1]

No full stop, because no termination for the tree's energies; but the poem, an eye's upward scan, is over. We have been carried through it by essentially narrative devices: from 'I must tell you' through suspensions and delays to 'and then', past vignettes and episodes ('hung with cocoons') to 'till nothing is left of it but'; and the terminal episode still secretes hidden force: 'bending forward | hornlike at the top'.

But the system contains energies left unaccounted, for the main clause it undertook with the words 'this young tree' was never completed. Though the whole poem has explicated this young tree, this young tree's syntactic circuit remains open. We may associate this unequilibrated energy with the poet's headlong generosity ('I must tell you . . .'), as though something had nevertheless escaped the telling. Or we may rhyme it with the failure of the trunk's gesture ('dividing and waning', after the integrated thrust that rises 'bodily'). For to rise bodily is to levitate. This levitation was an illusion, the trunk's vigor abetted by the poet's enthusiasm. The tree remains, we discover, tied to earth, toward which it bends back divided. The sentence arches, unarticulated, into ideal space.

The sentence offered, left not really finished, becomes a prime Williams strategy. In *The Sea Elephant*[2] gestures of sentences work like over-lapping planes. He wrote poems by dozens, consolidating this discovery.

(119–25)

1 *Collected Earlier Poems*, p. 331.
2 p. 71.

The Question of Measure

William Carlos Williams

from a letter to Richard Eberhart   23 May 1954 (reprinted in
J. C. Thirlwall (ed.), *Selected Letters*, 1957)

I have never been one to write by rule, even by my own rules. Let's
begin with the rule of counted syllables, in which all poems have
been written hitherto. That has become tiresome to my ear.

Finally, the stated syllables, as in the best of present-day free verse,
have become entirely divorced from the beat, that is the measure.
The musical pace proceeds without them.

Therefore the measure, that is to say, the count, having got rid of
the words, which held it down, is returned to the *music*.

The words, having been freed, have been allowed to run all over
the map, 'free', as we have mistakenly thought. This has amounted to
no more (in Whitman and others) than no discipline at all.

But if we keep in mind the *tune* which the lines (not necessarily
the words) make in our ears, we are ready to proceed.

By measure I mean musical pace. Now, with music in our ears
the words need only be taught to keep as distinguished an order,
as chosen a character, as regular, according to the music, as in the
best prose.

By its *music* shall the best of modern verse be known and the
resources of the music. The refinement of the poem, its subtlety, is
not to be known by the elevation of the words but – the words don't
so much matter – by the resources of the *music*.

To give you an example from my own work – not that I know
anything about what I have myself written:

count: – not that I ever count when writing but, at best, the lines
        must be capable of being counted, that is to say, *measured* –
        (believe it or not) – At that I may, half consciously, even
        count the measure under my breath as I write. –

(approximate example)
(1) The smell of the heat is boxwood
      (2) when rousing us
            (3) a movement of the air
(4) stirs our thoughts
      (5) that had no life in them
            (6) to a life, a life in which
(or)
(1) Mother of God! Our Lady!
      (2) the heart
            (3) is an unruly master:
(4) Forgive us our sins
      (5) as we
            (6) forgive
(7) those who have sinned against

Count a single beat to each numeral. You may not agree with my ear, but that is the way I count the line. Over the whole poem it gives a pattern to the meter that can be felt as a new measure. It gives resources to the ear which result in a language which we hear spoken about us every day.
(325-7)

Alan Stephens

from 'Dr Williams and Tradition', a review of
Pictures from Brueghel, *Poetry*, vol. 101, no. 5   1963

'I have wanted to link myself up with a traditional art,' Dr Williams explained in *Selected Letters*, and in this collection he calls attention to his new measure, which uses 'the variable foot' and gives us 'the counted poem, to an exact measure'. These phrases show his concern for the traditional, but I think they are misleading – not so much description as enthusiastic cries.

'Measure' calls for a unit of measurement, and in our verse you can select your unit from only a few possibilities: you can count beats, or syllables, or feet constructed of definite and recurrent combinations of stressed and unstressed syllables; the identity of the line is a matter of simple arithmetic, and you will search in vain for such a basis in Dr Williams's line. The concept of the variable foot no doubt has for Dr Williams a special analogical value, just as the concept of the eye of the phoenix had for Japanese painters when they sought to render the shape of one kind of bamboo leaf; but to speak of the variable foot as a unit of measurement is like speaking of an elastic inch. Although it is true that often in his verse there is a more or less regular beat, and that many lines take a more or less equal time, the attempt to find a metric in these facts will be occupied as much with exceptions as with any rule.

I believe that the identity of Dr Williams's line has no metrical basis, but that none the less the line has a definable identity. The general principle is this: a line is a line because, *relative to neighboring lines*, it contains that which makes it in its own right a unit of the attention; and it is as precisely various in its way as are the shadings of accent that play about the abstract norm of the metrical foot, for it too has a norm against which it almost constantly varies, allowing for feats of focusing on values that would be otherwise indistinguishable. The norm is the ordinary unit of the attention in language – the formal architecture of the sentence. This principle, it seems to me, also underlies verse with a metrical basis – is indeed the ultimate principle of all verse; if this is so, then audible rhythm, whether produced by a formal metric or by improvisation, is not the supreme fact of the verse line (though it is of course indispensable) and Dr Williams will have been working in the tradition all along.

(361)

Paul Fussell

from 'Some Critical Implications of Metrical Analysis',
Poetic Meter and Poetic Form 1965

Much of the contemporary ambition to 'break out' of inherited metrical schemes, as if they were traps rather than opportunities, is distilled in the theory and to some degree in the practice, of William Carlos Williams, who has sought to replace the idea of 'meter' with the idea of 'cadence'. The Imagists and the *vers librists* of the 1920s listened with devotion as Williams told them what was ailing in Georgian poetry and in its American counterpart. Beginning with the proposition that the American idiom is unique and that it thus requires a unique rhythmical garment, not one simply imported without alteration from the very different tonalities of the British language, Williams asserted:

We must break down the line, the sentence, to get at the
unit of the *measure* in order to build again. We have had a
choice: either to stay within the rules of English prosody, an
area formed and limited by English character and marked by
tremendous masterwork, or to break out, as Whitman did,
more or less unequipped to do more. Either to return to rules,
more or less arbitrary in their delimitations, or to go ahead;
to invent other forms by using a new measure.

This 'new measure' (a meter 'consonant with our day', Williams explains) is conceived of as a cadence midway in formality between traditional British accentual-syllabism, on the one hand, and, on the other, the whimsical rhythmical anarchy of totally unmetered free verse. In the latter part of his career, after the composition of *Paterson*, Williams came to think of the basic unit of this new cadence as what he called 'the variable foot', a unit of measure varying from one to four syllables with no specific pattern of stresses. As Williams explained in 1953, 'The iamb is not the normal measure of American speech. The foot has to be expanded or contracted in terms of actual speech.'

The difficulty of Williams's concept is its vagueness about the fundamental psychology of base and variation; its confusion about poetry's being based on the 'normal' rather than on the conventional and artificial; and its oversimplification, its creation of a revolutionary's false dilemma admitting of no compromises. Robert Frost, on the other hand, is one who has perceived that American idiom requires some special metrical treatment without, at the same time, rejecting like Williams, and rejecting for the sake of mere theory, the proven expressive resources of English prosody. The poet E. L. Mayo has appraised Frost's achievement in embodying metrically the unique tone of the American language. He writes:

Effective meter is closely bound up with the matter of living
idiom. . . . Frost's line from *Birches*,

Kicking his wáy dówn through the áir to the gróund,

never fails to give me pleasure because it accommodates itself
so well to the purpose it serves in the poem (sudden activity
after inhibited movement) without violating American
speech idiom at any point. Some of the most casual and
common idioms of the language have strongly developed
metrical elements; for example:

I tóld him hálf a dózen tímes

Whéther you líke it or nót

Is there ány reál reáson whý you cán't?

(the list might be endlessly prolonged) and I conceive it the
duty of the poet who desires authenticity of sound and
movement to cultivate his ear, avail himself of these riches
that lie so close to hand whenever they serve his purpose. In
this way his metrical effects become more than merely
personal; they become *native*. He thus clothes his naked
uniqueness (no fear – it will be civilized and intensified, not
smothered by the clothing) in the real spoken language of the
time.

And we can add that Frost not only registers the rhythms of 'the real
spoken language of the time' – not perhaps the real work of poetry:
consider Milton and Keats – but more importantly manages to subsume
these rhythms within the inherited meters of English. What he does
is to fuse the living language with the metrical inheritance, and what
he produces thereby is an illusion of faultless authenticity, a way with
rhythm which owes a complex allegiance at once to the past and to the
present. The nature of this achievement is such that it exposes
embarrassingly Williams's primitive and shallow metrical theorizings
in all their simplistic crudity.

(104–7)

A. Kingsley Weatherhead

'William Carlos Williams: Prose, Form and Measure',
English Literary History, vol. 33   1966

Williams always showed a consuming interest in the shape of poetry,
which he seemed to think was yet to be discovered. Sometimes he
spoke of form, sometimes of line, and most recently of measure and
a thing called the variable foot. Poetry to him was practically
synonymous with creation of new form; and the new line existed
in the rhythms of live American speech. In the fifties, after a career
of experiment and discussion, he thought he had discovered the line
he had been looking for, in a passage in his own *Paterson* written
years earlier, and he determined to use 'no other form for the rest of
[his] life'.[1] While he continually paid homage to poetic form, however, he sometimes played down the distinction between prose and
poetry. But on the occasions that he did so, there were particular
reasons; and his belief in poetic form is not injured. In the Mike
Wallace interview, for example, when he says, 'Anything is good
material for poetry',[2] he is implying not the familiar twentieth-
century belief that there are no specifically proper or improper
subjects for poetry but that material – the material in question being
a grocery list – can be made poetry with no change, except that it be
'treated rhythmically'. But the need for rhythm is the important
qualification: very often in Williams it is only the existence of rhythm
in a poem that distinguishes it from prose; and very often, incidentally,
that rhythm makes only the slightest impression on the ear. Then
elsewhere when he says, 'I want to say that prose and verse are to me
the same thing',[3] he is trying, as the context shows, to stamp out the
idea that the prose passages in *Paterson* are 'an anti-poetic device', and
he protests too much. In other remarks about them he clearly implies
that he recognizes a difference between poetry and prose.

There are non-poetic passages in other poems that are analogous
to the prose passages in *Paterson*. But the existence within a poem of
passages of prose or the existence of single prosaic pieces within a
volume does not of course preclude the co-existence of poetry. One

1 *Selected Letters*, p. 334.   2 *Paterson*, V, ii, p. 262.
3 *Selected Letters*, p. 263.

ready and easy way of dealing with Williams's poems has been to stretch them out into blocks of prose and discover that they are not poetry at all! But in certain of Williams's pieces, this kind of man-handling obliterates the only formal element – the rhythm which is perceptible by observing end-line pauses.[1] Such a rhythm, uninsistent though it may be, is the sole poetic agency that distinguishes some pieces from prose. One does not want to be 'had' by poems which are only poems by virtue of their shape on the page, of which there has been a good crop in recent years; and it must be said that Williams himself had an eye for the appearance of the printed poem. On the other hand, it is only by the shape on the page that the way in which a poem is supposed to sound can be communicated; and when this is mutilated, communication is corrupted. If even prose can be injured in its rhythms by printing,[2] how much more may poetry. According to Charles Olson,[3] the typewriter gives the poet a chance to make a fairly exact score, but it is of no advantage if editors or critics ignore it. In an early letter, Williams complains to Harriet Monroe that her rearrangement of his poem makes it 'physically impossible for anyone to guess how [he] intended it to be read'.[4]

Williams is characteristically unwilling to gather his images or his snatches of American idiom and shift them about until they are moulded into a sonnet or a ballad or any other prepared form. But it is equally clear from both his poetry and his repeated concern in the prose that he is certainly not satisfied to do without form alto-gether; he does not subscribe to what R. P. Blackmur calls the 'stultifying fallacy' D. H. Lawrence believed in, 'that if a thing is only intensely enough felt its mere expression in words will give it

---

1 I am assuming that there is normally an end-line pause in Williams. Of one period of his career, he says, 'When I came to the end of a rhythmic unit (not necessarily a sentence), I ended the line' (*I Wanted to Write a Poem*, p. 15). Naturally there is occasional enjambment.

2 Northrop Frye points out that prose rhythm may be injured when an emphatic word is printed at the end of a line instead of at the beginning of the next (*Anatomy of Criticism*, Princeton University Press, 1957, p. 263).

3 Charles Olson observes that the typewriter can 'indicate exactly the breath, the pauses, the suspensions even of syllables, the juxtapositions even of parts of phrases' ('Projective Verse *v.* Non-Projective', *Poetry New York*, no. 3, 1950, p. 19).

4 *Selected Letters*, p 39.

satisfactory form';[1] indeed, he feels the need for form so strongly that he even writes to James Laughlin recommending him to try using heroic couplets to avoid bare statements.[2] In Williams's best work the statement made by the rhetoric is not the total statement made by the poem, as is implied by those who reorganize the lines; form, in these poems, serves as an indissoluble part of the means of expression, and paraphrase is difficult. It is, for example, the formal elements, the changing rhythms, that make *By the Road to the Contagious Hospital*,[3] the success it is. Take away the variety of movement and you have a prose statement, rather disordered, of images of winter and the brink of spring. Given the changing rhythms, you have the scene charged and elevated to express the feelings of the observer; the form carries the feeling and makes it publicly available. The stark images are in themselves delightful; but the poem goes far beyond imagism, in the limited sense of that word. The first section, of six lines, describes a wintry scene; and this description is crowned and summed up in the short two-line section that follows. The inactivity of this scene, impressed by the use of 'standing' twice, though with different meanings, and enhanced by the contrast of the surge of the clouds above it, is the strongest feature. The scene that follows in the next section, of four and a half lines, is of the 'twiggy stuff of bushes'; this scene also, as the rhetoric presents it, is inactive: literally, there is no image of movement here. But the rhythms modify our experience of it: the regular trochaic beat of the first two and a half lines invests the images with life and activity:

All along the road the reddish
purplish, forked, upstanding, twiggy
stuff of bushes

The liveliness doesn't belong to the objective scene but is grafted on to it by the poet's excitement at the thought that spring, not yet manifest, is at hand. But the real situation, summed up in the following two-line section, is unexciting:

Lifeless in appearance, sluggish
dazed spring approaches –

1 *Form and Value in Modern Poetry*, Doubleday, 1957, p. 256.
2 Letter included in John C. Thirlwall, 'William Carlos Williams as a Correspondent', *Literary Review*, vol. 1, Autumn 1957, p. 17.
3 *Collected Earlier Poems*, p. 241.

The next four line section, 'They enter the new world naked, | cold, uncertain . . .' further deprives the bushes of the sense of upthrust and confidence with which the rhythm had endowed them.

The most noticeable rhythmical feature of this poem, the regular trochaic beat in the lines describing the bushes, works in counterpoint to the static scenery and gives the poem a complexity and an interest that the rhetoric itself would not give. In Williams's better poems the function of the form is apparent as it is here.

If in this matter of form Williams must be defended against such criticism as would turn his poems into prose in order to discover that they are not poetry, he must be defended also from his own gossipy, off-the-cuff dicta on the subject, in letters, lectures and essays, which may not be taken literally and accurately. His prose is, to a great extent, hit or miss. There are on the one hand the brilliant perceptions: no one, for instance, has said in so few words shrewder things about Marianne Moore; that she is like a 'secret Niagara'[1] is only one example of the various exactly right remarks Williams makes about her. Then, on the other hand, there is the kind of floundering around, the compulsive repetition with variations of a word that has a kind of numinous appeal to him, found for example in *The Poem as a Field of Action*,[2] where he doesn't rightly know what he's about at all. Much of the talk about the 'new line' and 'measure' comes into this latter category: it is excited talk, and one must look at it with no fundamentalist belief in the inspiration of every word. Sometimes the implications of the 'line' as Williams suggests them are staggering:

If the measurement itself is confined (he writes) every
dimension of the verse and all implications touching it suffer
confinement and generate pressures within our lives which
will blow it and us apart.'[3]

Or, 'When Einstein promulgated the theory of relativity he could not have foreseen . . . its influence on the writing of poetry.'[4] Or, '. . . something has got to be done with the line,' he says, '– it's got to be opened up . . . newly ordered. . . . When we do that we shall know why society is falling apart and how rebuilding itself. . . .'[5]

1 *Selected Essays*, p. 292.   2 pp. 280–91.
3 *Selected Letters*, p. 332.   4 p. 335.
5 'Letter to an Australian Editor', *Briarcliff Quarterly*, vol. 3, 1946, p. 207.

These long range reverberations, as imaginative as the ascription of the fall of Troy to the shudder in the loins, need not be gainsaid. But in more immediate matters pertaining to measure, the dicta are more confusing: 'By measure I mean musical pace,' Williams says in the most useful, analytical letter on the subject.[1] But then in another letter, he says,

The first thing you learn when you begin to learn anything about this earth is that you are eternally barred save for the report of your senses from knowing anything about it. Measure serves for us as the key: we can measure between objects; therefore, we know that they exist.[2]

In this last sentence, what had been time measurement has become space measurement. Mary Ellen Solt says that Williams is referring here to 'meaningful word groups (or phrases) as objects';[3] and if this is so, measure can be saved to mean pace. But it is more likely, because more characteristic, that as so often Williams is simply using words loosely or even just playing with them, in the hope that the game might come up with a piece of prosodic wisdom.

Then, again, much of the talk about the American idiom is unhelpful. In the letter to Kay Boyle in 1932 Williams says, 'It is a contortion of speech to conform to a rigidity of line. It is in the newness of a live speech that the new line exists undiscovered.'[4] The first sentence here speaks of Williams's consistent aim to do no violence to actuality, which is seen everywhere in his treatment of both speech and physical objects in both poetry and the novel. An object, of course, cannot but be distorted when it is brought into any art form. Speech, on the other hand, can be incorporated into literature without modification – the popular misconception about Hemingway's dialogue assumes that it has been. But of course, art does modify reality and poetry does modify speech. Williams has very much to say about American speech and about the fact that it is different from English – 'a language which has not been taught to us in our schools, a language which has a rhythmical structure thorough-

1 *Selected Letters*, p. 326.   2 p. 331.
3 'William Carlos Williams: Idiom and Structure', *Massachusetts Review*, vol. 3, Winter 1962, p. 314.
4 *Selected Letters*, p. 134.

ly separate from English.'[1] And during his whole life he paid close attention to these rhythms as he heard them from day to day. But his best poetry, *By the road to the contagious hospital*,[2] for one example, is not the speech of anybody in particular; it does not contain American rather than British rhythms. Poetry in general does not necessarily ring of a specific regional speech at all. Poetry in Williams may incorporate American speech by embedding a phrase of the real language of men that is not poetry within lines that are – the lines in *Paterson*, for instance, 'Geeze, Doc, I guess it's all right | but what the hell does it mean?'[3] Or it may be modified. If it were otherwise, we should have to conclude that the lower classes of Rutherford, New Jersey, bourgeois gentilshommes though they are not, have been speaking poetry all their lives! At length Williams discovered in his own work the line he had been searching for, and he cites the passage from *Paterson* beginning 'The descent beckons'[4] as representing 'the culmination of all [his] striving after an escape from the restrictions of the verse of the past'[5] and, though he later modified the form, '[his] final conception of what [his] own poetry should be'.[6] But this passage neither embodies nor reflects American as opposed to British speech rhythms. As one critic after another has observed, its rhythms are those of Eliot's *Four Quartets*; and this poem, in so far as it reflects any sectional speech at all, reflects that of the British upper classes. The important fact about the relation between Williams's poetry and speech is not that it embodies American but simply that it is close to speech in general.[7]

In most of the poetry he wrote in the last ten years of his life Williams used a line of three parts. During the fifties he spoke often of the 'variable foot', but in the letter, to Richard Eberhart,[8] which gives the fullest consideration to the three-part line form, he doesn't mention the foot at all. (A variable foot is a strange term to use when speaking of measure: as Alan Stephens says, it is like speaking of an elastic inch.[9]) In this verse form, an equal measure of time is given to

1 p. 335.   2 *Collected Earlier Poems*, p. 241.   3 III, ii, p. 138.
4 II, iii, p. 96.   5 *Selected Letters*, p. 334.
6 *I Wanted to Write a Poem*, p. 80.
7 On this score, Denis Donoghue has said all that need be said, in 'Poetry and the Behavior of Speech', *Hudson Review*, no. 14, Winter 1961–2, pp. 537–49.
8 See above, pp. 313–14.
9 See above, pp. 314–15.

each of the three parts of the line. In the letter, Williams quotes a few lines from two poems, numbering the parts of the line, and says, 'Count a single beat to each numeral.' If each part of the line is equivalent to a beat then the three parts are equal in length to each other and so are the full lines; to this extent the verse is regular. But since each part of the line and hence each full line may contain a widely variable number of syllables, the form is flexible.

One looks to Hopkins for comparison, as Williams himself did. Williams, however, found that Hopkins was 'constipated' and 'didn't go far enough'.[1] Actually, the main difference is that Hopkins's theory and practice are based on the disposal of accented syllables, whereas Williams, except that he denies that the American idiom is based on the iamb which has dominated traditional prosody, speaks little of the accents in this new measure and bases his form on the time taken by the individual parts of the line. Speaking generally of all the poems in the form of the three-part line, one may say that each part has one strongly accented syllable, one or more that receive secondary stress, and others that are unstressed; but there is rarely a repeated pattern of stressed and unstressed syllables. The significant feature of this form is the pause: since to each third of the line an equal measure of time is given and since some lines consist of only one or two syllables, pauses of varying length continually arrest the movement of the verse.

The typographical arrangement of the lines may not, once again, be considered arbitrary. In some cases it is demonstrable that Williams gains effects of emphasis by the disposition of words throughout the parts of a line. In the version of *Asphodel, That Greeny Flower* that appeared as *Work in Progress* in *Perspective*, Williams wrote that it was ridiculous

what airs we put on
            to seem profound
                        while our hearts gasp

dying
        for want of love.[2]

1 *Selected Letters*, pp. 321, 335.
2 *Perspective*, no. 6, Autumn–Winter 1953, pp. 175–6.

In *Journey to Love* the passage goes
              while our hearts

gasp dying
              for want of love.[1]

The ear can detect the difference, and the reason for it is clear
enough: in the first version 'hearts' shares a time unit with 'gasp'
and thus receives less emphasis than in the second version where it
does not so share time, and there, in addition, it is immediately
followed by the end-line pause. That 'hearts' should get more
emphasis is proper, since the lines are dealing with an antithesis
between head and heart. Often in Williams's latest poems what may
appear to sight as an arbitrary arrangement of words on the page is
revealed to the ear as a beautiful, that is, a meaningful disposition of
pause and emphasis. Sometimes the form is not thus accountable;
then it is like the non-organic forms in which most poetry in English
is written that may occasionally be shown to contribute to local
meaning but most often may not. But with both Williams's form
and the traditional ones, the possibility that they are functional must
be admitted even though we cannot articulate what that function
is.[2]

   The function of the form, however, is not only to be sought in the
local emphases, but is intimately bound up with Williams's total
style which embodies his concept of poetry. A poem of Williams's
is not perfected like one of Pope's – to choose an example of a style
from the other end of the spectrum; there is always the sense, felt
also in Stevens's poetry, that something has gone before the poem
and that something else is to follow it, indicated sometimes by the
omission of a final period.[3] Williams speaks variously of the imper-
fection of his form: 'no new thing comes through perfect,' he says
of his early work[4]; of the form of *Paterson* he says, 'I was aware that it

1 *Journey to Love*, 1955, p. 69.
2 For example of a description of the function of measure, see Denis Donoghue's
analysis of 'Daphne and Virginia' (*Pictures from Brueghel*, p. 75), in 'For a
Redeeming Language'. *Twentieth Century*, no. 163, June 1958, p. 540.
3 Glauco Cambon, 'William Carlos Williams and Ezra Pound: Two Examples
of Open Poetry', *College English*, no. 22, March 1961, p. 389.
4 *Selected Letters*, p. 24.

wasn't a finished form, yet I knew it was not formless.'[1] This is the form of a life itself: not planned ahead, but discovered later. Williams's poetic practice results in a poem which is not a completed statement but a field of possible choices; and to this kind of poem the loose movement described above is perfectly appropriate.

The relationship between the three-part line and Williams's concept of poetry may be pointed by studying it in an individual poem. The incompleteness of *The Mental Hospital Garden*[2] consists in the failure of two or three extended metaphors to be perfectly asserted as such; metaphoric equivalences remain on the brink of materialization, leaving a slight sense of mystery. Williams has always written poems of this kind of incompleteness. Incompleteness is itself, in a way, the subject of *The Mental Hospital Garden* (as it is of many other poems), in which the early, incomplete spring, which Williams here and everywhere prefers to the fully burgeoning summer, almost becomes a metaphor for the disease of the patients. They and the season have in common a limitation, not shared by the bounty of sanity and summer. Early spring is the season when nesting birds must needs make use of old nests for materials

> against the advent of that bounty
> > from which
> > > they will build anew.

The limitation, inflicted upon the patients, however, is itself a bounty of another kind: the young couples embrace because

> They are careless
> > under license of the disease
> > > which has restricted them
> to these grounds.
> > They are divided
> > > from their fellows.

but they enjoy this liberating confinement as 'a bounty | from a last year's bird's nest'. Spring with its limitations almost stumbles into

---

1 *I Wanted to Write a Poem*, p. 74. Quoted by Gordon Grigsby, who discusses the matter further, in 'The Genesis of Paterson', *College English*, no. 23, January 1962, p. 279.
2 *Pictures from Brueghel*, p. 97.

becoming a metaphor for mental disease. Later in the poem, summer similarly becomes or nearly becomes the equivalent of cure. The cured patients are baffled by the full bounty and unlimited summer of their freedom:

Filled with terror
          they seek
                    a familiar flower
at which to warm themselves,
          but the whole field
                    accosts them.

The argument I am trying to follow calls for some such crude statement as this about the poem; and the fact of its necessary crudeness is a part of that argument. It is because the metaphoric equivalences remain vague and inexplicit, like structures in a mist, that the poem is *not* the morbid-sounding statement above, but another thing which is not to be botanized in this way. And it is exactly the loose form that provides the permissive medium in which relationships need not be defined and argument need not come to a point. Unless one ignores the pauses between the parts of the lines and read this poem as prose, the hesitance of the movement reflects the inconclusiveness of the evolution of the poem and the relationships in it. But the movement is more than a reflection (one needs to go beyond Pope's facile formula about the sound merely echoing the sense); it is the actual movement of the meditating mind, pursuing its disjunctive course between images as it looks with hesitation for the metaphoric relationships by means of which the outside world might be made into poetry. For the particular operation Williams wishes to perform, a tighter verse form would be inappropriate, indeed unthinkable. One need only imagine this tentative thinking process confined in the couplet or in the kind of blank verse that rides in triumph through Persepolis to realize that the form it has actually taken is the only form possible. Many other poems in *Pictures from Brueghel* are in the same form, and it is appropriate to them for the same or similar reasons.

It might be claimed that many of Williams's earlier poems are incomplete, in the way that *The Mental Hospital Garden* is or in another, and that the verse form in which they are written is adequately loose. If this is so, why should Williams show such excitement over his new form? There are two important reasons, of very different kinds. First, one feature of the new line relates these last poems to modern painting and thus points back to the earlier work which is likewise related and to its ideals, specifically to Williams's loyalty to a world of discrete things and his anti-platonic aim to use them exclusively to present ideas: 'no ideas but in things'. One effect of the three-part line to which attention has been drawn[1] is that by giving to each element in a sentence a separate and equal part of a line Williams makes a particular of each element. It is not a brand new feature,[2] but its regularity is new. The effect is like that gained by printing Walter Pater in *vers libre*, as Yeats does in *The Oxford Book of Modern Verse*, remarking that Pater was accustomed to give each sentence a separate page of manuscript. The mind lingers on each part as a separate sensation. In Williams, emphasis falls equally on each part of the line; thus, for example, a subordinate clause may receive as much formal emphasis as a main one; it becomes 'another fact of the situation, instead of the familiar and consequently de-emphasized modifying clause'.[3] The implications of this observation are very interesting. The syntactical relations between parts of the sentence are weakened and the poem is at liberty to move according to association and fancy rather than according to logic: in many instances the poem moves on from a clause that is syntactically subordinate, not the main one: in *Asphodel, That Greeny Flower*, Williams is speaking of waste and attributing it to 'the bomb'. He asks

> What else was the fire
> at the Jockey Club in Buenos Aires ...
> when ...
> the hoodlums destroyed,
>   along with the books
>   the priceless Goyas.

1 Bernard Engel, 'The Verse Line of Dr Williams: A Fact of the Thing Itself', *Papers of the Michigan Academy of Science, Arts, and Letters*, no. 46, 1961, pp. 665–70.
2 Carl Rakosi, for example, observed early on the separation in Williams of key words from their modifiers ('William Carlos Williams', *Symposium*, no. 4, October 1933, p. 444).
3 Engel, p. 668.

But he doesn't develop the idea of waste; he goes on:

> You know how we treasured
>> the few paintings
we still cling to[1]

It is the pictures, which the rhythm has de-subordinated as it were, that he takes off from.

There is a similarity in this effect to that of the compound sentence in Hemingway and his so-called 'democracy of the "and"'. But in view of Williams's own interests, it is in pictures that the analogy seems nearer. The three-part line tends to break the rhetoric of the poem into its various parts, which we may think of as the equivalents of pigments. The poet, or for that matter the prose writer, who by pushing syntax to the margins of our attention makes us dwell more on images or particulars than on the relationships between them brings the literary form close to the condition of painting – at least to that of modern painting, the kind to which Williams's taste ran. Williams may well have shared the taste of Marianne Moore, which was for pictures that do not have a design on one and do not assert one thing at the cost of another: 'It must not wish to disarm anything; nor may the approved triumph easily be honoured – | that which is great because something else is small.'[2] The traditional presentation in older pictures of a central subject in a subordinated environment gives way in modern painting to the general spreading of significant items over the whole canvas. The change may be seen as reflecting a change in men's minds. The 'flattening out of climaxes' in art has been related to the 'radical transformation of the Western spirit' which this century has witnessed:

When mankind no longer lives spontaneously turned toward God or the supersensible world . . . the artist too must stand face to face with a flat and inexplicable world. This shows itself even in the formal structures of modern art. Where the movement of the spirit is no longer vertical but only horizontal, the climactic elements in art are in general levelled out, flattened.[3]

1 *Pictures from Brueghel*, p. 168.
2 'When I Buy Pictures', *Collected Poems*, Faber, 1959, p. 55.
3 William Barrett, *Irrational Man*, Heinemann, 1964, pp. 44, 42, 43.

Williams's new line, then, playing down syntactical relationships and submitting details without subordinating them to a central idea, seems to be related, in its own small, refracting manner, to a feature of the modern mind. It is a remote relationship, perhaps; but as we have seen above, it is the kind of thing Williams himself used to assert without batting an eye.

On the other hand there may be another reason for Williams's interest in this new line: in crying *Eureka* over a matter of form, he may be disguising what in fact the exciting innovation really is. When he says, 'I shall use no other form for the rest of my life',[1] he may conceivably mean by 'form' something more comprehensive than the shape of the poem. This may be so. If, as is most likely, he means form in its usual, limited sense (and indeed in the same letter a little earlier he is speaking of the variable foot and of free verse), then it seems possible that the attachment of his excitement to it is a case of displacement – the psychological trick by which an important feature of a situation is hidden by focusing upon another one. The measure of the passage from *Paterson* is new, but it is not so remarkably new as the departure the passage makes in its totality from the kind of poetry Williams had established as his own during the previous twenty-five years. Then, most typically, he forced concrete objects of the world, as perceived immediately in the present, into a poetic relationship with himself, by the agency of rhythm and metaphor: much depended upon insignificant concrete objects such as a red wheelbarrow, a grocery list, his wife's bedroom slippers, sparrows, a dish of plums, or whatever. The early Williams, though he explicitly departs from the limited imagist proposals, which, he says, do nothing for structure, does not cease to use the image of the quotidian thing seen here and now. All through his early career his eye, like that of the cubist painters he admired so much, was on the foreground – the small hard things of the suburbs – and he always fought down, though not always successfully, the romantic urge to remove it therefrom. Over and over again in one form or another we find him disdaining 'the light that never was on sea or land.' Similarly, although sometimes by protesting too much he reveals the attraction for him in what he is dismissing, in the early verse he dismisses memory. In *Good Night*,[2] he pits images from

1 *Selected Letters*, p. 334. 2 *Collected Earlier Poems*, p. 145.

memory – 'memory playing the clown' – against images of the present and defames memory to the extent that we recognize its power over him. In *Brilliant Sad Sun*,[1] he presents an image of a woman giving water to chickens and asks, 'What are your memories | beside that purity?'

In many of the poems in the three-part line, however, romantic qualities are more manifest: memory, for example, receives an increased dispensation: in *The Descent*, it presents reality with a deeper intensity – 'no whiteness (lost) is so white as the memory of whiteness'; *To a Dog Injured in the Street*[2] is informed by memories: in *Shadows*,[3] 'the world of memory' is greater than the present world 'we share with the | rose in bloom'. *Asphodel, That Greeny Flower*[4] is full of memories.[5]

Then in the last poems, those in the three-part line, there is another difference which also shows a weakening of Williams's resistance against romanticism: there is no prose; and because the rhythm steadily dominates the whole poem no distinct provision is made for images or statements which belong to the real world and exist beyond the poetry or are just coming over into it. Only a little previously, Williams had made much of his need, which is indicated by the prose passages in *Paterson* and the distinct passages of non-poetry elsewhere, to 'fight his way to a world which breaks through to the actual'.[6] Now the presence in the poem of 'the actual' is not so sharply marked as it was earlier. In these last poems, memories, old photographs, and other experience at second hand and sometimes the ideal quality these suggest are sanctioned, and the presence of the specifically non-poetic is no longer thrown into relief. There seems to be an appreciable shift in the balance – not necessarily a stark change in Williams's attitude – of the reality-romantic ratio: it is as if the poet were becoming aware in age that the memories that play about a concrete percept become part of its reality or that one's own concept of ideality is itself, paradoxically, a kind of reality.

1 p. 324.   2 *Pictures from Brueghel*, p. 86.   3 p. 150.
4 pp. 153–82.
5 Linda W. Wagner attributes Williams's turn to the realm of imagination and memory to the narrowing of the boundaries of the physical world in the poet's ill-health (*The Poems of William Carlos Williams: A Critical Study*, Wesleyan University Press, 1964, pp. 129–30).
6 *Selected Letters*, p. 324.

What we have in Williams's new line, then, is first and foremost a rhythmical form which means something and which changes into poetry what would otherwise merely be images, observations, and even, one may say, garrulous talk. Then, at least by implication, there is a movement on the part of the poetic form toward the condition of that kind of modern painting in which his poetry had always revealed interest. And finally, incidentally, there is a backing down from the stern discipline he had inflicted upon himself earlier. (118–31)

Ruth Grogan

'Swaying Form in Williams's *Asphodel*' 1970

Williams's later years were occupied in part by a continuing meditation on death. On one occasion, shortly after his first cerebral
accident, a carved East Indian mask hanging on his living room wall
provided a vehicle into the rare disinterested composure he could at
intervals achieve in this meditation:

I saw it last night while I was sitting listening to some music.
It came to life, complacent before death, complete peace. It
was a lesson to me – and no dogma to soften the blow. It had
the peace before violent death that is in the *Iliad*, and the
consciousness, the complete consciousness, before it that is in
the heroes of Greek legend.[1]

The Coda of *Asphodel, That Greeny Flower*,[2] written about two years
later and in the ever-present possibility of another stroke, expresses
again in poetic form this complete consciousness before violent death,
a moment of total illumination between lightning flash and thunderstroke. For a poet who had declared many years earlier that 'heaven
seems frankly impossible', this moment of peace and light, brief but
timeless, was the only heaven possible.

But the formal and meditative movement from the initial 'hell'
of *Asphodel* to its culminating 'heaven', from the negative to the
positive pole of Williams's fundamental 'resignation to existence',[3]
is neither easily achieved nor easily explained. It occurs by way of
apparently haphazard musings on memories and objects, on things
which hover between being real and symbolic, and which, taken
separately, are the same shape or structure as the poem in its entirety.
Its pivot is predictably a flower, the embodiment throughout

1 *Selected Letters*, p. 297. 2 *Pictures from Brueghel*, p. 153.
3 *Selected Letters*, p. 147.

Williams's poetry of that gentle force that splits rocks. He deliberately invites comparison of this poor weak greeny flower of hell with the crimson cyclamen whose tension and passion had informed an earlier poem on death, that of his friend Charles Demuth. Like the life forces of an old man, the asphodel exists only in memory and in a few faded petals. The taut energy and colour of the cylamen, exploding through leaves and flower, compelled belief in its existence and in its symbolic message, whereas 'too weak a wash of crimson | colors it [the asphodel] to make it wholly credible'. But it would be a mistake to conceive of this hell as entirely without satisfactions. In fact, the effect of the poem derives largely from the way Williams can move lightly back and forth from despair to some small mitigation of despair; he is in hell, but he is cheered to know that there are flowers in hell. By contemplation of the flower, humble as it is, he is led in various ways toward the final benediction.

With a curiously confused metaphor Williams once explained to Louis Martz that 'I begin to see what I have been after, by evidence of the sense of smell mostly, but which now is coming more and more into view'.[1] The mixed metaphor lingers in the poem:

I have forgot
       and yet I see clearly enough
              something
central to the sky
       which ranges round it.
              An odor
springs from it!
       A sweetest odor!
. . . .
It is a curious odor,
       a moral odor,
              that brings me
near to you.
       The color
              was the first to go.

As in To Daphne and Virginia, odour stirs the thoughts, establishes a mood, and eventually transforms the world, suggesting perhaps

[1] p. 299.

possible analogies between this 'olfactory world' and McLuhan's directionless, unfocused, 'auditive world'. The fragrance of the flower and the calm conscious breathing by which it is appreciated begin to establish the total, impartial, loving understanding of the Coda.

The energies of the flower are not always 'a love engendering | gentleness and goodness'; violence, evil and eventually death are encompassed in Williams's meditations on it:

I should have known
          though I did not,
                    that the lily-of-the-valley
is a flower makes many ill
          who whiff it.

The *Iliad*, for instance, tells the tale of

the sexual orchid that bloomed then
          sending so many
                    disinterested
men to their graves

'Disinterested' is a key word, allotted a line to itself, summing up the peaceful indifference before violent death of the *Iliad*, 'the complete consciousness, before it, that is in the heroes of Greek legend'. The flower of sexual love that doomed men produced at the same time its own antidote, the calm unconcerned control enabling them to meet their doom. This seems to have been a central truth for Williams in the *Iliad*, a complex knowledge without which, he says, the world would have called the whole Trojan legend simply murder; and it is the same knowledge which he passes on in his own poetry.

Since ultimately for Williams the flower is shaped or formalized energy, he can discover analogies between the flower and the bomb, even, bewilderingly, that both involve love:

I am reminded
          that the bomb
                    also
is a flower
          dedicated
                    howbeit

to our destruction.

> The mere picture
>> of the exploding bomb

fascinates us

> so that we cannot wait
>> to prostrate ourselves

before it. We do not believe

> that love
>> can so wreck our lives.

The atomic mushroom, shaped like the bloom of some monstrous flower and bursting forth against restrictions like so many of Williams's poetic flowers, exercises the same fatal fascination over men's minds as the 'sexual orchid'. Once it is grasped that 'shaped energy' lies behind most of the poem's images, as behind Williams's lifetime work, the relevance of Colleoni's sword, of the freight train thundering through the station, of the drill driven into the earth for oil, all becomes clear. They are 'pictures of crude force', unbridled mechanical, physical, or even spiritual drive, energy that Williams felt in himself and in the world around him, which he had to come to terms with, harness, release, and understand in some orderly way.

The poem in its entirety is a coming to terms with these elemental forces, but two images within it play a crucial interpretative role. One is the sea. The short history of love in which the first reference to the sea is embedded reveals through its dream-logic surface something of what the sea means to Williams. His youthful love is symbolically contrasted to his present love. When he first fell in love

Endless wealth,

> I thought,
>> held out its arms to me.

A thousand topics

> in an apple blossom.
>> The generous earth itself

gave us lief.

> The whole world
>> became my garden!

It was a mood in which the whole earth centred on the lover, bloomed for him alone. The apple blossom here is reminiscent of a very early love poem, *Portrait of a Lady*,[1] a delicately expansive and whimsical evocation of that youthful and now superseded attitude. 'But', he continues:

> ... the sea
>   which no one tends
>   is also a garden
> when the sun strikes it
>   and the waves
>   are wakened.

The mood changes, not by mechanical association of ideas, but by an implicit comparison of youth and age; if in youth he lived in a garden tended for him alone, seen from his personal persepective, now he inhabits the great indifferent sea, for which no individual matters and which no person tends. But it too comes to life, takes on a kink of shape when the sun of the imagination strikes it. This sun, as other poems testify, is not a subjective visionary light originating in the poet's mind and illuminating the world only for this eyes; it represents his participation in an objective, even scientific, world view, available to all and illuminating all, indifferent to the individual and yet offering sustenance to the individual

> I have seen it
>   and so have you
>   when it puts all flowers
> to shame.

These moments of self-transcendence when the sea of reality can be seen whole and shaped are not exclusive to Williams's later years; in a much earlier poem, *Flowers by the Sea*,[2]

> the sea is circled and sways
> peacefully upon its plantlike stem

But it is only in the later poems that these moods are taken out of isolation and enveloped with tacit relationships, as occurs here with the two kinds of 'oceanic consciousness', infantile and mature. This later kind of imaginative vision shines impassively on the waves, which it enlivens, and on the tidally abandoned starfish, which it

1 *Collected Earlier Poems*, p. 40.   2 *Collected Earlier Poems*, p. 87.

stiffens. Williams has come to accept the great tidal and periodic movement of his mental life, by which underwater creatures are alternately buried and sustained:

> ... We knew that
> along with the rest of it
> for we were born by the sea,

And just as he and his wife have gone from time to time to the sea shore, so he has found himself in hell from time to time in pursuit of love. The great indifferent sea of reality, like the impartial sun of the imagination, can be life-sustaining or life-destroying, just as the energies of the flower can be benevolent or malevolent. And yet, somehow or other, a part of the mind must rise above these ambivalences in order to understand them. The energies of the flower and the energies of the bomb are, after all, not the same. It is of the essence of Williams's poetry that he should insist upon immersion in the sea:

> The sea alone
> with its multiplicity
> holds any hope.

and at the same time upon inclusion and comprehension of these manifold energies:

> Love is something else,
> or so I thought it,
> a garden which expands,
> . . . .
> until the whole sea
> has been taken up
> and all its gardens.

From an earlier love, in which the world was a garden centred upon himself, in which all relationships in the world were understood with reference to him, he moves through a sea of non-relatedness, a death of love where there are no distinctions and differentiations, to a vast and mysterious garden which can include the sea and in which facts are flowers, flowers facts and all works of the imagination are interchangeable.

The second image by which the mind is laid to rest is that of the storm, representing the violent death which Williams at that time could expect momentarily. Driven by the same forces that drive a plant through stony soil, it piles up slowly,

> a flower
> > that will soon reach
the apex of its bloom.

even though it has once 'proven abortive' (a reference to the poet's recent severe stroke). How is the mind to contain the total and annihilating violence of death? A partial answer is found in 'the complete consciousness' before death that Williams saw in the Greek heroes. The moment of light between the flash and the thunderstroke is the moment of complete consciousness, when the sea of multiplicity is given shape, when total understanding brings 'the love that swallows up all else'. It is related in its breathless expectancy to the tensions of the earlier poetry, the excitement of waiting for a volcano to erupt, a child to be born or a flower to push through the earth. In youth, though, a man could afford in these moments to look toward the future, toward the new thing that would emerge after the inevitable rupture. In old age he must find total significance in the instant itself:

> In the huge gap
> > between the flash
and the thunderstroke
> spring has come in
> > or a deep snow fallen.
Call it old age.
> In that stretch
> > we have lived to see
A colt kick up his heels.

• • • • • • • • • •

This is that interval,
> that sweetest interval,
> > when love will blossom.

This is the same poise (to gather up other late images) of a bird glimpsed on outstretched wing or a little girl about to jump, an instant caught full and whole like a bubble ready to burst, only filled here not by the muscular pressure of his earlier poetry nor even by odour, but by light. Indeed, the entire poem can be read as a celebration of light:

Light, the imagination
       and love,
                 in our age,
by natural law,
       which we worship,
                 maintain
all in one piece
       their dominance.

In the Coda the passage of time no longer presses upon him as it did at the beginning of the poem; if his whole being is concentrated within the present moment, past and future can be remembered or speculated upon without projecting into them a desperate urgency to exist 'in actuality':

       So we come to watch time's flight
                 as we might watch
summer lightning
       or fireflies, secure,
                 by grace of the imagination,
safe in its care.

The moment can include paradoxically all time; in this moment of total understanding, the mind, like the Coda itself, contains memories lived as though the next moment would bring death, in a sense that life has been lived 'in the huge gap | between the flash and the thunder-stroke'. The value of the interval, though temporally succeeded by the annihilating heat, is never in itself destroyed or cancelled out.

From the 'shape' of certain images one is led to consider the shape of the poem as a whole. Donald Davie, to name one, is sceptical about Williams's ability to shape a long poem; for all his scruples about the possibility of mistaking 'structured coherence of an unforeseen kind' for incoherence, he comes to the conclusion that Williams's poems are only 'approaches' with no insides.[1] I would propose, in answer

1 Donald Davie, 'Poems in a Foreign Language', *Essays in Criticism*, vol. 7, no. 4, October 1957, p. 441.

to this view, that *Asphodel*, and many of Williams's later poems, have the underlying coherence of a certain kind of creative reverie; Williams is imitating *purposive* musing, preliminary thinking that deliberately heads for a discovery, though the exact terms of the discovery may as yet be unknown or only vaguely guessed at.

Its best analogy perhaps, bearing in mind Williams's medical training and his frequently expressed interest in great scientists such as Fabre, Mme Curie and Einstein, might be with one stage of scientific thinking, called by Koestler in his *Act of Creation* the 'period of incubation';[1] this is the period during which a problem, if it has evaded the efforts of conscious analysis, is temporarily pushed back into the darker recesses of the mind, to be followed if all goes well by the apparently miraculous flash of insight or solution. For some scientists, as for some poets, this anticipatory stage is a complete submersion in non-logical, non-verbal, unconscious modes of ideation; a more appropriate scientific parallel for the flow of images in *Asphodel* might be what Einstein termed in a description of his own thinking processes a 'combinatory play'[2] of images, the visual, sometimes even muscular play of images which precedes discovery and subsequent conventional systematization. *Asphodel*, with its apparently disconnected, spontaneous perceptions and memories, completed by the lightning institution of the Coda, has the fluidity and submerged purposiveness of the scientist's 'period of incubation' or Einstein's 'combinatory play'; the scientific analogy is useful in so far as it suggests the intent but detached quality of Williams's verse, the symbols less obsessively charged and the rhythms less incantatory than much verse claiming the sanctions of the unconscious. The mind here is working intensely, but not feverishly.

It is an underlying purposiveness in *Asphodel*, then, that removes it from the products of surrealism or self-abandonment.[3] The transi-

1 Pan Books, 1966, p. 182.
2 Quoted in Koestler, p. 171.
3 Williams had never wholly succumbed even in his 'improvisations' to the doctrine of poetry as the uncensored dredgings from the subconscious. In a letter of 1942 he mentions his attempt to find some sort of synthesis of spontaneity and control: 'It's all right to give the subconscious play but not *carte blanche* to spill everything that comes out of it. We let it go to see what it will turn up, but everything it turns up isn't equally valuable and significant. That's why we have developed a conscious brain' (*Selected Letters*, p. 194). And again in

tion from garden to sea, for instance, in the sequence already discussed, might seem a mental accident except for the word 'but' which invests the juxtaposition with some as yet undisclosed logic. The poetic means for this fusion of purposiveness and play can be deciphered if we make for the moment an artificial distinction between the poem's images and attitudes. The images – of flower, sea, storm, bomb and so forth – appear in an order unexplained by anything but mechanical suggestions:

> Approaching death,
>> as we think, the death of love,
>>> no distinction
> any more suffices to differentiate
>> the particulars
>>> of place and condition

The particulars, totally unrelated, might have been reshuffled without making any difference. The imaginative response, on the other hand, does almost imperceptibly progress. Beginning in urgency, 'fear in my heart', panic before passing time, the poem advances by the end of Book One to a calmer insistence that can be heard:

> Hear me out
>> for I too am concerned
> and every man
>> who wants to die at peace in his bed
>>> besides.

By the end of Book Two he has reached a unity with his wife in adoration of the 'single image'. This is followed by the revelation of Book Three that, far from being totally unrelated, particulars are totally interrelated:

> Are facts not flowers
>> and flowers facts

1944 he describes the 'scabby philosophers': 'I'm afraid that Freud's influence [sic] has been the trigger to all this. The Surrealists followed him. Everything must be tapped into the subconscious, the unconscious – as if poetry had ever been different. But poetry has also been a construction on the words – very strange news this is to the present day' (*Selected Letters*, p. 219).

or poems flowers
> or all works of the imagination,
>> interchangeable?

At this point he can affirm that

you will be my queen,
> my queen of love
>> forever more.

– all of which is preparatory for the illumination of the Coda. Even in the opening confusion and uncertainty, there is evidence of underlying confidence

> Of love, abiding love

it will be telling
> though too weak a wash of crimson
>> colors it

to make it wholly credible.

Even though the asphodel at that moment may be too weak to be wholly credible, he can dimly foresee its eventual message:

> There is something
>> something urgent

I have to say to you
> and you alone
>> but it must wait . . .

Such tentative predictions, couched in the future tense, of an as yet obscure finale, are in fact characteristic of Williams's later poems. It takes time, steady persistent contemplation of his memories and perceptions, before the Coda can be realized.

A comparison of the meditative shape of *Asphodel* to the scientific 'period of incubation' with its climactic explosion of discovery can be complemented by an account of the systole and diastole in Williams's line-to-line movement, his simulation on a more reduced level, adhering closely to the syntax or the tiny triadic stanza, of both purposiveness and play, frustration and release. For purposes of analysis this effect is most evident in another late poem, *The Ivy Crown*.[1] This poem is composed of a series of assertions whose force

1 *Pictures from Brueghel*, p. 124.

is constantly checked but not vitiated by modifications or partial contradictions. The frequent use of qualifying or conditional words – 'unless', 'or', 'though', 'but', 'whatever' and so on, is the grammatical reflection of a microscopic swing between negative and positive poles. For instance, the discouragement of the phrase 'the whole process is a lie' is retrieved by 'unless crowned by excess | it break forcefully ... from its confinement', with a subordinate pulsation in 'one way or another'. The secure assertion of 'I love you' is slightly unhinged by the following possibility, 'or I do not live | at all'. The pendulum swings from positive to negative –

> No doubts
> are permitted –
> though they will come

and back again from negative to positive in

> We are only mortal
> but being mortal
> can defy our fate.

Williams's methods vary. At one point the italicization of 'which' indicates that it should follow quickly and emphatically on the heels of 'cruelty' as if to temper its harshness. On the other hand, though people try to 'keep the briars of cruelty out'

> you cannot live
> and keep free of
> briars.

And so the poem continues, dancing between depression and exaltation, till the final certainty of

> We will it so
> and so it is
> past all accident.

Asphodel is constructed on the same pattern. Because it is a longer and more inclusive poem than *The Ivy Crown* the intervals between negative and positive poles are more elastic. It is clear enough in the following lines:

```
... our eyes fill
         with tears.
                  Of love, abiding love
it will be telling
         though too weak a wash of crimson
                  colors it
to make it wholly credible.
         There is something
                  something urgent
I have to say to you
         and you alone
                  but it must wait
while I drink in
         the joy of your approach,
                  perhaps for the last time.
And so
         with fear in my heart ...
```

The alternating charge in the images of garden and sea, wakened waves and stiffened starfish, rose-hedges and strawberries, wild plum and descent into hell, continues the movement.

For the movement of the poem on all levels, perhaps we could borrow a term from Howard Nemerov, who in turn borrowed it from Florio's translation of Montaigne:

There is no man (if he listen to himselfe) that doth not discover in himselfe a peculiar forme of his, a swaying forme, which wrestleth against the art and the institution, and against the tempest of passions, which are contrary unto him.[1]

A 'swaying form' penetrates all the crevices of Williams's poem, from syntax, to image, to theme, to total shape – an appropriate expression for an

```
         ... old man
                  whose bones
have the movement
         of the sea
```

1 Quoted in Howard Nemerov, 'The Swaying Form: A Problem in Poetry', in *To The Young Writer*, ed. A. L. Bader, 1965, p. 109.

It is a form which can accommodate all the eddies and currents of the mind, both the fury and the stillness, all the varieties of energy to be found in Williams's poetry, and yet paradoxically maintain a steadiness which Hillis Miller has compared to the sustained and dynamic motion of a fountain.

Hugh Kenner

'Dr Williams Shaping His Axe', *Hudson Review*, vol. 8, no. 1 1955
(reprinted in *Gnomon*, 1958)

Dr Williams, infinitely sympathetic with the purposefulness of
earnest coteries, is our champion contributor to the least-known
magazines, into which he empties his mind of its current obsessions.
Since he hasn't been all these years painfully developing a system
(which means trimming one's later ideas to fit the earlier ones: 'order
that cuts off the crab's feelers to make it fit into the box'): hasn't
feared to risk in his fifties and sixties the kinds of false starts that don't
matter in one's twenties; and has kept his mind at the moment of
writing fixed on some object or other that looms as oppressively as
the cat's head in the primitive painting ('a cat with a bird in his
mouth – a cat with a terrifying enormous head, enough to frighten
birds') – for all these reasons random samples of his fugitive writings,
gleaned from such copies of equally fugitive magazines as come one's
way, are apt to prove unfortunate. Hence the impression (on what has
been to date necessarily imperfect acquaintance) of a bush-league
avant-gardist, one foot still in the 1920s, apt to be sent gaga by the
latest surrealist. His tone isn't soothing; he is himself the archetypal
six-foot cat's head; even when he makes an appearance among the
statuary of more securely capitalized publications, virtually put on
his honor not to frighten the birds, commissioned for instance to
review Shapiro's *Essay on Rime*, he is apt to throw his overcoat onto
the grand piano ('I hadn't prepared a damn thing'[1]) and begin –

Suppose all women were delightful, the ugly, the short, the
fat, the intellectual, the stupid, the old – and making a virtue
of their qualities . . . made themselves available to men, some
man, any man, without greed! . . . Take for instance the fat:

1 Cf. his 1950 lecture at UCLA: *Autobiography*, p. 386.

If she were not too self-conscious, did not regret that she
were not lissome and quick afoot, but gave herself, full belly,
to the sport! What a game it would make!

The man who jammed a notion like that into the *Kenyon Review*
can be credited with having extended our notions of the possible,
but hardly with an Eliotic platform manner. It is no wonder that he
isn't known as a major critic, especially since he doesn't specialize in
putting into hierarchies an array of poems closed off forty years ago
(Wyndham Lewis's *Dead arrangements by the tasteful hand without*) but
concentrates on the *nature* of writing, especially the writing that
somebody ought to be doing right now. No critic senses more
urgently the immediate relevance of his subject to this year's necessary activities.

Poetry, for him, keeps thought clean; not by what is vaguely
called 'the humanizing influence of literary studies' but by virtue of
what it says, on the rare occasions when the writing is sufficiently
good. Just any poetry won't do; the sea contains many billionfold
more water than it does whale, but that is no reason for confusing the
two. Dr Williams writes to defend critic and practitioner alike
against 'belief in a complicated mystery of approach fostered by
those who wish nothing done'.

The trick is delay; to involve the mind in discussions likely
to last a lifetime and so withdraw the active agent from
performance. The answer is, an eye to judge. – When the
deer is running between the birches one doesn't get out a
sextant but a gun – a flash of insight with proof by
performance – and let discussion follow. If the result is a
work of art the effect is permanent.

Amid boulders his shots often ricochet; this wouldn't happen if he
were pelting his quarry with grapes, but it has condemned a good
deal of his prose to mere eccentricity. In retrospect, fortunately,
Williams can be trusted to identify his solid critical achievements,
though unlike Pound and Eliot he hasn't up to now troubled
to keep them pruned and in circulation. His *Selected Essays* – a
collection of pieces that should have been widely known years ago
(the gist of the book lurks in passages written before 1939, and the

contents date from 1920) ought to scatter a good many pigeons. Its advent is nicely timed to disturb the afternoon peace of a bureaucracy that has lately been supposing all the major criticism of the present time to be well known and sifted, the orthodoxies established, the hammocks slung, the returns in, and nothing to do but execute philosophical doodles – pointless as freshman themes – while the grad students work at tabulations. Williams has the timely virtue of being sufficiently aphoristic to focus attention – on his clumps of words, not on the phases of some wafty argument – and the conjoint virtue of having coined aphorisms as little suitable for ruminative mastication as so many bricks:

the usual 'poem', the commonplace opaque board covered
with vain curlicues. . . .

the coining of similies is a pastime of very low order,
depending as it does upon a merely vegetable coincidence. . . .

beauty . . . truth incompletely realized. . . . The beauty that
clings to any really new work is beauty only in the minds of
those who do not fully realize the significance. . . .

His best insights, like Mr Eliot's, whom he admirably complements, coagulate into aphorisms; with this difference, that to qualify Williams's *obiter dicta* one needs a cold chisel, not a scalpel. He isn't adjusting his absolutes to existing frailty; by and large, he is talking about writing so good it hasn't been done yet. His knowledge of what it will be like if anyone succeeds in doing it sustains his intensity of statement. Aspects of this unwritten writing he discerns in the contemporary work that interests him, work which he subjects (amid tut-tuts from the glowworms) to a scrutiny implacable as an electric furnace. The writing of this half-century will not find a more tenacious reader. Where Mr Pound reads his contemporaries to find out if they are alive, and Mr. Eliot to see if they merit introductions, Dr Williams reads and rereads them to find out what they mean. He tells his young contemporaries the simple truth: that he has 'a will to understand them that they will not find in many another'.

'The goal of writing is to keep a beleaguered line of understanding which has movement from breaking down and becoming a hole into which we sink decoratively to rest.' Hence the virtual non-existence of quotations in Williams's critical essays. He abhors the notion that the essential poetic *movement* can be represented by one or two of the points it traverses: as though a railway system were judged by its station architecture. The abhorrence sets him squarely against the tendency – not the principle – of nine-tenths of modern criticism: against the idea, originally a classroom strategy, that the poem is *in* a few of its detachable parts; that i t consists of gems, for the sake of which it exists, united by neutral bits; that one ponders this image (what does it mean?), this image, and this image, and stops with a sum of images. The whole incorruptible bulk of Williams's critical achievement is dropped squarely athwart the beaten track of the ants.

It is not to be supposed that for details he substitutes 'ideas'.

It is in the minutiae – in the minute organization of the words and their relationships in a composition that the seriousness and value of a work of writing exist – *not* in the sentiments, ideas, schemes portrayed.

It is here furthermore, that creation takes place. It is not a plaster of thought applied.

His point is that instances of this 'minute organization' can't be as readily detached from the whole composition's trajectory as we have been led to suppose. What takes place in a work of art is not an accumulation of beauties but 'an alertness not to let go of a possibility of movement in our fearful bedazzlement with some concrete and fixed present'.

Eschewing quotations, then, his method – which less skillful hands would be ill advised to imitate – is to exercise his inventive faculty and write a solid piece of prose which will serve as a sort of equivalent for 'what this writer's work amounts to'. This doesn't, in his practice, mean going back to Sainte-Beuve or Saintsbury. It means an intense concentration on the intentions implied by the subject, not on the urbanities of a public-relations job. Occasionally Williams thinks into the subject perfections probably not inherent in it; when he does this, as in the remarkable essay on Gertrude Stein, the result is not silliness but illumination not so much of Miss Stein as of the nature of writing. He notes, for instance, that

Music could easily have a statement attached to each note in the manner of words, so that C natural might mean the sun,

etc., and completely dull treatises be played – and even
sciences finally expounded in tunes.

Solid writing, however, tends to use the word 'as reality' rather than
'as symbol':

Bach might be an illustration of movement not suborned by
a freight of purposed design, loaded upon it as in almost all
later musical works; statement unmusical and unnecessary.
Stein's 'they lived very gay then' has much of the same
quality of movement to be found in Bach – the composition
of the words determining not the logic, not the 'story', not
the theme even, but the movement itself. As it happens,
'They were both gay there' is as good as some of Bach's
shorter figures.

Stein is a laboratory example; turning his method to writing one
willingly rereads, Dr Williams has produced, for instance, the only
enlightening pages in print on Marianne Moore, and the meatiest
comments on *A Draft of XXX Cantos* ever written. His ability to
drive a spike with one blow helps single him out from the critics one
wonders whether to take seriously or not. He writes when he knows
what there is to be said, and conveys his gists without periphrasis. Of
the Greek quotations in *The Cantos* ('knowing no Greek, I presume
they mean something') he divines correctly, 'They are no particular
matter save that they say, There were other times like ours – at the
back of it all.' When the Ur-critics of *XXX Cantos* were fussing about
Pound's pedantry or his aestheticism, Williams was staring hard at
Pound's theme. Twenty-four years before *Rock-Drill* he defined it:
'A closed mind which clings to its power – about which the intelligence beats seeking entrance': bull's-eye with one shot.

Preoccupied not by the standards of traditional excellence with
which Pound, to the confusion of most readers, retains contact, but
by his own hard-won perception of the nature of a responsible
modern American poet's job, Williams wasn't alarmed whenever
Pound stopped imitating a Grecian nightingale. He was able to see the
early Cantos as if the Van Buren and Adams sequences had already
existed, classicism not an inert norm but a key-signature, one of
several, controlling the movement of the poet's intelligence.

It is beside the question in my opinion to speak of Pound's versification as carefully and accurately measured. . . . His excellence is that of the maker, not the measurer. . . .

That is why he can include pieces of prose and have them still part of a *poem*. . . .

That is also, he might have added, why Pound could include pieces of 'poetry', When *Eleven New Cantos* at length appeared, Williams had nothing to unsay:

There is a good deal to say about money in this series, 9 per cent, thousands, millions of cash and the ways of men with it – to the exclusion of love. And love. . . .

It is the poet who has digested the mass of impedimenta which the scholar thinks to solve by sinking up to his eyes in it and shouting that he has found it.

In the earlier Pound essay (1931) he noted,

Pound's 'faults' as a poet all center around his rancor against the malignant stupidity of a generation which polluted our rivers and would then, brightly, give ten or twenty or any imaginable number of millions of dollars as a fund toward the perpetuation of *Beauty* – in the form of a bequest to the New York Metropolitan Museum of Art.

In America this crime has not been spread over a period of centuries, it has been done in the last twenty or twenty-five years, by the single generation, fifteen or twenty-five years older than I am, who have held power through that slobbery period.

This suggests the coordinates of Williams's rancor against 'Beauty', his abnegation of poetic attempts to secure it, and his suspicion of every proposal to endow it – expensive universities, for instance, 'for the propagation of something that passes for the arts', which he consigns to the bottom of a list of amenities beginning with dog hospitals, canine cemeteries and Palm Beach. 'Beauty at its best seems truth incompletely realized'; and to use 'beautiful' language 'is to confess an inability to have penetrated with poetry some crevice of understanding; that special things and special places are reserved for art, that it is unable, that it requires fostering. This is unbearable.'

What fascinates him about Marianne Moore is that while she is undeniably choosing the things she puts into her poems, the principle of choice has no relation to a notion of beauty inherent in the materials. 'The baby glove of a Pharaoh can be so presented as to bring tears to the eyes', but Miss Moore doesn't deal in baby gloves (Williams is careful to say that her poems wouldn't *therefore* be bad if she did). What Miss Moore does deal in is actions, intellectual progressions, the mind moving freely 'unencumbered by the images or the difficulties of thought. In such work there is no 'suggestiveness', no tiresome 'subtlety' of trend to be heavily followed, no painstaking refinement of sentiment'. Sentiments are blocks of emotional stuff; the poet envisaged by Dr Williams doesn't pause to refine what he encounters in transit, he passes through it like an X-ray.

A poem such as *Marriage* is an anthology of transit. It is a pleasure that can be held firm only by moving rapidly from one thing to the next. It gives the impression of a passage through. There is a distaste for lingering, as in Emily Dickinson.

This is not only an admirable statement of Miss Moore's quality, it implies, once we remove the coloration of the particular example, a poetic of great interest. Though poems, for Dr Williams, have a mode of being which differs from that of raw experience, they don't thereby inhabit a zone on the lower borders of the supernatural. Though the mystical quality 'still seems to many the essence of poetry itself', poetry is a secular art, deriving its illuminations directly from the quality of the mind that has done the work. 'There is a "special" place where poems, as all works of art, must occupy, but it is quite definitely the same place as that where bricks or colored threads are handled.' Since the poem is itself a force, it won't, while it remains chaste, incorporate objects by force. Though the characters, as Aristotle said, are included only for the sake of the action, we demand assurance that they are acting and not being pushed, and in the same way should demand images that aren't being conscripted. Again Miss Moore supplies the illustration; in her poems

an apple remains an apple whether it be in Eden or the fruit bowl. . . .

dazzled by the apple

The apple is left there, suspended. One is not made to feel that as an apple it has anything particularly to do with poetry or that as such it needs special treatment, one goes on. Because of this the direct object does seem unaffected . . . free from the smears of mystery. . . .

These remarks are as valuable as Mr Eliot's on the metaphysical poets: which prompts the reflection that nine-tenths of Eliot's vastly influential criticism is concentrated in a dozen or so formulations, some of them dangerously succinct and memorable, that have started people thinking, and frequently been applied with clumsy enthusiasm to all sorts of locks they were never intended to open. The home-made quality of Dr Williams's mental furnishings, if it wants ease, fends off glibness; it should be evident that his *Selected Essays* probably contains as many radioactive deposits as Mr Eliot's book of the same title, and that they really are intended to be useful generalizations, not *ad hoc* formulations (like the famous sentence about the objective correlative) which some readers allow the pervasive urbaneness to invest with inappropriate universality. Critical books also contain outcroppings of less valuable minerals, and of these Williams probably offers a higher concentration per ton of rock fill than does his eminent rival. His remarkable essay on *The American Background*, though not untinged with crankiness, should be required reading for anyone interested in American writing; Mr Eliot on comparably panoramic topics (Humanism, for instance, or Modern Education and the Classics) is after twenty-odd years chiefly interesting to students of Mr Eliot. The mind behind Williams's book is probably not less catholic, though certainly less urbane; to say that Matthew Arnold wouldn't have understood him is to bring out strength and weakness together. Against his impatience with much of the literary past one can weigh Eliot's rank incuriosity concerning the present. If Williams ignores Donne and is suspicious of Dante, Eliot was unable to say *why* he found the later Joyce impressive, and wrote of *The Cantos* that Pound's belief that they meant something was sufficient for him. There can be no question of the one writer superseding the other. But we are not likely to find two valuable critics each so perfectly the other's complement.

(144–50)

Thomas R. Whitaker

'The White Mule Trilogy', *William Carlos Williams* 1968

The trilogy *White Mule* (1937), *In the Money* (1940) and *The Build-Up* (1952), follows the Stecher family from the birth of their daughter Floss in 1893 through the American entry into the war in 1917. Williams began this work in 1927 partly because of his interest in a 'plain' style true to his 'sharpest, firmest present vision'. Aiming to 'write with attention to marshalling the words into an order which would be free from "lies",'[1] he kept clear of the rigidities of the obviously plotted novel. 'Plot is like God: the less we formulate it the closer we are to the truth'.[2] A formulated plot, like the snow that Joe Stecher sees blanketing New York, is 'peaceful to the ear and eye from the obliteration of meaningless detail', yet an 'unreality', the 'illusion of an imposed order'.[3] Such a plot acts as Joe sees a 'policy' act in human affairs: 'It uproots everything in its path. You make up your mind you're going to plow through. Then you go ahead and plow. . . . You stop paying attention to the truth of the detail.'[4]

But Williams also kept clear of the rigidities of the post-Jamesian or post-Joycean novel. Though in *White Mule* and *In the Money* the author seems almost refined out of existence, the fiction does not use strictly limited points of view or impersonal techniques of revelation. The result is no illusion of an independent world but a continuing sense of a truly human point of observation that does not call attention to itself – one that has become as transparent as possible. It is this transparency, rather than any technical substitution of impersonality for personality, that Williams later meant when he said: 'we've got first to annihilate ourselves also as artists. We've got to get ourselves out of the way of what we have to do and to say'.[5] As he had written to Pound, all he sought to do was 'to understand something in its natural colors and shapes. Since it must have some kind of shape to be seen by me at all it grows to be – if it please – a novel'.[6]

1 'White Mule versus Poetry', *The Writer*, vol. 50, no. 8, 1937, p. 244.
2 *Selected Letters*, p. 146.   3 *White Mule*, p. 124.
4 *In the Money*, pp. 141-2.   5 Talk at Briarcliff Junior College, 1945.
6 *Selected Letters*, p. 104.

White Mule gives equally careful attention to the worlds of new-born Floss, her mother, Gurlie, and her father, Joe – and, through those, to the larger worlds of immigrant family life and the wider American society. Williams sought in this way to transcend the limitations of such a story as Gertrude Stein's *Melanctha*, which, by its clinical focus on the individual, had done 'violence to the larger scene'. To deal with a Melanctha alone, he concluded, is less than human. It is 'to overlook the gross instigation and with all subtlety to examine the object minutely for "the truth".'[1]

But how can one attend to the 'gross instigation' without indulging in 'lies'? The answer in *White Mule* is a sequence of fitted narrative blocks, each examining minutely some portion of the much larger field of attention: the birth of Floss; Joe in the park, considering the meanings of family, business and America; Joe and Gurlie in an argument; the Negro girl Vinie playing with Floss; a visit from Joe's brother Oscar; a scene in the printing company where Joe is shop manager – and so forth. As the novel progresses, we follow simultaneously the development of the sensitive and tenacious (but partly rejected) baby, the social climb being made by the egocentric and ambitious Gurlie, the subtle compromising of Joe's integrity as he yields to Gurlie's pressures – and the whole process of family and social movement of which these lines of growth, hardening and decline are a part. The whole pattern (illuminated by many analogies, crosslights and interrelations) is a study of the burdens of success in American life. Early in the book Joe calls it a 'battle for something without value at the cost of all he knew that was worth while.'[2]

The pattern of this implicit sequel to *In the American Grain* partly arises from the shape of the narrative blocks themselves. A peculiar lack of perspective, causing all details to appear as in a close-up, realistically allows conflicts and crises to emerge unexpectedly (but after hidden preparation) from the seemingly random texture of experience. A visit from Oscar, beginning as a study in contrasting temperaments and modes of adjustment to America, gradually builds to a serious fight between Gurlie and Joe. Or a Christmas family gathering allows Joe's imperfectly admitted unhappiness to be revealed in his jocular responses and his response to his favorite violin piece.

1 *Selected Essays*, pp. 119, 120.   2 *White Mule*, p. 24.

Frequent counterpointing enriches this texture. A chapter concerned with the strike that Joe is trying to break moves from a domestic scene in which he unintentionally injures Floss's finger, through several scenes of tense inaction for the adults, accompanied by unusual mischief on the part of Floss and her older sister Lottie, to Joe's reports of actual violence involving him. On a larger scale, the last four chapters move through Gurlie's idyllic summer in Vermont (where her ambition appears as the serpent in the garden), Joe's interview with Mr Lemon (in which Joe rejects the dishonesty of stock-market speculation but makes a subtler compromise), Joe's watching of a Fourth of July doubleheader (which counterpoints details of the baseball games and of Joe's imperfect awareness of his own gradual capitulation), and a final Vermont episode, focusing on Floss and the Ferry children – which is, for the baby, a delighted exploration of a new world; for Gurlie, a mixture of bucolic adventure and distaste for poverty; and, for the reader, a complex image of what is happening to the Stechers. The closing vision of Floss, after a mud-pie-and-raspberry escapade, points also toward Gurlie and Joe in their adjustments to American success: 'the baby's face smeared with berry juice, her hands sooty, quite part of it all.'[1]

In their handling of naturalistic details, these chapters are related to much contemporary fiction – from Flaubert and Chekhov through Joyce and Hemingway. But, despite the counterpointing that I have mentioned, in Williams's fiction we are apt to feel less portentous symbolic pressure; indeed, the surface may often seem mere documentary rendering. We can understand that Williams should object to Hemingway's use of 'conversation': 'it is rarely as expressive as he makes it and almost twice as succinct.'[2] Certainly the drama of conversation is a major achievement in *White Mule* and *In the Money* – along with family group scenes that render a complex interplay of temperament, experience and awareness.

If Williams's use of the symptom rather than the bold symbol results in some dilution of meaning, this is balanced by two strengths that emerge from the pattern of the whole. We gradually are led to become aware of the rich significance of the 'actual', as the many small filaments that substitute for plot make their omnipresence felt. And we gradually discover the implications of the narrator's own

1 p. 234.   2 *Selected Letters*, p. 105.

state of open attention to the slightest detail, whether or not it may seem predictably 'significant'. For that is the state of attention toward which the characters move in their moments of harmonious growth and fullest self-knowledge, and from which they depart (either obviously or subtly) as they react into self-enclosure, self-deception and destructiveness.

In 1937 Williams promised a continuation of the chronological pace of *White Mule*, but also some shift of focus: 'In this volume the baby has her "pattern" set. In the next volume she learns how to dress herself, at about the age of three. In the last volume she gets as far as the first things she will remember later. That's all I want of her. While she is doing this the family makes money and moves into the country. The third volume will end without the baby as a principal character. It has to. The social theories of our day finally become arthritic and Joe dies among their rigidities.'[1]

In the Money does continue according to this plan. Floss is in her second and third years, and the major focus is now more continuously upon Joe. (The narrative pace is therefore more rapid and the structure closer to the usual conception of 'plot'.) We watch Joe's strategies and infer his compromises as he bids for the money-order contract and establishes his own printing business. By the last chapter, 'The Miracle', he has bought a new house in the suburbs; and the closing symbolic action is the family's discovery of the miraculous gift he had promised on the day before:

There was the dwarf plum tree they had planted in the yard
when they moved into the house in the spring and that
hadn't had a blossom on it or a sign of fruit the whole
season. But it had at least a dozen tremendous red plums on
it now, each at the end of a twig. Gurlie began to laugh.[2]

They remove the plums, strings and all: natural growth is yielding to engineered abundance.

This second volume of the American parable, however, has involved an unexplained shift of dates. The action occurs not in 1894-5 but in 1901-2 (or 1903-4) – apparently because Joe's dealings with the government (like those of his prototype, Paul Herman) must

1 *'White Mule* versus Poetry', p. 244.
2 *In the Money*, p. 299.

take place during Roosevelt's administration.[1] *The Build-Up* silently rectifies this situation: it begins in the summer of 1900 when Floss is seven. But some twelve years have altered Williams's conception of the necessary style and plan of the trilogy. Though still seeking solidity of rendering,[2] he gives less attention to detail.

The mode of this less successful book is closer to that of the recently written *Autobiography*. Narrative blocks are shorter; tone is more anecdotal; there is more explicit commentary; and the pace is much more rapid. In fact, *The Build-Up* briskly covers some seventeen years. Nevertheless, Williams does sustain the trilogy's larger contrapuntal structure. He now focuses primarily on Gurlie's climb up the ladder of suburban life, the meanings of which he expands by parallel treatment of Floss's and Lottie's entrances into the adult world. The tone is one of social comedy, darkening perceptibly toward the end. Floss's marriage and the birth of her first child occur against the background of a comprehensive wiping out of promise: Lottie's effective disappearance in Europe, the accidental self-killing of her younger brother, Paul, and the entry of the United States into the First World War. Gurlie's success dissolves in the wave of anti-German feeling, heightened by gossip about Joe's previous business activities. Though she again prevails in her insistence upon having a new house, Joe's building has now become frenzied: 'Blow the damned rock to hell and gone. We're going to have a house like nothing in the neighbourhood.'[3]

As part of this larger pattern, Charlie Bishop, the young doctor-poet, marries Floss only after being shattered by Lottie's refusal of him. New life must arise from such descent into despair and nothingness. That is the love that presents itself to Charlie's imagination: 'There is a sort of love, not romantic love, but a love that with daring can be made with difficultly to blossom. It is founded on passion, a dark sort of passion, . . . a passion of despair, as all life is despair.'[4] In its repetitive insistence, this is still a youthful romanticism. But, recognizing Charlie as a portrait of the artist as a young man, we can see the affinity between his love and that state of consciousness which has very largely determined the texture of these volumes. As an attentive and compassionate study of Floss and her family, the

1 pp. 44, 127. 2 *Selected Letters*, p. 312.
3 *The Build-Up*, p. 335. 4 p. 262.

White Mule trilogy is evidence of that new world which Charlie called 'a real thing'.[1]

Anonymous

'Local Boy' a review of *The Build-Up*, *The Times Literary Supplement*
13 March 1969

I'm writing a novel (said Williams of *The Build-up* in a letter
to Robert Lowell), it's a novel, as usual, about my local scene
(the scene is merely what I know) ... I want to write it so
that when I speak of a chair it will stand upon four legs in a
room. And of course it will stand upon a four-legged sentence
on a page at the same time.

Williams's way with prose writing – from the chair in the sentence
to the containing episode – eschews, as Pound put it, 'major form'.
The form of the trilogy, which began with *White Mule* and *In the
Money*, and is brought to an open-ended conclusion in *The Build-Up*,
admits plot chiefly in its awareness of time passing. A 'real' plot
would have interfered with Williams's sense of truth to life: there are
no parallel developments of groups of characters, no structural
ironies, and Williams is uninterested in the knowing asymmetries
of the *nouvelle vague*. So the trilogy is close to being a biography of
the Stecher family – the Herman family, that is, into which Williams
married – and *The Build-Up* overlaps, in some of its finest stretches,
with the *Autobiography*, published in the previous year.

A reluctance to trust oneself to the current of the thing can result
in the reader's imposing an alien form, and this happens in a significant
way on the dust jacket, where we read:

Joe Stecher and his wife have struggled from their early
poverty and strangeness into social acceptance and comparative
ease. But somewhere along the line they have not only lost the
magic of their youth. But the dream of America the golden
has become the taste of brass.

1 p. 263.

This kind of sentimental Spenglerism, so dear to the English with their comforting notion of America as a land of doomed hopes, tidies the book up no end, but its pop sociology takes no purchase on Williams's human actualities. Joe Stecher reaches ultimate misery because a war is threatening with Germany, his homeland, and – more poignantly – his son has accidentally shot himself. It is precisely Williams's avoidance of 'major form' and his refusal to drag in abstractions which give this close its felt weight. In a novel by Hardy the accident would be called on to prove something, but Williams has no interest in the President of the Immortals or in easy generalities about America the golden.

The 'ideological' centre of the book occurs when Gurlie Stecher, Joe's wife, invited South by a friend, is called on to talk to a group of Southerners, avid for aristocracy, about her Viking forebears. What she tells them is:

Your ancestors were immigrants, too, and many of them were poor. They had to work .... My Eva Anderson, who came to me three years ago, is a fine, healthy girl. Now she can speak English. She got married to a farmer in Minnesota, pretty soon her children will be the leading citizens, maybe doctors and lawyers and then you'll see. They have brains. But that is what America is for. ...

Mrs Stecher speaks in character, but Williams casts no shadow of irony on what she says and neither does the book's conclusion. He is with her here, although he knows more than she knows and exhibits her at times in all her crass insensitivity – particularly when she is instrumental in getting her elder daughter married to the wrong man. Yet, in some way, she remains admirable and her social getting-on, too, opens a field for praiseworthy energies and endeavours. The refusal to simplify what he knew into a plotted novel entails Williams's occasional loss of impetus. But it is of a piece with his refusal to simplify the quality, weave and outcome of human motive – from Mrs Stecher's almost mindless thrust of ego to his own proposal of marriage to the girl he is not yet in love with. Form for Williams is the difficult mimesis of such human waywardness.

(262)

Further Views

Wallace Stevens

'Rubbings of Reality'   1946 (reprinted in Samuel French Morse (ed.), *Opus Posthumous*, 1957)

If a man writes a little every day, as Williams does, or used to do, it may be that he is merely practising in order to make perfect. On the other hand he may be practising in order to get at his subject. If his subject is, say, a sense, a mood, an integration, and if his representation is faint or obscure, and if he practises in order to overcome his faintness or obscurity, what he really does is to bring, or try to bring, his subject into that degree of focus at which he sees it, for a moment, as it is and at which he is able to represent it in exact definition.

A man does not spend his life doing this sort of thing unless doing it is something he needs to do. One of the sanctions of the writer is that he is doing something that he needs to do. The need is not the desire to accomplish through writing something not incidental to the writing itself. Thus a political or a religious writer writes for political or religious reasons. Williams writes, I think, in order to write. He needs to write.

What is the nature of this need? What does a man do when he delineates the images of reality? Obviously, the need is a general need and the activity a general activity. It is of our nature that we proceed from the chromatic to the clear, from the unknown to the known. Accordingly the writer who practises in order to make perfect is really practising to get at his subject and, in that exercise, is participating in a universal activity. He is obeying his nature. Imagism (as one of Williams's many involvements, however long ago) is not something superficial. It obeys an instinct. Moreover, imagism is an ancient phase of poetry. It is something permanent. Williams is a writer to whom writing is the grinding of a glass, the polishing of a lens by means of which he hopes to be able to see clearly. His delineations are trials. They are rubbings of reality.

The modern world is the result of such activity on a grand scale, not particularly in writing but in everything. It may be said, for instance, that communism is an effort to improve the human focus. The work of Picasso is an attempt to get at his subject, an attempt to achieve a reality of the intelligence. But the world of the past was equally the result of such activity. Thus the German pietists of the early 1700s who came to Pennsylvania to live in the caves of the Wissahickon and to dwell in solitude and meditation were proceeding in their way, from the chromatic to the clear. Is not Williams in a sense a literary pietist, chastening himself, incessantly, along the Passaic?

There is an intellectual *tenue*. It is easy to see how underneath the chaos of life today and at the bottom of all the disintegrations there is the need to see, to understand: and, in so far as one is not completely baffled, to recreate. This is not emotional. It springs from the belief that we have only our own intelligence on which to rely. This manifests itself in many ways, in every living art as in every living phase of politics or science. If we could suddenly remake the world on the basis of our own intelligence, see it clearly and represent it without faintness or obscurity, Williams's poems would have a place there.

(257)

Charles Tomlinson

'Letter to Dr Williams', *Spectrum*, vol. 1, no. 3   1957

There being no immediate
           likelihood
                      of reading your poems

under the impress
           Faber and Faber,
                      may a poet

and (at that) an English
           poet, salute them?
                      For here

they are deaf to everything
           except the quatrain
                      which is virtually

as useless as the couplet.
           You chose
                      (so you say) 'the speech

of Polish mothers.'
           Whatever your means
                      or your intention, the end

has enriched us all
           whether we confess it
                      or no. We have gained

a world, and you
           have enlivened a discipline
                      by a propriety of cadence

that will pass
           into the common idiom
                      like the space

of Juan Gris
> and Picasso —

>> invented to be of use

and for the rearticulation
> of inarticulate facts.

(58–9)

William Empson

from 'Rhythm and Imagery in English Poetry', *Journal of the British Society of Aesthetics*, vol. 2, no. 1 1962

The English often feel that some Americans quack on with a terrible monotony and no pause for the opposite number to get in a word. For that matter, I have known American literature students who believed that regular metres if used by literate authors were always meant as a parody of the unsophisticated – the well-known Mock-pastoral. The Free Verse movement began in America, and this might simply be because their language is no longer stressed. Greek lost its tones during some Dark Age, and a similar thing may be happening to English. But it is clearly not true that all American accents are unstressed; perhaps only the Boston accent is. I should guess that Miss Marianne Moore really talks without stress, and only could be scanned by counting syllables, so that she was quite right to make her innovation. It is rather surprising, come to think of it, that American poets have not revived classical metres, as they feel them-selves forbidden the standard singing line. Forbidden does seem the word; the *vers libre* movement has meant, for many young poets, a struggle to renounce a pleasure which they feel perfectly capable of. Opinion about William Carlos Williams makes the position clear, I think; English critics don't feel he is a poet at all, but the most un-expected American critics will be found speaking of him with tender reverence; they feel he is a kind of saint. He has renounced all the pleasures of the English language, so that he is completely American; and he only says the dullest things, so he has won the terrible fight to become completely democratic as well. I think that, if they are such

gluttons for punishment as all that, they are past help. But then again, I am not sure that we English aren't the ones who are losing the singing line, as apart from renouncing it. Serious poetry written to be set to music would be a striking change in the literary scene, and may be, though we don't know it, already an impossible one.
(44-5)

Robert Lowell

'William Carlos Williams', *Hudson Review*, vol. 14, no. 4   1961-2

Dr Williams and his work are part of me, yet I come on them as a critical intruder. I fear I shall spoil what I have to say, just as I somehow got off on the wrong note about Williams with Ford Madox Ford twenty-five years ago. Ford was wearing a stained robin's-egg blue pajama top, reading Theocritus in Greek, and guying me about my 'butterfly existence', so removed from the labors of a professional writer. I was saying something awkward, green and intense in praise of Williams, and Ford, while agreeing, managed to make me feel that I was far too provincial, genteel and puritanical to understand what I was saying. And why not? Wasn't I, as Ford assumed, the grandson or something of James Russell Lowell and the cousin of Lawrence Lowell, a young man doomed to trifle with poetry and end up as President of Harvard or ambassador to England?

I have stepped over these pitfalls. I have conquered my hereditary disadvantages. Except for writing, nothing I've touched has shone. When I think about writing on Dr Williams, I feel a chaos of thoughts and images, images cracking open to admit a thought, thoughts dragging their roots for the soil of an image. When I woke up this morning, something unusual for this summer was going on! – pinpricks of rain were falling in a reliable, comforting simmer. Our town was blanketed in the rain of rot and the rain of renewal. New life was muscling in, everything growing moved on its one-way trip to the ground. I could feel this, yet believe our universal misfortune was bearable and even welcome. An image held my mind during these moments and kept returning – an old fashioned New England cottage freshly painted white. I saw a shaggy, triangular shade on the house, trees, a hedge or their shadows, the blotch of decay. The house might have been the house I was now living in, but it wasn't; it came from the time when I was a child, still unable to read and living in the small town of Barnstaple on Cape Cod. Inside the house was a bird-book with an old stiff and steely engraving of a sharp-shinned hawk. The hawk's legs had a reddish-brown buffalo fuzz on them; behind was the blue sky, bare and abstracted from the world. In the present, pinpricks of rain were falling on everything I could see, and even on the white house in my mind, but the hawk's picture, being indoors I suppose, was more or less spared. Since I saw the picture of the hawk, the pinpricks of rain have gone on, half the people I once knew are dead, half the people I now know were then unborn, and I have learned to read.

An image of a white house with a blotch on it – this is perhaps the start of a Williams poem. If I held this image closely and honestly enough, the stabbing detail might come and with it the universal that belonged to this detail and nowhere else. Much wrapping would have to be cut away, and many elegiac cadences with their worn eloquence and loftiness. This is how I would like to write about Dr Williams. I would collect impressions, stare them into rightness, and let my mind-work and judgements come as they might naturally.

When I was a freshman at Harvard, nothing hit me so hard as the Norton Lectures given by Robert Frost. Frost's revolutionary power, however, was not in his followers, nor in the student literary magazine, the *Advocate*, whose editor had just written a piece on speech rhythms in the *Hired Man*, a much less up-to-date thing to do then than now. Our only strong and avant-garde man was James Laughlin. He was much taller and older than we were. He knew Henry Miller, and exotic young American poetesses in Paris, spent summers at Rapallo with Ezra Pound, and was getting out the first number of his experimental annual, *New Directions*. He knew the great, and he himself wrote deliberately flat descriptive and anecdotal poems. We were sarcastic about them, but they made us feel secretly that we didn't know what was up in poetry. They used no punctuation or capitals, and their only rule was that each line should be eleven or fifteen typewriter spaces long. The author explained that this metric was 'as rational as any other' and was based on the practice of W. C. Williams, a poet and pediatrician living in Rutherford, New Jersey.

About this time, Laughlin published a review somewhere, perhaps even in the *Harvard Advocate*, of Williams's last small volume. In it, he pushed the metric of typewriter spaces, and quoted from a poem, *The Catholic Bells*,[1] to show Williams's 'mature style at fifty'! This was a memorable phrase, and one that made maturity seem possible, but a long way off. I more or less memorized *The Catholic Bells*, and spent months trying to console myself by detecting immaturities in whatever Williams had written before he was fifty.

The Catholic Bells

Tho' I'm no Catholic
I listen hard when the bells
in the yellow-brick tower
of their new church

ring down the leaves
ring in the frost upon them
and the death of the flowers
ring out the grackle

toward the south, the sky
darkening by them, ring in
the new baby of Mr and Mrs
Krantz which cannot

for the fat of its cheeks
open well its eyes, . . .

What I liked about *The Catholic Bells* were the irrelevant associations. I hung on the words 'frost' and 'Catholic', and still more its misleading similarity to the 'Ring out wild bells' section of *In Memoriam*. Other things upset and fascinated me and made me feel I was in a world I would never quite understand. Were the spelling 'Tho', strange in a realistic writer, and the iambic rhythm of the first seven words part of some inevitable sound pattern? I had dipped into Edith Sitwell's criticism and was full of inevitable sound patterns. I was sure that somewhere hidden was a key that would make this poem as regular as the regular meters of Tennyson. There had to be something outside the poem I could hang onto because what was

1 *Collected Earlier Poems*, p. 111.

inside dizzied me! the shocking scramble of the august and the crass in making the Catholic church 'new' and 'yellow-brick', the cherubic ugliness of the baby, belonging rather horribly to 'Mr and Mrs | Krantz', and seen by the experienced, mature pediatrician as unable to see 'for the fat of its cheeks' – this last a cunning shift into anapests. I was surprised that Williams used commas, and that my three or four methods of adjusting his lines to uniform typewriter spaces failed. I supposed he had gone on to some bolder and still more mature system.

To explain the full punishment I felt on first reading Williams, I should say a little about what I was studying at the time. A year or so before, I had read some introductory books on the enjoyment of poetry, and was knocked over by the examples in the free-verse sections. When I arrived at college, independent, fearful of advice and with all the world before me, I began to rummage through the Cambridge bookshops. I found books that must have been looking for a buyer since the student days of Trumbull Stickney: soiled metrical treatises written by obscure English professors in the eighteen-nineties. They were full of glorious things: rising rhythm, falling rhythm, feet with Greek names, stanzas from Longfellow's *Psalm of Life*, John Drinkwater and Swinburne. Nothing seemed simpler than meter. I began experiments with an exotic foot, short, long, two shorts, then fell back on iambics. My material now took twice as many words, and I rolled out Spenserian stanzas on Job and Jonah surrounded by recently seen Nantucket scenery. Everything I did was grand, ungrammatical and had a timeless, hackneyed quality. All this was ended by reading Williams. It was as though some homemade ship, part Spanish galleon, part paddle-wheels, kitchen pots and elastic bands and worked by hand, had anchored to a filling station.

In *The Catholic Bells*, the joining of religion and non-religion, of piety and a hard, nervous secular knowingness are typical of Williams. Further along in this poem, there is a piece of mere description that has always stuck in my mind.

(the

grapes still hanging to
the vines along the nearby

Concordia Halle like broken
teeth in the head of an

old man)

Take out the Concordia Halle and the grape vines crackle in the
wind with a sour, impoverished dryness; take out the vines and the
Concordia Halle has lost its world. Williams has pages and pages of
description that are as good as this. It is his equivalent of, say, the
Miltonic sentence, the dazzling staple and excellence which he can
always produce. Williams has said that he uses the forms he does for
quick changes of tone, atmosphere and speed. This makes him dangerous and difficult to imitate, because most poets have little change of
tone, atmosphere and speed in them.

I have emphasized Williams's simplicity and nakedness and have
no doubt been misleading. His idiom comes from many sources,
from speech and reading, both of various kinds; the blend, which is
his own invention, is generous and even exotic. Few poets can come
near to his wide clarity and dashing rightness with words, his dignity
and almost Alexandrian modulations of voice. His short lines often
speed up and simplify hugely drawn out and ornate sentence structures. I once typed out his direct but densely observed poem *The
Semblables*,[1] in a single prose paragraph. Not a word or its placing
had been changed, but the poem had changed into a piece of smother-
ing, magnificent rhetoric, much more like Faulkner than the original
Williams.

The difficulties I found in Williams twenty-five years ago are still
difficulties for me. Williams enters me, but I cannot enter him. Of
course, one cannot catch any good writer's voice or breathe his air.
But there's something more. It's as if no poet except Williams had
really seen America or heard its language. Or rather, he sees and
hears what we all see and hear and what is most obvious, but no
one else has found this a help or an inspiration. This may come
naturally to Dr Williams from his character, surroundings and
occupation. I can see him rushing from his practice to his typewriter, happy that so much of the world has rubbed off on him,
maddened by its hurry. Perhaps he had no choice. Anyway, what
others have spent lifetimes in building up personal styles to gather

1 *Collected Later Poems*, p. 244.

what has been snatched up on the run by Dr Williams? When I say that I cannot enter him, I am almost saying that I cannot enter America. This troubles me. I am not satisfied to let it be. Like others I have picked up things here and there from Williams, but this only makes me marvel all the more at his unique and searing journey. It is a Dantesque journey, for he loves America excessively, as if it were *the* truth and *the* subject; his exasperation is also excessive, as if there were no other hell. His flowers rustle by the superhighways and pick up all our voices.

A seemingly unending war has been going on for as long as I can remember between Williams and his disciples and the principals and disciples of another school of modern poetry. The 'beats' are on one side, the university poets are on the other. Lately the gunfire has been hot. With such unlikely Williams recruits as Karl Shapiro blasting away, it has become unpleasant to stand in the middle in a position of impartiality.

The war is an old one for me. In the late Thirties, I was at Kenyon College to study under John Crowe Ransom. The times hummed with catastrophe and ideological violence, both political and aesthetical. The English departments were clogged with worthy, but outworn and backward-looking scholars, whose tastes in the moderns were most often superficial, random and vulgar. Students who wanted to write got little practical help from their professors. They studied the classics as monsters that were slowly losing their fur and feathers and leaking a little sawdust. What one did one's self was all chance and shallowness, and no profession seemed wispier and less needed than that of the poet. My own group, that of Tate and Ransom, was all for the high discipline, for putting on the full armor of the past, for making poetry something that would take a man's full weight and that would bear his complete intelligence, passion and subtlety. Almost anything, the Greek and Roman classics, Elizabethan dramatic poetry, seventeenth-century metaphysical verse, old and modern critics, aestheticians and philosophers, could be suppled up and again made necessary. The struggle perhaps centred on making the old metrical forms usable again to express the depths of one's experience.

For us Williams was of course part of the revolution that had renewed poetry, but he was a byline. Opinions varied on his work. It was something fresh, secondary and minor, or it was the best that free verse could do. He was the one writer with the substance, daring and staying power to make the short free verse poem something considerable. One was shaken when the radical conservative critic, Yvor Winters, spoke of Williams's *By the road to the contagious hospital* as a finer, more lasting piece of craftsmanship than *Gerontion*.

Well, nothing will do for everyone. It's hard for me to see how I and the younger poets I was close to could at that time have learned much from Williams. It was all we could do to keep alive and follow our own heavy program. That time is gone, and now young poets are perhaps more conscious of the burden and the hardening of this old formalism. Too many poems have been written to rule. They show off their authors' efforts and mind, but little more. Often the culture seems to have passed them by. And once more, Dr Williams is a model and a liberator. What will come, I don't know. Williams, unlike, say, Marianne Moore, seems to be one of those poets who can be imitated anonymously. His style is almost a common style and even what he claims for it – *the American style*. Somehow, written without his speed and genius, the results are usually dull, a poem at best well-made but without breath.

Williams is part of the great breath of our literature. *Paterson* is our *Leaves of Grass*. The times have changed. A drastic experimental art is now expected and demanded. The scene is dense with the dirt and power of industrial society. Williams looks on it with exasperation, terror and a kind of love. His short poems are singularly perfect thrusts, maybe the best that will ever be written of their kind, because neither the man nor the pressure will be found again. When I think of his last longish autobiographical poems, I remember his last reading I heard. I was at Wellesley. I think about three thousand students attended. It couldn't have been more crowded in the wide-galleried hall and I had to sit in the aisle. The poet appeared, one whole side partly paralysed, his voice just audible, and here and there a word misread. No one stirred. In the silence he read his great poem, *Of Asphodel, That Greeny Flower*, a triumph of simple confession – somehow he delivered to us what was impossible, something that was both poetry and beyond poetry.

I think of going with Dr Williams and his son to visit his mother, very old, almost a hundred, and unknowing, her black eyes boring through. And Williams saying to her, 'Which would you rather see, us, or three beautiful blonds?' As we left, he said, 'The old bitch will live on but I may die tomorrow!' You could not feel shocked. Few men had felt and respected anyone more than Williams had his old mother. And in seeing him out strolling on a Sunday after a heart attack: the town seemed to know him and love him and take him in its stride, as we will do with his great pouring of books, his part in the air we breathe and will breathe.

(530–36)

J. Hillis Miller

from 'William Carlos Williams', *Poets of Reality* 1966

Williams's work expresses, quietly and without fanfare, a revolution in human sensibility. When he gives himself up to the world he gives up the coordinates and goals which had polarized earlier literature. Romantic poetry, like idealist philosophy, had been based on an opposition between the inner world of the subject and the outer world of things. Since the world is other than the self, that self can ground itself on something external. This tradition remains valid through the nineteenth and early twentieth centuries, down to Yeats and the early Stevens. In Williams it disappears. This is perhaps most apparent, to a reader steeped in romanticism, in a strange lack of tension in his work. Gone are both the profound abysses of subjectivity, so important in earlier poetry, and the limitless dimensions of the external world, through which Shelley's Alastor or Browning's Paracelsus sought a vanishing presence and strained every nerve to reach it. 'How foolish to seek new worlds,' says Williams, '. . . when we must know that any world warmed by the arts will surpass the very Elysian Fields if the imagination reaches its end there'.[1] Only in the *Poems* of 1909 does the image of fathomless space appear, the 'soundless infinite blue day',[2] and only there are found examples of the romantic theme of an unattainable presence in the landscape, as in the assertion that poetry will take the

1 'Introduction' to Byron Vazakas, *Transfigured Night*, 1946, p. xi.
2 *Poems*, (1909), p. 21.

reader 'to worlds afar whose fruits all anguish mend',[1] or in the last lines of *To Simplicity*:

... Hark! Hark! Mine ears are numb
With dread! Methought a faint hallooing rang!
Where art thou hid? Cry, cry again! I come!
I come! I come![2]

In Williams's mature work, if something exists at all, it dwells in the only realm there is, a space both subjective and objective, a region of copresence in which anywhere is everywhere, and all times are one time. 'What is time but an impertinence?' asks the poet.[3] Since there are no distances there is 'no direction',[4] no reason to go one way rather than another because there is no reason to go anywhere at all. To be in one place is already to be in all other places. 'I won't follow causes,' he said. 'I can't. The reason is that it seems so much more important to me that I *am*. Where shall one go? What shall one do?'[5] Byron Vazakas is an authentic American poet because he 'hasn't had "to go anywhere". There he is ... anywhere, therefore *here*, for his effects. And being here, he sees here; and hears here.'[6]

This situation means the disappearance of another characteristic of traditional philosophy and poetry: thinking in terms of causality. Western thought has been dominated since Aristotle by the idea of cause, whether this has meant a search for the ground of things in some transcendent being, or whether it has meant conceiving of nature as a chain of cause and effect, each element pushing the next in an endless series. Both kinds of causality vanish in Williams's work. All things exist simultaneously in one realm, and though they may interact they are not related causally. The idea of causal sequence is replaced by the notion of a poetry which 'lives with an intrinsic movement of its own to verify its authenticity'.[7] As in other areas of contemporary thought, linear determinism gives way to a system of reciprocal motions, 'intrinsic, undulant, a physical more than a literary character.'[8]

1 p. 11.   2 p. 9.   3 *Great American Novel*; *Imaginations*, p. 213.
4 *Paterson*, I, ii, p. 28.   5 *Selected Letters*, p. 147.
6 'Introduction' to *Transfigured Night*, p. xii.
7 *Selected Essays*, p. 257.   8 p. 256.

It is appropriate that Keats should have been the poet who most influenced Williams in his youth, for Williams might be said to begin where Keats ends. The leap into things of the sympathetic imagination is achieved by Williams at the beginning, and attained also is that perpetual present which is expressed in the epigraph adapted from the *Ode on a Grecian Urn* which the poet puts on the title page of his first book: 'Happy melodist forever piping songs forever new.' 'I quit Keats,' he says 'just at the moment he himself did – with Hyperion's scream'.[1] Williams means of course Apollo's scream. Keats's poetry reaches its climax with Apollo's attainment of immortal knowledge. With that climax it melts into the silence beyond poetry. Williams's work begins with the muteness of what he calls in *Spring and All* an 'approximate co-extension with the universe'.[2]

This silence will provide another definition of the place Williams enters when he resigns himself to existence. The romantic or idealist tradition in one way or another presupposes a separation of words from things. Words are instruments which the poet may use to reach and grapple objects in order to close the gap between himself and them. Through words the poet imposes his will on things and so transforms them. The naming of poetry is the creation of a cunning verbal replica which changes things into spiritualized stuff and so assimilates them into the mind. The idea that words 'represent' things is deeply a part of the tradition of metaphysical thinking of which romanticism is a version. Williams never uses words in this way. For him things are already possessed before being named. When he gives up he reaches a place which is before language: 'Things have no names for me and places have no significance.'[3] This loss of language is radically different from the aphasia of the prince in the early poem. The princes's mutism expressed his separation from other people and the land. Now all things have been assimilated and the need for words has disappeared. If language is the voice of consciousness in its isolation, union with everything can be reached only by leaving it behind. 'As a reward for this anonymity,' says Williams, 'I feel as much part of things as trees and stones.'[4] His new speechlessness is the silence which

1 *Autobiography*, p. 61.   2 p. 27.
3 *Selected Letters*, p. 147.
4 p. 147.

376 J. Hillis Miller

follows Apollo's scream. In it he belongs to 'a wordless | world | without personality'.[1]

If trees, flowers, mountains and meadows are for Wordsworth and Tennyson the dwelling places of a haunting presence, other romantic poets describe the search for a similar ideal incarnated successively in the women they love. To Gérard de Nerval all women are the same woman, and with each is experienced a failure to possess the ideal: 'La Treizième revient . . . C'est encore la première; | Et c'est toujours la seule.'[2] This theme too no longer has meaning for Williams. If everything is part of himself this includes men and women. The strangers speaking an alien tongue in his early poem are replaced by the men and women of *Paterson*. The latter exist within the man-city and are the poet's mind incarnated:

> Inside the bus one sees
> his thoughts sitting and standing. His
> thoughts alight and scatter –[3]

In the same way he says of one of the personae of *The Great American Novel*, a 'savior of the movies': 'his great heart had expanded so as to include the whole city'.[4] This expansion is anticipated in the last text of the *Poems* of 1909, where the poet affirms that with the help of 'Perfection' he has transcended the 'profusion | Of space' and 'o'errides all restriction'.[5] Perfection is ubiquity in space and possession of its contents, the 'fresh variety' of the world which, in another poem from the same volume, leaves the poet 'perplexed by detail'.[6] The celebrated slogan, 'No ideas but in things', is a shorthand expression of the identification of mind and universe presupposed in Williams's work. Other people are no different from inanimate objects and may just as well incarnate the poet's ideas. This obliteration of distances also takes place in the relation between the poet and his readers. 'In the imagination,' he says, 'we are from henceforth (so long as you read) locked in a fraternal embrace, the classic caress of author and reader. We are one. Whenever I say "I" I mean also "you".'[7] To accept the embrace Williams offers means the impossi-

1 *Collected Earlier Poems*, p. 280.
2 Gérard de Nerval, *Oeuvres, éd. de la Pléiade*, 1:31, 1952.
3 *Paterson*, I, i, p. 18. 4 p. 49; *Imaginations*, p. 198.
5 *Poems* (1909), p. 22. 6 p. 20. 7 *Imaginations*, p. 89.

bility of 'criticizing' his work, if criticism means viewing with the cold eye of analysis and judgement. The critic must resign himself to the poet's world and accept what he finds there.

If the poetry of the last century and a half has often assumed a distance between man and things or between man and man, an equally important theme has been the distance of God. Here too Williams differs from his predecessors. In his work there is no searching for the traces of a vanished deity, no frantic attempt to find a new mediator between heaven and earth. 'Heaven,' he says in one of his few references to the idea of another world, 'seems frankly impossible.'[1] The disappearance of a distinction between subject and object could be said to mark the end of a tradition which began in its modern form with writers like Montaigne, Pascal, Descartes and Locke, those explorers of the abyss of subjectivity. The absence of the idea of heaven means the rejection of an even older tradition, Christian and Platonic. Here is everywhere for Williams, and there is no other world to go to.

The resignation to existence which makes Williams's poetry possible is the exact reverse of the Cartesian Cogito. Descartes puts everything in question in order to establish the existence of his separate self, an existence built on the power of detached thinking. Williams gives himself up in despair and establishes a self beyond personality, a self coextensive with the universe. Words, things, people and God vanish as separate entities and everything becomes a unit. In *The Wanderer*[2] this obliteration of distinctions is poetically enacted. Under the aegis of a muse-lady (whom Williams has identified with his grandmother),[3] the poet is absorbed into the Passaic, swallowed up by 'the utter depth of its rottenness',[4] or it can be said that he takes the river into himself, for it is an interpenetration, both ways. After this plunge he possesses all time and space and has complete knowledge of everything: 'I knew all – it became me.'[5]

This phrase is quoted near the end of Book Five of *Paterson*, in a context which shows the poet's awareness of its seminal place in his work. After the absorption of the poet by the river the muse speaks once more to him: 'Be mostly silent!'[6] Here is attained that silence

---

1 *Selected Letters*, p. 147.   2 *Collected Earlier Poems*, p. 3.
3 *Autobiography*, p. 60.   4 *Collected Earlier Poems*, p. 11.
5 p. 12.   6 p. 12.

and anonymity which he describes in the letter to Marianne Moore. This silence is his marriage to all that is. . . .

Finally there is *Asphodel, That Greeny Flower*, the extraordinary love poem of Williams's old age. This poem has the quiet mastery of supreme attainment. Like *Paterson*, Book Five and *The Desert Music*, *Asphodel* gathers the world together and the lines rise continuously from a center which is everywhere. Since the lines ascend one by one from the same unfathomable ground, each is the equivalent of the others, the same and yet different. Flowers are facts, poems flowers, and 'all works of the imagination, | interchangeable'.[1] Each object could be substituted for any of the others, for all say the same thing, do that one thing which all poetic speech does – perpetuate the dance. In the extreme reach of his imagination the poet enters a space where:

> no distinction
> any more suffices to differentiate
> the particulars
> of place and condition[2]

Interchangeability enters in yet another way, for in *Asphodel* beauty is expressed not in a single image, of dance or music, but in a group of images all standing side by side in the poem to say the same thing, each saying it perfectly but in a unique way. The space of the poem is the poet's memory. Everything which has ever happened to him is brought back in its substantiality, 'a whole flood | of sister memories'.[3] It is also, and pre-eminently, the space of love, for *Asphodel* is a poem 'of love, abiding love',[4] the poet's final affirmation of his love for his wife and of the way the relation between them creates and sustains the world. The poem is also the space of language, of a murmuring speech which the poet prolongs defiantly and yet precariously, with infinite gentleness, against time and death:

And so

> with fear in my heart
> I drag it out

1 *Pictures from Brueghel*, p. 178.
2 p. 162.
3 p. 154.
4 p. 153.

and keep on talking
            for I dare not stop.
                        Listen while I talk on
against time.[1]

The space of the poet's sustaining speech is the realm of the imagina-
tion, 'the place made | in our lives | for the poem'.[2] This place is
also the sea, or rather the waves on the surface of the sea. The sea is
the profound depth from which all things have come to dance like
waves as the lines dance in the poem. The 'sea | which no one tends |
is also a garden',[3] earth giving birth to flowers as the sea to waves.
Sea, garden, poem, love and memory are equivalents, and 'the glint
of waves', 'the free interchange | of light over their surface',[4] is the
play of words in the poem, the blossoming of flowers in a garden.

These images lead to others. The poem is speech in defiance of
death. Here, at the very end of Williams's career, death appears in
his world for almost the first time. It is another name for the un-
fathomable ground. The poem flowers from it and yet contains it.
As Asphodel is the flower of hell but still triumphs over the darkness,
so the space of the poem is not hell but is the flower which rises
above death, for

    love and the imagination
            are of a piece,
                        swift as the light
to avoid destruction.[5]

This leads to a final group of images, once more interchangeable with
the others. Asphodel, the flower of hell, is the atomic bomb, since
'the bomb | also | is a flower'.[6] The exploding bomb is equated
with a distant thunderstorm over the sea which the poet watches
with his wife. The poem prolongs indefinitely the moment just
before death. It is speech in the shadow of death and dwells in the
light of a perpetual present, between the lightning and the thunder-
clap, between the sight of the exploding bomb and the coming of
annihilating heat. In *Asphodel, That Greeny Flower* light, the sea,
memory, speech, the garden, and love are the same, and the poem

1 p. 154.   2 p. 159.   3 p. 156.   4 p. 165.
5 p. 179.   6 p. 165.

maintains forever in living poise the moment between birth and death. As long as that moment lasts the flame of beauty is held in the open:

> The light
>
> > for all time shall outspeed
> > > the thunder crack.[1]

This radiant promise is the climax of Williams's writing, and the climax too of the development so far of twentieth-century poetry. Beginning with a heritage of romanticism and the dualism which usually accompanies it, twentieth-century literature has sometimes, as with Conrad, gone to the limits of nihilism, or sometimes, as with Eliot, recovered a new version of Christian immanence. Yeats, Thomas, Stevens and Williams have gradually developed a poetry beyond subjectivism and beyond dualism. This poetry presupposes a new understanding of reality. Only a reality which includes the human life that is lived in it makes possible a poetry which is 'the cry of its occasion, | Part of the res itself and not about it.'[2] In the work of Yeats, Thomas and Stevens can be witnessed the difficult struggle to go beyond the old traditions. Williams goes farthest. He begins within the space of immanence and his work is a magnificent uncovering of its riches. The section in Book Two of *Paterson* beginning 'The descent beckons | as the ascent beckoned'[3] is more than the poet's first use of the novel measure of his last poems. It also affirms his right to dwell in a new space and a new time. The poem describes the 'accomplishment', 'renewal' and 'initiation' of memory, but memory here is identical with the endless present of *Asphodel, That Greeny Flower*. In 'The descent beckons', as in Williams's other late poetry, space and the mind are identical. This space, a domain of plenitude and enlargement, coincides with a time which continually reaches out toward a goal of perennial freshness. Time is a dimension of space, a function of its life as it moves onward in the ever-new moment between origin and end. 'The descent beckons', in its expansive openness to the future, may be taken as a comprehensive description of the realm entered by the poetry of reality:

1 p. 181.
2 Wallace Stevens, *The Collected Poems*, Knopf, 1954, p. 473.
3 iii, p. 96.

> ... the spaces it opens are new
>
> places
>
> inhabited by hordes
> heretofore unrealized,
>
> of new kinds –
>
> since their movements
> are towards new objectives[1]
>
> (288–92, 356–9)

Yvor Winters

from 'Conclusions', *Forms of Discovery* 1967

William Carlos Williams (1883–1963), in his view of life and of poetry, was an uncompromising romantic. It is surprising, in the light of this fact, that he appears to have been a devoted husband, father and physician, eminently virtuous and practical in these capacities, and often naively shocked by the behavior of some of his Bohemian acquaintances who held the same ideas but acted upon them. He was a thorough bore in print except on a few occasions. He believed in the surrender to emotion and to instinct as the only way to wisdom and to art: *The Trees* is one of his many explicit statements of this notion. He believed that art is the product of a character which is 'automatically first-rate' (*Blues*, for May 1929); this is a version of Rousseau's doctrine of the 'beautiful soul', which Irving Babbitt discusses at length in *Rousseau and Romanticism* and which Jane Austen parodies in her first work of fiction, *Love and Freindship*. Williams, of course, believed that the doctrines originated with himself. Williams's artist would have no need for ideas and no awareness of them; in fact, he would display no signs of consciousness whatever. Williams distrusted all ideas and sought value as far as possible in the concrete; in an early poem called *Paterson* he reiterates the phrase 'no ideas but in things' (this idea, like Pound's imagism, is an end-product of eighteenth-century associationism); and he distrusted the entire range of emotion which is motivated by ideas, for he was in no position to distinguish good ideas from bad, and

1 *Paterson*, II, iii.

hence, in this realm, sound emotion from false. In *A Poem for Norman MacLeod* he writes:

The revolution
is accomplished
noble has been
changed to no bull[1]

Any emotion arising from the contemplation of an idea, whether moral, metaphysical or religious, appears to him merely sentimental. He distrusts traditional form, as a kind of restraint or inhibition: since he fails to grasp its meaning and uses, it appears to him, another mechanical sentimentalism; and he desires that the theme create its own form, like other believers in organic or imitative form from the eighteenth century onward, and like these believers he offers animal and vegetable comparisons – a poem moves as a crab moves or grows as a cabbage grows. But in this desire he was often frustrated by his congenital talent, for in his best poems he has made of free verse a complex accentual meter, very difficult to control and creating very binding conventions of feeling.

His poetry, therefore, concentrates on the concrete; the only ideas which it occasionally expresses are those which I have outlined, and since the ideas are bad, the poetry which deals with them is bad. At his best, Williams offers merely sharp impressions of objects observed, either in isolation or in accidental sequence, or forced by a purely rhetorical violence, as in *Romance Moderne*, into some kind of formal unit. In such a poem as this last – and there are many such – the form, or emotion, which enacts the violence is unmotivated, and the whole effect, in spite of any interesting details, is one of excited over-statement. Sometimes the sharp impression of the object observed, however, may have an intrinsic meaning, and when it is offered in isolation, in a single poem, the poem may have power: *Complaint* and *The Great Figure* from *Sour Grapes* (1921)[2] are such poems; they are not great, but they are far better than the poem about the red wheelbarrow. *Pink confused with white* from *Spring and All* (1923)[3] is another such poem. *By the road to the contagious hospital* from *Spring and All* is his best poem:[4] it deals with the force of vegetable

1 *Collected Earlier Poems*, p. 114.   2 pp. 199, 230.   3 p. 242.
4 p. 241.

nature and the season behind it coming to life in the spring; it could have been sentimentalized, but it is not. *To Waken an Old Lady* from *Sour Grapes* and *To a Dead Journalist*[1] complete the list of his best pieces. All are very fine work, but are very small; they are more serious and are better executed than anything by Pound or Miss Moore. But it is foolish to think of Williams as a great poet; the bulk of his work is not even readable. He is not even an anti-intellectual poet in any intelligible sense of the term, for he did not know what the intellect is. He was a foolish and ignorant man, but at moments a fine stylist.

(318-19)

Denis Donoghue

from 'Williams, a Redeeming Language', *The Ordinary Universe: Soundings in Modern Literature* 1968

I often think that Williams is best understood as a grammarian; skilled in reading the signs. He had no interest in the kind of thing that interested Stevens: philosophy, ontology, epistemology, gorgeous nonsense of the mind; but he was engrossed in history, because he thought of history as signs, footprints, tracks in the mud, proof that someone has lived there. He was much closer to Davy Crockett than to Bergson, Berkeley or Plato: one never thought of him as a suitable correspondent for Jean Wahl or Paul Weiss. When he saw a footprint he had no interest in the meaning of the experience as knowledge, perception, vision or even truth: he just wanted to find the foot. If he saw a blackbird, he had no interest in the thirteen ways in which Stevens saw it: one way was enough, given reasonable lucidity. This is to say that Williams was a moralist, not a philosophic poet. If he was a little weak in consecutive thought, the reason was that he believed the pure reasoning powers had been in office too long; besides, his own mind worked best by pointing to things. This is what gives *In the American Grain* its remarkable animation. These things were done, Williams is constantly saying, and if we can only understand why they were done and the spirit in which they were

1 pp. 200, 416.

done and the expense of that spirit, we can probably begin to understand ourselves. Conrad speaks, in a letter, of the silence of fact:
Williams understood that silence, and listened to it; he wrote
thousands of words, but he never thought them more important
than fact. . . .
(181-2)

Many readers of Williams feel that he is weak in structure, and they
say that his breath is short, a matter of fragmentary epiphanies, as in
So Much Depends. And yet I should be surprised to find that the
epiphanies are isolated, without the determination of some fine idea
or 'moral universal' which, in their partial way, they enact. Recall
that it was Williams who wrote:

It is hard to say what makes a poem good, but if it is not in
the detail of its construction, it is in nothing. If the detail of
the construction is not to the smallest particular distinguished,
the whole poem might as well be thrown out.[1]

It is difficult to reconcile this with the big lumpkin who, we are told,
would not be caught dead in the company of an idea. Besides, there
is the constructive evidence of *Tract, These, Dedication for a Plot of
Ground, The Lonely Street, A Coronal*.[2] In these poems we find Williams's life-long devotion to measure, craft, the resources of speech,
the redeeming language. Behind, there is his idea of culture as the
density of particular life.

The burning need of a culture (he says) is not a choice to be
made or not made, voluntarily, any more than it can be
satisfied by loans. It has to be where it arises, or everything
related to the life there ceases. It isn't a thing: it's an act. If
it stands still, it is dead. It is the realization of the qualities of
a place in relation to the life which occupies it; embracing
everything involved, climate, geographic position, relative
size, history, other cultures – as well as the character of its
sands, flowers, minerals and the condition of knowledge
within its borders. It is the act of lifting these things into an

1 *Selected Letters*, p. 318. Letter of 14 May 1953 to Richard Eberhart.
2 *Collected Earlier Poems*, pp. 129, 433, 171, 227, 38.

ordered and utilized whole which is culture. It isn't something
left over afterward. That is the record only. The act is the
thing. It can't be escaped or avoided if life is to go on. It is in
the fullest sense that which is fit.[1]

Stevens said. 'The natives of the rain are rainy men': what Williams
adds is the need of a sense of rain, a life of rain and action. This is to
say that Williams, in poems, essays, fiction, letters, has undertaken to
provide a grammar of American culture; American because he is
American, a man with a stake in the country, not because he thinks
America is better than Athens or Rome. If the grammar seems
incomplete, the reason is, I suggest, that it lacks a religious dimension.
Put Eliot's *Notes towards the Definition of Culture* beside Williams's
grammar and the point is made. But Williams's achievement remains
heroic in its dedication, its energy, its largesse.

To delight: the ingratiation of style. Williams's best poems delight
the mind because they show the continuing possibility of grace,
delicacy, even when the *materia poetica* is ordinary. These poems
offer a language, at its best, lithe, vivid, close to the contour of
speech. They choose the living world for text, as Yeats said of
Synge. So we read them as we read Chaucer, Wyatt, Fulke Greville,
Jonson, Swift, Crabbe, Clough, Pound. But Williams, who was
prepared to learn from anyone, needed someone nearer home;
Whitman, who would sustain him in the belief that American
speech constituted a new language, American as distinct from English
and sometimes as opposed to English. In *The American Language*, a
book Williams admired, Mencken quotes Whitman: 'The appetite
of the people of These States, in popular speeches and writings, is for
unhemmed latitude, coarseness, directness, live epithets, expletives,
words of opprobrium, resistance ... I like limber, lasting, fierce
words.' This is part of Williams, too; his poems seek in resistance a
new decorum, not to destroy the past but to place beside the past, in
respect, the new thing, the invention. 'I live where I live,' Williams
says, 'and acknowledge no land of opportunity because of that to be
alert to facts, to the music of events, of words, of the speech of
people about me.' So the task in hand is to use this speech as the
ground bass of a new measure, not only for the 'music' but for the

1 *Selected Essays*, p. 157.

sake of modes of being, otherwise dumb: 'It is in the newness of a live speech that the new line exists undiscovered.'

In his later years the new measure came to him, he believed, when he wrote in the second Book of *Paterson* the passage beginning

The descent beckons
    as the ascent beckoned
        Memory is a kind
of accomplishment . . .[1]

So he wrote other poems in the same measure, including *To Daphne and Virginia*.[2] I quote a fragment to show how it runs:

The smell of the heat is boxwood
    when rousing us
        a movement of the air
stirs our thoughts
    that had no life in them
        to a life, a life in which
two women agonize:
    to live and to breathe is no less.
        Two young women.
The box odor
    is the odor of that of which
        partaking separately,
each to herself
    I partake also
        . . . separately.

Williams counts each of these short lines as a foot. What he wants is 'a *relatively* stable foot, not a rigid one', a foot expanded to allow a freer handling of the measure. Williams's thought on questions of metre and prosody is closely related to the world-view of physics since Einstein; as one might say that the poetic aim is to convert the mass of daily speech into energy. In the fourth Book of *Paterson* he speaks of

hydrogen
the flame, helium the
pregnant ash[3]

1 *Paterson*, iii, p. 96.   2 *Pictures from Brueghel*, p. 75.   3 *Paterson*, ii, p. 207.

and the Mendelief chart was fascinating to him because of the magic, the alchemy, implied. He saw himself as a poet-scientist changing one element into another, the poem a cyclotron, the last grace, hey presto: hydrogen. So his new measure is as deeply part of his poetry as, say, his praise of the Curies in *Paterson*. To my ear the lines of the measure are equivalent only in duration, and their determining factor is a movement in phrases, close to speech, with the free movement of rhetorical stresses as counterpoint. The words have the movement of bars in music; each bar may contain any number of syllables, in keeping with the tendency of the language 'to squeeze units into relatively equal time spans'. The pattern gets its dynamics from the discreet use of internal rhymes, assonance, complex alliteration and pauses. Thus the pause of depressed insight before the second 'separately': as Daphne and Virginia live by weathering separate agonies. Again:

I have two sons,
>   the husbands of these women
>   who live also
> in a world of love,
>   apart.
>   Shall this odor of box in
>   the heat
> not also touch them
>   fronting a world of women
>   from which they are
> debarred
>   by the very scents which draw them on
>   against easy access?

This is verse at least as well written as prose. The measure is just sufficiently positive to ensure that the writing is exact and scrupulous. It is not imperative. The pattern, once established, allows the poet to pay down the single, final word 'apart' and to have its bar filled with a pause of sorrowful recognition, without rancour. Auden says that American poetry differs from English poetry in its 'fingering'; a good word. It is the fingering which allows for that special load placed here upon 'debarred'. Williams is using a measure not to intensify but to control, to test the feeling as it meets the edge of the language; and he prefers the control to be as light as possible. This is why his best poems can be so individual, so unexpected, so quirky, without a trace of exhibitionism.

It does not particularly matter how we approach these poems; provided we approach them. It is good to meet them with a sense of their historical pressure, the sense of the weight of feeling behind them. Some readers are first attracted by Williams's personality, the impression of being at ease, informal, taking high risks: there are no Sabbaths in his week. Others simply listen to the words as they come. The 'propriety of cadence' which Charles Tomlinson admired in Williams is a constant delight. Reading him is like going through a diary, skipping here and there when the voltage of the writing is low, but marking the passages which are wonderfully charged with feeling.

(184–8)

Select Bibliography

Books on Williams

James E. Breslin, *William Carlos Williams, An American Artist*, Oxford University Press, 1970.

John Malcolm Brinnin, *William Carlos Williams*, University of Minnesota Press, 1963.

Bram Dijkstra, *The Hieroglyphics of a New Speech: Cubism, Stieglitz, and the Early Poetry of William Carlos Williams*, Princeton University Press, 1970.

James Guimond, *The Art of William Carlos Williams; A Discovery and Possession of America*, University of Illinois Press, 1968.

Vivienne Koch, *William Carlos Williams*, New Directions, 1950.

J. Hillis Miller, (ed.), *William Carlos Williams: A Collection of Critical Essays* (Twentieth Century Views), Prentice-Hall, 1966.

Alan Ostrom, *The Poetic World of William Carlos Williams*, Preface by Harry T. Moore, Southern Illinois University Press, 1966.

Sherman Paul, *The Music of Survival, the Biography of a Poem by William Carlos Williams*, University of Illinois Press, 1968.

Walter Scott Peterson, *An Approach to Paterson*, Yale University Press, 1967.

Linda Wagner, *The Poems of William Carlos Williams*, Wesleyan University Press, 1963.

Emily Mitchell Wallace, *A Bibliography of William Carlos Williams*, Wesleyan University Press, 1968.

Thomas R. Whitaker, *William Carlos Williams*, Twayne Publishers, 1968.

Books Containing Discussions of Williams

Conrad Aiken, *Collected Criticism*, Oxford University Press, 1968.

Hugh Kenner, *Gnomon*, McDowell, Obolensky, 1958.

Frederick J. Hoffman, *The Twenties: American Writing in the Postwar Decade*, revised edn, Collier-Macmillan and the Free Press, 1965.

Randall Jarrell, *Poetry and the Age*, Faber, 1955.

J. Hillis Miller, *Poets of Reality: Six Twentieth-Century Writers*, Oxford University Press and the Belknap Press of Harvard University Press; 1966.

Roy Harvey Pearce, *The Continuity of American Poetry*, Princeton University Press, 1961.

Sister M. Bernetta Quinn, *The Metamorphic Tradition in Modern Poetry*, Rutgers University Press, 1955.

M. L. Rosenthal, *The Modern Poets, A Critical Introduction*, Oxford University Press, 1960.

M. L. Rosenthal, *The New Poets; American and British Poetry since World War II*, Oxford University Press, 1967.

Karl Shapiro, *In Defense of Ignorance*, Random House, 1952.

Tony Tanner, *The Reign of Wonder*, Routledge & Kegan Paul, 1965.

René Taupin, *L'Influence du Symbolisme Français sur la Poésie Américaine*, Champion, 1929.

Yvor Winters, *In Defence of Reason*, Routledge & Kegan Paul, 1960; University of Denver Press, 1943.

Louis Zukofsky, *Prepositions*, Rapp & Carroll, 1967.

Articles

(Articles for which reference has been supplied in the Introductions, pp. 27-37, 145-50 and 205-14 are not repeated here.)

Kenneth Burke, 'The Methods of William Carlos Williams', *Dial*, vol. 82, February 1927, pp. 94-8.

Kenneth Burke, 'William Carlos Williams 1883-1963', *New York Review of Books*, vol. 1, no. 2, May 1963, pp. 45-7.

Thomas Clark, 'Moving Images', *New Statesman*, 23 July 1965, p. 126.

Robert Creeley, 'In Conversation with Charles Tomlinson', *Review*, no. 10, 1964, pp. 24-35.

Denis Donoghue, 'Poetry and the Behaviour of Speech', *Hudson Review*, vol. 14, no. 4, Winter 1961-2, pp. 537-49.

Robert Duncan, 'A Critical Difference of View', *Stony Brook*, no. 3¼, 1969, pp. 360-63.

Richard Ellmann, 'The Doctor in Search of Himself', *Kenyon Review*, vol. 14, no. 3, Summer 1952, pp. 510-12.

Leslie Fiedler, 'Some Uses and Failures of Feeling', *Partisan Review*, vol. 15, no. 2, 1948, pp. 924-31.

Ruth Lechlitner, 'The Poetry of William Carlos Williams', *Poetry*, vol. 54, September 1939.

Neil Myers, 'Sentimentalism in the Early Poetry of William Carlos Williams', *American Literature*, vol. 37, no. 4, January 1966, pp. 458-70.

Vittorio Sereni, 'William Carlos Williams: An Italian View', *Prairie Schooner*, vol. 38, 1964, pp. 307-16.

Benjamin T. Spencer, 'Dr Williams's American Grain', *Tennessee Studies in Literature*, vol. 8, 1963, pp. 1–16.

John C. Thirlwall, 'The Lost Poems of William Carlos Williams', *New Directions* 16, 1957, pp. 3–45.

John C. Thirlwall, 'Two Cities: Paris and Paterson', *Massachusetts Review*, vol. 3, no. 2, Winter 1962, pp. 284–91.

Charles Tomlinson, 'Dr Williams's Practice', *Encounter*, vol. 29, November 1967, pp. 66–70.

Gael Turnbull, 'A Gesture to be Clean', *Satis*, no. 2, Spring 1961, pp. 15–24.

Michael Weaver, 'William Carlos Williams', *Cambridge Review*, 30 May 1964, pp. 465–6.

A. Kingsley Weatherhead, 'William Carlos Williams: Poetic Invention and the World Beyond', *English Literary Practice*, vol. 32, March 1968, pp. 126–38.

N. M. Willard, 'A Poetry of Things: Williams, Rilke, Ponge', *Comparative Literature*, vol. 17, no. 4, 1965, pp. 311–24.

Acknowledgements

For permission to use copyright material acknowledgement is made to the following:

For 'Introduction to *The Tempers*' by Ezra Pound to the author, Bircham & Co. and New Directions Publishing Corporation; for *Prologue to Kora in Hell* from *Selected Essays* by William Carlos Williams copyright 1931, 1954 by William Carlos Williams, all rights reserved, reprinted by permission of New Directions Publishing Corporation; for *Kora in Hell* by Marianne Moore to the Viking Press; for 'Heaven's First Law' by Kenneth Burke to the author; for 'The Mechanics for a Literary "Secession"' by Gorham B. Munson to the author and Doubleday & Co. Inc.; for 'William Carlos Williams' from *Port of New York* by Paul Rosenfeld to the University of Illinois Press; for 'Subjective History' by Kenneth Burke to the author; for 'American Heroes' by D. H. Lawrence to Laurence Pollinger Ltd and to the Estate of the late Mrs Frieda Lawrence; for 'A Poet of the Quattracento' by Marianne Moore to the Viking Press; for 'William Carlos Williams, a United States Poet' by Gorham B. Munson to the author; for 'Dr Williams's Position' from *Literary Essays of Ezra Pound* by Ezra Pound copyright 1918, 1920, 1935 by Ezra Pound, to the author, New Directions Publishing Corporation and Faber & Faber; for 'William Carlos Williams' from *Prepositions* by Louis Zukofsky to Rapp & Whiting; for 'Preface to *Collected Poems*' from *Opus Posthumous* by Wallace Stevens to Alfred A. Knopf Inc. and Faber & Faber; for 'Things Others Never Notice' from *Predilections* by Marianne Moore to the Viking Press; for letters to Marianne Moore, Babette Deutsche and Richard Eberhart from *Selected Letters* by William Carlos Williams, copyright 1957 by William Carlos Williams, reprinted by New Directions Publishing Corporation, agents for Mrs William Carlos Williams; for *White Mule* by Alfred Kazin from the *New York Book Review* to the *New York Times*; for the extract from 'John Wheelwright and Mr Williams' and from 'Notes from Seven Poets' by R. P. Blackmur to the author, George Allen & Unwin Ltd and Harcourt Brace, Jovanovich Inc.; for the Introduction to *The Wedge* from *The Wedge* by William Carlos Williams, copyright 1944 by William Carlos Williams, reprinted by permission of New Directions Publishing Corporation, agents for Mrs William Carlos Williams; for the extract from 'The Poet and his Public' by Randall Jarrell to *Partisan Review* and Alfred A. Knopf Inc.; for the extract from 'The Poet of *Paterson* Book One' by Parker Tyler to the author and the *Briarcliff Quarterly*; for the extract from 'Thomas, Bishop and Williams' by Robert Lowell to the author and the University of the South © 1947; for the extract from *I Wanted to Write a Poem* by William Carlos Williams to Jonathan Cape and the Beacon Press; for the extract from '*Paterson* Book Two' by Robert Lowell to *Nation*; for 'The Paterson Impasse' by Edwin Honig to the author and *Poetry*; for the extract from 'A View of Three Poets' by Randall Jarrell to *Partisan Review* and Alfred A. Knopf Inc.; for the extract from 'The Lyre and the Sledgehammer' by Joseph Bennett to the *Hudson Review* Inc.; for 'With the Bare Hands' by Hugh Kenner to the author and *Poetry*; for 'Word-Sick and Place-Crazy' from *Alms of Oblivion* by Edward Dahlberg to the author and the University of Minnesota Press; for the article 'William Carlos Williams's *Spring and All*' by Neil Myers to the author and *Modern Language Quarterly*; for the extract from 'The Legacy of Fenimore Cooper' by Donald Davie to the editors of *Essays in Criticism*; for '*In the American Grain*: William Carlos Williams on the American Past' by Alan Holder to the author and the *American Quarterly*; for the extract from 'The Influence of French Poetry and American' from *Assays* by Kenneth Rexroth copyright 1961 by Kenneth Rexroth to the author and New Directions Publishing Corporation; for the extract from 'French Silence and American Poetry' from *Tradition of the New* by Harold Rosenberg © 1960 to Horizon Press; for the article 'Influence of Painting on William Carlos Williams' by Ruth Grogan to the author; for the extract from 'Modern Verse: Diffusion as a Principle of Composition' by Albert Cook to the author and the *Kenyon Review*; for the extract from *The Language Poets Use* by Winifred Nowottny to the author and the Athlone Press; for 'Syntax in Rutherford' from *The Pound Era* by Hugh Kenner to Faber & Faber and the University of California Press; for the extract from 'Dr Williams and Tradition' by Alan Stephens to the author and *Poetry*; for the extract from 'Some Critical Implication of Metrical Analysis' by Paul Fussell to the author and Random House Inc.; for 'William Carlos Williams: Prose Form and Measure' by A. Kingsley Weatherhead to the author and Johns Hopkins Press; for the article 'Swaying Form in Williams's *Asphodel*' by Ruth Grogan to the author; for 'Dr Williams Shaping his Axe' by Hugh Kenner to the author and Astor-Honor Books; for 'The White Mule Trilogy' by Thomas R. Whitaker to the author and Twayne Publishers Inc.; for the extract 'Local Boy' to the Times Newspapers Ltd; for 'Rubbings of

Reality' from *Opus Posthumous* by Wallace Stevens to Alfred A. Knopf Inc. and Faber & Faber; for the extract from 'Rhythm and Imagery in English Poetry' by William Empson to the British Society of Aesthetics; for 'William Carlos Williams' by Robert Lowell to the author and the *Hudson Review* Inc.; for 'William Carlos Williams' from *Poets of Reality* by J. Hillis Miller to the author and Harvard University Press; for the extract from *Forms of Discovery* by Yvor Winters to the author and the Swallow Press Inc.; for the extract from 'Williams, a Redeeming Language' by Denis Donoghue to the author and the Macmillan Co.; for the extracts from the poetry of William Carlos Williams: *Collected Earlier Poems*, copyright 1938, 1951 by William Carlos Williams; *Collected Later Poems*, copyright 1944, 1948, 1949, 1950, 1963 by William Carlos Williams; *Paterson*, copyright 1946, 1948, 1949, 1951, 1958 by William Carlos Williams, 1963 by Florence Williams; *Pictures from Brueghel and Other Poems*, copyright 1949, 1951, 1952, 1953, 1954, 1955, 1956, 1957, 1959, 1960, 1961, 1962 by William Carlos Williams; reprinted by permission of New Directions Publishing Corporation and MacGibbon & Kee.

Plates

For plate 1 to Metropolitan Museum of Art, New York; plate 2 to Museum of Modern Art, New York; plate 3 to Art Institute of Chicago; plate 4 to Worcester Museum, Massachusetts, Dial Collection; plate 5 to Whitney Museum of American Art, New York; plate 6 to Mrs Edsel B. Ford.

Index

Extracts included in this anthology are indicated by bold page references.

References to individual poems by Williams are listed together under his name.

Penguin Critical Anthologies

Penguin English Poets

Instead of offering selections of the works of English and American poets, the Penguin English Poets will consist of the complete poems, in one or more volumes depending on the length of the *oeuvre*. The aim of the series is to provide a sound, readable text with helpful annotation which does not intrude on the text itself.

The first six titles

Christopher Marlowe: The Complete Poems and Translations
Edited by Stephen Orgel
Associate Professor of English, University of California at Berkley

John Donne: The Complete English Poems
Edited by A. J. Smith
Professor of English Literature, University of Keele

Samuel Johnson: The Complete English Poems
Edited by J. D. Fleeman
Tutorial Fellow of Pembroke College, Oxford

William Wordsworth: The Prelude (A Parallel Text)
Edited by J. C. Maxwell
Reader in English Literature and Fellow of Balliol College, University of Oxford

Lord Byron: Don Juan
Edited by T. G. Steffan and W. W. Pratt
Professors of English, University of Texas at Austin
and E. Steffan

Robert Browning: The Ring and the Book
Edited by Richard D. Altick
Regents' Professor of English, Ohio State University

Forthcoming

Sir Gawain and the Green Knight
Edited by J. A. Burow
Fellow of Jesus College and Lecturer in English, University of Oxford

Andrew Marvell: Complete Poems
Edited by Elizabeth Story Donno
Associate Professor of English, Columbia University

Penguin Modern Poets

Already published

Pelican Biographies